THE CAMBRIDGE COMPANION TO
DANTE

This second edition of *The Cambridge Companion to Dante* is designed to provide an accessible introduction to Dante for students, teachers, and general readers. The volume has been fully revised to take account of the most up-to-date scholarship and includes three new essays. The suggestions for further reading now include the most recent secondary works and translations as well as online resources. The essays cover Dante's early works and their relation to the *Commedia*, his literary antecedents, both vernacular and classical, biblical and theological influences, the historical and political dimensions of Dante's works, and their reception. In addition there are introductory essays to each of the three canticles of the *Commedia* that analyze their themes and style. This new edition will ensure that the *Companion* continues to be the most useful single volume for new generations of students of Dante.

RACHEL JACOFF is Margaret Deffenbaugh and LeRoy Carlson Professor of Comparative Literature and Italian Studies at Wellesley College.

THE CAMBRIDGE
COMPANION TO
DANTE
Second Edition

EDITED BY
RACHEL JACOFF

CAMBRIDGE
UNIVERSITY PRESS

CAMBRIDGE UNIVERSITY PRESS
Cambridge, New York, Melbourne, Madrid, Cape Town, Singapore, São Paulo,
Delhi, Mexico City

Cambridge University Press
The Edinburgh Building, Cambridge CB2 8RU, UK

Published in the United States of America by Cambridge University Press, New York

www.cambridge.org
Information on this title: www.cambridge.org/9780521605816

First published 1993
Second edition 2007
6th printing 2012

Printed and bound at MPG Books Group, UK

A catalogue record for this publication is available from the British Library

ISBN 978-0-521-84430-7 Hardback
ISBN 978-0-521-60581-6 Paperback

CONTENTS

NOTES ON CONTRIBUTORS

ALBERT RUSSELL ASCOLI is Terrill Distinguished Professor of Italian Studies at the University of California, Berkeley. He is the author of *Ariosto's Bitter Harmony: Crisis and Evasion in the Renaissance* (Princeton: Princeton University Press, 1987) and co-editor of *Machiavelli and the Discourse of Literature* (Ithaca: Cornell University Press, 1993) and of *Making and Remaking Italy: Cultivating National Identity around the Risorgimento* (Oxford: Berg Press, 2001).

TEODOLINDA BAROLINI is Da Ponte Professor of Italian at Columbia University. She has written *Dante's Poets: Textuality and Truth in the Comedy* (Princeton: Princeton University Press, 1987) and *The Undivine Comedy: Detheologizing Dante* (Princeton: Princeton University Press, 1992). She is preparing a new edition of Dante's *Rime*.

PIERO BOITANI is Professor of Comparative Literature at the University of Rome "La Sapienza." He is the author of numerous books including *The Tragic and Sublime in Medieval Literature* (Cambridge: Cambridge University Press, 1991), *Chaucer and Boccaccio* (Oxford: Society for the Study of Medieval Languages and Literature, 1977), *The Shadow of Ulysses: Figures of a Myth* (Oxford: Oxford University Press, 1994), *The Bible and its Rewritings* (Oxford: Oxford University Press, 1994), and *The Genius to Improve an Invention* (Notre Dame: University of Notre Dame Press, 2002). His most recent book, *Parole alate* (Mondadori, 2004) will appear in English as *Winged Words*.

KEVIN BROWNLEE, Professor of Romance Languages at the University of Pennsylvania, is the author of *Poetic Identity in Guillaume de Machaut* (Madison: University of Wisconsin Press, 1984). He is the co-editor of *L'espositione di Bernardino Daniello da Lucca sopra la Commedia di Dante* (Hanover, NH: University Press of New England, 1989) and has also co-edited several collections of essays, including *The New Medieval-ism* (Baltimore: The Johns Hopkins University Press, 1991).

CHARLES TILL DAVIS was Professor of History at Tulane University and served as president of the Dante Society of America from 1991 to 1997. His major works on Dante are *Dante and the Idea of Rome* (Oxford: Claren-don Press, 1957) and *Dante's Italy* (Philadelphia: University of Pennsylvania Press, 1984).

JOAN FERRANTE, Professor of Comparative Literature Emerita at Columbia University, is the author of *The Political Vision of the Divine Comedy* (Princeton: Princeton University Press, 1984), *Woman as Image in Medieval Literature* (New York: Columbia University Press, 1975), and *The Conflict of Love and Honor: The Medieval Tristan Legend in France, Germany and Italy* (The Hague: Mouton, 1973). She has also translated and co-edited several texts and is a past president of the Dante Society of America.

JOHN FRECCERO is Professor of Italian Literature and Comparative Liter-ature at New York University. His essays on Dante are collected in *Dante: The Poetics of Conversion* (Cambridge, MA: Harvard University Press, 1986). He has edited *Dante: A Collection of Critical Essays* (Englewood Cliffs, NJ: Prentice-Hall, 1965) and has written on St. Augustine, Petrarch, Donne, and Antonioni. He has received the Award of the President of Italy for Italian Literature in 1994.

ROBERT POGUE HARRISON, Rosina Pierotti Professor of Italian at Stan-ford University, is the author of *The Body of Beatrice* (Baltimore: The Johns Hopkins University Press, 1988), *Forests: The Shadow of Civiliza-tion* (Chicago: University of Chicago Press, 1992), and *The Dominion of the Dead* (Chicago: University of Chicago Press, 2003).

PETER S. HAWKINS, Director of the Luce Program in Scripture and the Literary Arts and Professor of Religion at Boston University, is the author of *The Language of Grace: Flannery O'Connor, Walker Percy, Iris Murdoch* (Cambridge, MA: Cowley, 1985). He has edited *Civitas: Religious Interpre-tations of the City* (Atlanta: Scholars Press, 1986) and co-edited *Ineffability: Naming the Unnamable from Dante to Beckett* (New York: AMS Press, 1984). He is co-editor of *The Poets' Dante: Twentieth Century Reflections* (New York: Farrar, Straus, and Giroux, 2001), and the author of *Dante's Testaments: Essays in Scriptural Imagination* (Stanford: Stanford University Press, 1999).

ROBERT HOLLANDER, Professor in European Literature, Emeritus, at Princeton University, is the author of *Allegory in Dante's Commedia* (Princeton: Princeton University Press, 1969), *Studies in Dante* (Ravenna: Longo, 1980), and *Il Virgilio dantesco* (Florence: Olschki, 1983), as well as several books on Boccaccio. He co-edited *Studi americani su Dante* (Milan: Franco Angeli, 1989) and *L'espositione di Bernardino Daniello da Lucca sopra la Commedia di Dante*. He and his wife, Jean, have published their verse translation of *Inferno* and *Purgatorio* (Doubleday/Anchor), and are preparing their *Paradiso*. He is a past president of the Dante Society of America and has received the Gold Medal from the City of Florence for his contribution to Dante studies. Professor Hollander is founding editor-in-chief of the *Electronic Bulletin of the Dante Society of America* and founding director of both the Dartmouth and Princeton Dante Projects.

RACHEL JACOFF, Margaret Deffenbaugh and LeRoy Carlson Professor of Comparative Literature and Italian Studies at Wellesley College, co-authored (with William Stephany) *Lectura Dantis Americana: Inferno II* (Philadelphia: University of Pennsylvania Press, 1989). She edited *Dante: The Poetics of Conversion* (Cambridge, MA: Harvard University Press, 1986) and co-edited (with Jeffrey T. Schnapp) *The Poetry of Allusion: Virgil and Ovid in Dante's Commedia* (Stanford: Stanford University Press, 1991). She and Peter Hawkins co-edited *The Poets' Dante: Twentieth Century Reflections*.

GIUSEPPE MAZZOTTA, Sterling Professor of Italian at Yale University, is the author of *Dante, Poet of the Desert* (Princeton: Princeton University Press, 1979) and *Dante's Vision and the Circle of Knowledge* (Princeton: Princeton University Press, 1993). He has also written *The World at Play in Boccaccio's Decameron* (Princeton: Princeton University Press, 1986) and *The Worlds of Petrarch* (Durham, NC: Duke University Press, 1993) and edited the collection *Critical Essays on Dante* (Boston, MA: G. K. Hall, 1991).

JOHN M. NAJEMY is Professor of History at Cornell University. He is the author of *Corporatism and Consensus in Florentine Electoral Politics, 1280–1400* (Chapel Hill: University of North Carolina Press, 1982) and *Between Friends: Discourses of Power and Desire in the Machiavelli–Vettori Letters of 1513–1515* (Princeton: Princeton University Press, 1993).

LINO PERTILE is Professor of Italian at Harvard University. He is the author of *La puttana e il gigante: dal Cantico dei cantici al Paradiso terrestre di Dante* (Ravenna: Longo, 1998) and *La punta del disio: Semantica del desiderio nella Commedia* (Fiesole: Cadmo, 2005). He is also the co-editor of *The Cambridge History of Italian Literature* (Cambridge: Cambridge University Press, 1999) and of *The New Italian Novel* (Toronto: University of Toronto Press, 1997).

JEFFREY T. SCHNAPP is the founder/director of the Stanford Humanities Lab and Pierotti Professor of Italian and Comparative Literature at Stanford University. He is the author of *The Transfiguration of History at the Center of Dante's Paradise* (Princeton: Princeton University Press, 1986) and the co-editor of *L'espositione di Bernardino Daniello da Lucca sopra la Commedia di Dante*. He has also co-edited (with Rachel Jacoff) *The Poetry of Allusion: Virgil and Ovid in Dante's Commedia*. He has written widely on Italian Fascism as well.

DAVID WALLACE is Judith Rodin Professor of English at the University of Pennsylvania and the current President of the New Chaucer Society. His books include *Chaucer and the Early Writings of Boccaccio* (Cambridge: D. S. Brewer, 1985), *Giovanni Boccaccio: Decameron* (Cambridge: Cambridge University Press, 1991), *Chaucerian Polity* (Stanford: Stanford University Press, 1997), and *Premodern Places* (Oxford: Blackwell, 2004). He edited *The Cambridge History of Medieval English Literature* (1999, 2002), and co-edited *The Cambridge Companion to Medieval Women's Writing* (2003).

A. N. WILLIAMS is Lecturer in Patristic and Medieval Theology at Cambridge University. She has written *The Ground of Union: Deification in Aquinas and Palamas* (Oxford: Oxford University Press, 1999) and the forthcoming *The Divine Sense: The Intellect in Patristic Theology*.

PREFACE

This second edition of *The Cambridge Companion to Dante*, like the first one, is designed to be an accessible and challenging introduction to Dante for students, teachers, and general readers. Seventeen essays by distinguished scholars provide contemporary perspectives on Dante's life and work, offering readings of his major texts and of various aspects of his cultural context. Contributors to the first edition were asked to update their essays and bibliographies, and there are three new essays as well. The essays concentrate on five general areas: Dante's early works and their relation to the *Comedy*; the literary antecedents, both vernacular and classical, of Dante's poetry; biblical and theological influences and their poetic implications; the historical and political dimensions of Dante's work; and selected reception history (the commentary tradition and Dante's presence in English-language literature). In addition, there are introductory essays to each of the three canticles of the *Comedy* that analyze their particular themes and strategies. The book aims to provide both insightful readings of specific textual practices and useful background material.

Because Dante's work is so capacious and multi-faceted, it is impossible to address all of the issues it raises and all of the areas of classical and medieval culture with which it intersects. Many of the essays conclude with suggestions for further reading, and there is a section at the end of the book that provides information about translations, web sites, critical works, and other aids to further study. The selective list of critical works includes many books that have appeared in the years since the first edition was published.

Indeed, there seems to be no end in sight of work on Dante or of Dante's presence in works by other writers, artists, musicians, and in popular culture.

NOTE ON TRANSLATIONS

Quotations from the *Divina Commedia* are taken from *La commedia secondo l'antica vulgata*, edited by Giorgio Petrocchi, 4 vols. (Milan: Mondadori, 1966–67), and reproduced, with very few changes, in *The Divine Comedy*, translated by Charles S. Singleton (Princeton: Princeton University Press, 1970–75). Translations are either by, or based on, that of Singleton in this edition.

CHRONOLOGY

1265	Dante born under the sign of Gemini
1283	Dante's father dies and Dante comes of age. He is married shortly thereafter to Gemma Donati with whom he has four children (Jacopo, Pietro, Giovanni, and Antonia)
1289	Dante takes part in the battle of Campaldino against Arezzo
1290	June 8, death of Beatrice
1293–94	*Vita nuova* written
1294	Dante meets Charles Martel, king of Hungary, and heir to the Kingdom of Naples and the country of Provence, in Florence
1295	Dante enters political life
1300	Boniface VIII proclaims Jubilee Year. June 15, Dante becomes one of the six priors of Florence for a term of two months. Easter 1300 is the fictional date of the journey of the *Divina Commedia*
1301	As Charles of Valois approaches Florence, Dante is sent on an embassy to Pope Boniface VIII
1302	January 27, the first sentence of exile against Dante reaches him in Siena. On March 10, Dante is permanently banished from Florence
1303–05	*De vulgari eloquentia* and *Convivio*, both unfinished, written
1303	Guest of Bartolomeo della Scala in Verona
1304	Birth of Francesco Petrarca
1309	Papacy moves from Rome to Avignon
1310	Henry VII of Luxemburg descends into Italy. Dante writes Epistle to him. Possible date of *Monarchia* (others think it may have been written as late as 1317)
1312–18	Guest of Cangrande della Scala in Verona
1313	Death of Henry VII. Birth of Giovanni Boccaccio
1314	*Inferno* published. Epistle to the Italian cardinals

I

GIUSEPPE MAZZOTTA

Life of Dante

The life of Dante is such a tangle of public and private passions and ordeals experienced over the fifty-six years he lived that it has always been a source of inexhaustible fascination. It is as if everything about his life – its innumerable defeats and its occasional and yet enduring triumphs – belongs to the romantic and alluring realm of legend: a love at first sight that was to last his whole life and inspire lofty poetry; the long, cruel exile from his native Florence because of the civil war ravaging the city; the poem he wrote, the *Divina Commedia*, made of his public and private memories; the turning of himself into an archetypal literary character, such as Ulysses, Faust, or any of those medieval knights errant, journeying over the tortuous paths of a spiritual quest, wrestling with dark powers, and, finally, seeing God face to face.

Many are the reasons why generations of readers have found the story of Dante's life compelling. His relentless self-invention as an unbending prophet of justice and a mythical quester for the divine is certainly one important reason. The fact that in his graphic figurations of the beyond (rare glimpses of which were available in only a few other legendary mythmakers – Homer, Plato, and Virgil) he was an unparalleled poet also greatly heightens our interest in him. Yet none of these reasons truly accounts for what must be called – given the extraordinary number of biographies Dante has elicited over the centuries – the literary phenomenon of "The Life of Dante."

Stories of mythical heroes of literature deeply absorb us either because these heroes are rarely, if ever, wholly human (Gilgamesh, Achilles, Aeneas), or because they display noble, exceptional gifts (Beowulf, Roland, El Cid) that transcend the practice and measure of ordinary life. By the same token, truly great poets have so quickly entered the domain of myth that they leave readers doubtful about the very reality of their existence; did Moses or Homer really exist or are they imaginary authors of actually anonymous texts? In the case of Shakespeare, arguments still rage as to whether or not he truly was who we may like to think he was.

But no such skepticism is warranted for the reality or legal identity of Dante's existence. One suspects that it is exactly this unquestioned reality, the knowledge that he was part of our history and was so much like us, that he was so thoroughly human while at the same time so thoroughly extraordinary as only fictional characters are, that accounts for the persistent fascination he exerts on us. The disparity between, on the one hand, his ordinariness (he was married, had children, was notoriously litigious, unable at times to pay his rent or find credit, craved recognition), and, on the other hand, his larger-than-life visionary powers (his unrelenting sense of justice, his unique ability to stretch the boundaries of the imagination, and the conviction, at once humble and proud, of a prophetic mission) repeatedly triggers the questioning and the desire to know what he was really like.

Accordingly, biographers have tried to define Dante's involvement with the Florentine intellectuals and poets of his time, as well as his role in local politics, which unavoidably reflected and shared in the larger struggles between pope and emperor. They have also tried to assess how real were the shifts in his philosophical and theological allegiances (whether or not he was ever an "Averroist" and what were the limits of his Thomism). And they have not neglected to unearth numberless details about his family circumstances in the effort to grasp the elusive essence of his life.

There is not yet, however, a full-fledged literary biography of Dante that evokes simultaneously the poetic, intellectual, and social topography of both Florence *and* the larger cultural world conjured up in his works. Existing biographies, in effect, beg the question. Is there really a correspondence between life and work? Can we take obscure details Dante writes about himself as clues to his life? And even if we could, what was Dante's relation to his friends, to his wife, to his children, and, perhaps more importantly, to himself? Where did he learn all he knew? When did he discover his poetic vocation? What did "to be a poet" mean to him and to those around him?

These questions have not been altogether ignored by biographers, but, right from the early biographies of Dante to those written in the last few years, they have drawn forth a predictable variety of answers. The answers, no doubt, are chiefly determined by the rhetorical assumptions shaping the biographical genre in itself. One such assumption is that the biographer has grasped the inner, authentic sense of the life to be told and will, thus, make it the principle of the narrative trajectory. Another assumption is that the history of a great poet coincides with the history of his own times; Dante, for instance, to adapt a statement by T. S. Eliot, is part of the consciousness of his age which, in turn, cannot be understood without him. A third assumption is the illusory belief, shared by almost all Dante biographers, that there is a solid, ascertainable correspondence between the facts of the poet's life and his art. From this standpoint the role of the biographer consists in sifting the documentary evidence and removing all obscurities and ambiguities from the record – did Dante really go to Paris during the years of his exile? Was Brunetto Latini an actual teacher of Dante? Was Dante ever a Franciscan novice? Did he attend both the theological schools of Santa Croce and Santa Maria Novella in Florence? And who was the "montanina" for whom Dante, late in his life, wrote exquisite poems?

The only remarkable exception to this pattern of the biographical genre is Giovanni Boccaccio's *Vita di Dante*, a self-conscious fictional work akin to Dante's own *Vita nuova* which responds imaginatively to Dante's steady self-dramatization in his works. Modern biographers of Dante, on the other hand (notably Michele Barbi and Giorgio Petrocchi), have given brilliant and dependable accounts of Dante's life and works, but these accounts are limited, paradoxically, in the measure in which, first, they are not speculative or imaginative enough, and, second, they refrain from giving what can only be, as Boccaccio lucidly grasps, the novelistic sense of Dante's life. It does not come as a surprise to discover, then, that these modern biographical reconstructions deliberately follow in the mold of the highly influential biography of Dante written by the Florentine historian Leonardo Bruni (1369–1444). Bruni's own version of the *Vita di Dante* was written specifically to correct and root in the reality of history the legend concocted by Boccaccio.

Boccaccio's *Vita di Dante*, which was written roughly around 1348 and is, thus, the earliest available biography of Dante, follows an altogether different path. His text has the structural complexity of both a personal poetics and of a romance telling the marvelous birth of the poet (accompanied, as happens in hagiographies, by an omen, such as the mother's prophetic dream). The two rhetorical strands converge in the central, exalted, narrative of the poet's fated growth and of the splendor of his imagination in the face of the severe encroachments of daily cares on the exercise of his craft. Because Boccaccio so often strays and digresses from the presentation of his material to relate his ideas about the sublime nature and essence of poetry, and because he chooses fiction as the dominant mode of his narrative, its literal trustworthiness has been much doubted or maligned since Bruni's stringencies. Nonetheless, in spite of some overt incongruities in Boccaccio's account, the legend he constructs fixes steadily on his central perception of Dante's life as pulled in antithetical directions.

One of these pulls was Dante's insight into the implacable demands of poetry as a total, all-encompassing activity which could provide the metaphysical foundation of the world. The other pull was Dante's experience of the burdens of the daily realities of family, of financial difficulties, of a marriage that, in point of fact, was far less unhappy than Boccaccio himself thought, and his naive decision to yield to the siren call of involvement in the shadowy, violent perimeter of city politics. The power games of politics, so Boccaccio infers, were Dante's deluded, even if provisional, choice and inexorably brought about his exile. Yet, this tragic mistake notwithstanding, Dante still clung to his faith in his own comprehensive visionary powers to recall the muses from their banishment.

To a civic humanist such as Leonardo Bruni, Boccaccio's celebration of Dante's heroic poetic temper seemed too partial an invention (much like, Bruni says wryly, the *Filocolo* or the *Filostrato* or even the *Fiammetta*). Bruni found Boccaccio's intimation of the poet's necessary disengagement from the responsibilities of the history of Florence an unacceptable way of bypassing the vital, empirical force of poetry, and of confining it to the realm of abstract metaphysical generalizations. Thus, in reaction to Boccaccio, Bruni's *Vita di Dante* presents Dante in the context of the particularities of Florentine intellectual and political life. It is possible that a transaction between Boccaccio's and Bruni's respective narrative techniques and understanding of the poet would convey a sharper view of Dante's life. Yet it must be acknowledged that the biographical paradigm inaugurated by Bruni and deployed by the historical scholarship of a Barbi or a Petrocchi has made a considerable contribution to the preliminary establishment of the facts of Dante's life.

The facts we know for certain are relatively few, but they are firmly established. Dante Alighieri was born in Florence in 1265 (between May 14 and June 13). Of his childhood, spent in Florence, most people recall only what he himself records in his *Vita nuova*, that when he was nine years old he met Beatrice, then eight years old, who died in 1290 (on either June 8 or 19), but whose memory never faded from the poet's mind and who was destined to play a providential role in his poetic vision. But many other things happened to and around Dante during his early years which were bound to affect a precocious and sensitive young man, as he no doubt was, to judge by the intensity of his response to Beatrice.

One can only speculate, for instance, what impression the meeting that took place in Florence in June 1273 between Pope Gregory IX and Charles of Anjou to establish peace between the city's warring factions of Guelfs and Ghibellines made on Dante. One can easily imagine the city's mood on those early summer days (which coincided with the feast of Florence's patron saint, St. John the Baptist), celebrating the dramatic event and calling for a general reconciliation. Everywhere, and for everybody, in Florence it was a feast marked by processions, songs, dances, laughter, jousts, tumblers, clowns, colorful young women and young men, as the poets' recitations of their verses mixed with the clamor of street vendors. Dante himself never refers to this extraordinary public episode which turned out to be nothing more than a brief interlude in Florence's endless bloody civil wars. But who can say the extent to which, if at all, this spectacular experience of the ritual of peace shaped his imagination of the pageantry at the top of *Purgatorio* or of *Paradiso* as the vision of peace and play? Who can say whether or not it was in the middle of that feast that he discovered his vocation to be a poet?

One would expect this sort of question to be asked by a biographer in the mold of, say, Boccaccio. A sober-minded biographical narrative of the life of Dante, however, would be expected to focus on ascertained, objective events of his early life. Some of these events, like the schooling he received, were fairly ordinary. He went to a grammar school where he was trained in classical Latin and medieval Latin texts, but because at this time his family was of moderate means, he had access both to the poetry and literature that came from Provence and France, and to the medieval vulgarizations of classical material. There were other events in his childhood, however, that could in no way be called ordinary. He lost his mother, Bella, between 1270 and 1273; his father remarried soon after and had three other children who remained close (especially Francesco) to Dante throughout his life. In 1283 Dante's father died, and his death forced Dante to take legal charge of the family. This circumstance, in turn, meant that he could not but become involved in the tense and even exciting realities of Florentine public life.

The Florentine meeting of 1273 between the pope and the emperor, arranged to mark the reconciliation of the popular factions, had no noticeable practical effects on the mood of the city, nor did it manage to efface the tragic memories of the defeat of Montaperti (1260), recalled in *Inferno* 10. Montaperti meant the defeat of the Guelfs, and also that Dante, a Guelf, came to life in a Ghibelline city. In terms of Florence's public mood, moreover, the defeat simply crushed the spirit of the city and marked Florence's loss of its hegemony over its neighboring cities. Public life was a persistent danger zone punctuated by the almost daily battles between the Guelfs and the Ghibellines. At the same time, the implacable, bitter resentments of the popular social classes against the entrenched interests of the magnates added a new and generalized turbulence, beyond the rivalries and feuds of the nobility (the Donati versus the Cerchi), to the city's political tensions. Dante, who had entered by necessity this political arena with its intractable problems, was soon to stumble against a host of unpredictable snares.

There is no doubt that Dante at first responded with enthusiasm and genuine excitement to the lure and prestige of public life. Public life was characterized in the Florence of the 1280s by the mingling of aristocrats, office-holders of the commune, men of letters and educators, poets and rich merchants. In concrete terms, it meant, for Dante, friendship with the prominent, cosmopolitan intellectual Brunetto Latini, the highly valued intimacy with the poet and aristocrat Guido Cavalcanti, and with Cino da Pistoia, and admission to the exclusive social circles of Nino Visconti and Guido da Polenta. It also meant recognition among the bourgeois and academic coteries of Bologna, where Dante journeyed and lived for several months (and where he possibly met the physician Taddeo Alderotti). At any rate, from Bologna he brought back to Florence the poetry of Guido Guinizelli, a master whom he was to hail later as the founder of the "sweet new style."

The decade from 1280 to 1290, the year of Beatrice's death, was immensely rich in Dante's life. In 1285 he married Gemma Donati with whom he had four children: three boys (Giovanni, Pietro, and Jacopo – named after the apostles who witnessed Jesus' transfiguration) and a girl (Antonia), who reappeared late in the poet's life in Ravenna where she was a nun who had taken the name of Sister Beatrice. Family life had its public counterpoint in what later came to figure as a central experience: the military campaign of Campaldino (June 1289) against the Aretines. Florence's victory reversed the mood as well as the internal balance of power that had been determined by the defeat of Montaperti. The Ghibellines were now defeated, and the popular classes strengthened their power; yet the victory gave rise to new social tensions between the popular government and the magnates. Kept out of the government of the city until they agreed to enroll in the various guilds, the magnates felt entitled to seek more political influence because of their decisive role in the city's military victory over Arezzo.

It is extraordinary how, even in the midst of so many demands made on him by family and civic responsibilities, Dante did not abandon the world of poetry. On the contrary, during this period he composed *Il Fiore*, a series of sonnets adapted from the *Roman de la Rose*. He also wrote *Il Detto*, only lately, and correctly, attributed to Dante. This work can be defined as a general synopsis, as it were, of the conventions of courtly love, but it also shows deep traces of the influence disparate literary traditions had on him: the *Roman de la Rose*, Provençal poetry, the Sicilian School, Guittone, and Brunetto Latini.

These early literary experiments can objectively be viewed as phases in Dante's technical-poetic apprenticeship, but the story of the apprenticeship itself, of the discovery and the necessity to be a poet, is told in the *Vita nuova*. As Dante's love story for Beatrice, which the text primarily purports to be, it relates few sensuous, empirical signs of her presence – the elegance (a bit showy but never tawdry) of her clothes; her stride; her eyes; her silence; her smile; her aura; her (violent) gestures of disdain. But it is certain that Beatrice's enigmatic presence, a sort of dematerialized body which casts her as an extraordinary, unique apparition, sets the lover on the path of self-discovery.

There must be, Dante soon finds out, a more profound means of exploring the sense of Beatrice's meaning in his life than those provided by the traditional, formulaic, Provençal poetic conventions. If Beatrice is a unique figure of love, it must follow that the poetry that celebrates her cannot but be a unique form of poetry. This poetic quest for a *new style*, which takes place in the shadow of Cavalcanti's literary-philosophical concerns, turns into the central theme of the narrative. Oriented at first to the past and to the unveiling of the secrets of memory, the *Vita nuova* quickly confronts memory's limits, seeks to transcend those limits, and strains for a mode of vision no longer that of mere reminiscences of the past. Dante must move, as the last chapters of the *Vita nuova* tell us, beyond the contingent revelations of objective, empirical knowledge to a realm of imagination and vision.

But Dante was not to keep immediately to this plan. While writing the *Vita nuova* he began reading the works of Boethius and Cicero, and attended the theological and philosophical schools (*Convivio* ii, xii, 1–7) where he became familiar with radical Franciscan and Thomistic speculation, with apocalyptic literature (tied to the names of Ubertino da Casale and Giovanni Olivi), and political theology (Remigio dei Girolami). This deepening of the intellectual horizon of his youth meant that the idea of poetry embodied in the *Vita nuova* appeared now as a coiled cipher, as a severely limited experience because it was predicated on the exclusion of other worlds from the realm of the personal. A new idea of poetry, one which would neither forfeit public realities nor transfigure those realities into a private phantasmagoria, now emerged. The reasons for this poetic shift, discernible in the writing of the allegorical-philosophical *Rime*, are several. But the primary reasons are both Dante's awareness of the city's political-moral climate in the 1290s, and the consciousness of his new responsibilities as a family man and a member of a middling social class.

The decade was marked by a number of contradictory signs for the future of Florence. In the aftermath of the battle of Campaldino there were many hopeful, scandalously utopian attempts to establish a bipartisan government, such as an alliance of Guelfs and Ghibellines to secure peaceful conditions in the city. This bold, provocative scheme never had a chance to become reality. Yet the passage of Charles Martel through Florence (1294) kept awake in Dante the dream that his own voice and ideas of how to bring order to the city could one day be heard by the emperor. There were, however, other events which signalled ominous and disastrous consequences. Chief among them was the inauguration of Boniface VIII's theocratic papacy (1294) in the aftermath of the collapse of Celestine V's ideals of evangelical pauperism. The new papal policy presaged difficult times for Florence's hegemonic claims, since the theocratic scheme entailed nothing less than the submission of the whole of Tuscany to papal control. This factor alone possibly constitutes the background against which Dante's further political involvement is to be seen. In this same year (1295) he enrolled in a guild, and on several occasions opposed Boniface's exactions on Florence.

Dante's political career reached its acme in 1300 (June 15–August 15) when he was one of the city's six priors. Leonardo Bruni's biography records a lost epistle of Dante in which the by-now exiled poet, taking stock of his life's disappointments, sees the cause of all his misfortunes in the decisions taken while he was a prior. In his *Cronica* (I, xxi) Dino Compagni, himself both a witness and protagonist of the times, registers the crisis that crippled the city's political life during these months: the violent clashes between the magnates and the representatives of the popular government. As a punitive measure for the violence, the priors agreed to send the leaders of the warring factions (Black and White Guelfs) into exile. Among the exiles was Dante's own friend, Guido Cavalcanti, who died late in August of that year.

The events that followed the priors' momentous decision are so muddled and complex that a simplification is necessary. As soon as Dante's tenure expired, his successors recalled the Whites from their exile. Pope Boniface VIII, angered by the decision which he saw as favoring his enemies, solicited Charles of Valois, the brother of Philip, then king of France, to intervene militarily in Italy. When Charles was in Italy, the Florentines dispatched three emissaries to the papal court in Rome to persuade the pope to keep the French king from entering Tuscany. One of the ambassadors was Dante who, perhaps while in Rome, was sentenced to death on March 10, 1302. Dante went into exile, which was to last until his death in 1321.

The remaining nineteen years of his life were the most painful for the poet. So dark were they, that the romantic image of the fugitive poet, roaming around like a "rudderless ship" and a "beggar" (*Convivio* I, iii, 4–5), captures the fact that we cannot even trace with any great precision his constantly shifting, precarious whereabouts. We know that at first he variously plotted and conspired a military seizure of Florence; and that he went from one city to another: Forlì in 1302; Verona in 1303; Arezzo, where, according to Petrarch, he met his exiled father, Ser Petracco; Treviso; Padua, where in 1305 he met Giotto at work in the Scrovegni Chapel – and one is left to imagine the exchanges between them; Venice; Lunigiana, where he worked for a time for the Malaspinas; Lucca in 1307–09; and many other places – only some of which are real – until he settled once again in Verona in 1312, and from Verona moved in 1319 to his last refuge in Ravenna.

But for all its harshness, exile turned out to be for Dante a blessing in disguise, nothing less than the central, decisive experience of his life. His texts always speak of his exile as a darkening time and as a ravage of the spirit. But from 1302 to 1321, from the year of his exile to the year of his death, Dante's history is essentially the history of his works, and they cannot be understood without understanding the bleak clarity exile brought to his vision. He knew despair and almost certainly he contemplated suicide. But because everything was now lost, nothing was lost. He abandoned the shallow illusion of a return to Florence by military action, and retreated from the grim, squalid quarters where other Florentine expatriates spun endless, wicked conspiracies of revenge.

Dante soon discovered, or simply accepted, that the exile they all bewailed as a tragic fatality need not be construed as a hopeless, unalterable condition. In the depths of his despair he saw the futility and falseness of despair. For his friend Guido Cavalcanti, the exile to Sarzana that Dante himself had a few years earlier decreed was the irremediable experience of no return, tantamount to the premonition of an imminent death. Guido's great exilic poem, "Perch'i' no spero di tornar giammai, ballatetta, in Toscana," is the tragic figuration of a mind yielding to despair's grip and ultimate unreality. For Dante, on the contrary, as his own exilic song, "Tre donne," exemplifies, hopelessness is illusory because it denies the reality and the possibilities of the future, and exile becomes the providential condition wherein he recognizes the necessity to transcend the particularisms of local history. The way out of the darkness of partial and relative viewpoints, as he was ceaselessly to argue in the two major works he started but never finished in the early stages of his nomadic existence, the *De vulgari eloquentia* and the *Convivio*, is a universal standpoint.

He must have longed during this time for an impossible restoration of his honor and his property, for the irrevocably lost security of a family life, for the conversations with his sweet friends along the banks of the river at the hour of dusk, and for a world of ordinary concerns. But he never let nostalgia stand in the way of his obstinate and absolute moral convictions. He continued to weave his voice into the web of intellectual-practical discourses, and undertook to write the *De vulgari eloquentia* and the *Convivio*. In the *Convivio*, the lyrical fluidity and cadences of the *Vita nuova* are now bracketed as the provisional, radiant compulsion of a solitary mind. He never rejects his past, but now strives for a new discipline of thought and for the rational bounds of a universalizing philosophical-theological discourse. The *De vulgari eloquentia* envisions the vitality of the vernacular as the root and bark of the politics, law, poetry, and theology of the whole of Italy. The *Convivio*, on the other hand, presents itself as an ethics and, as such, recalls both the teachings Dante received from Brunetto Latini and the commentary of St. Thomas Aquinas on Aristotle's *Ethics*. From the viewpoint of Dante's own existential concerns, the *Convivio* addresses the issue of the relationship between philosophy and political power (the intellectual and the emperor), and focuses on the range of moral values that shape the fabric of our life.

From 1308 to 1313, a historical enterprise dominated the stages of international politics and was at the center of Dante's own political passions and dreams. He seems to have all along understood the necessity of the empire as the sole reasonable warranty against the sinister spirals of violence splintering all cities. He sensed in the event at hand a real possibility for his abstract design. In November of 1308, the electors of Germany agreed to have Henry VII of Luxemburg crowned as emperor. Henry, who was on his way to Rome where in 1312 he would be crowned by the pope, was expected to redress the political imbroglios in the various Italian cities of the north and of Tuscany. Dante himself hailed his arrival as a new messianic advent. He met the emperor, and this meeting renewed and nourished, at least for a while, as one can infer from his political *Epistolae*, Dante's moral vision of the necessity of empire that comes to maturation in the political tract, *Monarchia*, perhaps written around 1316.

By the time of Henry's descent to Italy, Dante had finished writing both *Inferno* and most of *Purgatorio*. Around June of 1312 he moved back to the court of Cangrande in Verona, drawn to it, no doubt, by the legendary hospitality of the prince and by his devotion to the Ghibelline cause whose legitimacy Dante endorsed. During his stay in Verona, a city of great culture that celebrated, for instance, the arrival of a manuscript of the Veronese Catullus' *Carmina*, he started (in 1315) *Paradiso*, and when he was halfway through (*Paradiso* 17 is a glittering celebration of Cangrande's generosity and, retrospectively, a farewell to him) he took his leave. In 1319 Guido Novello of Polenta invited him to move to Ravenna, and Dante accepted.

Why did he leave Verona and go to Ravenna? We do not really know. In a famous letter to Boccaccio, Petrarch sharply suggests that it had become intolerable to Dante to be confused with the Veronese court's actors, buffoons, and parasites. Their bibulousness and hoaxes were as far a cry from his childhood memories of Florence's spontaneous feasts as they were from his understanding of *theologia ludens*, the insight into the deeply "comic" essence of God's creation and grace, which the whole of the *Divina Commedia* unveils and represents over and against the vast pageant of horrors it foregrounds. Nonetheless, the break with Cangrande was not definitive. It was to Cangrande that Dante addressed the letter (the attribution of which, by what must be termed academics' recurrent suspicions, has again been contested) that masterfully explicates the complex principles of composition of *Paradiso* and, implicitly, of the whole poem. And he was also to return to Verona to read on January 20, 1320, a Sunday, his *Quaestio de aqua et terra*.

We do not know exactly why he agreed to come to Ravenna, but, in hindsight, it was inevitable that he should come. By this time Ravenna was like an after-thought of the Roman empire and lived in the after-glow of its Byzantine art. For a man like Dante, who more than ever roamed in a world of internal phantasms and broken dreams, and who needed the most concentrated effort to finish the *Divina Commedia*, the dreamy immobility of Ravenna, the quality of posthumousness it conveyed, was the right place for his imagination. The dense woods of pine trees near the city; the tombs and reliquaries of the Caesars; the memory of Boethius and of the Emperor Justinian; the spiritual presence of the contemplative Peter Damian in the Benedictine abbeys surrounding the city; the riddle of shadows and the prodigy of the golden light in the mosaics of San Vitale and Sant' Apollinare in Classe (replicas of which Dante saw in Venice and Torcello) – these are the images of Ravenna that Dante evokes and crystallizes in the conclusive part of *Purgatorio* and in those parts of *Paradiso* he wrote or revised while in Ravenna.

It would not be entirely correct to suggest that the *genius loci* of Ravenna was merely the twilight, sepulchral sense that emanated from it and spoke so powerfully to the inward-looking, ageing poet. In the mosaics of Ravenna's basilicas, with their figurations of the Pantocrator (God as the all-ruling Father) hovering over the hierarchies of angels and saints, the Virgin Mary, and the extended narrative of the life of Christ (altogether different from that in the Scrovegni Chapel), Dante saw a confirmation of the esthetic-theological principles that shape his poem: his poetic vision, like Byzantine art, is the microcosmic recapitulation of the totality of the world.

Dante's poem, like the liturgical representations of the Ravenna basilicas, is an esthetic theology of the totality of history, eclectically made up of elements from the theologies and philosophies of Augustine, Albert the Great, Aquinas, Aristotle, and so on, but never reducible to any of them. If anything, actually, like the Greco-Byzantine art of the Ravenna basilicas and like Giotto's frescoes Dante had seen in Padua, all of which aim at inducing contemplation, his poem has its inevitable foundation in the contemplative theology of Benedict, Peter Damian, and Bernard of Clairvaux. As these contemplatives fully understood, and as Dante lucidly shows in his poem, poetry opposes the political world of partisan and partial interests and can only stem from the contemplation of the whole.

Dante's theoretical attitude, so marked in the final years of his life, never meant that he forgot the world and its cares. To presume this would be to falsify or altogether miss the essence of contemplation which always encompasses and underlies the sphere of moral action. This contemplative mode, however, accounts for the relative tranquility and for the real, if narrow, quiet the poet enjoyed in the last years of his life in Ravenna. His material needs were generously handled by Guido Novello for whom Dante undertook a number of missions; all of his children, even some of his grandchildren, and most likely his wife, Gemma Donati, were finally with him. Because of Guido Novello's generosity, his children's economic future looked bright, and this no doubt somewhat placated the poet's anxieties. He was also surrounded, as Giovanni Boccaccio reports, by disciples such as Pier Giardino, Giovanni Quirini, and Bernardino Canaccio; academics from Bologna, such as Giovanni del Virgilio, acknowledged his achievements and were eager to see him – the two of them even exchanged *Eclogues* that give a direct view into Dante's detachment from the idyllic pursuits of bland academic games called for by Giovanni and into his steady adherence to the summons of his sumptuous vision of glory.

It was here in Ravenna that, his poem finally completed, on returning from a trip to Venice, Dante died on September 13, 1321. It is usually said that death is the irreducible experience that unveils the meaning of a life. But because we do not know how Dante died – the fear and the joy this poet of the afterlife experienced at the point of his own death – the inner core of his life seems destined to remain impenetrable. Its public dimension, on the other hand, is a matter of record: the funerals he received, like the elegies written for the occasion by his admirers, were spectacular tributes to the passing of a rare man.

It cannot surprise us to find out that Dante's death marked the beginning of an effort to bring him back into the mythical memories of the living and to capture the vanished shape of his physical reality. Possibly as a way of tempering the dominantly legendary tone in his *Life of Dante*, Boccaccio goes out of his way to evoke the traits of Dante's physical appearance – his middle height, aquiline nose, large eyes, dark complexion, thick, black hair – as if the portrait could both root him in the reality of fact, and lead us to grasp the elusive secret of Dante's soul. Sometime later Domenico di Michelino drew a portrait of Dante, now hanging in Florence's Duomo, which figures the distance between the poet and his city. In his left hand the poet holds open the *Divina Commedia* as a gift to Florence, while with his right hand he points to the three realms of the beyond. The gates of the city, by contrast, remain shut. The secret of his soul, no doubt, is to be found in that gift.

SUGGESTED READING

Boccaccio's and Bruni's lives of Dante are available in *The Early Lives of Dante*, translated by Philip H. Wicksteed (London: Alexander Moring, 1904) and in a 1901 translation by James Robinson, published by Ungar (Milestones of Thought) in 1963 and frequently reprinted, most recently by Haskell House in 1974. Vincenzo

Zin Bollettino has translated Boccaccio's "Tratatello" for Garland (1990). Michele Barbi's own account of Dante's life is also available in English. See Michele Barbi, *Life of Dante*, trans. Paul Ruggiers (Berkeley and Los Angeles: University of California Press, 1960). See also Giorgio Petrocchi, *Vita di Dante* (Bari: Laterza, 1983), which extends his entry in the *Enciclopedia dantesca*, ed. U. Bosco, 6 vols. (Rome: Istituto dell'Enciclopedia Italiana, 1970–78).

More recent biographical studies include Stephen Bemrose's *A New Life of Dante* (Exeter: University of Exeter Press, 2000) and R. W. B. Lewis' *Dante* (New York: Penguin Viking, 2001). Biographical information also informs Robert Hollander's *Dante: A Life in Works* (New Haven and London: Yale University Press, 2001) and John A. Scott's *Understanding Dante* (Notre Dame: University of Notre Dame Press, 2004).

2

TEODOLINDA BAROLINI

Dante and the lyric past

Dante is heir to a complex and lively Italian lyric tradition that had its roots in the Provençal poetry nourished by the rivalling courts of twelfth-century southern France. The conventions of troubadour love poetry – based on the notion of the lover's feudal service to *midons* (Italian *madonna*), his lady, from whom he expects a *guerdon* (Italian *guiderdone*), or reward – were successfully transplanted to the court of Frederick II in Palermo, which became the capital of the first group of Italian vernacular lyric poets, the so-called Sicilian School. The centralized imperial court did not offer a suitable venue for the transplantation of Provence's contentious political poetry, which was left behind. The "leader" (or *caposcuola*) of the Sicilian School was Giacomo da Lentini, most likely the inventor of the sonnet (while the Provençal *canso* was the model for the Italian canzone, the sonnet is an Italian, and specifically Sicilian, contribution to the various European lyric "genres"). Giacomo signs himself "the Notary," referring to his position in the imperial government; this is the title Dante uses for him in *Purgatorio* 24, where the poet Bonagiunta is assigned the task of dividing the Italian lyric tradition between the old – represented by Giacomo, Guittone, and Bonagiunta himself – and the new: the avant-garde poets of the "dolce stil novo" or "sweet new style" (*Purgatorio* 24, 57), as Dante retrospectively baptizes the lyric movement that he helped spearhead in his youth. Like Giacomo, the other Sicilian poets were in the main court functionaries: in the *De vulgari eloquentia* Guido delle Colonne is called "Judge of Messina," while Pier della Vigna, whom Dante places among the suicides in Hell, was Frederick's chancellor and private secretary. Their moment in history coincides with Frederick's moment, and the demise of their school essentially coincides with the emperor's death in 1250.

At the heart of troubadour poetry is an unresolved tension between the poet-lover's allegiance to the lady and his allegiance to God; the love-service owed the one inevitably comes into conflict with the love-service owed the other. The conflict is rendered with great clarity in this sonnet by Giacomo da Lentini:

Io m'aggio posto in core a Dio servire,
com'io potesse gire in paradiso,
al santo loco ch'aggio audito dire,
u' si mantien sollazzo, gioco e riso.

Sanza mia donna non vi voria gire,
quella c'ha blonda testa e claro viso,
ché sanza lei non poteria gaudere,
estando da la mia donna diviso.

Ma no lo dico a tale intendimento,
perch'io peccato ci volesse fare;
se non veder lo suo bel portamento

e lo bel viso e 'l morbido sguardare:
ché lo mi teria in gran consolamento,
veggendo la mia donna in ghiora stare.

(I have proposed in my heart to serve God, that I might go to paradise, to the holy place of which I have heard said that there are maintained pleasure, play, and laughter. Without my lady I do not wish to go, the one who has a blond head and a clear face, since without her I could not take pleasure, being from my lady divided. But I do not say this with such an intention, that I would want to commit a sin; but rather because I would want to see her beautiful comportment and her beautiful face and her sweet glance: for it would keep me in great consolation, to see my lady be in glory.)

This poem both exemplifies the courtly thematic of conflicted desire, and provides an object lesson in the deployment of the sonnet as a formal construct. The Sicilian sonnet is divided into two parts, set off from each other by a change in rhyme: the octave rhymes ABABABAB, and the sextet rhymes CDCDCD. While there are possible variations in the rhyme scheme of the sextet (it could be CDECDE, for instance), there is always a switch at this point from the A and B rhymes to a new set of rhymes; there is always, in other words, a cleavage, created by rhyme, between the first eight verses and the latter six. It is this cleavage that "Io m'aggio posto" exploits in such paradigmatic fashion. Giacomo has perfectly fused form and content: the divisions inherent in the sonnet form express the divisions experienced by the poet-lover, who is himself "diviso" in the octave's last word. Moreover, subdivisions within the octave, divisible into two quatrains, and the sextet, divisible into two tercets (or, in this case, just as plausibly into three couplets), are also fully exploited in order to render the two poles of the poet-lover's divided allegiance.

As compared to the canzone, the lyric genre that allows for narrative development and forward movement, the sonnet's compact fourteen-verse form epitomizes a moment, a thought, or a problematic by approaching it from two dialectical perspectives: in a classic Italian sonnet, an issue is posed in the octave, and in some way reconsidered or resolved in the sextet. Looking at Giacomo's poem, we see that the first quatrain identifies one pole of the poet's desire: he wants to serve God, to go to paradise. His yearning does not at this stage seem conflicted, and the entire first quatrain could be placed under the rubric "Dio": "Io m'aggio posto in core a *Dio* servire." With hindsight we can see that the potential for conflict is already present in the fourth line's very secular – and very courtly – definition of paradise as a place that offers "sollazzo, gioco e riso": a trio lexically and morally associated not with the pleasures of paradise, but with the pleasures of the court. But the fact that there is an alternative pole of desire, an alternative claim on the lover's fealty, is not made evident until we reach the second quatrain, which belongs to the "donna" as much as the first quatrain belongs to "Dio": "Sanza mia *donna* non vi voria gire." Without her he does not want to go to paradise; the octave has neatly posed the problem with which the sextet must now deal. And in fact there is a sharp turn toward orthodoxy in the sextet's first couplet, in the initial adversative "Ma," and in the recognition that the lover's stance harbors a potential for sin, "peccato"; but a second adversative, "se non," follows on the heels of the first, negating its negation and reestablishing the poet's will to let the lady dominate. What follows is the listing of those literally "dominant" attributes (as in attributes pertaining to the *domina*) whose absence would render paradise intolerable, a concatenation of three adjective plus noun copulae that gains in momentum and power by being somewhat (in contrast to the otherwise relentlessly clipped syntactical standards of this poem) run on from line 11 to line 12: "lo suo bel portamento/e lo bel viso e 'l morbido sguardare." The lady is in the ascendant, and the poem concludes with a poetic resolution that makes the point that there is no ideological resolution to be had. Although the last line brings together the two terms of the conflict (the lady and "glory," or the lady and paradise), they are yoked in a kind of secularized beatific vision that affirms the poet-lover's commitment not to "Dio," but to the "donna": paradise is only desirable if it affords the opportunity to see "la mia donna in ghiora stare."

From Sicily the lyric moved north to the communes of Tuscany, where it was cultivated by poets like Bonagiunta da Lucca, Dante's purgatorial poetic taxonomist, and Guittone d'Arezzo (d. 1294), the *caposcuola* of the Tuscan School. Although consistently reviled by Dante for his "municipal" language and excessively ornate and cumbersomely convoluted verse, Guittone set the standard for Tuscan poets to follow, or – in the case of Dante and his fellow practitioners of the "sweet new style" – to refuse to follow. (From a lexical and stylistic perspective, in fact, the new style is best characterized precisely in terms of its rejection of the rhetorical and stylistic norms popularized by Guittone, through a process of winnowing that generated a refined but limited lexical and stylistic range.) A genuinely important poet who rewards study on his own terms, Guittone is responsible for key innovations in the Italian lyric: his *ornatus* derives not just from the Sicilians, but from first-hand appreciation of Provençal language, meter, and rhetoric; as a politically involved citizen of Arezzo, he is the first Italian poet to use the lyric as a forum for political concerns, in the tradition of the Provençal *sirventes*; he experienced a religious conversion (becoming a member of the Frati Godenti *c.* 1265) that is reflected in his verse, which moves, by way of the conversion canzone "Ora parrà s'eo saverò cantare," from love poetry to moral and ethical poetry, and even to religious lauds in honor of St. Francis and St. Dominic. Guittone is thus the first Italian poet to trace in his career a trajectory like that of Dante's (albeit without the epic dimension), and to embrace in his lyrics issues as diverse as the nature of love, in both its secular and divine manifestations, the moral code, with its virtues and vices, and the vicissitudes of Aretine and Florentine politics. Perhaps most significantly, Guittone's thematic innovations are at the service of his bourgeois didacticism, his view of himself as a moral *auctoritas*, a teacher; it is this stance that particularly infuriates his younger rivals, not only Dante but Guido Cavalcanti, who in the sonnet "Da più a uno face un sollegismo" scorns the notion of Guittone as a source of "insegnamento" ("teaching").

As we can see from the first two stanzas of "Ora parrà," Guittone deals with the problem of the lover-poet's dual allegiance by rejecting the troubadour ethos and what he brands carnal love for God and moral virtue:

> Ora parrà s'eo saverò cantare
> e s'eo varrò quanto valer già soglio,
> poi che del tutto Amor fuggh' e disvoglio,
> e più che cosa mai forte mi spare:
> ch'a om tenuto saggio audo contare
> che trovare – non sa né valer punto
> omo d'Amor non punto;
> ma' che digiunto – da vertà mi pare,
> se lo pensare – a lo parlare – sembra,
> ché 'n tutte parte ove distringe Amore
> regge follore – in loco di savere:
> donque como valere
> pò, né piacer – di guisa alcuna fiore,

poi dal Fattor – d'ogni valor – disembra
e al contrar d'ogni mainer' asembra?

Ma chi cantare vole e valer bene,
in suo legno a nochier Diritto pone
e orrato Saver mette al timone,
Dio fa sua stella, e 'n ver Lausor sua spene:
ché grande onor né gran bene no è stato
acquistato – carnal voglia seguendo,
ma promente valendo
e astenendo – *a* vizi' e *a* peccato;
unde 'l sennato – apparecchiato – ognora
de core tutto e di poder dea stare
d'avanzare – lo suo stato ad onore
no schifando labore:
ché già riccor – non dona altrui posare,
ma 'l fa lungiare, – e ben pugnare – onora;
ma tuttavia lo 'ntenda altri a misora.

(Now it will appear if I know how to sing, and if I am worth as much as I was accustomed to be worth, now that I completely flee Love and do not want it, and more than anything else find it very hateful. I have heard it said by a man considered wise that a man not pierced by Love does not know how to write poetry and is worth nothing; but far from the truth this seems to me, if there is concord between thought and word, for in all parts where Love seizes madness is king, in place of wisdom. Therefore how can he have worth or please in any way at all, since from the Maker of all worth he diverges and to the contrary in every way he resembles?

But he who wants to sing well and be worthy should place Justice in his ship as pilot, and put honored Wisdom at the helm, make God his star and place his hope in true Praise: for neither great honor nor great good have been acquired by following carnal desire, but by living as good men and abstaining from vice and from sin. Therefore the wise man must be prepared at all times with all his heart and power to advance his state to honor, not shunning toil; since indeed riches do not give anyone repose but rather distance it, and good striving brings honor, as long as one pursues it with measure.)

This poem displays essential Guittonian traits. Stylistically, the syntax is anything but clear and limpid, and it is rendered even more convoluted by the complex rhyme scheme with its *rimalmezzo*, or rhyme in the center of the verse (marked by modern editors with dashes). Thematically, a bourgeois ethic comes into play, as the poet, following his rejection of the troubadour equation between Love and true worth, exhorts us to pursue civic morality and virtuous moderation: although he tells us on the one hand to reject carnal desire (which is what courtly love becomes when stripped of its sustaining ideology), he does not tell us on the other to embrace monastic contemplation. The Guittonian ideal is a life of measured toil and measured gain, leavened by the pursuit of "orrato Saver" and the advancement of one's "stato ad onore": an honored position in the community and a wisdom conceived in terms less metaphysical than practical and ethical.

Our historical assessments of the various alliances that both bound these early Italian poets into schools and polarized them as rivals are not merely the product of an arbitrary need to order the unruly past; in the instance of the emerging Italian lyric, the record shows a keen – and frequently barbed – self-consciousness of such groupings on the part of the poets themselves. Thus, in a sonnet attributed to the Tuscan Chiaro Davanzati ("Di penne di paone"), a fellow poet, perhaps Bonagiunta, is accused of dressing himself in poetic finery stolen from the Sicilian Giacomo da Lentini; the same Bonagiunta will accuse Guido Guinizzelli, the Bolognese poet whom Dante hails as the father of the new style in *Purgatorio* 26, of having altered love poetry for the worse, of having "changed the manner of elegant verses of love" ("Voi, ch'avete mutata la maniera/de li plagenti ditti de l'amore"). Considered a "Siculo-Tuscan" for his use of both Sicilian and Guittonian mannerisms, Bonagiunta is unhappy with the newfangled directions in which Guinizzelli is heading: he does not understand what the "wisdom of Bologna" (a reference to that city's university, noted as a center of philosophical study) has to do with love poetry, and he accuses Guinizzelli of writing pretentious, obscure verse whose philosophical subtleties make it impossible to decode. For modern readers, who find Guittone's rhetorical virtuosity so much more of a barrier than Guinizzelli's modest importation of philosophy into poetry, Bonagiunta's critique may seem misdirected, but his sonnet provides an important contemporary view of the poetic movement that Italian literary historiographers, following Dante, have continued to call the *stil novo*. The exchange between Bonagiunta and the forerunner Guinizzelli will be echoed in later exchanges between conservatives and full-fledged *stilnovisti*; we think of the correspondence between Guido Cavalcanti and Guido Orlandi, for instance, or the parodic indictment of the new style found in the sonnets addressed by Onesto degli Onesti to Dante's friend and poetic comrade Cino da Pistoia.

So, what is this new style that created such consternation among those contemporary poets who were not its adherents? Initiated by the older and non-Florentine Guinizzelli (who seems to have died by 1276), the core practitioners are younger and, with the exception of Cino, Florentine: Guido Cavalcanti (the traditional birth year of 1259 has recently been challenged in favor of *c.* 1250; he died in 1300), Dante (1265–1321), Cino (*c.* 1270–1336 or 1337), and the lesser Lapo Gianni, Gianni Alfani, and Dino Frescobaldi.

In characterizing this movement, Bonagiunta was right to point to the yoking of philosophy – indeed theology – to Eros. What Bonagiunta could not foresee was the fertility of a conjoining that would effectively dissolve the impasse that drove troubadour poetry and give rise to a theologized courtly love, epitomized by the figure of Dante's Beatrice, the lady who does not separate the lover from God but leads him to God.

But we are getting ahead of ourselves. Bonagiunta's complaint regarding the theologizing of love was directed at Guinizzelli, and Guinizzelli's canzone "Al cor gentil rempaira sempre amore" is an excellent case in point: its fifth stanza argues that the noble lover should obey his lady in the same way that the angelic intelligence obeys God, thus implicitly setting up analogies between the lover and the heavenly intelligence on the one hand, and the lady and God on the other. As though to acknowledge – and simultaneously defuse – the radical thrust of his argument, in the *congedo* Guinizzelli dramatizes an imagined confrontation between himself and God, by whom he stands accused of having dared to make vain semblances of the divine, of having presumed to find traces of God's love in what can only be a "vano amor," a vain earthly love:

> Donna, Deo mi dirà: "Che presomisti?,"
> siando l'alma mia a lui davanti.
> "Lo ciel passasti e 'nfin a Me venisti,
> e desti in vano amor Me per semblanti;
> ch'a Me conven le laude
> e a la reina del regname degno,
> per cui cessa onne fraude."
> Dir Li porò: "Tenne d'angel sembianza
> che fosse del Tuo regno;
> non me fu fallo, s'in lei posi amanza."

(Lady, God will say to me: "How did you presume?," when my soul will be in front of him. "You passed through the heavens and came all the way to me, and you rendered me through the likenesses of vain love; for to me belong the praises and to the queen of the worthy kingdom, through whom all wickedness dies." I will be able to say to him: "She had the semblance of an angel that was of your kingdom; it was no fault in me, if I placed love in her.")

In other words, Guinizzelli has God tell him that he has gone too far. This poet, who has in fact transgressed, pushing to new latitudes the boundaries of the tradition in which he works, finds a supremely witty way of solidifying his gains, of sanctioning his boldness and concretizing what could have seemed merely a whimsical passing conceit: he stages the trial of his presumption ("Che presomisti?" is God's opening argument), registering the indictment but also therefore the self-defense, the justification that he offers before the divine tribunal. It is simply this: the lady possessed the semblance of an angel, of a creature of God's realm; therefore it was not his fault if he loved her. Thus Guinizzelli both acknowledges the dangers of his audacious yoking of the secular with the divine, and brilliantly defends his analogical procedure. If his original "fault" was a too expansive definition of the likenesses through which we can know God ("e desti in vano amor Me *per semblanti*"), the defense will rest on just such a likeness ("Tenne d'angel *sembianza*"). Guinizzelli justifies himself with the same analogies which were his sin in the first place, throwing the blame back on the original writer, God, who in his book of the universe made ladies so like angels.

In fact, the *congedo* of "Al cor gentil," with its stated likeness between ladies and angels, backs off somewhat from the canzone's fifth stanza, with its implied likeness between the lady and God himself. The net result of the poem, nonetheless, is to take the possibility of similitude between the lady and the divine much more seriously than it had been taken heretofore, to take her "angelic" qualities out of the realm of amorous hyperbole and into the realm of bona fide theological speculation. With respect to the impasse of troubadour poetry, evoked by Guinizzelli in the "Donna, Deo" conjunction with which the *congedo* begins, we could say that the explicit dramatization of the conflict in "Al cor gentil" goes a long way towards removing it as a problem. In sharp contrast to the troubadours, whose careers are frequently capped by recanting both love and love poetry and retiring to a monastery; in contrast to Giacomo da Lentini, who airs the conflict at its most conflictual in the sonnet "Io m'aggio posto in core a Dio servire"; in contrast to Guittone, who in a bourgeois Italian variation of the troubadour model rejects love but without retiring from secular life; in contrast to all the above, Guinizzelli provides a first step toward the "solution": he begins the process of making the lady more like God so that the two poles of the dilemma are conflated, with the result that the lover does not have to choose between them.

Likeness and similitude are Guinizzelli's modes of choice, paving the way for the *Vita nuova* and ultimately the *Commedia*, where similitude will give way to metaphor, as Dante conflates into one the two poles of his desire, making the journey to Beatrice coincide with the journey to God, and collapsing much farther than theology would warrant the distinction between the lady – the luminous and numinous sign of God's presence on earth – and the ultimate being whose significance she figures forth. In the sonnet "Io vogl' del ver la mia donna laudare" ("I want in truth to praise my lady"), Guinizzelli's theologically ennobled lady possesses literally beatific effects: when she passes by, she lowers pride in anyone she greets, makes a believer of anyone who is not, serves as a barometer of moral worth, since she cannot be approached by anyone base, and prevents evil thoughts, since no man can think evilly while he sees her. This poetics of praise, owed to the lady as a literal beatifier, is the Guinizzellian feature that Dante will exploit for his personal *stil novo* as distilled in the *Vita nuova*. In that work Dante builds on and further radicalizes Guinizzelli's theologized courtly love to confect his Beatrice, a lady whose powers to bless (people know her name, "she who beatifies," "she who gives *beatitudine*," without having ever been told) and whose links to the divine are beyond anything yet envisioned within the lyric tradition:

> Ella si va, sentendosi laudare
> benignamente d'umiltà vestuta;
> e par che sia una cosa venuta
> da cielo in terra a miracol mostrare.
> ("Tanto gentile e tanto
> onesta pare")

(She passes by, hearing herself praised, benignly dressed in humility; and she appears to be a thing come from heaven to earth to show forth a miracle.)

The sacramental and Christological dimensions of the *Vita nuova*'s Beatrice, the fact that she has come from heaven to earth as a manifest miracle, that the portents of her death are the portents of Christ's death, that she *is* the incarnate number nine, take Guinizzelli's solutions an enormous step further along the road from simile ("Tenne d'angel sembianza") to metaphor ("d'umiltà vestuta"), from assimilation to, to appropriation of, the divine.

Along this road that leads in a straight line from the theologized courtly love of the *stil novo* to the incarnational poetics of the *Commedia* there is a magisterial detour, a magnificent dead end (a *"disaventura,"* to use his word), and this is the path called Guido Cavalcanti. Guido's poetic *disaventura* can be considered a dead end in two ways: first, with respect to its ideology, which conceives love as a dead-end passion, a sub-rational natural force that leads not to life but to death; second, with respect to its impact on a lyric genealogy that was retroactively pulled into line by the gravitational force of Dante's achievement, which conceives love as a super-rational force that leads not to death but life. So Guido – the "best friend" of the *Vita nuova*, the poet whom both his contemporaries and modern scholarship know as the leader and originator of the *stil novo* movement, a man whose influence over Dante was not just poetic but personal and biographical – was rendered a detour on the highroad of the lyric by the poet of the *Commedia*, a work that bears the traces of its author's need to define himself as *not* Guido Cavalcanti.

The negativity that Dante worked so hard to negate is expressed most explicitly and theoretically in the famous canzone "Donna me prega," where Guido assigns love to that faculty of the soul that is "non razionale, – ma che sente" ("not rational, but which feels"), that is, to the seat of the passions, the sensitive soul, with the result that love deprives us of reason and judgment, discerns poorly, and induces vice, so that "Di sua potenza segue spesso morte" ("from its power death often follows"). But one need not look only to the philosophical canzone for Cavalcanti's tragic view of love. Although he sings throughout his verse of a lady who is, like Guinizzelli's lady, supremely endowed with worth and beauty, there is a tragic catch. Yes, she is an "angelicata – criatura" ("angelic creature") and "Oltra natura umana" ("Beyond human nature") in the early *ballata* "Fresca rosa novella," "piena di valore" ("full of worth") in the sonnet "Li mie' foll'occhi," possessed of "grande valor" ("great worth") in the sonnet "Tu m'hai sì piena di dolor la mente," and the litany could go on: Cavalcanti's lady is no less potent than Guinizzelli's. The problem is that she is *too* potent with respect to the lover, whose ability to benefit from her worth has been degraded while she has been enhanced. Thus, in the canzone "Io non pensava che lo cor giammai," Love warns the lover of his impending death, caused by her excessive worth and power: "Tu non camperai,/ ché troppo è lo valor di costei forte" ("You will not survive, for too great is the worth of that lady"). The poet-lover is dispossessed, stripped of his vitality, integrity, "valore," his very self: "dirò com'ho perduto ogni valore" ("I will tell how I have lost all worth"), he says in "Poi che di doglia cor." Because of her *troppo* valore, he will lose "ogni valore." From the lover's perspective, therefore, her worth is worthless because he has no access to it; it is in fact worse than worthless because it destroys him. As a result, the education of the lover is not an issue for Cavalcanti: in a context where the will is stripped of all potency, its redirection from the carnal to the transcendent becomes a moot point.

The education of the lover is, however, very much the point in the *Vita nuova*: Beatrice is a living lady of this earth, and yet the lover has to be weaned from desiring even as non-carnal an earthly reward as Beatrice's greeting. Unlike Cavalcanti's lady, a carrier of death, Beatrice is truly a *beatrice*, a carrier of life, but the *beatitudine* she brings is not of easy access. To find the blessedness/happiness offered by Beatrice the lover must redefine his very idea of what happiness is. It can have nothing to do with possession (even of the most metaphorical sort), since the possession of any mortal object of desire will necessarily fail him when that object succumbs to its mortality – in short, when it dies. Like Augustine after the death of his friend, he must learn the error of "loving a man that must die as though he were not to die" ("diligendo moriturum ac si non moriturum," *Confessions* 4, 8). Similarly, and painfully, the lover of the *Vita nuova* must learn to locate his happiness in "that which cannot fail me" ("quello che non mi puote venire meno," *Vita nuova* 18, 4), a lesson that constitutes a theologizing of the troubadour *guerdon* along Augustinian lines: because the lady and thus her greeting are mortal and will die, they are objects of desire that – for all their relative perfection – will finally fail him. Therefore the lover must learn to redirect his longing to that which cannot fail him, namely the transcendent part of her with which he can be reunited in God, the part that may indeed serve to lead him to God. Viewed from this perspective, the *Vita nuova* is nothing less than a courtly medieval inflection of the Augustinian paradigm whereby life – new life – is achieved by mastering the lesson of death. The *Vita nuova* teaches us, in the words of Dylan Thomas, that "after the first death there is no other" (from "A Refusal to Mourn the Death, by Fire, of a Child in London"); having encountered the lesson of mortality once, when Beatrice dies, the lover should not need to be taught it again. This is in fact the burden of Beatrice's rebuke to the pilgrim when she meets him in the Earthly Paradise: "e se 'l sommo piacer sì ti fallio/per la mia morte, qual cosa mortale/dovea poi trarre te nel suo disio?" ("and if the supreme pleasure thus failed you, with my death, what mortal thing should then have drawn you into desire?," *Purgatorio* 31, 52–54).

Formally, the *Vita nuova* is a collection of previously written lyrics that, sometime after the death of Beatrice in 1290, most likely in 1292–94, Dante set in a prose frame. The lyrics are chosen with an eye to telling the story of the lover's development, his gradual realization of Beatrice's sacramental significance as a visible sign of invisible grace. They also tell an idealized story of the poet's development, tracing Dante's lyric itinerary from his early Guittonianism (see the so-called double sonnets of chapters 7 and 8), through his Cavalcantianism (see the sonnet that begins with the hapax "Cavalcando" in chapter 9, the *ballata* – Cavalcanti's form par excellence – of chapter 12, and the Cavalcantian torments of the sonnets in chapters 14–16), to the discovery – with some help from Guido Guinizzelli – of his own voice in the canzone "Donne ch'avete intelletto d'amore." Prior to the inspired composition of "Donne ch'avete," the poet-lover undergoes the inquisition that induces him to declare that he no longer desires that which is bound to fail him, but instead has centered his desire "in those words that praise my lady" ("In quelle parole che lodano la donna mia," *Vita nuova* 18, 6). The lover's conversion, from one desire (the possession of her greeting) to another (the ability to praise her, to celebrate the miracle of her sacramental existence), is here explicitly stated in poetic terms, is indeed presented as a poet's conversion as well, since his desire for a transcendent Beatrice is formulated as a desire for the words with which to laud her. The *Vita nuova*'s key spiritual lesson is thus aligned with a poetic manifesto for what Dante will call "the style of her praise" ("lo stilo de la sua loda," *Vita nuova* 25, 4).

The first poem we encounter after the conversion of chapter 18 is the canzone "Donne ch'avete," whose incipit is visited upon the poet in a divine dictation akin to that described by Dante as the source of his "nove rime" in *Purgatorio* 24; "la mia lingua parlò quasi come per sé stessa mossa" ("my tongue spoke almost as if moved by itself," *Vita nuova* 19, 2) adumbrates the *Purgatorio*'s famous profession of poetic faith: "I' mi son un che, quando/Amor mi spira, noto, e a quel modo/ch'e' ditta dentro vo significando" ("I am one who, when Love inspires me, takes note, and in that fashion that Love dictates goes signifying," *Purgatorio* 24, 52–54). "Donne ch'avete" is canonized in the purgatorial encounter with Bonagiunta as the prescriptive example of the *stil novo*, the fountainhead and beginning of the "new rhymes," as though the lyric tradition had no past but originated with "le nove rime, *cominciando*/'Donne ch'avete intelletto d'amore'" ("the new rhymes, *beginning* 'Ladies who have intellect of love,'" *Purgatorio* 24, 50–51; my italics). The authorized version of Dante's lyric past recounted implicitly by the *Vita nuova* is thus confirmed by the *Commedia*, where a selective view of the lyric tradition is put forward through the network of presences and absences, encounters, statements, and echoes that make up the complicated tissue of the *Commedia*'s vernacular memory.

In brief, the *Commedia*'s version of Dante's lyric past is as follows. The influence of previous moral/didactic/political poetry is discounted. Dante denigrates the strongest Italian precursor in this vein, Guittone, first in the generic distancing of himself from all "old" schools that is put into the mouth of Bonagiunta in *Purgatorio* 24, then again in *Purgatorio* 26, where – using Guinizzelli as his spokesperson this time – he singles out the Aretine for attack, ascribing Guittone's erstwhile preeminence to outmoded tastes. In the same passage, Guinizzelli takes the opportunity to refer in less than glowing terms to Giraut de Bornelh, the Provençal poet whose treatment of moral themes Dante had cited with approbation in the *De vulgari eloquentia*, calling him a poet of "rectitude" and as such the troubadour equivalent of himself. *Purgatorio* 26 thus handily liquidates Dante's major vernacular lyric precursors in the moral/didactic mode. Dante also fails to acknowledge Guittone's political verse, championing as a political lyricist instead the lesser poet Sordello in an episode that is not without clear intertextual links to the displaced Aretine. With regard to the influence of previous vernacular love poets, the history of Dante's poetic indebtedness is rewritten in a way that gives disproportionate importance to Guinizzelli: the poetic "father" of *Purgatorio* 26 absorbs some of the credit due to Guido Cavalcanti as the major stylistic force in the forging of the *stil novo*. Dante's tribute to the love poet Arnaut Daniel, on the other hand, also in *Purgatorio* 26, is not inconsistent with the influence of the inventor of the sestina on the poet of the *petrose*; but it is worth noting that the exaltation of the Provençal love poet, Arnaut, is at the expense of the Provençal moral poet, Giraut.

Neither the *Vita nuova* nor the *Commedia* intends to tell the full story regarding Dante's lyric past. For that, we have to turn to the lyrics that Dante left as lyrics, that he never pressed into the service of any larger enterprise or ordered among themselves in any way, and that scholars refer to as the *Rime*. This wonderful collection of eighty-nine poems of definite attribution – sonnets, *ballate*, and canzoni written over a span of approximately twenty-five years (from *c.* 1283 to *c.* 1307–08), that is, from Dante's teens to after the *Inferno* was already begun – brings us as close as we can come to the poet's inner workshop, to glimpsing the ways by which Dante became Dante. These poems testify to the paths not taken, and also help us to see more freshly and vividly when, how, and by what slow process of accretion he embarked on the paths he did take. Moreover, the *Rime* embody the essence of a poetic adventurer; they remind us that Dante's hallmark is his never-ceasing experimentalism, his linguistic and stylistic voracity.

Because they vary so greatly among themselves, editors have found it convenient to order them under rough chronological headings, as follows: very early poems written in the Tuscan manner (e.g., the *tenzone* with Dante da Maiano); early poems experimenting in a variety of manners, from the Sicilian (e.g., the canzone "La dispietata mente"), to the playful realism associated with poets such as Folgòre da San Gimignano (e.g., the sonnet "Sonar bracchetti"), to the light strains of the Cavalcantian *ballata* (e.g., the *ballata* "Per una ghirlandetta"); poems of the time of the *Vita nuova*, and – whether or not included in the *libello* – written in the style we associate with the *stil novo* (a style that includes, for instance, the love poems dedicated in the *Convivio* to, but in my opinion not originally written for, Lady Philosophy). Through the *stil novo* phase, Dante's poetic agenda is, as Foster and Boyde point out in their edition, one of contraction and refinement; he eliminates both lexically and stylistically to achieve the refined purity of the high *stil novo*. The phase of contraction gives way around 1295 to the expansion, both lexical and stylistic, that will characterize the rest of Dante's poetic career and that is pioneered in the following groups of lyrics: the *tenzone* with Forese Donati, written before Forese's death in 1296; the so-called *rime petrose*, or "stony" poems, about a stony, hard, and ice-cold lady, "la pietra," dated internally by "Io son venuto" to December of 1296; moral and doctrinal verse, written most likely between 1295 and 1300, such as the canzone on true nobility, "Le dolci rime," and the canzone on the esteemed courtly quality of *leggiadria*, "Poscia ch'Amor." Finally, there are the great lyrics of exile: the canzone that treats Dante's own exile, "Tre donne"; powerful late moral verse, such as the canzone on avarice, "Doglia mi reca"; and late love poetry, such as the correspondence sonnets exchanged with Cino da Pistoia and the canzone "Amor, da che convien." Although Dante's lyrics are sometimes valued less than the more mono-tonal and unified productions of, say, Cavalcanti or Petrarch, it is precisely their infinite variety that is the key to Dante's greatness. They are – with the prose works written during these years – the worthy and necessary prerequisites for a work as non-finite as the great poem.

The *Rime* contain the traces of Dante's stylistic and ideological experimentation. The *tenzone* of scurrilous sonnets exchanged between Dante and his friend Forese Donati, for instance, was long denied a place among Dante's works because of its base content, considered inappropriate for the refined poet of the *Vita nuova*; and yet, without it, we would be hard put to trace the passage from the tightly circumscribed world of the *Vita nuova* to the all-inclusive cosmos of the *Commedia*. Nor does the *tenzone*'s lowly content obscure the archetypal signs of Dante's poetic mastery, evidenced by the compact vigor and concise force of his diction, and the effortless energy with which one insult springs from another. Whereas Forese requires a full sonnet to accuse Dante of being a bounder who lives off the charity of others, Dante characteristically packs an insult into each verse of the opening quatrain of "Bicci novel," which tells Forese that (1) he is a bastard, (2) his mother is dishonored, (3) he is a glutton, and (4) to support his gluttony he is a thief:

> Bicci novel, figliuol di non so cui
> (s'i' non ne domandasse monna Tessa),
> giù per la gola tanta roba hai messa
> ch'a forza ti convien tòrre l'altrui.

(Young Bicci, son of I don't know who [short of asking my lady Tessa], you've stuffed so much down your gorge that you're driven to take from others.)
(Foster and Boyde, *Dante's Lyric Poetry*, I, p. 153)

Stylistically, the *Rime* demonstrate continuities converging in the *Commedia*: thus, we can discern in the *tenzone* the seeds of a later vulgar and realistic style associated with *Inferno*. Ideologically, however, the *Rime* offer fascinating examples of discontinuities: thus, the early and generically *stilnovist* canzoni "E' m'incresce di me" and "Lo doloroso amor" testify to the possibility of an anti-*Vita nuova*, a Cavalcantian *Vita nuova*, whose Beatrice brings not life but death. In "Lo doloroso amor" Dante declares "Per quella moro c'ha nome Beatrice" ("I die because of her whose name is Beatrice"), a scandalous enough assertion for a poet whose career is forged on the notion that "Per quella vivo c'ha nome Beatrice." And in "E' m'incresce di me," the birth of a lady who possesses "homicidal eyes" ("occhi micidiali") is described in language resonant of the *Vita nuova*:

> Lo giorno che costei nel mondo venne,
> secondo che si trova
> nel libro de la mente che vien meno,
> la mia persona pargola sostenne
> una passïon nova,
> tal ch'io rimasi di paura pieno . . .

(The day that she came into the world, according to what is found in the book of my mind that is passing away, my childish body sustained a new emotion, such that I remained full of fear.)

From the perspective of the *Vita nuova* or the *Commedia*, where Cavalcanti is ideologically discounted, what we find here is an impossible hybrid, a fusion of elements that in the more canonical texts are kept separate. There are elements typical of the *Vita nuova*: the treatment of Beatrice's presence, in this case her birth, as a historically and literally miraculous event; the reference to the protagonist's "book of memory," in which the events of his life have been recorded; his juvenile susceptibility to a "passïon" defined as "nova," that is, miraculous, unexpected, totally new. But these elements are joined, as they would not be in the *Vita nuova*, to Cavalcantian stylemes: the book of his mind is failing, passing away, while the "passïon nova" fills the lover with that most Cavalcantian of emotions, fear.

Dante cannot be pigeonholed; his lyrics are salutary reminders that the dialectical twists of his itinerary cannot be flattened into a straightforward progress. We must remember Dante's sonnet to Cino da Pistoia, written most likely between 1303 and 1306, and thus a decade or so after the spiritualized love of the *Vita nuova*, in which he characterizes love as an overriding force that dominates reason and free will, and admits to having first experienced such love in his ninth year, that is vis-à-vis Beatrice:

> Io sono stato con Amore insieme
> da la circulazione del sol mia nona,
> e so com'egli affrena e come sprona,
> e come sotto lui si ride e geme.
> Chi ragione o virtù contra gli sprieme,
> fa come que' che 'n la tempesta sona . . .

(I have been together with Love since my ninth revolution of the sun, and I know how he curbs and how he spurs, and how under him one laughs and groans. He who puts forth reason or virtue against him does as one who makes noise during a tempest.)

"Sotto lui si ride e geme": here the lover is literally "beneath" love's dominion, literally *sommesso*, to use the verb that in *Inferno* 5 characterizes the lustful, those who submit reason to desire: "che la ragion sommettono al talento" (*Inferno* 5, 39). As Foster and Boyde comment: "This is the more remarkable in that Dante is now about forty years old and has behind him not only the *Vita nuova* with its story of an entirely sublimated 'heavenly' love, but also the series of canzoni that more or less directly celebrated a love that had its seat in the mind of intellect" (*Dante's Lyric Poetry*, II, p. 323). By the same token, Dante's last canzone is no tribute to sublimation, but "Amor, da che convien pur ch'io mi doglia," a Cavalcantian testament to deadly Eros that has been infused with a decidedly non-Cavalcantian vigor. The poet finds himself in the mountains of the Casentino, in the valley of the Arno where Love's power exerts its greatest strength; here Love works him over (the untranslatable "Così m'hai concio"), kneading him, reducing him to a pulp:

> Così m'hai concio, Amore, in mezzo l'alpi,
> ne la valle del fiume
> lungo il qual sempre sopra me se' forte:
> qui vivo e morto, come vuoi, mi palpi,
> merzé del fiero lume
> che sfolgorando fa via a la morte.

(To this state, Love, you have reduced me, among the mountains, in the valley of the river along which you are always strong over me; here, just as you will, you knead me, both alive and dead, thanks to the fierce light that flashing opens the road to death.)

The love-death of "Amor, da che convien," the ineluctable force against which (as explained in "Io sono stato") neither reason nor virtue can prevail, resurfaces in the *Commedia*'s story of Paolo and Francesca, wherein unopposable passion leads to death and damnation. Nor is the condemnation that awaits those unruly lovers without antecedents in the lyrics; roughly contemporaneous with "Io sono stato" and "Amor, da che convien" is the canzone "Doglia mi reca ne lo core ardire," whose indictment of passion ungoverned by virtue and reason inhabits a moral framework that is highly suggestive vis-à-vis the *Commedia*. The breadth and complexity of this canzone can be inferred from its juxtaposition of a courtly discourse with a more strictly ethical and moralizing bent; like Guittone in "Ora parrà," but much more systematically, Dante links carnal desire to desire for wealth, thus exploding the courtly ethos that would privilege love over baser desires and illuminating the common ground of all concupiscence. In the second stanza of "Ora parrà," cited earlier, Guittone rejects the pursuit of "carnal voglia" ("carnal desire") and recommends a life of abstinence from vice and willingness to toil; then, in an apparent non sequitur, he tells us that "riches do not give anyone repose but rather distance it, and good striving brings honor, as long as one pursues it with measure." Guittone is concerned lest, having exhorted us to reject carnal desire, he may seem – in his pursuit of the good life – to endorse the equally pernicious desire for material gain. The recognition that a repudiation of carnal desire – lust – must not be an endorsement of material desire – avarice – leads to the second stanza's concluding injunction against "riccor" ("riches"), and sets the stage for the fourth stanza's dramatic assertion that it is not we who possess gold but gold that possesses us: "Non manti acquistan l'oro,/ ma l'oro loro" ("Not many acquire gold, but gold acquires them"). In other words, Guittone first demystifies courtly love, calling it lust, carnal desire, and then links it to other forms of immoderate and excessive desire, all rooted in cupidity. It is this conflation between lust and greed, love and avarice, that is the key to "Doglia mi reca," a canzone which, although frequently and not incorrectly referred to as Dante's canzone on avarice, and therefore characterized as "stumbling" upon its main theme rather late (Foster and Boyde, *Dante's Lyric Poetry*, II, p. 305), in fact deliberately sets out to graft a discourse on avarice onto its courtly (actually anti-courtly) introduction.

"Doglia mi reca" begins, aggressively enough, by refusing to exculpate women from their share of the moral blame in matters of love; it is their duty to deny their love to men who cannot match in virtue what women offer in beauty. Acknowledging that he will speak "parole quasi contra tutta gente" ("words against almost everyone"), Dante inveighs, in the poem's first stanza, against the "base desire" ("vil vostro disire") that would permit a woman to love an unworthy man. He then announces, in the second stanza, that men have distanced themselves from virtue, and are therefore not men but evil beasts that resemble men ("omo no, mala bestia ch'om simiglia"); although virtue is the only "possession" worth having, men enslave themselves to vice. The submerged logical link between the phases of this argument is desire: we move from the ladies' "vil disire" for non-virtuous men in the first stanza, to virtue, the "possession che sempre giova" ("possession that is always beneficial"), that is, the only possession worth desiring, in the second. The point is that men enslave themselves through their desire; by not desiring to possess virtue, the only possession of real worth, and by desiring to possess what is not virtuous, they are doubly enslaved, being, as the third stanza puts it, slaves "not of a lord, but of a base slave": "Servo non di signor, ma di vil servo." Once we grasp the logic that links the two phases of the argument, the courtly to the moral, both viewed as discourses of desire, the fourth stanza's engagement of issues not normally associated with poems addressed to "donne" is less startling: the man whom the ladies are not supposed to love, the man enslaved to vice, is now compared to the miser in pursuit of wealth. In verses whose irascible energy adumbrates the *Commedia*, Dante depicts the "mad desire" ("folle volere") that induces a man to run after that which can never give him satisfaction:

> Corre l'avaro, ma più fugge pace:
> oh mente cieca, che non pò vedere
> lo suo folle volere
> che 'l numero, ch'ognora a passar bada,
> che 'nfinito vaneggia.
> Ecco giunta colei che ne pareggia:
> dimmi, che hai tu fatto,
> cieco avaro disfatto?
> Rispondimi, se puoi, altro che "Nulla."
> Maladetta tua culla,
> che lusingò cotanti sonni invano;
> maladetto lo tuo perduto pane,
> che non si perde al cane:
> ché da sera e da mane
> hai raunato e stretto ad ambo mano
> ciò che sì tosto si rifà lontano.

(The miser runs, but peace flees faster: oh blind mind, whose mad desire cannot see that the number, which it seeks always to pass, stretches to infinity. Now here is the one who makes us all equal: tell me, what have you done, blind undone miser? Answer me, if you can, other than "Nothing." Cursed be your cradle, which flattered so many dreams in vain; cursed be the bread lost on you, which is not lost on a dog – for evening and morning you have gathered and held with both hands that which so quickly distances itself again.)

The force and vitality of this passage alert us to the fact that Dante has here tapped into a wellspring of his poetic identity. Indeed, the same miser recurs in the *Convivio*, presented in very similar terms: "e in questo errore cade l'avaro maladetto, e non s'accorge che desidera sé sempre desiderare, andando dietro al numero impossibile a giugnere" ("and into this error falls the cursed miser, and he does not realize that he desires himself always to desire, going after the number impossible to reach," *Convivio* III, xv, 9). The miser is a figure through whom Dante explores the possibility of expanding the problematic of desire from the courtly and private to the social and public; from this perspective, the miser is an emblem of the transition from the *Vita nuova* to the *Commedia*. When, in the final stanza of "Doglia mi reca," Dante readdresses himself to the ladies, and denounces anyone who allows herself to be loved by such a man as he has described, he also ties together the poem's threads of desire into one knot of concupiscence: the depraved call by the name of "love" what is really mere bestial appetite ("chiamando amore appetito di fera"); they believe love to be "outside of the garden of reason" ("e crede amor fuor d'orto di ragione"). Dante has here welded the lover and the miser, and in so doing he has created a node of enormous significance for his future, no less than an adumbration of that she-wolf whose cupidity subtends both the lust of Paolo and Francesca and the political corruption of Florence. Courtly literature offers us many examples of lovers whose passion is outside of reason's garden, who are impelled by the "folle volere" that drives the miser, but courtly literature never dreams of calling the immoderate lover a miser; nor would the protagonist of Dante's sonnet "Io sono stato," which boldly proclaims that reason has no power against love, expect to find himself compared to an *avaro maladetto*! By making the comparison, Dante skewers courtly values, as Guittone had done before him, and then goes further: the comparison of the lover to the miser lays the foundation for the moral edifice of the *Commedia*, which is based on the notion of desire or love as the motive force for *all* our actions. Misdirected or immoderate desire leads to sin, and is therefore the distant origin for what we witness in Hell, where the misshapen desire has crystallized into act, as well as the more proximate origin for what we witness in Purgatory, where the soul's desires and dispositions are still visible in uncrystallized form. Love is, in fact, the impulse to which we can reduce all good action and its contrary: "amore, a cui reduci/ogne buono operare e 'l suo contraro" (*Purgatorio* 18, 14–15).

I will conclude this discussion of the significance of "Doglia mi reca" with a formal coda. The *Commedia* is a poem of epic dimension, epic scale, and yet it is also the most lyric of epics: it is the epic of the "I." Not only its first-person narrator, but also the lyricized narrative texture that is ever more present (for, with due respect to Croce, the "lyrical" canticle is not *Inferno*, but *Paradiso*) are indices of a lyric past that Dante chose never to leave behind. One feature of the *Commedia* that points to Dante's vernacular and lyric roots is the canto: why does Dante choose to invent the division into cantos, rather than divide his epic into long books of the sort Virgil uses in the *Aeneid*? Conceptually, I believe that the choice of the canto is connected to Dante's obsession with the new; the division into cantos renders the spiralling rhythm of new dawns and new dusks, the incessant new beginnings and endings that punctuate the line of becoming, the "cammin di nostra vita." Formally, I believe that the roots of the canto are to be sought in Dante's vernacular apprenticeship. A long canzone is roughly the length of a canto;

indeed, at 158 lines "Doglia mi reca" is longer than most cantos. When we think of the *Commedia* as 100 canzoni stitched together, we can better grasp both the later Dante's vertiginous distance from, and his remarkable fidelity to, his lyric past.

SUGGESTED READING

The twentieth century produced three great editions of Dante's lyrics, each magisterial in its own way. The fruits of Michele Barbi's long philological and historical labors are to be found in two volumes published after his death: M. Barbi and F. Maggini, eds., *Rime della Vita nuova e della giovinezza* (Florence: Le Monnier, 1956); M. Barbi and V. Pernicone, eds., *Rime della maturità e dell'esilio* (Florence: Le Monnier, 1969). Gianfranco Contini's *Rime* of 1946 (Milan: Einaudi, 2nd edn., 1965) remains unsurpassed for the pithiness and elegance of its formulations. Most useful for its comprehensiveness and for the clarity of the portrait that emerges of the early Italian lyric schools is the edition of Kenelm Foster and Patrick Boyde: *Dante's Lyric Poetry*, 2 vols. (Oxford: Oxford University Press, 1967).

This editorial enterprise culminated with the publication in 2002 of Domenico De Robertis' monumental five-volume edition of Dante lyrics: *Dante Alighieri: Rime*, in *Le Opere di Dante Alighieri*, Edizione Nazionale a cura della Società Dantesca Italiana, ed. Domenico De Robertis, 5 vols. (Firenze: Le Lettere, 2002). The five *tomi* are divided into three *volumi*: Volume I, *I documenti*, consisting of two *tomi*, offers a full review of the hundreds of manuscripts and early print editions in which Dante's lyrics were transcribed; Volume II, *Introduzione*, consisting of two *tomi*, comprises De Robertis' critical introduction to the *rime*; and Volume III, *Testi*, consisting of one *tomo*, presents the texts. De Robertis has added to the canon eight poems whose attribution was classified as dubious by previous editors. The enormous value of the documentary evidence he makes available is, however, compromised by what I consider a serious error in the matter of ordering the poems: De Robertis forsakes the chronological criterion for ordering adopted by his twentieth-century predecessors in favor of a bow to the editorial tradition, which divided the poems by genre, beginning with canzoni. For a full discussion of these editions, their choices, and the hermeneutical and cultural implications thereof, see Teodolinda Barolini, "Editing Dante's *Rime* and Italian Cultural History: Dante, Boccaccio, Petrarca . . . Barbi, Contini, Foster-Boyde, De Robertis," *Lettere Italiane* 56 (2004): 509–42.

On Dante's lyrics in general, see Patrick Boyde, *Dante's Style in His Lyric Poetry* (Cambridge: Cambridge University Press, 1971). On the *rime petrose* in particular, see the impressively encyclopedic study by Robert M. Durling and Ronald L. Martinez, *Time and the Crystal: Studies in Dante's Rime petrose* (Berkeley: University of California Press, 1990). On the *tenzone* with Forese Donati, see Susan Noakes, "Virility, Nobility, and Banking: The Crossing of Discourses in the *Tenzone* with Forese," in Teodolinda Barolini and H. Wayne Storey, eds., *Dante for the New Millennium* (New York: Fordham University Press, 2003), pp. 241–58. Christopher Kleinhenz provides a thorough review of the cultivators of the early sonnet in *The Early Italian Sonnet: The First Century (1220–1321)* (Lecce: Milella, 1986). On the material aspects of the lyric tradition and the implications for interpretation, see H. Wayne Storey, *Transcription and Visual Poetics in the Early Italian Lyric* (New York: Garland Press,

1993); for the development of lyric subjectivity in the Italian tradition, see Olivia Holmes, *Assembling the Lyric Self: Authorship from Troubadour Song to Italian Poetry Book* (Minneapolis: University of Minnesota Press, 2000).

For the *Commedia*'s handling of the vernacular tradition, see Teodolinda Barolini, *Dante's Poets: Textuality and Truth in the Comedy* (Princeton: Princeton University Press, 1984), chapters 1 and 2. In the years since the *Cambridge Companion to Dante* was first published, I have elaborated on some of the issues treated in this piece in the following essays: "Guittone's *Ora parrà*, Dante's *Doglia mi reca*, and the *Commedia*'s Anatomy of Desire," in Z. Baranski, ed., *Seminario Dantesco Internazionale: International Dante Seminar* 1 (Firenze: Le Lettere, 1997), pp. 3–23 (rpt *Italian Quarterly* 37 [2000]: 33–49); "Dante and Cavalcanti (On Making Distinctions in Matters of Love): *Inferno* 5 in its Lyric Context," *Dante Studies* 116 (1998): 31–63; "Beyond (Courtly) Dualism: Thinking about Gender in Dante's Lyrics," in *Dante for the New Millennium*, pp. 65–89; "Editing Dante's *Rime* and Italian Cultural History." Readings of specific lyrics, to be incorporated into the commentary of the *Rime* I am preparing for the *Biblioteca Universale Rizzoli*, have appeared as: "Saggio di un nuovo commento alle *Rime* di Dante. 1. *La dispietata mente che pur mira*: l'io al crocevia di memoria e disio; 2. *Sonar bracchetti e cacciatori aizzare*: l'io diviso tra mondo maschile e mondo femminile; 3. *Guido, i' vorrei che tu e Lippo ed io*: l'io e l'incanto della non-differenza," in *Dante: Rivista internazionale di studi danteschi* 1 (2004): 21–38.

3

ROBERT POGUE HARRISON

Approaching the *Vita nuova*

Dante's first book (his *libello*, or "little book," as he calls it), marks the beginning of a tendency that will dominate his literary career as a whole – the tendency to edit the self. All of Dante's major works – the *Vita nuova*, the *Convivio*, the *De vulgari eloquentia*, and of course the *Divina Commedia* – share this pattern of self-commentary on the part of an author who, for some reason, was never content merely to write poetry, but who also felt the need to instruct his reader about how that poetry came into being and how it should be read. Dante's work has been taken seriously by his readers over the centuries, to be sure, but it is fair to say that no one has ever taken it more seriously than the author himself.

The most striking aspect of the *Vita nuova*, for those who do not merely take its canonical stature for granted, or whose perception of the work is not mystified by the fact of its authorship, is the utter seriousness with which the author sets out to dignify and solemnify the rather innocent (and often mediocre) lyric poems that he composed in his youth. The *Vita nuova* gives the impression that Dante was unwilling to allow the poems to stand on their own but strove, through his prose commentary, to give them the sort of weight they lacked in their own right. There is far more to the *libello* than this, as we shall see, but it is important to state at the outset that we are dealing here with an author who had an inordinate anxiety about defining, self-consciously and for the most part retrogressively, the nature and ambitions of his literary vocation.

Taken on their own, the poems of the *Vita nuova* tell a somewhat different story than the one Dante narrates in the prose. It is the story of a young poet whose first experiments in the lyric medium were largely determined by the literary traditions he inherited in the late 1280s. These traditions include the Sicilian School (which in effect invented a literary language for Italy by transcribing the Provençal lyric conventions into a courtly, supra-regional idiom); Guittone d'Arezzo's inelegant but linguistically innovative municipal verse (later derided by Dante, but whose influence was considerable at the time); Guido Guinizzelli's refined, intellectualistic love poetry; and, most important for the *Vita nuova*, Guido Cavalcanti's exquisitely abstract and rarefied lyricism of the self. With respect to these influences, Dante's early poetry does not reveal any great originality. Only on occasion does a truly distinct voice break through in some of the lyrics. Nevertheless, it is clear that, from the very beginning, this voice was seeking to find itself – to express its own singularity, as it were – and the *Vita nuova*, in its sustained effort at self-commentary, testifies to the earnestness of this quest on the part of the young poet.

From this perspective it also seems clear that the prose dimension of the *Vita nuova* confesses, quite openly and dramatically, that Dante's first attempts to find his poetic voice were not altogether successful, indeed, that they were marked by an intrinsic failure. The last chapter of the *libello*, in which Dante declares that he has decided to remain silent until he finds a way to say of Beatrice what has never been said of any woman, indicates that the author is looking to the future for the true fulfillment of his literary vocation. In other words, the *Vita nuova*, as a self-editing document, ends with the author's gesture of cancelling or disqualifying his literary endeavors up until that time. It announces, in effect: "I was mistaken. I did not understand what I was really up to. My efforts have led to an impasse, at which I now find myself, and I have written this little book in order to say that, whatever my love for Beatrice was all about, I have not yet been able to express it adequately." In short, the prose narrative of the *Vita nuova* is ultimately "palinodic," or self-revisionary. Thus it is a typically Dantean work insofar as Dante never ceased, throughout his career, to revise, and in some sense rewrite, his past. Up until the end, when he finally embarked upon the *Divina Commedia*, he was forever trying to find his way out of a "dark wood" of past errors.

What is fascinating about the *Vita nuova* is the complex and subtle story it tells of Dante's youthful errors. These errors are manifold in nature and in what follows we shall examine the ways in which the *libello* seeks to represent them, interpret them, and recount the ways the author went about overcoming them. On the basis of Dante's own critical self-commentary, then, we shall try to delineate certain essential features of the work that every reader of the *Vita nuova* should keep in mind when approaching its elusive, and at times bizarre, narrative.

For a book composed in the thirteenth century, the *Vita nuova* is at bottom shocking, even blasphemous, in the way it glorifies a mortal woman named Beatrice. The daring of Dante's liberal use of the language of sacrality with reference to Beatrice does not abash us sufficiently, since we take it for granted by now, but the fact is that such a work, in its historical context, approaches the limits of sacrilege. As far as we know, the *Vita nuova* was never condemned or burned by the authorities (probably because it had a very restricted audience – Dante's fellow poets, for the most part); nevertheless we should keep in mind that, at the time, it was potentially as scandalous a work of literature for the general public as, say, D. H. Lawrence's *The Rainbow*, which in 1915 was banned in England because of its obscenity.

Here too, however, there is a considerable discrepancy between the poems and the prose of the *Vita nuova*. In some of the poems Dante indeed uses religious or Christological analogies to speak of Beatrice (see, for example, the canzone "Donna pietosa," in chapter 23), but the degree to which he does so is minimal compared to the all-out glorification of Beatrice that occurs in the prose. Taken in their own right, the poems merely further the idealizing rhetoric of the medieval lyric tradition. The troubadours, for instance, were masters at such rhetoric when they praised the perfections of their ladies; the poets of the Sicilian School took over this same rhetoric and gave it an Italian inflection. Shortly thereafter Guido Guinizzelli, in his famous canzone "Al cor gentile," took the idealizing rhetoric even further when he spoke of his lady as a divine angel; yet even in his case the analogies between love and the cosmic order remained on the level of poetic tropes. Given these precedents, Dante's angelification of Beatrice in the canzone "Donne ch'avete" (chapter 19), for example, exasperates but does not break with this well-established tradition. Even the Christological analogies in "Donna pietosa," though daring in themselves, implicitly appeal to the poetic license of the idealizing lyric.

In the case of the *Vita nuova*'s prose, however, we can no longer assume that we are in the realm of mere rhetoric when Dante assures us that Beatrice was a miracle (as evidenced by her associations with the number nine), or that her greeting had a salvific power. Dante's glorification of Beatrice in the prose goes beyond the bounds of mere idealization. It asks us to take seriously the suggestion that she was no ordinary woman, that she was the singular incarnation of transcendence, and that she was nothing less than Dante's spiritual salvation itself. These are weighty, and somewhat shocking, claims to make about a mortal woman, yet the *Vita nuova* insists on their truth-value. In short, the *Vita nuova* represents, among other things, Dante's resolute attempt to *literalize* a poetic trope (the ideal woman) and to equate Beatrice with the prospect of transcendence itself.

However, one of the great paradoxes of this text (there are more than one) is that the narrative deliberately strains the reader's credibility, not only by virtue of its extravagant claims about Beatrice, but also because it belies at the same time that it affirms these claims. The story of Dante's blunders and errors with regard to Beatrice while she was alive cast into doubt the author's reliability as a witness to the events he lived through at the time. Let us see why this is so.

In the early chapters of the *Vita nuova*, for example, we are told that his vision of Beatrice on the streets of Florence had an overwhelming effect on the young Dante, and that from the moment he first saw her, love took complete possession of his soul and lorded over it with "the faithful counsel of reason." This claim promptly reveals its irony in the subsequent chapters, which recount Dante's decision to use so-called "screen ladies" to help conceal the identity of the woman he loved. We are asked to believe that these screen ladies were nothing more than that – screens – but the narrative in fact reveals that the author here is merely trying to screen the truth of these parallel love affairs, if we may call them that, from his reader. In chapter 7, for example, Dante admits that when his first screen lady left Florence, he was "distraught at the loss of my beautiful defense." He says that he became dispirited, "more than I myself would have thought [possible]" before the departure. He then records a sonnet of lament he wrote on that occasion, claiming that he wrote it merely to preserve appearances, yet the sonnet is a persuasive confession of lovelornness. Where is the boundary here between appearance and reality? Are we really to believe that this lady was no more than a screen, or is it not more likely that Dante's devotion to Beatrice at the time was less than total – that his amorous sentiments were aimed in more than one direction?

The case of the second screen lady, described in chapter 10, seems to confirm the latter suspicion. Here Dante admits that in a short time he turned her into such an effective screen for his true love that many people began to gossip about the brashness of his behavior with regard to this new woman – behavior, we are told, which went beyond the bounds of courtesy. We are not informed of the precise nature of Dante's behavior, but it was obviously scandalous or distasteful enough to cause Beatrice to deny her greetings to Dante in public, whether out of jealousy or moral indignation we cannot say. The least we can say about it is that it was not typical of someone who was utterly and totally devoted to Beatrice at the time. Nor can we say that love was lording over him with the "faithful counsel of reason" in this case (it was the lord of love, after all, who advised Dante to take up with this new woman – chapter 9).

Finally, after Beatrice's death Dante falls in love with yet another woman, the so-called "gentle lady," who threatens to supplant Beatrice in Dante's affections altogether. It is not clear how long his new affair lasted (I use the term "affair" in the sentimental sense), but Dante tells us that one day he had a vision of Beatrice in which she appeared to him in the guise in which he had seen her for the first time, at nine years of age, and that this image was overwhelming enough to cause him to repudiate his new love and turn all his thoughts and affections to the memory of Beatrice. Shortly thereafter the *Vita nuova* ends with Dante having had yet another "miraculous vision" of Beatrice, a vision which inspires him to remain silent until he can speak of her more adequately.

There is no doubt that Beatrice triumphs over her rivals by the end of the *Vita nuova*, yet this outcome should not be allowed to obscure the fact that Dante's "book of memory" is at once a testimony of his singular love for Beatrice as well as the story of his multiple loves both before and after her death. Meanwhile it turns out that the "lord" of love, who presumably dictated Dante's behavior with the "faithful counsel of reason," made a mess of his tutelage. At one point, we recall, he advised Dante to seek out a new screen lady (chapter 9), but when it became clear that this (bad) advice led to Beatrice's alienation from Dante, he reversed his counsel and advised him to lay aside the simulations ("tempus est ut pretermictantur simulacra nostra," chapter 12). In other words, this lord is revealed in due course as an impostor. He is the very figure of Dante's blunders and errors with regard to Beatrice, and in fact he disappears from the narrative in chapter 24 after announcing to Dante, in unambiguous terms, that Beatrice herself is love – thus rendering himself superfluous.

The foregoing remarks have put us in a position where we can begin to approach the deeper core of the *Vita nuova*. This core is pervaded by a simple, yet obsessive, question: "What is love?" It is the question that engaged Guido Guinizzelli (whom Dante cites as an authority in the sonnet of chapter 20) when he presumed to define love in speculative, cosmic terms in his canzone "Al cor gentil." Thanks to Guinizzelli, the question of love's nature became the dominant preoccupation of the younger generation of learned, intellectual poets to which Dante belonged – the so-called *stilnovist* poets (Cavalcanti, Dante, Cino da Pistoia, Lapo, and others). Guido Cavalcanti – Dante's "first friend" to whom the *Vita nuova* is dedicated – was particularly obsessed with the question, so much so that his entire poetic corpus represents a continuous effort to define, describe, and come to terms with the essence of this "accident," as he calls it in his famous poem "Donna me prega."

It is impossible to understand the *Vita nuova* (a story about Dante's multiple loves which ends with Beatrice's glorious triumph) without understanding the extent to which this question – "What is love?" – utterly absorbed the literary community of which Dante was a member at the time. The *Vita nuova* is nothing less than Dante's own answer to that question. It is an answer that goes by the name of Beatrice. But to understand the meaning of Dante's answer it is necessary to fathom the question, which requires some knowledge of what exactly it is that Dante is responding to in the *Vita nuova* when he equates Beatrice with love itself. He is responding above all to his "first friend," Guido Cavalcanti.

There is irony in the fact that Dante dedicates the *Vita nuova* to Cavalcanti, for the book figures ultimately as his polemic with his older friend on the nature of love. When Dante began writing lyrics, Cavalcanti was the most original and compelling of Italian poets to date. He was Dante's senior by seven years, and, in addition to his lyric genius and recondite knowledge of philosophy, he was also a dashing aristocrat who belonged to one of the most powerful Florentine families. In short, Dante's literary career began under the spell of Cavalcanti. The poems of the *Vita nuova*, if not the prose, show that the "first friend" was by far the most decisive influence on him at the time. Dante's initial experience of love, as it is figured in the *Vita nuova*, is so Cavalcantian in nature as to be merely derivative and, in that sense, banal. There is every indication that, at the start, Dante wholly adopted and thus reconfirmed Cavalcanti's answer to the question "What is love?" Let us consider that answer.

Cavalcanti portrays love almost exclusively in negative terms, as a force of bewilderment, disorder, and dissolution. The lyric subject that speaks in his poems about the effects of love on the lover invariably describes a drama of self-dispossession. Love is a form of violation, if not violence, shattering the fragile core of the self and leading it to the brink of death. In the lover who suffers its effects occurs an upheaval of the equilibrium of the various "spirits" that regulate life (see Dante's description of such an upheaval in chapter 2 of the *Vita nuova*, which recounts his first vision of Beatrice). The lover pales, languishes, despairs, and sighs his life away when this passion takes possession of his body and soul. In essence, love figures in Cavalcanti's poetry as the overwhelming experience of one's own precarious finitude, if not death.

Cavalcanti elaborated his conception of love in abstract, philosophical terms in his poem "Donna me prega," which assigns love to the realm of the appetites. By arousing an inordinate and anarchic desire in the lover, love leads to states of ire, blindness, and *tristitia*, or melancholy. The danger of this passion lies in the fundamental misunderstanding it brings about in the lover's psyche, for the lover has a tendency to confuse the true object of love with the woman who inspires it. While the woman *inspires* love, she cannot answer its longings. For Cavalcanti, the beloved is nothing more than a bewitching illusion. She *seems* to possess in her person the ideal beauty that love desires, but in truth the beauty she manifests does not belong to her at all. Like all ideal qualities (truth, virtue, beatitude), her beauty belongs to a radically transcendent realm of universality which has no substantial links with the realm of materiality (this, in a highly over-simplified formula, is Cavalcanti's so-called Averroism). This transcendent realm is accessible only to abstract contemplation, which must remain free from the compulsions of appetition. The love passion is potentially destructive to the degree that it arouses the lover's appetites – which seek possession – and hence disturbs the serenity of reflection. In a word, the passion engendered by love *misdirects* the lover's desire toward the woman herself, thus disabling reason's capacity to contemplate the universals in all their abstract ideality.

Hence Cavalcanti did not believe that any woman could embody love in the absolute sense, given that all her admirable qualities (which inspire love in the first place) are impersonal attributes which other women may also exhibit and which ultimately pertain to the non-material order. This is a form of Platonism, to be sure, but in Cavalcanti's poetry it takes on a uniquely lyrical pathos as the lover laments, in exquisite verse, the psychic disorder and victimization he suffers at the hands of a sinister and destructive passion.

The *Vita nuova* rehearses, in a persuasive way, the drama of love as Cavalcanti conceived of it. Dante's description of the disruption of his "spirits" on the occasion of his first vision of Beatrice is Cavalcantian through and through. So is the "marvelous vision" in chapter 3, in which Beatrice lies in the arms of the lord of love, who holds Dante's flaming heart in his hand – a heart which he then feeds to Beatrice against her will (Cavalcanti had used the image of a burning heart in one of his poems, "Perché non fuoro a me gli occhi dispenti"). The rigorous association of love with death in his vision is strictly Cavalcantian – an association that also recurs in many of the poems – and hence it is no accident that Dante's friendship with the older poet was inaugurated as a result of this dark and dubious dream.

With the exception of a brief interlude, during which Dante resolves to write only poems that praise Beatrice, almost all of the poems of the *Vita nuova* describe Dante's experience of love in Cavalcantian terms of disruption and discombobulation. Even the lexicon is Cavalcantian: words like "sbigottito" ("bewildered"), "struggere" ("to destroy"), "grave" ("grave"), "plorare" ("to cry"), "orranza" ("honor"), and so on. Dante's "battle of the thoughts," which occurs both toward the beginning and at the end of the narrative, is also typically Cavalcantian. And last but not least, the obsessive theme of death, which pervades both the poems and the prose, is as sure an indication as any that we find ourselves here in Cavalcanti's psychic theater of self-dispossession and victimization.

And yet despite the Cavalcantianism that haunts it, or perhaps even because of it, the *Vita nuova* remains Dante's polemical declaration of independence from his "first friend." In her salvific status Beatrice contradicts and disqualifies the pessimistic notion of love as victimization. Dante's insistence on her miraculous grace, her utter singularity, and her non-substitutability by other women, as it were, conveys a message to Cavalcanti to the effect that Dante repudiates the despair that characterizes his friend's psychology and stakes his very salvation on his woman's incarnation of love. This is why it is essential that the *Vita nuova* should both glorify Beatrice and at the same time tell the story of how she triumphed over all her rivals in love. It is only through Dante's multiplication of his loves that Beatrice's singularity and authenticity can be effectively dramatized and confirmed. The episode of the "gentle lady" is especially crucial to Dante's declaration of faith, for it affirms that, even in her absence, Beatrice cannot be replaced by another woman.

It is not by chance, therefore, that Dante's polemical gestures toward Guido Cavalcanti became most poignant at precisely that moment in the text when Beatrice's incarnational status is affirmed most decisively. The reference is to the dramatic scene in chapter 24 of the *Vita nuova*. Let us turn to it.

Dante is sitting in some public place and feels a tremor in his heart. He has a vision of the lord of love, who tells him to be joyous. Then he sees a woman named Giovanna walking down the street, followed by Beatrice. Giovanna was the woman loved by Cavalcanti, who gave her the nickname "Primavera" in one of his poems. The lord of love tells Dante that he inspired Cavalcanti to give her that name for this occasion alone, when she would *precede* Beatrice on the streets of Florence ("prima verrà" in Italian means "she will come first"). He then interprets her real name, Giovanna, by reference to John the Baptist, the prophet who preceded Christ. Finally, he tells Dante that anyone who considers Beatrice properly would call her love itself, "because of the great similitude she bears to me." With these words this figure of speech – the lord of love – disappears from the *Vita nuova* altogether. Love and Beatrice have become absolutely identified with one another, and at the heart of this identification lies an analogy with Christ.

In this passage Dante makes a point of mentioning that, at the time, he believed that Cavalcanti still loved Giovanna. He was in fact mistaken. Dante's "first friend" ("first" like Giovanna, who "comes first" or precedes Beatrice) had already become disillusioned with Giovanna. His heart was already elsewhere. Such inconstancy on Guido's part was of course consistent with his disillusioning conception of love, for, as we have seen, he believed that what one admired in a noble woman were transcendent qualities that did not belong to her person in any inherent or substantial way. It is significant, therefore, that precisely at this critical juncture of the *Vita nuova* Dante affirms Beatrice's personhood most forcefully – a personhood that is in every way incarnational and hypostatic. It is here, in a chapter that evokes the presence of Cavalcanti most deliberately, that Dante stakes his claim. The claim is that Beatrice does not manifest love merely accidentally or temporarily (as Cavalcanti would have it), but that she is the substantial embodiment of love itself.

From this point on, until her death, Beatrice's splendor attains its height. In the next two chapters Dante goes on to describe the bliss that he, as well as others, experienced in her presence – a presence that he assures us was miraculous in nature. Unfortunately it was also a presence of which he would soon find himself deprived. When her early death removes Beatrice from the world, Dante succumbs to grief, confusion, and paralysis. He even lapses back into a sombre Cavalcantianism, as in the episode with the "gentle lady," but by the end of the *Vita nuova* the memory of Beatrice intervenes to put him on a new track. After his "miraculous vision" of Beatrice in heaven, a whole new prospect – existential, spiritual, and no doubt literary – seems to open up for him. We do not know the precise nature of this prospect, for the book ends with Dante's vow of silence and his promise to write of Beatrice in the future what has never been written of any woman. Does this promise allude to the *Divina Commedia*? It is impossible to know. We are told only that a revelation took place. The most we can conclude from this suspended ending is that it does not terminate the story as much as project it into a new, unrealized horizon altogether. In other words, the "book of memory" ends at the threshold of a new beginning that transcends memory insofar as it extends into the future. Since the *Vita nuova* cannot presume to record what lies beyond the bounds of memory, it ends in a silence that is full of anticipation of future speech.

Whatever the nature of the new life promised by such a future, such a prospect, there is no question that it stands in a decisive relation to the past. The new life in question has been rendered possible (if not actual) by Dante's retrospective coming to terms with (and overcoming of) the errors and mis-understandings of his past. The book we have just read is precisely that retrospective self-editing digest that prepares the way for another itinerary altogether. To speculate about the future itinerary is feckless and superflu-ous (Dante scholars have all too readily assumed it was nothing less than the *Divina Commedia*, but there is no basis for such speculation in the text). All we can say is that, in the *Vita nuova*, Dante acknowledges, and claims to have overcome, his past errors, not the least of which, as we have seen, was his tendency to confuse his vocation, both as a poet and a lover, with that of his "first friend."

What is love? We have seen that for Cavalcanti it amounted to the drama of the lover's intimations of his own finitude. Cavalcanti's poetry is a prodigous phenomenology of the effects of disorder and privation which love brings about in the self, foreshadowing its death. The poetry of the *Vita nuova* for the most part shares Cavalcanti's preoccupation with the self's finitude, yet the prose narrative revises the postures adopted by Dante in his poems and offers a radically different answer to the question of love's nature. That answer did not come easily. It came as the result of a profound crisis in Dante's life. That crisis was the death of Beatrice.

The death of Beatrice came as a shock to Dante. The fact that he refuses to comment on the event in the *Vita nuova* (see chapter 28) indicates to what extent he was at a loss to account for its meaning. The difference between Dante and Cavalcanti is that Dante experienced the death of the other, namely Beatrice, while Cavalcanti remained obsessed with the *idea* (unrepresentable in itself) of his own death. Beatrice's death was thus something of a scandal, in the sense that it exposed the fact that death was not merely a poetic trope for a subjectivistic poetry, but a brutal reality that put life as a whole into crisis.

The *Vita nuova* is Dante's response to the crisis of finitude which Beatrice's death revealed as the human condition as such. It is fair to say that, for the rest of his career, Dante continued to respond to this crisis in one form or another. It is also fair to say that his aggravated sense of such a crisis made of him the most profoundly Christian of poets in our literary tradition. In the final analysis, the *Vita nuova* is Dante's account of how he discovered the prospect of salvation in the death of Beatrice. The Christological associations that accrue around the figure of Beatrice in the book serve to emphasize Dante's faith that her life was not in vain, that her personhood was not accidental, that her beauty was not a bewitching illusion but rather was congruent with the cosmic order as such. In other words, for Dante, Beatrice was the evidence of grace in the midst of a condition of disgrace. Cavalcanti despaired of the possibility of such saving grace, which explains, among other things, why Dante evokes his presence in the circle of the heretics in *Inferno*, where those who believed that the soul dies with the body are punished.

Expressed otherwise, we could say that the crisis that informs the *Vita nuova* takes the form of two alternatives: either Beatrice's life was nothing more than a passing illusion, in which case we are all damned; or else the grace she manifested in her person while alive was a revelation of some prospect that lies ahead, in which case the possibility of salvation remains open. It is this latter alternative that the *Vita nuova* embraces (thus it is one of the most risky works of literature in history). The prospect that lies ahead is the same one that interrupts the narrative of the *Vita nuova* so abruptly, inspiring Dante to remain silent. But even as he vows to remain silent in the last chapter, he promises to continue his speech once he has found a way to speak of this woman more adequately. That is Dante's way of saying the story is over only for those who decide to foreclose its ending.

SUGGESTED READING

Book-length studies of Dante's *Vita nuova* in English include Charles S. Singleton's classic, *An Essay on the Vita nuova* (Cambridge, MA: Harvard University Press, 1949; rpt, Baltimore: The Johns Hopkins University Press, 1977); J. E. Shaw's *Essays on the Vita nuova* (Princeton: Princeton University Press, 1929); Jerome Mazzaro's *The Figure of Dante: An Essay on the Vita nuova* (Princeton: Princeton University Press, 1981); and Robert P. Harrison's *The Body of Beatrice* (Baltimore: The Johns Hopkins University Press, 1988). For a classic book-length study in Italian, see Domenico De Robertis' *Il libro della Vita nuova* (Florence: Sansoni, 1961). A fine collection of diverse essays on the *Vita nuova* is to be found in the special issue of *Dante Studies* 92 (1974), as well as the special issue of *Texas Studies in Literature and Language* (Spring 1990) edited by David Wallace. One of the best individual essays on the *Vita nuova* in English is Giuseppe Mazzotta's "The Language of Poetry in the *Vita nuova*," *Rivista di studi italiani* 1 (1983): 3–14.

4

ALBERT RUSSELL ASCOLI

From *auctor* to author: Dante before the *Commedia*

Before, during, and after the writing of his *Commedia*, surely the most "authoritative" work of the Western canon, Dante composed a considerable number of poetic, prose, and prosimetrum works, both in Italian and in Latin. Of these, several – *Vita nuova* (*The New Life*), *Convivio* (*The Banquet*), *De vulgari eloquentia* (*On Eloquence in the Vernacular*), and the *Monarchia* (*Of World Empire*), not to mention the four great canzoni known as the *rime petrose*, and two Latin eclogues, the first written since late antiquity – would in the absence of the masterwork still have been recognized as among the most significant and distinctive writings of the later Middle Ages, for a combination of historical, aesthetic, intellectual, and broadly cultural reasons. Just to start with, there is no contemporary poet writing in Italian whose range of topics and forms, and whose intellectual, moral and political ambition, begin to compare with those of Dante's "other" works. Because of the immense shadow cast by the *Commedia*, however, these works are less studied and appreciated than they deserve and, even when they are, it is usually in subordinate relation to *the* Dantean masterpiece.

In this essay I will focus on three of the principal "minor" works, *Vita nuova*, *Convivio*, and *De vulgari eloquentia*, using as a touchstone a fundamental concern of Dante that, indeed, culminates in the *Commedia*, namely the appropriation of what the Middle Ages called *auctoritas*, or cultural authority, for a person (Dante Alighieri) and a language (the romance vernacular on its way to becoming what we now call Italian) that would not ordinarily have been considered entitled to claim such status. In the process I hope to give some indication of why one might be interested in these works for their own sakes. I will suggest as well how they light the way to a better understanding of the immensely difficult process undergone by Dante as he readied himself to become the unassailable canonical figure – author of the *Commedia* – we know today.

In a now famous, or infamous, essay of 1968, Roland Barthes declared "the death of the author," rather prematurely, most would now say. The personage Barthes hoped to kill off was the "author-god," the autonomous creative self who, like an omniscient deity, spun out imaginary universes whose significance he, and he alone, dictated. From our point of view, what matters here is that this author, this personal yet "universal" figure, is generally said to have emerged on the scene of Western culture shortly after the time that Dante composed the *Commedia* – "he" (and indeed the figure is normatively male and patriarchal, like the God he is modeled on) is very often specifically identified with Francesco Petrarca, the "first modern man/ first modern author," a younger product of the same Florentine political diaspora that both traumatized Dante and mobilized his creative energies. This figure, in many ways, remains our "naturalized" idea of what a literary author universally, essentially, is. Yet my premise here is that Barthes's contemporary, Foucault, was absolutely right, in his own fundamental essay, "What is an Author?," to insist that what an "author" is, and what textual significance amounts to, changes continuously according to mutable historical and cultural factors, and is frequently shaped more by social expectations and institutional constraints than by personal creativity.

Dante, then, began with one notion of what authorship might be, embodied in the largely impersonal, ahistorical category of the medieval "auctor," which included both greats from the classical tradition, such as Aristotle and Virgil, and the human authors of the Bible, from Moses to St. John. In the process of appropriating the attributes of that figure to himself, however, Dante made substantial, if at least in part unintentional, progress toward inventing the new modern, vernacular, individualized "author" who would become the darling of Renaissance studies and forerunner of Romantic expressionism, and then the *bête noire* of post-structuralist critiques of Western culture. In other words, Dante's career as a whole can be understood, from one angle, as a progressive, if not always linear, struggle with the nature and function of the poetic calling, in a time when the writing of literature was a distinctly secondary occupation in relation to, say, theology; when the most authoritative poetry, and the title of *auctor*, was the exclusive domain of long-dead ancients rather than of "moderns" like Dante Alighieri; and when the unpolished, impermanent, irregular vernacular was understood to be inferior to the permanent, because rule-governed and tradition-tested, expressive powers of Latin *grammatica*.

Anyone who has read the *Commedia* recognizes that Dante has these categories and problems explicitly in mind from the outset, and that, at least by this point in his evolution, his basic strategy is to represent himself and his (Italian) poetry as the linear offspring and heir of the greatest of Latin poets, Publius Virgilius Maronis, author of the imperial epic, the *Aeneid*, as well as of the pastoral *Eclogues* and the agricultural *Georgics*. Consider these three lines from the first canto of the *Inferno*, in which the character Dante first registers his surprise and delight at finding himself in the presence of the shade of Virgil:

> You are my teacher and my author; you alone are he from whom I took the beautiful style that has brought me honor.   (*Inferno* 1, 85–87)

This is the best known by far of Dante's many uses of the language of *auctoritas* throughout his *oeuvre*. Its importance is unquestionable: it introduces the personage who will guide Dante during approximately three-fifths of his extraordinary journey through the afterlife; it makes the first substantial reference in the poem to the fact that the character Dante is also a well-known poet of his day.

Most importantly, these words set in motion an elaborate staging of Dante's relationship to Virgil, which at once betokens immense respect for the greatest of Latin poets and aims to appropriate Virgil's authority for Dante's language, his poem, and himself, and, indeed, to supersede it. A widely accepted, and quite compelling, account of the function of this reference in the economy of the poem exists, though it does not serve for Dante's *oeuvre* as a whole. As Robert Hollander first demonstrated, the *Commedia*'s five, carefully positioned references to "autore" and "autorità" open and close the poem and define a conceptual itinerary that leads from poetry to theology, from human writer to divine creator. The first two references evoke the classical, pagan *auctores* near the beginning of the poem, in the cited line from *Inferno* 1 and in the related encounter, in *Inferno* 4, with the finest classical poets (Homer, Horace, Lucan, Ovid, and, of course, Virgil). The latter are said to possess "grande autorità ne' loro sembianti" (great authority in their countenances; 4, 113), and it is into their company that Dante is humbly exalted as "the sixth among such wisdom" (4, 102).

The last three references come at the culmination of Dante's interrogation, modeled on the typical scholastic "bachelor's examination" of the great medieval universities (notably, Paris and Bologna), by three apostles who are also biblical *auctores* (Saints Peter, James, and John) in cantos 24 through 26 of *Paradiso*. The examination sequence is a high-point in the process of "authorizing" Dante, putting an apostolic and ecclesiastical (since Peter is the founder of the papacy) seal of approval on his thought and his writing, and incidentally remedying the absence from his ad hoc educational curriculum of the normal intellectual credentials of the day. This scene, and these references, explicitly subordinate the "autoritade" derived from human reason (*Paradiso* 26, 26 and 47) to the higher authority of the human biblical scribes and thence to "the voice of the truthful [or true] Author" (26, 40), God, the absolute and transcendent Author of authors. Coming long after

Virgil's disappearance from the poem (*Purgatorio* 30), the episode shows a "Dante" who now possesses an authority comparable to that of prophets and apostles, one which descends to him directly from God, and which thus removes him from the taint and contingency of historical, human authorship, taking him far, far beyond the accomplishments of his avowed "maestro e autore."

The *Commedia*, in short, tells the story of how the character-poet "Dante" went from humble disciple of the classical *auctor* Virgil, to a poetic author in his own right, to someone who is not out of place in the company of the most prestigious of all medieval authors, those who were authorized to transcribe the words of God himself in the New Testament. Nonetheless, it does not recount the whole story of how Dante Alighieri arrived at the point of writing a work of such stunning ambition, or accurately reflect his complex contingent situation as "subject of history" wrestling with the impersonal constraints of what Foucault called "the author function." What, then, for the Dante of the *Commedia*, is an "autore"? Why does he want to be one?

In order to answer these questions we will need to go back to those earlier Dantean texts that constitute a largely effaced backdrop to the discourse of authority in the *Comedy*. But before that, let me put my principal conceptual cards on the table.

(1) Dante, from at least the *Vita nuova* (1293) forward, expresses keenly both the desire to possess "authority" and an understanding of the imposing obstacles to acquiring it. And he becomes increasingly explicit and articulate about that desire and the strategies to be used in overcoming those obstacles in the great, unfinished treatises of his early exile (1303–06), the Italian *Convivio* and the Latin *De vulgari eloquentia*.

(2) The principal obstacles, as I believe Dante understood them, to acquiring the standing of *auctor* in the terms that word was used in the later Middle Ages are the interrelated traits of contingency, personality, and modernity. In other words, Dante, largely following the lead of the "official discourse" of medieval culture, posited authority as a quality at once impersonal, ancient, and transhistorical, and thus antithetical to his own existential position as a modern (i.e., living), mortal and mutable, first-person subject of writing.

(3) In the process, stretching through several works, of defining and redefining, acknowledging and appropriating "autorità," Dante took considerable liberties with the received conceptual framework of medieval authorship, and, in the process, displaced it significantly, both definitionally and "performatively" in the direction of what we now consider

to be "modern" authorship – the individual, creative, willful "author-function" usually identified, as noted above, with Petrarca.

Dante's first uses of a language of authority, and his first systematic attempts to assimilate himself and his vernacular writings to the cultural authority of poetic, philosophical and theological Latinity, come only after his exile from Florence, that is, in the early part of the first decade of the fourteenth century, during the relatively brief run-up period to the writing of the *Commedia*. In order to mark the full trajectory of his relationship to *auctoritas*, however, we should begin by looking at the youthful *Vita nuova*, a composite text put together when Dante was about twenty-eight years old, which surrounds poems, most of which were written earlier for specific occasions, with new prose that is itself distinguished into explanatory narrative and analytical commentary on the poems. Despite scattered references to "high" Latin culture (in the use of occasional Latin tags, in eclectic borrowings from the normative text/commentary arrangement, and so on), the *Vita nuova* is concerned primarily with defining, and then redefining, Dante's place within the emergent tradition of vernacular love poetry.

The agenda of the *libello* can be measured out, heuristically, in the space between two episodes, to be found in the conventionally numbered chapters 3 and 24–25. In chapter 3, Dante recounts having sent around for interpretation a poem ("To every soul captured by Love and to each noble heart") recounting a cryptic vision of Love personified to a group of vernacular poets, whom he calls the "fedeli d'amore" (the faithful of love). These included, perhaps, Cino da Pistoia and, explicitly, Dante's "first friend," Guido Cavalcanti, to whom he later says the book as a whole is directed (chapter 30). The chapter defines a poetic community, describes Dante's novitial exordium within it, and claims a place for him at its center. Chapter 24 then returns to the figure of Love personified (for the last time in the book, as it turns out), now transfigured from the equivocal, eroticized figure of chapter 3 into a transcendent emanation of spiritual love. The rest of the "fedeli d'amore" have disappeared, with only Dante himself and Guido Cavalcanti remaining. Even between these two a hierarchy has been established, by virtue of an analogy between John the Baptist and Guido's beloved, Giovanna, nicknamed "Primavera" (Spring), cast as precursor to Dante's Christ-like Beatrice. In other words, having begun the book as the last and least among the "faithful of love," Dante has now established himself, qua praiser of the extraordinary Beatrice, as the messianic telos toward which all contemporary vernacular poetry, even that of the formidable Guido, has tended.

It is no accident, then, that the following chapter, 25, marks a first, tentative, assimilation of Dante to the world of classical literary authorship, as if he, and his poetry, had moved beyond the limitations of "vulgarity" and modernity and onto another plane altogether. The pretext with which this chapter begins is what seems to most modern readers a pedantic quibble: Dante imagines an objection to his representation of a personified "Amore" on the grounds that love is not a "substance," an autonomous intellectual and corporeal subject, but rather an "accident," that is, an emotional condition experienced by a human subject, i.e., himself. He then goes on to justify this exercise in "poetic license" by arguing that the "dicitori d'amore," the poets of romance vernaculars (Occitan and proto-Italian) who have emerged over the past 150 years, are entitled to the same privileges of figuration as the classical "poete": Homer, Virgil, Lucan, Horace, and Ovid. Having placed himself at the "head of the class" of the "dicitori," and having, for that matter, made it perfectly clear that his "amore" is a different and far better thing than theirs, Dante thus makes a strong first bid to assimilate himself into the company of the ancients – the same five, in fact, who will appear in person and add him explicitly to their number in *Inferno* 4.

At the same time, clear limits are still in place: (1) the "dicitori" and the vernacular are specifically limited to the subject of love and love only (though since the Love in question is arguably an aspect of the triune God, this is potentially not so much of a limitation as he makes it out to be); (2) the key words *auctoritas* and *auctor* are nowhere to be seen; (3) the "dicitori," and Dante in particular, are specifically said to be constrained to show that they know what they are doing when they personify Love – i.e., they are *not* entitled to the automatic belief and assent, supported by servile commentary of "modern," i.e., medieval, exegetes, which the classical poets are, and must explicitly prove their artistic intentions in prose explanations, like those in the *Vita nuova*.

This brings us back to the question of "personality" around which, as suggested above, Dante's problematic relationship to authority pivots. In introducing the need for the modern writer to explain his intentions, Dante at once aligns himself with the ancients (like them he speaks figuratively) and separates himself from them (they do not need to explain their intentions, given their status as confirmed *auctores*). He, the living, must supply a first-person singular explanation; they, the honored dead, can, indeed must, rely on the third-person, depersonalized, claim upon blind readerly faith codified in their canonical names. At the same time, since, with the possible and very different exception of Cavalcanti's great didactic canzone, "Donna me prega" ("A lady asks me"), none of the other contemporary "dicitori" has undertaken this explanatory mission, certainly not in the form of an explicit prose self-commentary, Dante further distinguishes himself from the other modern poets.

The issue of personality is also raised by the problem of the *prosopopeia* (that is, the allegorical personification) of Amore which was the initial pretext for the digression on ancient and modern poetry. Dante's point is that Love, the central – first destructive, then salvific – force that, in conjunction with Beatrice, dominates Dante's life, is not an externalized being at all, but a part of himself. To the extent that Love has now been transformed into a positive, inspiring force, with roots in divinity, the function of this masking is to represent as an impersonal, visionary impetus something located personally in Dante-*dicitore* on his way to true authorial status.

The complex relationship between personality and authorship is far more explicitly articulated in the post-exilic, pre-comedic, work, *Convivio*, where Dante deploys for the first time the technical terminology of authority most commonly used in late medieval Latin culture. The declared aim of the treatise is far higher than that of *Vita nuova*. Having previously restricted vernacular poetry to the subject of heterosexual love, with (relatively uneducated) women as the primary audience, Dante now claims for a series of his vernacular canzoni the power to transmit to an Italian-speaking audience, primarily male, the ethical truths articulated in classical philosophy, and especially in the works of *the* philosophical author, Aristotle. This, he says, will appear in a series of prose commentaries on his canzoni that expose an allegorical, ethical content hidden beneath literal songs of love.

In book 1 of *Convivio*, Dante sets out to explain two constituent features of his treatise, both of which tend to compromise whatever "authority" he may possess. First, he needs to explain his pervasive first-person singular presence in the work, when (classical) rhetoric excludes this on the grounds that personalized discourse compromises the credibility of any argument (1, 2–4). Second, he needs to explain the use of vernacular (i.e., proto-Italian), a contingent, historically mutable, non-prestigious language, rather than *grammatica*, i.e., Latin, a rule-governed language that transcends time, place, and person, whose character as the normative language of intellectual authority he particularly stresses (1, 5–13). Ironically, his explanation of the former problem only emphasizes the question of the incompatibility of personality with authority. He says that his exile, which has brought him personally into the presence of many people who had only known him through his works, has diminished his own stature and that of the said works, precisely because personal presence compromises credibility. The remedy, however, can only be that of a protracted self-justification: a first person singular writing to counter the negative effect of personal presence.

The justification of the use of Italian is far more lengthy and elaborate, and I only have space here to call attention to a couple of important issues it raises. First of all, despite Dante's deferential subordination of the vernacular and his own use of it to *grammatica*, and notwithstanding his ostensible focus on the prose commentary as humble "servant" of poetic discourse, the book clearly works indirectly to assert exceptional authority for Dante and his Italian poetry. For example, in chapter 9 he observes that while Latin has often been used for purposes of commentary, the vernacular never [sic] has:

> the vernacular will give an unasked-for gift [in commenting upon these canzoni], which Latin would not have given: since it will give itself in the form of commentary, which no one ever asked for; and this cannot be said of Latin, which has already been requested to comment upon and gloss many writings [or "scriptures"], as can be seen clearly at the beginnings of many of them [where medieval manuscripts often placed the "accessus ad auctorem," or introduction to the author, which accompanied many commentaries].
>
> (1, 9)

In calling attention to the lack of commentary on and in the vernacular, Dante at once reminds his readers of the cultural inferiority of his language to Latin, and implicitly affirms that his poems, uniquely to this point among "vulgar" works, merit the kind of attention traditionally reserved for Latin *auctores*. Here again, as in the *Vita nuova*, he marks both the resemblance of his work to, and its difference from, the traditional medieval text-commentary model:

> only a cogent reason will justify setting aside what has long served others well, as has the use of Latin in composing commentaries. This requires a clearly justifiable reason, because new ways of acting have no guarantee of success, since in their case that experience is completely lacking which has proven the worth of what has been tried and found useful. That is why the Law ["Ragione," which also means "Reason"] takes pains to command men to think carefully before setting out on a new path . . .

Again we see the curious mixture of attitudes: deference to a tradition, equated with a completely rationalized Law, the central figure of which is the impersonal, Latin *auctor* whose works are surrounded by commentaries; affirmation of his own radical, first-person singular innovation in that tradition; implicit indication of the profound breach that he has effected between the humble modern commentator and august classical author, as he has, again almost uniquely, taken both roles upon himself.

In this light, then, it is not so surprising that book 1 culminates with a double, apparently contradictory, assertion. First, Dante claims that that the Italian vernacular is, after all, capable of achieving something very close to the authority of Latin: "through this commentary people will be led to recognize the great goodness of the Italian vernacular: they will see the power it has to make plain the highest and newest [or strangest] ideas, decorously, fully and attractively, almost as well as Latin" (1, 10). And, Dante adds, his specific aim in writing poetry is to confer on the vernacular, through the binding force of "rhyme and rhythm," the same transhistorical, transpersonal coherence and permanence that distinguish Latin:

> Everything naturally pursues its own perpetuation, and this I may demonstrate in the following manner: thus, if the vernacular were able to pursue its own ends, it would pursue that one, and it would consist in preparing itself for greater stability, and greater stability could not be obtained than in binding itself with numbers [meter] and with rhymes. And this same pursuit has been my own . . . (1, 13)

In the second place, and on the other hand, as the last phrase of this quotation already suggests, Dante makes himself personally, historically, responsible for providing the Italian language with the attributes of impersonal, ahistorical authority, to the point of near-complete identification of himself with that language. Significantly, he argues that Italian is responsible for his very existence as an individual, since it was the vehicle of communication that brought his parents together and thus led to his conception, as well as to whatever moral and intellectual perfection he has now achieved:

> The fact is that man has two perfections . . . – the first makes him *be*, the second makes him *be good* – and if my own speech was the cause of both in me, then I have received the greatest benefit from it . . . This my vernacular was the uniter of my parents [those who generated me], because they spoke using it . . . Clearly then it participated in my generation. Furthermore, this my vernacular introduced me into the ways of knowledge, which is the final perfection, inasmuch as with it I entered into the knowledge of Latin, which was expounded to me using it.

Here again, then, Dante places himself on the risky boundary between impersonal "medieval" authority and personal "modern" authorship.

Still, only in book 4 of *Convivio* does the language of authority itself become central to Dante's discourse, at the very point when he is first claiming for himself a truly original contribution to philosophy (as against a "vulgarization" of the knowledge produced by others, above all Aristotle; 1, 1). The focus of the book is on a definition of "nobility" as an individual quality, the ground of all eleven ethical virtues (those that, presumptively, would have been treated in the omitted/unwritten canzoni and commentaries). This definition is opposed to another view, which derives nobility from ancestry and/or "ancient wealth" and which is attributed by Dante to Emperor Frederick II Hohenstauffen (1194–1250) and, indirectly, to Aristotle himself. In this context, Dante feels the need to account for his apparent contradiction of two great *auctores*, political and philosophical, and he begins the process with an etymologically grounded exploration of the nature and types of *auctoritas*.

As Dante explicitly notes (4, 6), his discussion of the origins and meaning of the word "auctor" derive from a specific source, the late medieval etymological dictionary written by Hugutio of Pisa, known as the *Magnae derivationes*. Hugutio gives three separate definitions, which both indicate the "state of the art" in the discourse of authority in the later Middle Ages and open the way for Dante to make further innovations on the topic. Hugutio's first definition, "auctor" from "augeo," "to amplify or augment," concerns political authority, which seeks to increase the territory under its control. His second, "autor," comes from a Greek word, "autentim," which means "worth of belief and imitation," and is applied to "philosophers and the inventors of the arts." This, he says, is the definition of the *auctor* proper. Finally, there is a third meaning, one which had not been much reported in earlier medieval discussions of authority, namely "avitor" from "avieo," or "to bind," which is applied to poets like Virgil who "bind their verses with feet and with meter." Authority, according to Hugutio, has political, philosophical, and poetic dimensions, and each of these is clearly distinguished from the others. As we will now see, when Dante picks up Hugutio's categories, he makes some subtle and not so subtle changes that reflect both the rhetorical and conceptual needs of his treatise and, of course, his own ill-concealed desire to appropriate some or all of these types of authority for himself.

In *Convivio* 4, Dante is overtly concerned with two of these types of authorities – an emperor (Frederick II) and *the* philosopher, Aristotle – and implicitly with the third (the issue at hand is the content of a *poem* and Dante himself is evidently a poet). At the same time, in chapter 6, he rehearses two of Hugutio's definitions, the poetic author, from *avieo*, with which, he says, disingenuously, he is not at present concerned, and to which I will return in short order, and the philosophical/intellectual, from *autentim*, which *is* the focus of his discussion:

> [T]he other source from which "author" – as Hugutio bears witness in his *Derivationes* – descends is a Greek word *autentin*, which in Latin means "worthy of faith and obedience." As thus derived, "author" refers to every person worthy of being trusted [worthy of faith] and [of being] obeyed. From this comes the word with which we are concerned now, namely "authority," so we see that "authority" is equivalent to "an act worthy of faith and obedience." Whence, given that Aristotle is most worthy of faith and obedience, it is obvious that his words are the supreme and highest authority. (4, 6, 5)

Both in his citation of Hugutio's authority on authority and in his declared intention to demonstrate the compatibility of his argument with the authorities of Frederick II and of Aristotle, Dante is trying to demonstrate his mastery of the cultural discourse of authority, to affirm his subscription to its values, and to place himself in the naturally subordinate position to which he – as modern, unofficial, vernacular writer – is relegated by it.

Dante, in other words, is attempting to demonstrate his own "faith and obedience" even as he apparently contradicts the *dicta* of two *auctores*. The attempt itself is a curious one, however, since in it Dante freely arranges to his own purposes the categories he received from the tradition through Hugutio's text. He omits the etymology of the political *auctor* from *augere*, perhaps because his ideology of empire posits the universal dominion of the monarch, who is concerned with administering justice rather than with conquering new territories (see *Convivio* 4, 3–5, and the later treatise, *Monarchia* [On Universal Empire]). At the same time, he (implicitly) brings imperial authority under the same rubric as philosophical authority, stressing the definitional shift by adding the politically-juridically charged "obedience" to the Hugutian "belief." Having put these two authorities on parallel footing, he then proceeds to delimit the scope of their respective dominions – Frederick, as any emperor, has authority over the governance of human will, but not over the rational exposition of truth – thus he has no special authority to define nobility and thus the discrepancy between his account and Dante's makes no difference. Aristotle, and any philosopher, while master in the domain of reason, requires the emperor in order to translate understanding into practice – in other words, *obbedienza* is only assured with the imperial imprimatur (4, 6, 17). Having affirmed both types of authorities, Dante has also limited both, leaving a space, what Etienne Gilson long ago called the "aporia dantesca," into which he drives the critical wedge of his own intellectual innovations.

Let me note one further implication of the relationship between Dante's definitional excursus and Hugutio's treatment of *autor* from *autentim*: Hugutio specifically claims that the author in this sense is entitled to the adjective "autenticus," which he glosses as "nobilis," noble. If we then consider that Dante's "digression" on authority concerns the question of how seriously we should take his discourse on nobility, a hermeneutic circle begins to close. And if we further note that his thesis concerning nobility is that it is an individual quality, responsible for the generation of virtuous actions in unique persons, we can infer that even as he argues for personal nobility he is also implicitly, impersonally, affirming an oxymoronically personal *autorità*.

Perhaps just as significant, from this point of view, is the digression within a digression dedicated to the poetic *autore* from *avieo* that immediately precedes the etymology of *autore* from *autenim*:

> This word, namely "autore," can descend from one of two sources. One is a verb no longer much used in grammar [i.e., Latin], namely "auieo" which means as much as "to bind words." And whoever looks carefully at it *in its first person singular form* will see that it openly demonstrates this meaning, because it is made up only of the bonds of words, that is, only of the five vowels, that are the soul and bond of every word, and composed of them in a mobile form that figures the image of a bond . . . And inasmuch as "autore" derives from this verb, it is taken to refer to the poets alone, who with musical art have bound together their words: and with this meaning we are not concerned at present. (4, 6)

The ostensible function of the digression is to separate the purely formal "authority" of the poet from the moral and intellectual content offered up under the aegis of the philosophical "autore" from *autentim*. This is a curious, and curiously self-deprecating, gesture, however, since (1) Dante is nothing if not a poet, but there is no overt indication that this type of authority concerns him or his canzoni at all; and (2) the whole point of the *Convivio* is to argue for the philosophical content of Dante's canzoni, so that the separation of poetic and philosophical *autori* seems counter-productive.

There are, however, compelling internal reasons to think that the disclaimer Dante offers is disingenuous, part of the ongoing rhetorical process of concealing and revealing his ambitions simultaneously. Notably, if we look back at the discussion of poetic language at the end of book 1, we see that this definition responds very closely to Dante's affirmation of his mission to bind together the vernacular into an authoritative language through the use of "rhythm and rhyme," which he there clearly posits as the *sine qua non* for proving that Italian is capable of expressing the same (philosophical) concepts as Latin. In other words, at the very moment when he distinguishes one kind of authorship from another, he is implying their inextricable connection. Similarly, at the very moment when he is defining the role of the *autore* in impersonal terms and placing himself in the role not of the *auctor* but of one who humbly believes and obeys authoritative words, he also leaves a hint, hidden in plain sight, of a very different role for himself as individual author. The etymon, *avieo*, he carefully emphasizes, is the first-person singular form of this Latin verb. In other words, he is saying, in quotation marks, "I [Dante] author."

A complementary process of self-authorization, similarly conflicted between depersonalized and personalized concepts of authorship, is found in the roughly contemporaneous, and similarly incomplete, treatise, *De vulgari eloquentia*. Where in *Convivio* Dante suggests that the writing of vernacular poetry will elevate Italian to a stylistic and semantic level close to that of *grammatica*, in *De vulgari eloquentia* he moves in the opposite direction, defining an "illustrious vernacular" (book 1), which can then be used in writing Italian poetry, and particularly the noblest of its forms, the canzone. Where in *Convivio* he writes in self-effacing Italian and deferentially insists on the precedence of Latin, in *De vulgari eloquentia* he writes in authoritative Latin (flatly contradicting his assertion in the other treatise that "grammatica" should not be put in the service of "volgare"), and insists from the outset on the greater nobility of the vernacular, which everyone, including women and children, learns from her/his wet-nurse:

> And of these two languages, the nobler is the vernacular: to begin with because it was the first language used by the human race [in Eden]; then because the whole world enjoys its benefits, even though it is differentiated in diction and pronunciation [from place to place and from time to time]; and, finally, because it is natural, while the other is, instead, artificial. (1, 1)

The language described is at once personal and universal, and is linked to the perfection of Edenic human origins. The balance of the first book, however, is spent in redefining the Italian vernacular, so that it becomes, very much like Latin, an elite, rule-governed language that is specific to no place and no time, that is, in other words, impersonal and transcendent:

> . . . the noblest actions carried out by Italians are specific to no Italian city, but common to all; and among these we can identify that vernacular which we have pursued throughout this book, and which, although it leaves its trace in every city, dwells in none of them . . . It is thus like the simplest of substances [i.e., beings], namely God. (1, 16)

As in *Convivio*, too, the authority of this language is multi-dimensional, qualified by the adjectives "illustrious, cardinal, regal, and curial" (1, 17–19). Specifically, Dante says, this language is the one that *would* be found in the court of an Italian king if there was one, and employed by the "curia" of that court, namely the elite cadre of literate intellectuals who advise the king and carry out his business. In other words, as in *Convivio*, book 4, it is the language of both "rational" and "political" authorities as these would operate together in ideal collaboration.

Dante recognizes at least two problems with this fantasy of a perfectly impersonal, authoritative, "vulgar" tongue. First, at a general world-historical level, vernaculars may be like the "natural language" of prelapsarian Eden, but they are, more immediately, the products of the fall from Eden and the related episode of the Tower of Babel, which resulted in a chaotic multiplication of languages throughout the world, a situation in which, at an extreme, every individual person has his own, incomprehensible, way of speaking. Secondly, and more pressing, at least since the time of Emperor Frederick II (d. 1250), no central Italian court, no established *curia*, and thus no centralized, authorizing institution exists to cultivate and house an "illustrious vernacular." Instead, the *curia*, and with it the vernacular, wander the peninsula "in exile": "our illustrious vernacular wanders like a stranger and finds hospitality in lowly refuges, since the regal court is empty" (1, 18, 3).

It is thus, willy-nilly, that Dante himself reappears, personally, in the picture. Earlier in the treatise he had stressed his own unhappy situation of exile, but also its role in making him familiar with the range of "municipal" vernaculars throughout the Italian peninsula, and thus giving him the authority to treat this unprecedented subject. He, like the *curia*, like the illustrious vernacular, wanders in exile through the peninsula (1, 6, 3 and 1, 17, 7). The parallel, in fact, suggests that in many ways Dante himself personally embodies the vernacular in its highest form.

That he here, once again, both claims and effaces this oxymoronically personal authority and authorship is evident, finally, in the complex and evolving strategies by which he refers to himself in the treatise. *Qua* author of the prose treatise, he refers to himself in the first plural "nos" (we, us), thus adopting the impersonal "voice of reason." At the same time, he consistently refers to himself, obliquely, as a privileged exemplar of the best qualities of the vernacular, several times coyly placing himself in the final position of a list of illustrative poetic passages, but referring to himself obliquely in the third person, usually as the "friend of Cino [da Pistoia, the law professor-poet who may be one of the 'fedeli d'amore' in *Vita nuova*, chapter 3]" (1, 10, 2; 1, 13, 4; 1, 17, 3; 2, 2, 8 [twice]; 2, 5, 4; 2, 6, 6).

This depersonalizing pose, however, eventually drops away, and in an extremely telling fashion. In book 2, having established the existence of an "illustrious [Italian] vernacular," Dante begins what was apparently to have been a three-book sequence giving an encyclopedic review of the different kinds of Italian poetry and the language appropriate to them. The treatise, however, ends abruptly as it nears the conclusion of his treatment of the first form, the canzone, which is also the noblest of forms, worthy of the highest style ("tragedy") and the greatest subjects (love, war, and "rectitude," i.e., ethics), thus leaving intact the impression that the "illustrious vernacular" and (Dante's) Italian poetry are essentially the same thing.

That this is so, and that Dante is appropriating personally to himself and his works the authority he impersonally attributed to the "illustrious vernacular," appears in a series of steps in book 2: in the first place, when he says that poets of the "vulgare illustre," whom (following the first Hugutian etymology of *Convivio* 4, 6) he refers to as "binders of language" ("avientibus"; 2, 1), provide the model for prose writers rather than the reverse; secondly, when he offers himself, still as the "friend of Cino," as the sole example of the highest subject matter treated in the illustrious vernacular, the "poetry of rectitude" (2, 4 [twice]); thirdly, four chapters further on, when he refers to the writers of vernacular canzoni, specifically, and on an equal footing with Virgil himself, as "autores" (2, 8 [twice]); and finally when, later in the very same chapter, he suddenly shifts his exemplary rhetoric and now refers to himself as poet and model for the noblest form (canzone) of the noblest mode (poetry) of the noblest vernacular ("vulgare illustre"), no longer in the impersonal third person, but in the same first person plural that he has used in authoring the treatise:

> Thus we say [nos dicimus] that the canzone, which is called in this way because of its supreme excellence [since "cantio," "canzone," means "song," the species taking on the name of the poetic family as a whole], which is the quality we have been seeking for – is a concatenation in equal stanzas, without refrain, serving the expression of a unified concept, as we ourselves [nos] showed when we say [dicimus]: "Donne che avete intelletto d'Amore."
>
> (*Vita nuova*, chapter 19; compare *Purgatorio* 24, 49–51)

In the five remaining chapters of the treatise, Dante refers to himself as poet six more times, each time in the first person (2, 10, 2; 2, 11, 5 & 7–8; 2, 12, 3; 2, 13, 2 & 13). Slowly, almost imperceptibly, then, Dante has first moved Italian from the humble status of a language spoken even by women and children (see again *Vita nuova*, chapter 25), to a universal, impersonal vehicle of the authoritative "poetry of rectitude," to an ideal language and an exalted poetic genre with which he is personally equated.

This, then, is the fundamental paradox in Dante's developing concept of himself as poet – at once participating in the culture of impersonal *auctoritas* and anticipating the advent of a modern, personalized, "individualistic" authorship. Dante, clearly, feels the cultural tension pressing on his claims concerning himself, his language, and his verse, and he adopts a variety of conceptual and rhetorical strategies, explicitly as well as implicitly, both to conceal and to justify his apparent "usurpation" of *auctoritas*. It should now be evident that the apparently straightforward "discourse of authority" in the

Commedia emerges precisely from the rhetorical-conceptual "selva oscura" (dark woods; *Inferno* 1, 1) of Dante's earlier career. I have, however, not yet touched on what may be the decisive strategy that makes the *Commedia* possible, and which is already coming into view in the works examined here.

We can find a dim hint of this in the language quoted above from *De vulgari eloquentia*, book 1, chapter 17, where Dante compares the transcendent unity of the "vulgare illustre" to the "simplest of substances," i.e., God, shortly before he then implicitly identifies it with himself as an exile wandering homeless through the Italian peninsula. In other words, Dante as unifier of language through the binding words of poetry is analogous to (not identical with, evidently), God as the unifier of Creation itself.

The same analogy lies behind the definition of the poetic *autore* from *avieo* in *Convivio* 4, 6, although this only becomes really clear when seen retrospectively, in light of the *Paradiso*. In canto 33, the created universe is described as a book "bound together with love in one volume," creating (as Giuseppe Mazzotta first noticed) an implicit connection between the poetic *autore* who binds together poetic language with "the vowels of authority" and God as Author of authors, the Logos who unites the "book of creation." In canto 26, where, as seen earlier, God is specifically identified as the "verace Autore" of the Bible, Dante also refers to the Creator through a vocalic metaphor:

> The Good which makes this court content is A and O[mega] of all the writing
> that Love reads to me . . .   (16–18)

And later in the same canto Dante has Adam, the first human "binder of words," designate Him with two more vowels:

> the highest Good . . . was called 'I' on earth: and afterward he was called 'E[l].'
> (133–35)

The triune God of Christianity combines absolute power with total knowledge in a perfect "poetic" creativity, fusing the three types of human authority distinguished by Hugutio. By implying that the poetic author from *avieo* has a synthetic capacity analogous to divinity – and in fact in basing his representation of divine creativity in terms that he has previously used to describe the human poet – Dante seems well on the way to instantiating the Renaissance "author-God," the very personage so virulently attacked by Barthes and Foucault. With additional space we could also show that Dante goes beyond analogy to suggest that his authority can exceed the temporal, institutional, linguistic and other limits to which it properly ought to be subjected because it is conferred on him by divine, prophetic – evangelical – apocalyptic, inspiration.

This then, is the complex background, of medieval traditions and of Dante's own earlier wrestling therewith, against which we can better understand the problem of authority as it unfolds in the *Commedia*. From early on, Dante attacks the problem on a number of fronts simultaneously, at once conserving, outwardly, his own respectful and distanced stance toward the "impersonal" authorities, poetic, philosophical, imperial, and, ultimately, theological, that his culture sets over him, and at the same time negotiating in impersonal terms what is fundamentally a personal space of authorship and authority for himself. He also anticipates in the earlier works the possibility of an ad hoc infusion of directly inspired authority into a human person, like the human authors of the Bible, whose writings "channel" the will of the divine Word (God as Logos).

Let me now turn back briefly to the key passage in which the problem of the human *autore* is introduced into the *Commedia*:

> While I was falling down into a low place, before my eyes one had offered himself to me who through long silence seemed hoarse. "Miserere – on me," I cried to him, "whatever you may be, whether a shade or true man!" "Not a man, I was formerly a man, and my parents were Lombards, Mantuans both by birth. I was born sub Iulio, though it was late, and I lived in Rome under the good Augustus in the time of the false and lying gods. I was a poet, and I sang of that just son of Anchises who came from Troy, when proud Ilion was destroyed by fire." . . . "Now are you that Virgil, that fountain which spreads forth so broad a river of speech?" I replied with shamefast brow. "O honor and light of the other poets, let my long study and great love avail me, that has caused me to search through your volume. You are my master and my author; you alone are he from whom I have taken the [beautiful] style that has brought me honor." (*Inferno* I, 61–73, 79–87)

What, if anything, has changed as we consider this passage in the light of the four prior works discussed here? No doubt that we still see "Virgilio" as the vehicle by which authority, especially human authority deriving from ancient times, is first defined and then appropriated by Dante over the course of the first sixty cantos of the *Commedia*. But we see more as well. We recognize, for example, that the epic poet Virgil is only the latest in a lengthy line of authoritative personages and textual sites which have served as a "local habitation and a name" for Dante's interest in the problem of *auctoritas*. We recognize, as well, that through the character of Virgil Dante has brought together and reconciled all of the previously disparate strands of human authority laid out by Hugutio. He is, as commentators have long asserted, an *autor* from *autentim*, who has taken over from the *Convivio*'s Aristotle as the "voice of reason," "worthy of faith and obedience." He is also, it should now be obvious, the poetic *avitor* from *avieo*, who had already prior to this meeting taught Dante the "beautiful style" that has brought him "honor." Finally, as the protégé of Caesar Augustus and the author of the poem that describes the foundation of Rome and predicts its Augustan apotheosis, he is also bound up with the imperial *auctor*. For the first time, then, in Dante's *oeuvre*, all of the various domains of authority (with one, transcendent, exception), come together under the umbrella of an Italian word, "autore," that simultaneously translates Latin *autor*, *auctor*, and *avitor*. And when, in the final lines of canto 27, *Purgatorio*, Virgil's tutelage comes to an end, as he "crowns and miters" Dante over himself (140), he indicates not only the completion of an individual moral-intellectual education that reverses the effects of the Fall, but also, as a consequence, his pupil's liberation from institutional authorities, both political (crown) and spiritual (miter) to which he and all living persons are properly subjected. Finally, the figurative crown should also be understood as a version of the laurel wreath, emblem of all true poetic *auctores*.

Our itinerary through the *opere minori* should make evident another crucial feature of Dante's use of Virgil in the *Commedia*. It is not just that he serves the abstract function of allegorically conflating the three major types of authority with which an earlier Dante wrestled so long and so hard – more important, he does so in the guise of a historical person, with a specific biography and an individual history. According to the *Vita nuova* and *Convivio*, only "modern" poets like Dante are in the awkward position of having to "explain themselves," justifying their practices of signification, in the first person, while the illustrious authorities of antiquity are to be taken on faith and blindly obeyed. In *Inferno* 1, Virgil has been personalized, and thus brought down to Dante's level, even as Dante is being raised up to his. In *Purgatorio* 22, in fact, we will learn that, unlike Dante, Virgil could not have explained the truest (Christian) meanings of his poetry even if he had wanted to. As "Statius" says to him:

> You first directed my steps toward Parnassus to drink from its grottos, and first illuminated me concerning God. You did as one who walks at night, who carries the light behind him and does not help himself, but instructs the persons coming after . . . (67–69)

In other words, the most salient fact about "Virgil," from the point of view of Dante's career-long quest for authority, is simply that he is there at all, and that the character, "Dante," is conversing with him face-to-face.

In *Vita nuova*, in *Convivio*, and elsewhere, "Virgil" is "become a name," serving as an impersonal site of trustworthy language, and moral truths. In the *Commedia*, instead, he is a "person" – the mask or shadow of an excellent but imperfect individual with a precisely defined, though indeed unhappy, eternal destiny – while at the very same time he is also the personification of ancient authoritative books (the *Aeneid*, but also the *Eclogues* and *Georgics*). Indeed, like the Amore of *Vita nuova* 25, he serves as a projection from and of Dante's own authorial personality (and, of course, in this sense Dante is *his* author). In other words, if Dante's contingent historical personality (precisely located "in the middle of the way of [his] life," that is, Good Friday, 1300) is the primary obstacle to the achievement of impersonal authority, the solution is to encounter the *auctor* in person. However deferential his tone may be in speaking to his "maestro e autore," the very fact that he is *talking to Virgil*, and then to Homer, Lucan, Horace, and Ovid, sweeps away in a moment the chasm that is still not completely bridged by the end of *Convivio*.

This strategy has a second, and equally simple, element, which enables the chiasmus, the crossing, between authority and personality to take place, as Erich Auerbach seems to have recognized first, in his formulation of the concept of "figura." The point is that even as Dante personalizes, and thus in a sense historicizes, the ancient *auctores*, he simultaneously, and conversely, confers on himself a condition basic to medieval notions of *auctoritas*: namely, a comprehensive view of history which is grounded outside of history. He accomplishes this feat by removing himself, literally, from the domain of temporal contingency and asserting as his own, from *Inferno* 3 forward, the perspective of an *altro mondo* beyond time and corporeal death, from which he can draw less and then more and more directly on the supreme authority of the "verace Autore," God himself. This basic strategy, embodied, or, perhaps, shadowed forth, in the face-to-face encounter between "Dante" and "Virgil," sutures together past and present, personality and authority, time and eternity. Crucially, both of these features – the personalizing of the ancients and the depersonalizing, or rather, the de-historicizing, of Dante himself – are presented as simple predicates of the poem, although they will then, as the *Commedia* unfolds, serve as the indispensable foundation for a narrative dramatization of the poet's transcendence of those personal and historical attributes that impede his access to authority.

SUGGESTED READING

As regards *auctoritas* and the *auctor* in medieval culture, see, *inter alii*, Ernest Robert Curtius, *European Literature in the Latin Middle Ages*, trans. W. R. Trask (Princeton:

Princeton University Press, 1953, first published in German, 1948), esp. pp. 48–54 *et passim*; as well as A. J. Minnis and A. B. Scott, eds., *Medieval Literary Theory and Criticism, c.1100–c.1375: The Commentary Tradition* (Oxford: Clarendon Press, 1988), and the bibliography included there. For the late twentieth-century debate on the significance of authorship in the Western tradition, see Roland Barthes, "The Death of the Author," in *Image, Music, Text*, trans. S. Heath (New York: Hill and Wang, 1977, first published in French, 1968), pp. 142–48; Michel Foucault, "What is an Author?," in *Language, Counter-Memory, Practice: Selected Essays and Interviews*, ed. Donald F. Bouchard, trans. Donald F. Bouchard and Sherry Simon (Ithaca: Cornell University Press, 1977, this essay first published 1968), pp. 113–38. As regards Dante generally and the *Commedia* specifically, see Erich Auerbach, "Figura," in *Scenes from the Drama of European Literature: Six Essays* (New York: Meridian Books, 1959, first published in German, 1944), pp. 11–76; Robert Hollander, *Allegory in Dante's Commedia* (Princeton: Princeton University Press, 1969), esp. pp. 76–79; Giorgio Stabile, "Autore" and "Autorità," in vol. 1 of the *Enciclopedia dantesca*, 6 vols., Dir. Umberto Bosco (Rome: Istituto dell'Enciclopedia Italiana, 1970–78), pp. 454–60; Giuseppe Mazzotta, *Dante, Poet of the Desert* (Princeton: Princeton University Press, 1979); Kevin Brownlee, "Why the Angels Speak Italian," *Poetics Today* 5 (1984): 597–610; Rachel Jacoff and Jeffrey Schnapp, eds., *The Poetry of Allusion: Virgil and Ovid in Dante's Commedia* (Stanford, CA: Stanford University Press, 1991); various essays by Zygmunt Baranski, including "Dante Alighieri: Experimentation and (Self-)Exegesis," in Alastair Minnis, ed., *The Cambridge History of Literary Criticism. Volume 2. The Middle Ages* (Cambridge: Cambridge University Press, 2005), pp. 561–82.

For an extended consideration of these topics, see Albert Russell Ascoli, *Authority in Person: Dante and the Making of a Modern Author* (Cambridge: Cambridge University Press, 2007). For additional general information and bibliography on the *opere minori*, see the entries under *Vita nuova, Convivio, De vulgari eloquentia*, and *Epistles* in Lansing, ed., as well as the following items of special relevance to the individual works: for the *Vita nuova*, see the essays of Barolini and Harrison in this volume and the bibliographies cited there, as well as Thomas C. Stillinger, *The Song of Troilus: Lyric Authority in the Medieval Book* (Philadelphia: University of Pennsylvania Press, 1992); various books and essays by Michelangelo Picone, especially "Dante and the Classics," in Amilcare Iannucci, ed., *Dante* (Toronto: University of Toronto Press, 1997), pp. 51–73; Olivia Holmes, *Assembling the Lyric Self: Authorship from Troubadour Song to Italian Poetry Book* (Minneapolis and London: University of Minnesota Press, 2000); and Robert M. Durling, "Guido Cavalcanti in the *Vita Nuova*," in M. L. Ardizzone, ed., *Guido Cavalcanti tra i suoi lettori* (Florence: Cadmo Editore, 2003), pp. 177–85. For *Convivio*, Etienne Gilson, *Dante and Philosophy*, trans. D. Moore (New York: Sheed and Ward, 1949); Ulrich Leo, "The Unfinished *Convivio* and Dante's Rereading of the *Aeneid*," *Medieval Studies* 13 (1951): 41–64. For *De vulgari eloquentia*, Zygmunt Baranski, "Notes on Dante and Plurilingualism," *The Italianist* 6 (1986): 5–18; Marianne Shapiro, *De Vulgari Eloquentia: Dante's Book of Exile* (Lincoln, NB: University of Nebraska Press, 1990); Steven Botterill (Introduction," in Dante Alighieri, *De Vulgari Eloquentia*, ed. and trans. S. Botterill (Cambridge: Cambridge University Press, 1996), pp. ix–xxvi; Gary Cestaro, *Dante and the Grammar of the Nursing Body* (Notre Dame: Notre Dame University Press, 2003).

Competent English translations exist for all the major texts cited: *Vita nuova* by Mark Musa (Oxford and New York: Oxford University Press, 1992); *Convivio* has been translated both by Christopher Ryan (Saratoga, CA: Anma Libri, 1989) and by Richard Lansing (New York: Garland, 1990); for *De vulgari eloquentia*, the Botterill translation cited above; for the *Epistles*, Paget Toynbee, ed. and trans., *Dantis Alagherii: The Letters of Dante* (Oxford: Clarendon Press, 1920 [out of print]).

5

LINO PERTILE

Introduction to *Inferno*

A dark and menacing forest dominates the *Comedy*'s opening scene:

> In the middle of the journey of our life,
> I came to myself in a dark wood,
> for the straight way was lost.

The character who says "I" does not tell us how he got there. He himself does not seem to know; indeed he only suddenly becomes aware of the alien, nightmarish reality that surrounds him. But who is this character? He is both the protagonist of the story and its narrator, a character who has survived his adventure and is now in the process of writing it down: a character-poet. Unlike Homer and Virgil who always say "he," never "I," and unlike Ulysses and Aeneas who went to Hell but did not write the stories of their own journeys, the protagonist and the narrator of the *Comedy* are one and the same.

They are one but they undertake separate journeys within the poem: the journey of the character from the dark forest to the Empyrean heaven, where God dwells with all the blessed; and the journey of the narrator through the one-hundred cantos of the poem, from canto 1 of the *Inferno* to canto 33 of the *Paradiso*. The first journey lasts one week; the second, to the best of our knowledge, took at least a dozen years (circa 1307–20). In fact, we are given to understand along the way that, whereas the experience of the journey was willed and facilitated by Divine Providence, the poem, the work of the narrator, is in a sense a far more difficult undertaking, a task that costs him "hunger, cold *and* vigils" (*Purgatorio* 29, 37–38): the poet's daunting task is to find words adequate to his experience, "so that the word may not be different from the fact" (*Inf.* 32, 12).

Not until *Purgatory* 30, line 55 will we discover that the protagonist and narrator of the journey is called "Dante." Indeed the poem leaves us with no doubt that he is the Florentine poet Dante Alighieri. The character Dante, the narrator Dante, and the historical Dante are all intertwined and overlapping, but we cannot assume that they are identical. Nor are they three discrete entities. Dante's identity in the poem is ultimately an irresolvable ambiguity, an interlacing the poet fully exploits.

The journey

Dante does not say "In the middle of the journey of *my* life," but "In the middle of the journey of *our* life." This sentence denotes both a point in time and a point in space. The question of time is easily resolved: the ordinary duration of an individual life in Dante's culture was believed to be the biblical "threescore years and ten" (Psalms 90:10). Therefore, "in the middle of our life" indicates the age of thirty-five, that is for Dante in the year 1300, a date that will be confirmed later in *Inf.* 21, 112–14. At the same time, by placing *his* awakening in the context of the journey of *our* life, Dante stresses the universal value of his experience. Not by chance, 1300 was also the first Jubilee Year, and a time in which Dante believed that the church was led by an unworthy pope, while the empire had no leader at all – a time of grave crisis, therefore, not just for Dante the character, but for the entire world.

The issue of space is more complicated, for the journey of our life is a journey only in a metaphorical sense. This metaphor, however, is one which, for Christian culture, defines the most intrinsic meaning of life, the quintessence of the human condition. Ever since Adam and Eve were banished from the earthly Paradise, we live in a state of exile in a land that was not meant for us. In this "region of unlikeness,"[1] we are travelers, or pilgrims, longing to return home. What drives us is our desire to recover our lost happiness – an innate desire, good in itself, but capable also of leading us astray.

The journey in the middle of which Dante wakes up at the beginning of *Inferno* is this metaphorical journey. The magic of Dante's poetry is that, as he wakes up, the metaphor becomes literal, the journey real. In one week Dante will travel from the dark forest to the Empyrean; from exile to his spiritual home. Intriguingly enough, Dante was actually in exile from Florence when he wrote the story of his journey home, and it is to this double exile, from heaven and from Florence, that we owe the *Comedy*.

Virgil

At the beginning of the story, Dante does not see beyond the forest, nor does he know what direction to take in order to get out of it. He is prey to a crisis whose nature robs him even of the minimum of knowledge necessary to free himself. If it depended on him, the forest would swallow him up again and forever. Only an outside agent can save him.

And just as he is fleeing in despair from three fearful beasts, the figure of a man appears before him in the waste land. "*Miserere* on me," he cries, "whatever you may be, whether shade or true man!" (*Inf.* 1, 65–66). The forest, the hill, the three wild animals were stylized figures, suspended between nightmare and reality; this apparition, however, though he presents himself as a "shade," is a real man. He is the Latin poet Virgil, who, on Good Friday of the year 1300, more than thirteen centuries after his death, materializes out of nowhere: Virgil, the author of the *Aeneid* and the master of poetry and wisdom revered by Dante and by the entire Middle Ages. He is the outside agent who now invites the hopeless wayfarer to "hold to another path," a third way that opens, paradoxically, downwards, between the she-wolf and the forest. It is he who will guide Dante to safety. Not an angel, a saint, a philosopher, a scientist or a theologian, but a poet – the poet of the Roman empire.

But first, something far more astonishing occurs to faze the naive reader: the very same Virgil speaks of the she-wolf, confirming that the beast is indeed alive and real and invincible to all save to a mysterious greyhound who will one day come "to make her die in pain," and, better yet, drive her back to Hell, "whence envy first sent her forth." And, as if that were not enough, Virgil adds that, in so doing, the greyhound will bring salvation to the whole of Italy, "for which the virgin Camilla died of her wounds, and Euryalus, Turnus, and Nisus" (1, 107–08). But aren't the virgin Camilla – we may ask – and Turnus, Euryalus, and Nisus all legendary pagan characters in Virgil's poem? Why then does Dante make Virgil treat them as if they were historical figures who died for Italy? Before Dante has even entered the world beyond, we are fascinated and disoriented by a poetic texture involving both dream and reality, legend and history, personal story and world events.

Moral and physical structure

When Dante began the *Comedy*, there already existed a vast body of narrative concerning the afterlife. There were stories of journeys to, and of visions of, the hereafter, as well as allegorical poems and rudimentary literary texts, both in Latin and in several European vernaculars.[2] Dante knew most of these written texts, and was probably familiar with other stories that were transmitted only orally. His *Comedy* is the point of arrival of this thousand-year-old tradition; it is also a point of departure so total and definitive that, by completely absorbing and surpassing everything that preceded it, it rendered impossible any future sequel.

No other narrative about the afterlife is as complex and coherently structured as the *Comedy*. Dante's journey from the dark forest down into the great funnel of Hell is all in one direction. On the evening of Good Friday, 1300, he enters the funnel in the northern hemisphere and proceeds through the entirety of Hell until he reaches the centre of the earth. Then he climbs back up a "natural cavern" inside the southern hemisphere until he resurfaces at the antipodes of Jerusalem, on the shore of the mountain of Purgatory, just before dawn on Easter Sunday. Thus the time Dante spends "buried," as it were, underground, corresponds to the time that, in the liturgy of the church, Christ spent in His tomb from burial to resurrection. Dante will take the next three days to climb up to the Garden of Eden at the summit of the mountain of Purgatory, and from there he will fly through the heavens to the Empyrean; thus his journey will take him across the entire known universe. It will also take him, through the whole of human history, back to where time began.

The moral system of the *Inferno*, which Virgil explicates in canto 11, is based on a broadly Aristotelian-Ciceronian scheme, but with variations and adaptations that depend on popular traditions, as well as occasional inventions for which the poet alone is responsible. The damned are punished in nine circles from the top to the bottom of the funnel in exact proportion to the increasing gravity of their sins.

We enter Hell at the beginning of the third canto when Dante and Virgil cross the threshold of a gate situated below ground in an unspecified place. What we see, from the threshold of the canto, is not the gate itself, but rather, the epigraph inscribed above it:

> THROUGH ME THE WAY INTO THE GRIEVING CITY,
> THROUGH ME THE WAY INTO ETERNAL SORROW,
> THROUGH ME THE WAY AMONG THE LOST PEOPLE.
> JUSTICE MOVED MY HIGH MAKER;
> DIVINE POWER MADE ME,
> HIGHEST WISDOM, AND PRIMAL LOVE.
> BEFORE ME WERE NO THINGS CREATED
> EXCEPT ETERNAL ONES, AND I ENDURE ETERNAL.
> ABANDON EVERY HOPE, YOU WHO ENTER.

These words are "spoken" not by Dante, but by the gate itself. The inscription is a piece of Hell transported onto the page by the poet who says that he saw and read it with his own eyes: a "photograph" from the other world, a divine intertext expressed, not by coincidence, in the *terza rima* rhyme scheme of the poem. The creator of the gate and the author of the words is God Himself, one and three according to the doctrine of the Trinity, exactly as the inscription itself is one in three tercets, and each tercet is one in three lines. In fact, the gate declares itself to have been made in the name of justice by the Trinity of the Father, the Son, and the Holy Spirit. We must imagine that it was erected and that the inscription was dictated at the moment in which Lucifer, the first and greatest sinner, fell from Heaven and crashed down into the center of the earth, creating the crater of Hell that would contain all future sinners. Whoever enters this gate may not hope to leave ever again.

Beyond this gate and before arriving at the river Acheron is the Vestibule of Hell, or *Antinferno*, a strip of no-man's-land where the neutral, uncommitted spirits dwell: "so many [T. S. Eliot translates in the *Waste Land*], I had not thought death had undone so many" (see *Inf.* 3, 55–57). These are the despicable souls who, while living, refused to choose between good and evil, and therefore are now equally rejected by Hell and Heaven. The poet, who invents them without any narrative or theological precedent, refuses to classify them, while condemning them to one of his most repulsive punishments. They run furiously behind an unidentified banner, pursued by hornets and wasps which sting and suck their blood as, mingled with their tears, it trickles from their wounds down to their feet, where it becomes food for disgusting worms.

The river Acheron separates the Vestibule from Hell proper. All the souls of the damned gather by its bank to be ferried across by Charon. Not however Dante, who, as the ground shakes, loses consciousness to wake up on the other side of the river: a symbolic death which he must endure in order to travel through the world of the dead.

Even the first circle of Hell, which Dante visits after leaving the Vestibule and crossing Acheron, is not, strictly speaking, "infernal," since the souls confined to it are not punished except insofar as they are deprived of the sight of God. What is striking here, alongside the traditional Limbo of unbaptized infants, is a theologically unprecedented castle, in which dwell the great souls of the past who never knew the Christian God. It is here that Dante the character-poet places himself firmly in the company of Homer, Virgil, Horace, Ovid, and Lucan and speaks of himself as "sixth among so much wisdom": a move of extreme audacity and self-confidence for a poet who has not yet gotten his major poem under way. Already, however, we can observe how the character Dante interacts with the creatures of the poet Dante's imagination. The construction of the poem proceeds in fact along a double track: every episode has its own autonomous life, but at the same time it tells a story in which Dante the character becomes involved, in such a way that the general effect transcends each single episode. Thus, the conflict between resolution and diffidence in the mind of the protagonist in the second canto, unsure as to whether or not to embark upon his journey, is made further manifest, on the one hand, in the cowards of the third canto and, on the other, in the great souls of the fourth. And when Dante subsequently presents himself as the successor of the five great ancient poets, we understand that the poet too, not merely the hesitating character, has finally accepted the challenge of the one-hundred-canto journey.

Hell proper begins here, and it is divided in two major regions, conventionally known as Upper and Lower Hell, lying respectively outside and inside the walls of the City of Dis. Outside the walls are the sins of incontinence, inside the sins of malice – a distinction which Dante borrows from Aristotle's *Nichomachean Ethics*. The incontinent are the souls who are unable to control their passions or desires for earthly goods (circles two through five); the malicious offend and injure others by force (the violent, circle seven) or fraud (the fraudulent, circles eight and nine): these distinctions Dante borrows from Cicero's *De officiis* (1, 13).

Being natural, the sins of incontinence offend God less, and therefore they are punished in the first four circles. In the second circle, the lustful are relentlessly buffeted by stormy winds; among them are Paolo and Francesca, the most famous couple of Dante's *Comedy*. By virtue of their position at the start of Hell proper and its punishments, their sin acquires a founding value, so to speak. Just like the sin of Adam and Eve at the dawn of human history, the sin of Paolo and Francesca presents itself, at the beginning of Dante's journey, as a catastrophe from which all other evils follow, even if not out of necessity. There is no good that love, unrestrained by reason, does not destroy; there is no evil to which such love does not lead. We begin by yielding to passion, and we end betraying and murdering Caesar and Christ: this is the story of humanity and the map of Dante's Hell.

In the third circle the gluttonous wallow in mud while a fetid rain drenches them; in the fourth the avaricious and the prodigal roll weights in opposite directions around the perimeter of the circle, until they crash into one another, turn back and collide again on the other side of the circle; and finally, immersed in the filthy marshes of the river Styx, the wrathful repeatedly attack each other, while the sullen sigh and gurgle beneath the muddy waters.

Beyond the river Styx stand the walls of the City of Dis with their burning towers, a parody of the heavenly Jerusalem, the City of God. As soon as we enter, we encounter the tombs of those who did not believe in the immortality of the soul (sixth circle, canto 10). These are the heretics, a category unknown to antiquity (Virgil in fact will not mention it in his moral topography in canto 11). They occupy the borderline between Upper and Lower Hell, between the incontinent and the violent. They burn "alive" in open sepulchers.

Lower Hell begins, to all effects, right here: in it are assembled the souls of the violent and fraudulent, to whom Dante dedicates twenty-three cantos: six to the violent punished in the seventh circle (cantos 11–17), and seventeen to the fraudulent, crammed in two separate circles: the eighth, with the deceivers (cantos 18–30) and the ninth, with the traitors (cantos 31–34).

The violent (seventh circle) are those who pursued their unjust ends with force. They are subdivided into three *gironi* or rings, according to whether they practised violence against others (tyrants and murderers, submerged in the boiling blood of the river Phlegethon), against themselves (suicides, whose souls are transformed into thorn bushes, and squanderers, torn to bits by hounds), or against God, nature, and art (blasphemers, sodomites, and usurers: they lie supine, perambulate, or crouch on burning sands under a rain of fire).

The eighth circle, a dark, deep crater separated from the circles above it, contains those who were guilty of simple fraud, the broadest and most varied of Hell's categories. This circle has a name, Malebolge (Evil Pouches), that has no precedent either in the established theology of Hell or in the preceding tradition of visions of or journeys to the afterlife. The most compendious of all the circles, it is subdivided into ten "pouches," moats or concentric ditches, connected, for the most part, by stone bridges. Reserved for the souls of those who in their wrongdoing exercised their God-given reason and intelligence, it is guarded, not by mythological hybrids like the previous circles, but by "modern" devils, the so-called Malebranche (Evil Claws). Malebolge is an inferno within the *Inferno*, a penal colony of industrial proportions, so to speak. The sinners, even though they are all deceivers, are punished in the most diverse forms within the individual pouches.

In the first bolgia pimps and seducers are lashed with whips by horned devils; in the second, flatterers are submerged in foul excrement, and in the third, simonist popes are "pocketed" head-down in the rocky ground, their legs poking out from the holes, the soles of their feet constantly on fire. Sorcerers and diviners follow in the fourth bolgia: their heads twisted back to front on their shoulders, they walk backwards, tears streaming down their buttocks. In the fifth, the barrators (those who practice political graft) are kept under boiling pitch, and, if they dare to surface, the Malebranche pounce on them with grappling hooks. In the sixth, the hypocrites walk weeping under gilded capes of lead, while in the seventh the thieves are relentlessly possessed by, and transformed into, all manner of reptiles. In the eighth, the so-called fraudulent counselors are consumed within tongues of fire, and in the ninth, the schismatics and sowers of discord are constantly butchered and mutilated. In the tenth, revolting diseases torment the falsifiers: leprosy disfigures the alchemists, a furious madness deranges the impersonators, dropsy swells the counterfeiters, and the liars burn with a hectic fever which causes them to steam and stink.

Finally, in the last circle we find the worst of all sinners, the traitors. The difference between the deceivers and the traitors is that the latter used fraud against those who were tied to them by a special bond of trust. According to the special nature of this bond, the traitors are punished in four separate sections in which they are immersed differently in the ice of Cocytus: traitors against relatives in *Caina*, traitors against party or city in *Antenora*, traitors against guests (and hosts) in *Tolomea*, and traitors against lords and benefactors in *Giudecca*.[3] Here, an anti-Trinitarian Lucifer grinds for all eternity in his three mouths the three worst traitors of all times: Judas who betrayed Christ, and Brutus and Cassius who betrayed the Roman empire in the person of Julius Caesar. Cocytus is the bottom of the abyss, where all the tears of Hell are collected and frozen by the wind that Lucifer produces with his six wings that recall those of a giant bat. Betrayal, the worst sin of all, coincides with total absence of movement and warmth: it is the heart of darkness, the center of the region of unlikeness.

Dante, judge and witness

Dante's Hell is a complex, all-inclusive construction, which combines the different philosophical, theological, literary, and psychological strands of Dante's high cultural inheritance with the desires and fears of popular culture so well represented in the afterlife vision literature tradition.

What is deeply disturbing for the modern reader is the endlessness of the state of being in which victims and tormentors are caught by the eye of the passing visitor: the notion that "great hailstones, filthy water, and snow" will never cease to teem over the gluttons' naked bodies; that the Harpies will forever bite and feed on the leaves that clothe the limbs of the suicides; that a drop of water will never fall upon the parched lips of the counterfeiters; that, in sum, in the kingdom of death no one will ever be allowed not to live on and suffer. As he runs through the wood of the suicides desperately trying to escape the fangs of the ravenous hounds that pursue him, the squanderer Lano da Siena implores: "Now hurry, hurry, death!" (13, 118). In Hell, existence itself is the most implacable punishment. Faced with the "reality" of never-ending punishments, the reader is dismayed at the thought of a justice that can *never* be satisfied. The text does indeed compel us to react and respond to its provocations. The reasons for this are at least two, and both have to do with Dante's extraordinarily original conception and consummate art.

First, outdoing all the visionaries and preachers of his time by leaps and bounds, Dante portrays not sins, but sinners. He gives form to a Hell in which theological and ethical principles, abstract and inaccessible to the many, are embodied in, and totally absorbed by, the stories of concrete men and women, for the most part Florentines or Tuscans – not necessarily "great" individuals, but certainly "true," and known at least by name to his readers. A Hell where, even while sharing a common destiny, each character represents a specific sin, without however forfeiting any part of his or her own unique personal story, his or her own irrepressible individuality. All of the characters of the *Inferno* are defeated individuals, but each one is vanquished in his or her own unique way. The penal conditions to which they are subjected, the unchangeable form of their new existence, instead of dulling or extinguishing their individuality, illuminates it with unanticipated sparks and unsuspected complexity. Thus Dante reveals the actions of his friends and his enemies alike, he gives a voice to their thoughts; they in turn are given access to understanding life in a way they were unable to while living it.

In the second place, Dante does not limit himself merely to cataloguing sinners according to their crimes, but rather he explores human actions in their most secret motivations. A most original and compelling trait of Dante's Hell is the notion that, while being all equally damned, the souls of the sinners are not all entirely nor equally reprehensible. Next to perfectly "evil" figures (for example, Filippo Argenti or Vanni Fucci or Pope Boniface VIII), there are others in whom evil presents itself as a tragic flaw that either sudden death has rendered fatal or no virtue has been capable of conquering or compensating for: this is the case, for example, of Francesca da Rimini, Pier della Vigna, and Brunetto Latini.

But Dante does not stop here. His *Inferno* also shows that, if good people can lose their way forever, the "bad" can have positive characteristics that, while not saving them, nevertheless render their identity more rich and complex. Farinata, for example, is an "Epicurean" (for Dante, a denier of the soul's immortality), a Ghibelline, arrogant, and bloodthirsty, but his magnanimity and his love for his native city confer a dignity upon him that in part redeems him. Likewise, Cavalcante de' Cavalcanti's paternal love may well be obsessive and blind, but it is not contemptible: his desperation seizes in a flash the anguish of any father at the thought that the door of the future is closed forever for his son, that the dreams he had dreamed for him are no longer possible. Master Adam is a hardened and ugly counterfeiter of coins, but the elegiac tenderness with which he recalls "the little streams that from the green hills of the Casentino come down into Arno, making their channels cool and moist" (30, 64–66), is so heart-rendingly lyrical, and reveals such an acute and delicate sensibility on his part, that, for a moment at least, the reader is completely overcome.

This is why the feelings of Dante the character towards the "lost souls" (*Purg.* 30, 138) are not always and exclusively negative. As he descends deeper into Hell, Dante's reactions range from compassion to aggression, from respect to contempt, from curiosity to revulsion, from pity to pitilessness. He swoons at the tale of Francesca's fatal desire but, wilfully or by accident, he kicks Bocca degli Abati in the face; he delights at the torments inflicted on Filippo Argenti and Vanni Fucci, but feels filial affection for the disfigured Brunetto Latini. Before Farinata he is in awe, and spellbound before Ulysses. Dante's journey through Hell is a discovery of how deeply intertwined good and evil can be, in ourselves as well as in others, and how difficult and painful it is for any human being to reach, without proper guidance (see *Purg.* 16, 85–96), any kind of moral clarity.

There is only one group of sinners which Dante seems to hold in absolute contempt: the corrupt popes of his times, whom he condemns to Hell as simonists. Not content with predicting, in one of his most brilliant inventions, the damnation of Pope Boniface VIII (canto 19), Dante portrays him again as "the prince of the new Pharisees" (27, 85), the evil mind who, being a more astute and adept deceiver than the canny Guido da Montefeltro himself, inveigles Guido back into his old sinful ways, and, ultimately, condemns him to Hell.

Naturally, it is Dante who guides the minds and hearts of his readers; it is only through his eyes and responses that we perceive the particular nature of each sinner, reacting with revulsion or sympathy, fear or nervous laughter, as the case may be. In fact, we identify with the pilgrim Dante to the point that we forget that, whatever the figure, incident, or scene to which the character reacts, it is Dante the poet himself who has created it. For example, the pilgrim Dante seems genuinely shocked as he unexpectedly comes across his old teacher, Brunetto Latini, in the *girone* of the sodomites. He remembers Brunetto's "dear, kind paternal image" when, in the world, he used to teach him how man makes himself eternal; he declares his devotion and love for him, and he wishes that he could still be part of the community of the living. And yet, this is the same Dante who, by "finding" Brunetto among the sodomites, reveals to the whole world, present and future, a flaw in his master which was scarcely, if at all, known among Brunetto's closest friends and contemporaries. We see here Dante's synchronized double approach: on the one hand, the pupil's compassion for his master's scorched face, and his enduring loyalty and affection beyond and despite Brunetto's newly discovered flaw; on the other, the inflexible eye of the judge who, for all of Brunetto's civic virtues and scholarly accomplishments, sees a man guilty of sodomy, and does not let him get away with it. Dante does not flinch from putting himself in God's place as judge, nor does he question what he sees as God's judgments; nevertheless, this sternness does not prevent him from feeling pity and involving his readers in his sorrow. The message is definitely mixed, but the lack of moral clarity on the part of the frightened, confused, and uncertain pilgrim is part of a strategy designed to affirm the absolute necessity of such clarity for the pilgrim's (and our own) ultimate salvation.

Crime and punishment

The exploration mapped in the *Inferno* is a voyage through the immense historical archives of the world's evils, ordered according to type and severity in the subsoil of the dark forest. On the surface of the earth, evil can manifest itself in disorderly ways and in complex forms that do not always allow themselves to be fully fathomed by the eyes of the living. In Hell, however, the deeply rooted motivations as well as the extreme consequences of human actions are revealed. Outward appearances have no place here; every choice appears in its barest, most essential truth, and is judged as such. Evil is without remedy, truce, or hope of relief; it has no other boundary than its everlasting present. One cannot even say that evil triumphs on its own ground, since what triumphs over it is Divine Justice, which reduces everything to order and employs evil against itself.

Two general conditions apply to all the souls in Hell: their deprivation of the sight of God (*poena damni*), and the perpetual torment which each soul (with the exception of those in Limbo, who suffer only the first condition) must undergo as punishment for his or her sin (*poena sensus*). The principle which determines the form that this second type of suffering takes is called by Dante the "counterpass" or *contrapasso*. With this term (from the Latin *contra pati*) Dante sums up the retributive principle, which establishes that every soul must suffer (Latin *pati*) in the afterlife according to the sin he or she has committed on earth.

The concept is illustrated in exemplary fashion in canto 28. The sinners of the ninth bolgia, when they were living, sowed scandal and discord in communities and among previously united individuals. As a consequence, they are punished for all eternity by a devil who, each time they pass by him, slashes them with his sword. Thus Mohammed, who was (inaccurately) said to have been a Christian before founding Islam, is shown to be split from chin to anus, and the decapitated Bertran de Born walks holding up his head by the hair like a lantern. The same Bertran explains that, just as he "parted" those who were joined (he fomented division between the king of England, Henry II, and his son, Henry III), he now carries his own head "parted" from his trunk: "thus," he concludes, "one may observe in me the *contrapasso*" (*Inf.* 28, 142).

As a principle of justice, the *contrapasso* derives from the biblical law of retaliation (*lex talionis*) which required that "anyone who inflicts an injury on his neighbor shall receive the same in return."[4] A similar concept is present also in classical authors such as Virgil (*Aeneid* 6, 654) and Seneca (*Hercules furens* 735–36). However, the idea of a divine punishment suited to the crime can also be found, albeit in a rudimentary form, in other, less learned, Christian and non-Christian narratives of the Middle Ages, for instance in the Irish *Vision of Tundale* (vv. 290 ff.), as well as in the Arab *Book of the Ladder of Mohammed* (§§ 199–201). In this popular tradition the *contrapasso* responds, as it does in Dante, to the universal desire to see justice done and the wicked punished. What distinguishes its appearance in the *Comedy* is that, in the poem, it does not function merely as a form of divine revenge, but rather as the fulfilment of a destiny freely chosen by each soul during his or her life. In the *Comedy* the state of the souls after death does not seem to have been devised and enforced by an external agent; rather, it seems to be "a continuation, intensification and definitive fixation of their situation on earth."[5]

There are a number of cases in which the *contrapasso* appears to function as the tragic fulfillment and realization of a metaphorical discourse, that is to say, as the transposition into everlasting "reality" of a common metaphor, habitually used to describe an inner, spiritual condition. For example, the metaphorical storm of passion that possessed the lustful while alive is turned in Hell into a "real" storm that will torment them forever (5, 31–45); the wasting and dispersion of their substance, which marked the behavior of the squanderers on earth, is now inflicted literally upon them by the hounds, which hunt and tear them apart, scattering the fragments of their bodies through the forest (13, 109–29); the unnatural distortion whereby the diviners, looking to the past, fraudulently claimed to be seeing the future, has now become the perpetual condition of their bodies (20, 10–15).

In other cases the literal condition of the sinners after death appears to be the continuation of a real choice made by them while alive: for instance, the momentary act by which the souls of the suicides violently repudiated their bodies is ironically extended to last forever, even beyond the day of the Last Judgment and the resurrection of the flesh (13, 106–08). However, the relationship between crime and punishment does not always stand out in such a clear and direct manner. For example, the panders and the seducers are incessantly whipped by demons (18, 34–39), the flatterers are plunged in human excrement (18, 112–14), the fraudulent counselors are enveloped in tongues of fire (26, 40–42; 27, 7–15). We assume that some compelling reason must dictate these particular forms of punishment, though what they might be remains a matter for speculation.

The *contrapasso* is traditionally said to function either by analogy or by antithesis or by a combination of the two. In fact, if the basic doctrinal principle remains the same throughout the *Inferno*, the ways in which it works in the narrative are as many as the sins, if not as many as the sinners, to which it is applied. Beyond its theological significance, it acts as a magnificent structuring device whereby, at the narrative level, the poem naturally acquires both order and variety.

Myth, history, and poetry

As is the case with all well-ordered realms, Dante's Hell works smoothly because it employs a large staff of devils and monsters who take care of its operation. Thus, old Charon ferries the souls across the Acheron (3, 82–87), and Minos assigns them to their proper places (5, 4–6). Both figures are frozen in time: Charon the demon is, and will always be, "white with the hairs of age," and around his eyes he has, and will always have, "wheels of flame"; Minos stands, and will always stand, "bristling and snarling," on the threshold of the second circle, judging and passing sentence according to how many times he wraps his tail around himself.

Most circles have their special guardians and enforcers – mythological creatures, hybrids half-bestial, half-human, intended to embody the moral features of the sinners they rule over and torment. Barking with his three throats, Cerberus flays and rends the gluttonous (6, 13–18); Pluto protests with grating unintelligible syllables ("*Pape Satàn, pape Satàn aleppe!*", 7, 1–2) against the descent of the two travelers into the circle of the avaricious and prodigal, while Phlegyas hurtles over the Stygian marsh beside himself with blind rage (8, 13–18). The Minotaur, the "infamy of Crete," is stretched out guarding the violent (12, 11–15); and watching over the bloodthirsty, who are immersed in the hot blood of Phlegethon, are the Centaurs, led by Chiron (12, 73–78). The foul Harpies, with their broad wings and necks, and women's faces, make their nests in the trees of the wood of the suicides (13, 13–15), and Geryon, ship/ plane, man-reptile-lion-scorpion, the "filthy image of fraud," transports the two journeyers through the clammy air, and deposits them in *Malebolge* (17, 10–15).

Most of the demons, like the topography of Hell generally, are derived from classical sources, especially from the description of Avernus in the sixth book of Virgil's *Aeneid*. However, Dante transforms the fables of the classical past into organic components of the Christian afterlife. In their original forms, by the end of the Middle Ages, these demons were essentially extinct, except perhaps for a few learned readers still familiar with the works of Ovid and of Virgil. It is Dante who resuscitates them and finds employment for them in his Hell, at the same time endowing them with such vitality and energy, such functionality, that we hardly remember having encountered them elsewhere.

Dante's recovery of these bugbears succeeds beyond all expectations, out-weighing the technical project of recycling pagan materials to fit the Christian mould. For instance, Cerberus not only crushes with his three mouths, and scrapes with his claws, but he flays and quarters his victims with a degree of participation – he has an oily, greasy beard – that goes well beyond the terms of his job. The gesture with which Chiron, making use of an arrow as if it were a pen, parts his beard back from his chin, transforms him in our eyes from a slender devil to a reflective intellectual. The Malebranche are vulgar, quarrelsome, and ostensibly ferocious, but also rather jovial and amateurish in the execution of their duties: they are more amusing than frightening. And then there is Geryon, the most polyvalent figure in all Hell: a ship that lands, a beaver lying in ambush, an aircraft in reverse, a darting eel, a falcon that turns around and descends, an arrow that shoots out and vanishes. Geryon is proof that Dante has not only learned Virgil's lesson, but has also surpassed his master in creating a phantasmagoric hybrid, never seen before, an incredible being, just like his *comedia*. The journey bursts out of an imagination that mixes the high with the low, the old with the new, the scholarly with the popular, Ovid with Lenten sermons, and Virgil with Alberico da Cassino.[6]

In addition to monsters and demons, Dante includes other figures from the classical world that are a novelty for his time, completely foreign to the restricted horizons of the previously extant popular visions. Whether these are historical men and women or mythological creatures, Dante treats them all as if they had really existed. In the noble castle, specially built as the dwelling of the magnanimous ancients, along with "Caesar in armor with hawklike eyes" (4, 121–23) reside Electra, Hector, and Aeneas; along with Cicero and Seneca, the mythological Orpheus and Linus, "and alone, to the side, Saladin" (4, 129). The same combination of myth and history recurs throughout *Inferno*, sometimes in far more colourful and noticeable forms. Next to Saint Paul, we have Aeneas; next to Francesca da Rimini, Dido and Helen of Troy; next to Guido da Montefeltro, Ulysses and Diomedes. On the burning sands of the third ring of the violent, under an incessant rain of fire, Capaneus, the mythological blasphemer of Jove, "lies scornful and frowning" (14, 46–72), paradoxically the only historical example of blasphemous violence against the Christian God. And, for good measure, presiding over the abyss of the traitors, alongside the biblical character Nimrod, stand the pagan giants Ephialtes, Briareus, and Antaeus (canto 31).

All events and characters – mythological, legendary, and historical – become equally real and contemporary in Dante's afterlife. The reason for this, rather than a lack of historical perspective on Dante's part, is his belief in an eschatology to which history itself is subservient. There is however something else, too: the intense aesthetic pleasure of evoking those glorious characters and reciting their ancient names, often for the very first time, in the new tongue of Italy: "Lucrezia, Iulia, Marzia and Corniglia" (4, 128), "Euclide geomèter and Tolomeo,/ Ipocràte, Avicenna and Galieno,/ Averoìs who made the great commentary" (4, 142–44). Virgil himself is at the same time a supreme example of the mystery of God's justice, and the most cherished object of Dante's creativity. All in all, the poet is led by the power of the word and of the image just as much as he is driven by the idea of saving the world.

Dante storyteller

Our journey through Dante's *Inferno* is a journey through dozens of "true" stories. In every circle, detaching themselves from the crowds of Hell's denizens, individual figures come into focus. Interacting or conversing with Dante, they tell their stories and the obsessions that gnaw and define each one of them. These are often tales never heard before, and of which no independent evidence remains. Dante's journey fills the gaps left unfilled by history, chronicle, or legend. His dialogues with the dead shed light on their last days, hours, and minutes, revealing secrets that they took with them to their graves. What persuaded Francesca to yield to her desires? What compelled Pier della Vigna to take his own life? How and where did Ulysses end the journey of his life? What happened in Ugolino's tower after the door was nailed shut once and for all? Most of Dante's great characters tell the stories of their deaths; they satisfy the reader's desire to be taken back in time and see how the inevitable happened in Francesca's chamber, Piero's jail, Ulysses' ship, Ugolino's tower. The poet's astonishing ability to give each of his characters a unique voice means that we willingly suspend our disbelief, and fully identify with them, forgetting that the stories they tell are no more than poetic fabrications. In *Paradiso* (17, 124–42), we will learn that these stories are told so that we may learn from them. Each story in fact serves some didactic purpose; yet, what engages the reader, as well as Dante the character, is the extent to which they go beyond that purpose. Once they are created, the most memorable of Dante's characters cannot be neatly contained within their teleological boundaries, their vitality cannot be repressed.

Take Francesca. Her story shows that lust has tragic consequences in this life, and leads to perpetual suffering in the next. Francesca herself, however, even before she sins, is aware of the consequences of sinning, and so are we; and yet she sins, and so do we. The heart of the story lies in the unequal struggle between natural desire and moral inhibition, and we never tire of hearing it because Dante focuses entirely on the tragic inevitability of its course. Critics have attempted to exorcise Francesca by dismissing her as a provincial dreamer, fatally affected by second-rate literature. But what about Virgil's long list of queens and warriors, the "ancient ladies and knights" (5, 71), all overcome by the power of love? What about "the great Achilles," who was defeated by love in the end? If love defeated Achilles, how may we resist it? Who is strong enough not to be subjugated by it? The defeat of the Greek hero exposes the fragility of human nature; it exposes the intrinsic weakness of our wills. If anything, Francesca's drama makes those lofty tragedies much more significant and alarming than they would otherwise be; it brings the stuff of literature into everyday experience.

Or take Ulysses. Generally speaking, despite its crowdedness and the number of cantos it occupies, the eighth circle of *Malebolge* does not contain any major character. The habit of fraud not only diminishes its practitioners, it takes away that thread of human empathy that, in other circles, brings the visitor closer to some of the great characters. Dante's disdain for the fraudulent is such that it prevents his imagination from "locating" any figure in the eighth circle worthy of our pity or of the distinction of tragic greatness. *Malebolge* is a place in which the comic register (ironic, sarcastic, grotesque) degrades everything and everyone, a more subhuman than inhuman place. But there is one major exception: the character of Ulysses.

Dante finds Ulysses in the eighth bolgia, enveloped in a tongue of fire within which he is tormented along with another Greek warrior, Diomedes. The sinners punished in this bolgia, though traditionally said to be fraudulent counselors, are more likely to be astute men of action (politicians and *condottieri*), prepared to stop at nothing in order to achieve their ends – leaders who, two centuries later, will attract Machiavelli's open admiration, qualified though it may be. The purpose of Dante's visit to the eighth bolgia is for him and us to learn that the use of intelligence unrestrained by virtue is self-destructive. The two examples given are Ulysses who, in his search for knowledge, dares to sail to the forbidden mountain island of Earthly Paradise, and Guido da Montefeltro who tries to win Paradise while at the same time doing the evil bidding of Pope Boniface VIII. However, while Guido, the calculating biter bit, is at home in the vulgar and vile context of *Malebolge*, Ulysses stands out as an exception, not just because he is the only great mythological figure in a poem in which all the other major characters are contemporary, but because, despite all his crafty deceits, his pursuit of knowledge at all costs is so compelling that the reader cannot help identifying with him. Ulysses is a truly tragic character. We see him sailing for five months towards the desert island of ultimate knowledge; we know that he is going in the right direction, and yet we also know that he will be stopped before he reaches the new land – the Earthly Paradise cannot be taken by storm, what Adam lost cannot be recovered by willpower alone. Ulysses is a character in whom subjective innocence and objective guilt appear to be in conflict with each other – if not quite the "pyramid planted in the mud of Malebolge" that Francesco De Sanctis wrote about in 1870, nonetheless a noble figure whose longing to reach beyond our restricted horizon still strikes us as quintessentially human.

There are other episodes too, not necessarily tied to great characters, which seem to have a vitality of their own. The encounter with Filippo Argenti on the river Styx begins abruptly as a squabble between the boat-borne Dante and Filippo who is wallowing in the swamp. It soon degenerates into physical violence when Filippo tries to capsize Dante's boat. It ends when the other sinners in the mire, unknowingly doing Dante's bidding, viciously attack Filippo who by now is in such a fit of rage that he turns his teeth upon himself (8, 31–63). Something similar happens to Vanni Fucci, the Pistoian thief previously mentioned who, not satisfied with inflicting psychological pain on Dante (24, 151), brandishes his hands in an obscene gesture against God Himself (25, 1–3): just as the sinners immersed in the Styx attack Filippo, in the same way the snakes of the seventh bolgia (themselves transformed sinners) attack Vanni, binding him so tightly that he can no longer raise his arms. In both cases, these action-packed episodes are meant to be examples of what happens in Hell to arrogant people who thought too highly of themselves on earth. However, Dante's art is so consummate that, like Dante the character, we too become thoroughly engrossed in the action, and the last thing we think of is the humiliation that lies in wait in Hell for the proud.

As we reach canto 21 and the fifth bolgia, we are ready for some comic relief, and Dante obliges us in a superb fashion by staging a grotesque farce enacted by a band of spirited Malebranche with deliciously fearsome, untranslatable vernacular names (Malacoda, Scarmiglione, Alichino, Calcabrina, Cagnazzo, Barbariccia, Libicocco, Draghinazzo, Ciriatto, Graffiacane, Farfarello, Rubicante). These devils play a game of cat and mouse with their charges, clearly enjoying their job, which consists in tormenting the barrators whom they must keep under boiling pitch (cantos 21–23). When Virgil and Dante appear on the scene the demons become uncontrollably excited at the prospect of having them too, for a while, as their favorite toys; their leader Malacoda can hardly restrain them. The farce almost turns to drama when, to escape the Malebranche's grappling hooks, Virgil himself, with Dante in his arms, is obliged to scramble on his backside down the bank of the next bolgia. Hardly a dignified way out for the "altissimo poeta"! In the battle of wit and deception, a barrator like Ciampolo turns out to be a better match for the Malebranche than wise Virgil himself. But is this the message of the episode and the reason why it is there, or is it there because Dante is carried away by his imagination and creativity?

What makes Dante's Hell so vivid and credible is, perhaps more than anything else, the poet's brilliant and pervasive use of dialogue. After one thousand years in which it had been virtually absent from literature, dialogue erupts as one of Dante's most powerful tools in the *Comedy*'s narrative representation of reality. Direct speech is not rare either in classical Latin literature or in the early Italian lyric, but neither in the one nor in the other does it aim at reproducing ordinary conversation in all its subtlety and complexity. This is what Dante does, not just tentatively or experimentally, but with consummate self-confidence. Indeed his dialogue has both the freshness of a new invention and the ripeness of a well-tested device. The examples in the *Inferno* are countless. See for instance how, as he is traversing the river Styx, Dante replies to Filippo Argenti's challenge by picking up, and then turning against him, first one ("vieni": "vieni–vegno–non rimango") and then another of his words ("piango": "piango–piangere–ti rimani"), while at the same time carrying through the increasingly taunting theme of Filippo's muddiness/ugliness ("un pien di fango," "sí se' fatto brutto," "ancor sie lordo tutto"): Dante's counter-challenge is so effective that it enrages Filippo to the point that, frustrated by the verbal sparring, he resorts to physical violence, only to be beaten back once again. In the end Filippo finds that he can safely exercise his wrath only upon himself (8, 31–63).

Almost all of Dante the poet's characters, Dante the character included, whether they speak or, as sometimes happens, choose to remain silent, are defined by their ongoing relationship to others. They are described in terms of actions that link them, in a new verbal and social structure, to other characters in the afterlife, while at the same time excluding us readers, almost as if their existence did not depend either on the eye of Dante the character or even on ours.

Dante's Hell is, to use Bakhtin's phrase, a "polyphonic world" made up of many distinct voices – loving, abusive, doleful, insulting, petulant, blasphemous, sarcastic, gentle, pathetic, obscene – that do not, and will not, harmonize. However, verbal language is not the only tool Dante employs to construct characters and situations; body language is equally present from the beginning to the end of the *Inferno*. By virtue of it, we have the impression that characters are autonomous agents, not marionettes in the hands of a puppeteer. Charon's woolly jowls fall silent only after Virgil has spoken (3, 97–98); Paolo and Francesca look into each other's eyes timidly, longingly, and their faces turn pale (5, 130–31); Pluto falls to earth like the tangled sails of a cracked mast (7, 13–15); Farinata rears himself up with his chest and forehead (10, 35–36); Barbariccia makes a trumpet of his ass (21, 139); the thief Buoso Donati stares fascinated at the snake that has just bitten him, and he yawns, as if in a trance (25, 88–90); Mohammed opens wide his split breast with his hands (28, 29); Ugolino wipes his mouth on the hair of Archbishop Ruggeri (33, 2–3). In a world populated exclusively by disembodied shades, Dante employs the language of the body to convey an astonishing array of feelings and moods – constantly changing the narrative tempo and register: love, hatred, rage, pride, fear, dismay, grief, sadness, irony, vulgarity, inhumanity, and so on and so forth. Indeed, Dante's creativity seems to be inexhaustible, or to be only matched by his ability to contain it within the formal structures of the poem.

Florence

In psychological and moral terms, Hell presents itself as the final result of man's attempt to attain, while still alive, completeness and happiness through the satisfaction of his desires and the affirmation of his individuality in the world. For this reason, the "culture" of Hell, namely, the culture which Hell draws upon, is most similar to that of the world of our own experience. It is a culture that promises and allows, indeed encourages, material growth and progress, social mobility, fulfillment of desire through the free use of individual initiative, enterprise, and talent. It is indeed a dynamic, unprejudiced culture, potentially democratic according to a modern political vision, inasmuch as it stimulates the progress of society towards the material equality of its most active members; but repugnant to Dante inasmuch as it foments disorder, restlessness, anxiety, and forever new desires that cannot be satisfied in this life. Accordingly, the object lesson that *Inferno* intends to impart is that the society to which the culture of desire gives rise is ultimately overwhelmed by it; in other words, it reveals the tragically self-destructive nature of the culture of desire.

Nowhere is this more true than in Dante's treatment of contemporary politics. The political theme is inscribed into the poem from the very beginning; it is indissolubly intertwined with the moral and theological theme. The "restless beast" that blocks Dante's ascent of the hill in canto 1, driving him back "to where the sun is silent"; the wild animal that "makes his veins and pulses tremble," is neither leopard nor lion, but "a she-wolf laden with all cravings." Not a private animal, then, associated with such secret vices as lust, gluttony, and wrath, but a public animal, whose nature is "so evil and cruel that her greedy desire is never satisfied, and after feeding she is hungrier than before" (1, 97–99). Immediately upon arriving on the scene, Virgil identifies her as an otherwise incurable evil that only a mysterious

Greyhound, the saviour of wretched Italy, "will make die in pain." An evil, therefore, that impedes Dante from reaching the light glimpsed at the top of the hill, but that, at the same time, afflicts the whole world. The she-wolf is none other than human greed, responsible, according to Dante, for the crisis in which Italy and the world in 1300 find themselves and, shortly thereafter, for the exile in which the poet will be forced to spend the rest of his life.

Dante believed that, possessed by an insatiable craving for material goods and power, contemporary society had become utterly corrupt: popes, bishops, monks, kings, princes, barons, ordinary men and women, communes and republics – everyone was fighting for individual success, advantage, and gratification. In this belief he was hardly unique. Many of his contemporaries felt that the degeneration of humanity had reached its nadir, and were therefore awaiting the end of the world and the definitive reaffirmation of God's justice over the evil forces of the Antichrist. This belief gripped not only the naive, the uncultured, and the fanatical, but also mystics, such as Joachim of Fiore, and theologians, such as the Franciscan Pietro di Giovanni Olivi, who taught at Santa Croce in Florence between 1287 and 1289. Even apart from these apocalyptic expectations, a longing for peace and justice was widespread in Italy, a country torn by internal strife and in the throes of social upheaval. In the *Comedy*, Dante gives a voice to this longing, and Florence provides a poetic and political focus for it. Hell does indeed seem to be a penal colony of Dante's native city.

Dante attacks many Italian cities in the *Inferno* – Pistoia (25, 10–12), Pisa (33, 79–84), Genoa (33, 151–53), the Rome of the simonist popes (19, 106–11) – but reserves his most bitter words, his most virulent invectives, his most sarcastic tones, for his beloved Florence. Even the original title of the poem *(Comedia Dantis Alagherii florentini natione sed non moribus*: The Comedy of Dante Alighieri, a Florentine by birth, not by conduct) conceals a political gibe against the city that had exiled him. The love that Dante feels for Florence is immense and immensely frustrated: it is the love of a rejected lover, of a disinherited son, of an unheeded father, of a banished politician, of a reviled prophet, of an underrated poet; a love that would not stop at violent measures for the sake of freeing the beloved from her ills, as witnessed by the political letters, which Dante wrote on the occasion of the descent of the heir to the Holy Roman Empire, Henry VII, into Italy.

It is no mere coincidence that, after the allusions in the opening scene, the political theme takes center stage with the appearance of the first Florentine character, Ciacco the glutton. In the *Comedy*, the political theme is *par excellence* autobiographical and Florentine, and all it takes to trigger it is for any of the characters to notice Dante's origin. Thus, when Ciacco introduces himself, instead of dwelling upon the pleasures of the table which had been his ruin, he decisively places the moral condemnation of Florence at the centre of his discourse, as will the heretic Farinata, Brunetto Latini, and the other three noble Florentines whom Dante meets among the sodomites.

In fact, the poem turns out to be more ambiguous here than ever. The sodomites appear naked under the incessant rain of fire, punished in an undoubtedly atrocious Hell. The attitude of Dante the character in relation to them, however, is one of great respect, if not admiration; moreover, it is endorsed by none other than Virgil who, as soon as he sees them rush forward shouting, bids Dante to stop and to "be courteous" with them. "And if it were not for the fire that the nature of the place pours down" – he adds – "I would say that haste would more become you than them" (16, 14–18). The reason for such respect, a respect that has no parallel in *Inferno* except for the case of the magnanimous spirits of Limbo, is clear: these souls are the only ones in Hell to be anguished not by the loss of power on the part of their political party or their families, but by the decay of the old Florentine civil and moral virtues. This is, in fact, the subject on which the three spirits ask Dante to speak as soon as they see him:

> tell us if courtesy and valor
> dwell in our city as they used to do,
> or if they have utterly forsaken it . . .
> (16, 67–69)

Now we understand why, in the realm of villainy, Virgil had urged Dante to "be courteous." Values fundamental to the well-being of mankind and the achievement of earthly happiness are at stake here, principles that the city has by now forgotten. And it is precisely the city that, responding to his interlocutors, Dante the character addresses directly and with extraordinary vehemence:

> The new people and the rapid gains
> have generated pride and excess, Florence, in you,
> so that you already weep for it.   (16, 73–75)

Dante will focus again and at greater length on Florence and the political theme in the central cantos of the other two canticles. Here in Hell, for the first time in the *Comedy*, he contrasts two antithetical lifestyles, two opposite ethical and political models. On the one hand, "courtesy and valour," virtues of the past; and on the other, "pride and excess," vices of the present, the evils of the Florentine "depraved city" (16, 9). The root and cause of this process of degeneration, evoked precisely in the middle of the

Inferno, was for Dante a historical phenomenon of an economic and social nature: the rage for wealth that had devastated the civil and moral life of the city.

"And what else," Dante had written in his *Convivio*, "day after day, endangers and destroys cities, regions, individuals so much as yet another amassing of wealth by someone? This very amassing releases further desires, which cannot be satisfied without someone paying the price" (*Convivio* IV, xii, 9, trans. Ryan). Dante was not against the human search for happiness, but he objected most vehemently to the notion that the acquisition of wealth and power could make people happier and more fulfilled. He saw the inner contradictions of what we call "progress," the sufferings it brought to people's lives, rather than the benefits. He never entertained the idea that the social conflicts of his time could pave the way for a new, more just and democratic, society, or that any movement, individual or collective, which aimed at earthly well-being independently of humanity's eternal destiny, could be good. The ultimate good for civil society does not lie, according to Dante, in equality or in social progress, concepts that are foreign to the beliefs of his time and to his world view, but, rather, in universal peace, inasmuch as "universal peace is the best of those things which are ordained for human happiness" (*Monarchia* I, iv, 2, trans. Shaw). Florence, on the contrary, with her "accursed florin," was for him the embodiment of a society that had lost its way, a society that had sacrificed conscience and virtue to intelligence, integrity to effectiveness and success, the good of the community to the interests of powerful individuals: in short, a society which, by obsessively seeking heaven on earth, had made a Hell of life on earth.

Conclusion

The story that Dante recounts in the *Inferno* is almost entirely set in the world of the dead, yet its real target is the world of the living – the innumerable ways, all of them morally wrong, in which men and women attempt in this life to satisfy their desires for knowledge, power, and happiness. There is a progression in this negativity ranging from the love that binds Paolo and Francesca together in the infernal storm to the bestial hatred that keeps Count Ugolino gnawing at the skull of his enemy. Lucifer is the living sum of this negativity – his angelic beauty turned into extreme ugliness, his six wings incapable of lifting him one inch above the prison of ice they constantly create, his three mouths chewing forever without ever satisfying his hunger. An emblem of monstrous desire, colossal impotence, gigantic frustration.

Virgil, with Dante clinging to his neck, clambers down Lucifer's hairy flanks and then, once they have passed the centre of all gravity, he starts climbing upward along his shanks. Lucifer, however, does not react. Unlike any of the other infernal functionaries, Lucifer seems to be completely unaware of what goes on. His six eyes weep, his tears and bloody slobber dribbling down his three chins, his six batlike wings flapping incessantly. He is a machine totally desensitized and dehumanized, that is to say, totally deprived of either emotions or intelligence. Despite what Dante says, this is not the emperor of malice, not the source of all sorrow, but rather the ultimate outcome of all evil – a machine symbolizing and putting on display the supreme stupidity, futility, and hopelessness of evil – except perhaps as a ladder to goodness. This is why, once Dante is out of the "natural cavern" (34, 98), we look back and ask ourselves how Hell could, indeed why it should, last forever – a point which Dante does not discuss.

The *Inferno* is rich in characters but, compared to the other two canticles, relatively lacking in scientific, philosophical, and theological discourse. So many are the characters who demand to be seen and heard by the unusual visitor that Dante has hardly any time for indulging in theory. However, the first canticle's theoretical shortcomings are also its dramatic greatness, a fact that generations of readers have underlined through seven centuries by overwhelmingly favouring *Inferno* over both *Purgatorio* and *Paradiso*. Why do readers of all ages and of so many diverse cultures and backgrounds keep going back to the *Inferno* with so much empathy? The reason, I submit, is not Hell's graphic display of divine justice, but rather the tragically flawed humanity of its inhabitants. Of course, Dante condemns all mortal sinners to perpetual suffering. Yet the manner and justness of their condemnation does not engage us as much as the universal nature of their faults. Dante's Hell is so enduring because, like the earth we know, it is so much about love gone wrong: Francesca's love for Paolo, Farinata's love for Florence, Piero's love of self, Ulysses's love of knowledge, Ugolino's love for his children.

However, the true significance of Dante's Hell can only be grasped within the *Comedy* as a whole. Divine justice shows its inflexible face in Hell, its readiness to forgive in Purgatory, and its boundless grace in Paradise. At the beginning and the end of the earthly part of Dante's journey, Virgil and Beatrice respectively prophesy the coming of a Saviour, possibly a new emperor, who will soon deliver the world from all evil. God's Providence, which ensures the happy ending of Dante's journey, will ultimately bring about the happy ending of the world, too. Despite the *Inferno*'s remorseless catalogue of human weakness and wickedness, the *Comedy*, as its title implies, remains a poem of hope.

NOTES

1 See Saint Augustine, *Confessions*, VII x 2, and Saint Bernard, *Sermones de diversis*, 42, 2.
2 See Morgan and, for a wide selection of texts about the afterlife, Gardiner.
3 In Ptolomea Dante finds another category of sinners unacceptable to theology but not unknown to popular culture: traitors whose souls, upon sinning, are sent to Hell while their bodies, inhabited by devils, go on living on earth for their appointed lifespan.
4 Leviticus 24: 19; see also Exodus 21: 23–25 and Deuteronomy 19: 21; but also Matthew 5: 38–40 and 7: 1–2 and 12.
5 Auerbach, *Dante*, p. 88.
6 Alberico, a monk at Monte Cassino, wrote in the 1230s an account of a vision he had had as a boy.

SUGGESTED READING

Armour, Peter, "Dante's *contrapasso*: Context and Texts," *Italian Studies* 55 (2000): 1–20.
Auerbach, Eric, *Dante, Poet of the Secular World*, trans. R. Manheim (Chicago: University of Chicago Press, 1961).
Baranski, Zygmunt G., "La lezione esegetica di *Inferno* I: allegoria, storia e letteratura," in M. Picone, ed., *Dante e le forme dell'allegoresi* (Ravenna: Longo, 1987), pp. 79–97.
Freccero, John, *Dante: The Poetics of Conversion*, edited and with an introduction by R. Jacoff (Cambridge, MA: Harvard University Press, 1986), pp. 180–85.
Gardiner, Eileen, *Visions of Heaven and Hell Before Dante* (New York: Italica, 1989).
Morgan, Alison, *Dante and the Medieval Other World* (Cambridge: Cambridge University Press, 1990).
Nardi, Bruno, *La caduta di Lucifero e l'autenticità della Quaestio de aqua et terra* (Turin: SEI, 1959), pp. 5–28.
Ó Cuilleanáin, Cormac, "'Quell'arte': Dramatic Exchange in the *Commedia*," in J. C. Barnes and J. Petrie, eds., *Word and Drama in Dante* (Dublin: Irish Academic Press, 1993), pp. 27–53.

6

JEFFREY T. SCHNAPP

Introduction to *Purgatorio*

Of the three otherworldly kingdoms which the *Divina Commedia* represents, Purgatory is Dante's most original creation. Hell and Paradise were already well-established places within the medieval imagination. Each possessed a standard set of topographic and iconographic attributes which, accrued in the course of many centuries of patristic tradition, rendered them instantly recognizable to prince and pauper alike. Hell was a dark, subterranean place where eternal torments were administered by demons under the guidance of Satan, the ruler of the underworld. Paradise was Hell's positive counterpart: a luminous celestial palace where eternal blessings were administered by the angels under the guidance of God, the emperor of the universe. In both cases the author of the *Commedia* felt called upon less to alter preexisting traditions, than to extend and systematize them: establishing, for instance, a much more precise hierarchy of the degrees of damnation or blessedness endured or enjoyed by souls in the afterlife; and finding a place for specifically Christian categories of error, like heresy, within an Aristotelian moral system.

But as regards the intermediate realm between Paradise and Hell, the visual, literary, and patristic precedents were far less rich. Christian theologians had long recognized that there existed a logical necessity for a place in between Hell's eternal torments and Paradise's eternal beatitude. To them it seemed inconceivable that a soul like that of Buonconte da Montefeltro (*Purgatorio* 5), saved thanks to a single tear of contrition after a lifetime of sin, should simply be lifted up into heaven and placed in the company of the blessed without some additional purifying process. Such an instantaneous form of beatification would, in effect, have raised ordinary sinners, saved at the moment of death through God's grace, to the status of saints and martyrs, whose souls were to be transported directly up into heaven because they had lived and died in a state of spiritual perfection. No less of a stumbling block were the moral and psychological implications of uniform beatification: if saints and repentant sinners were to be saved without distinction, there would remain no incentive for living Christians to lead saintly lives while still on earth. No price would have to be paid for a lifetime of errancy; no reward would result from a lifetime of virtue. As a solution to this problem, theologians came to envisage an intermediate realm, a realm of process and exchange, where ordinary souls could be cleansed (or "purged") of their remaining sins and be spiritually reshaped in preparation for their admission to Paradise proper. To this spatially and topographically unspecific realm they assigned the label "Purgatory."

The task of fully imagining this intermediate kingdom would rest on the shoulders of a poet. Before Dante's *Commedia*, Purgatory was often little more than a theologian's abstraction; after it, Purgatory bears a universally recognized structure. The structure in question repeats and reverses that of Hell both on the literal and symbolic levels. Dante's Hell is a mock fortified city, a topsy-turvy hilltop town. A hollow cone made up of nine concentric circles, each representing an increasingly grave category of sin, it is surrounded by a disorderly assemblage of gateways, battlements, walls, and moats, all of which presume to limit access to the lowermost circle. Yet, despite the martial trappings, Hell's doors are wide open. Hell proves to be the easiest, the most "natural" city to enter in a postlapsarian world. Souls simply "rain down" into Hell following the natural inclination of their fallen bodies to gravitate towards sin.

Purgatory, on the contrary, is a genuine fortified city, at once impermeable and remote. Formed from the very soil that Satan displaced in his fall from Heaven (*Inferno* 34), it assumes the form of a conical mountain: a positive countertype to Hell's empty concavity. The mountain is so tall that it extends up beyond the sublunar realm of generation and corruption into the heavens' lowermost circle, made up of air and fire.[1] Its slopes are therefore immutable and eternally fruitful (whereas Hell's landscape embodies sterility, decay, and flux). The mountain is steep and is protected by two rings of walls. One, a cliff, divides the Ante-Purgatory (cantos 1–9), from Purgatory proper (cantos 9–28); the other, a wall of fire, separates Purgatory from Eden (cantos 29–33), which lies atop the summit. Between the walls, seven concentric terraces rise up, each of which represents, in decreasing order of gravity, one of the seven deadly sins: pride, envy, wrath, sloth, avarice, gluttony, and lust.[2] Purgatory's gateway is equally forbidding. Narrow ("like the eye of a needle") and barred with a double lock, it is always guarded by an angel.[3] To such obstacles to access must be added the remote location. Whereas Hellmouth lay within easy reach of the habitable world (as then conceived), Mount Purgatory is situated in the southern hemisphere at the earth's antipodes.[4] Precisely opposite the city of Jerusalem, it is surrounded by the fierce ocean waters that ensured Ulysses' shipwreck in *Inferno* 26.

For all of the above reasons it is not possible simply to "rain down" into Purgatory. To reach the mountain's shores is an arduous task. To conquer its summit is more arduous still. At a matter of fact, Dante believed that both tasks were *impossible* between the time of Adam's Fall and the Harrowing of Hell. During that era the gate to Paradise was closed. According to Christian doctrine, only after the coming of Christ was it reopened for souls whose humility was sufficient to earn them the grace of God. Ulysses' journey, or any other journey that would rely upon human resources alone, thus remains impossible (as does the sort of unguided climb attempted by Dante-pilgrim in *Inferno* 1). To reach and ascend Mount Purgatory requires human effort *and* superhuman support. Both are necessary if the gravitational pull of sin is to be transmuted into the levitational, "God-ward" pull of sacred love. (To emphasize these prerequisites is not to imply that Dante's God wishes to bar the way to salvation. The opposite is true: a mere tear of repentance can atone for a lifetime of evil. "Orribil furon li peccati miei," states Manfred speaking for much of the cast of the second canticle, "ma la bontà infinita ha sì gran braccia,/che prende ciò che si rivolge a lei" ("horrible were my sins, but the Infinite Goodness has such wide arms that It receives all who turn to It," *Purgatorio* 3, 121–23).

The transformation of gravity into levity entails the recovery of the pristine nature that was humankind's before the Fall. According to the book of Genesis, man was created in the image of God and then disfigured – "made ugly," as Dante puts it – through sin.[5] Having reached Purgatory's shores, he now seeks to undo the damage by means of a step by step process of purification whose end point is Eden: the place of origins, humankind's first home. The process is analogous to the restoration of a unique artwork. Sin is akin to the layers of soot, varnish, later additions, and imperfections that accumulate over time and diminish the value and beauty of an old master painting. Once these sorts of accretions are stripped away one after another, the image reverts to its original splendor. The master's hand once again becomes visible. The image is reborn.

Purgation accomplishes just such a rebirth. A case in point is Dante-pilgrim. He begins the climb with seven "p"s traced on his forehead (*Purgatorio* 9, 112). Standing for the deadly *peccata* or wounds of sin borne by all human beings after the Fall, these disfiguring marks weigh him down literally and figuratively. They oblige him to wage both an outer and an inner war: to struggle against his body's downward pull and against his will's resistance. In the course of the climb the marks are cleansed away one by one, each erasure bringing increasing levity as a deadly sin is overcome. When he reaches his destination, Dante has been remade. He is a new man, a double of Adam before the Fall. Freed from the disfiguring burden of sin, he feels so light as to be able to soar into the heavens: "Io ritornai . . . rifatto sì come piante novelle/rinovellate di novella fronda,/puro e disposto a salire a le stelle" ("I came forth . . . renovated, even as new trees renewed with new foliage, pure and ready to rise to the stars," 33, 143–45). The ascent into the celestial Paradise can now begin.

The case of Dante-pilgrim is telling because purgation is a time-bound, dynamic process. Unlike Paradise or Hell but in the image of our world, souls in Purgatory are on the move. They are not bound for eternity to the terrace, pouch, or celestial seat in which they appear, but rather are "strangers in a strange land," pilgrims on a temporal and spatial journey in which, paradoxically, the course of time is reversed, sin erased, the divine image restored. This mobility accounts for the new tone of urgency set by Cato in canto 2 and maintained throughout the canticle: "correte al monte" ("[make] haste to the mountain," 2, 122), the Roman patriot commands the laggard spirits, reminding them that in Purgatory, as in Benjamin Franklin's America, time is money. Here time cannot be squandered as it was in Hell, where, in a sense, all time is "wasted time." Nor can it be taken for granted, as will be the case in Paradise, where temporality is cast aside like a broken toy. Time is precious for Dante-pilgrim because, granted only a three-day stay, he must always keep in mind that "'l tempo che n'è imposto . . . utilmente compartir si vuole" ("the time that is allotted us must be . . . usefully apportioned," 23, 5–6). Time is precious for souls undergoing purgation inasmuch as, like inmates in a reform school, they have been assigned a sentence in exact proportion to the quantity and quality of sins they have committed. Once they have "served their time" on a given terrace, they eagerly press on to the next one, attaining freedom only when they have paid off their "debt" to God and completed the re-education process.

Purgatory's pilgrims measure out their sojourns in the same units that the living do their existences: units defined by the daily and annual circling of the stars and planets. As a result, astronomical references abound in Dante's account of his spiral ascent as nowhere else in the *Commedia*. Some are purely symbolic, like the constellations that appear in cantos 1, 23–24 and 8, 89–90, representing the four cardinal and three theological virtues. The great majority, however, function as time markers. They record the precise movements of the sun with respect to Dante-pilgrim's position on the mountain, often playing upon liturgical traditions that associate the sun with divine guidance, sunrise with resurrection, and nightfall with death and temptation. The notion of the sun as guide is more than a literary conceit. This is largely due to the fact that Purgatory's terrain is unfamiliar to Virgil. His authority somewhat diminished, the Latin poet repeatedly appeals to the sun – symbol of God and reason, as well as of imperial and papal Rome – for assistance: "per lo novo cammin, tu ne conduci" ("on this new road, do you guide us," 13, 17). How might the sun offer guidance? Literally speaking, by providing light. Without the sun's rays no forward motion is possible: "andar sù di notte non si puote" ("to go up by night is not possible," 7, 44), declares Sordello, because "ben si poria con lei tornare in giuso" ("truly by night one might return downwards," 7, 58). The law of the mountain permits no exceptions: daytime is for circling and climbing; nighttime is for sleep.

To sleep means to dream. Accordingly, Dante's three-day stay on the mountain yields a sequence of interlocking allegorical dreams. Of pivotal importance to *Purgatorio*'s meditation on the perils and powers of images – a matter to which this essay will soon have occasion to return – these dreams are at once prophetic and poetic in character. "False" at least to the degree that their content is either mythological or imaginary, they require a subsequent decoding in order to yield a prophetic truth. The first occurs in canto 9. It involves the myth of Ganymede's rapture/rape at the hands of Jove. Dante imagines that, like the most beautiful of mortal youths, he too was "ratto al sommo consistoro" ("caught up to the supreme consistory," 9, 24) – a fantasy that turns out to be doubly true. As he was sleeping, Lucy had lifted him up to Purgatory's door. To this first "rapture" will correspond a second: a flight into the Empyrean where he will meet up with the Christian Jove. The protagonist of the second dream (in canto 19) also derives from ancient myth: a "dolce serena" ("sweet Siren," 19, 19). Transformed by the dreamer's imagination from a hag into a beautiful woman, she is unmasked by Virgil as an image of corruption and putrefaction. The unmasker furnishes an explanation: "Vedesti . . . quell'antica strega/che sola sovr' a noi omai si piagne" ("You have seen . . . that ancient witch who alone is now wept for above us," 19, 58–59). The siren/hag reveals the essence of the sins purged on the next three terraces: avarice, gluttony, and lust are all symptoms of an immoderate, even idolatrous, love for evanescent goods. The third and final dream (in canto 27) is of biblical origin. Far more transparent than its predecessors, its deeper meaning is disclosed only by subsequent events. Its subject is Laban's daughters, Leah and Rachel, traditional representatives of, respectively, the active and the contemplative virtues. Dreaming of these two Old Testament figures, Dante hints at the meaning of the two ladies he will encounter in Eden: Matelda and Beatrice. Broadly concerned with the psychology of love and with the role of female intercessors, this tripartite sequence forms a kind of crescendo. Moving from ancient myth to biblical typology, it performs two essential structural functions. On the one hand, it sets up and foreshadows the action of succeeding cantos and the succeeding canticle; on the other, it divides up the narrative action of *Purgatorio* into three distinct temporal units.

One last category of astronomical references deserves special mention before moving on, if only because it has given rise to frequent scholarly disputes. In a series of remarkably complex prologues found in cantos such as 9, 1–9, 15, 1–9, and 25, 1–3, Dante summons his reader to adopt an extraterrestrial or "God's-eye" perspective on the planet Earth. The reader is asked to envisage the planet as an interconnected whole such that, for instance, if it is noon in Jerusalem, it is midnight in Purgatory, and nine p.m. on the shores of Italy. Whatever their precise astronomical significance, these kinds of time markers serve as reminders that the cosmic clock ticking on Mount Purgatory is the same as that ticking in the northern hemisphere. Their purpose is to drive home a didactic point: namely, that if time is so precious to the dead, it ought to be all the more so to living beings whose salvation or damnation remains uncertain until the moment of death. The purgatorial pilgrimage provides a model of time "well spent" for the latter's benefit: time lived as a bridge to beatitude, time transformed into a sacrifice and sacrament, liturgical time.

The temporal reciprocity that binds together the northern and southern hemispheres also corresponds to a mutual exchange of prayers. Praying for the souls of the dead, the living can reduce the duration of their sentences on each terrace; they can help "repay" the sinners' debts. Praying for the souls of the living, the dead can try to keep them on the straight and narrow path, "pre-paying" debts that are not yet due. This reciprocal relation, founded on the doctrine of divine intercession, changes the nature of Dante-pilgrim's interactions with *Purgatorio*'s cast of characters. Whereas in Hell he had often been obliged to seek out his interlocutors, now it is they who pursue him. Once the shadow cast by his body of flesh and blood is noted, Dante finds himself surrounded by dense crowds, like a winning gambler getting up from the gaming table (6, 1–12). (Virgil is left behind, as if a loser.) The throng's eagerness is inspired neither by a longing for earthly infamy or fame, nor by nostalgia for our world. The souls of Purgatory have but one desire: they wish to be remembered in the prayers of the loved ones they left behind them so that they may accelerate their journey heavenward. More-over, when they pray for "color che dietro a noi restaro" ("those who remain behind," 11, 24), they are not looking backward, but forward: anticipating the moment when they will be reunited in the City of God.

Reunion is one of *Purgatorio*'s great themes: not only the reuniting of indi-viduals with their Creator, but also the reconvening of broken families and dispersed communities, whether political, spiritual, moral, or linguistic. Old friends and lovers are brought back together on the mountain slopes: friends like Dante and Casella (canto 2); lovers like Dante and Beatrice (canto 30). Bitter political enemies such as the Holy Roman emperor Rudolf I (1218–91) and Ottokar II, king of Bohemia between 1253 and 1278, forge eternal friendships (see canto 7). The citizens of cities rent by civil wars embrace one another as brothers, like Virgil and his fellow Mantuan Sordello in canto 6, separated by centuries but joined together by a common origin. Warring polities make their peace. And the codes of civility which render harmonious coexistence possible are reborn: the laws of the mountain are courtesy, hospitality, honor, respect, compassion, and piety. The political, moral, and spiritual rebirth carried out in Purgatory finds its highest earthly expression in the ideal of the Roman empire – an ideal which informs Dante's *Commedia* from start to finish and which largely accounts for Dante's choice of Virgil as his first guide. Hopes for an imperial resurgence had suffered a severe blow with the condemnation for heresy in *Inferno* 10 of the greatest of the Hohenstaufen emperors, Frederick II. But, as is so often the case in *Purgatorio*, when a father must be damned, a son is spared, implying the survival of the hopes embodied by the father. Accordingly, the dream of empire may be said to return to life in Manfred, Frederick's son. A gruesome wound across Manfred's brow suggests that the dream of empire has been injured and humbled (*Purgatorio* 3, 108). Nonetheless, it remains very much alive: Manfred greets the pilgrim with a beaming smile (3, 112). Similar hopes are touched upon again, notably in Dante's famed speech on "serva Italia" ("servile Italy," 6, 76–151), though in the mode of invective. They persist throughout the second canticle, reaching their climax in Beatrice's final prophecy that a certain "cinquecento diece e cinque" ("Five Hundred, Ten, and Five," 33, 43) – a DXV or DUX (the Latin word for leader) – will right the wrongs of human history.[6]

As indicated by Dante's incorporation of political matters into the *Commedia*, poetry has a key role to play in civilization's renewal. And nowhere more so than on the slopes of Mount Purgatory, where the rebuilding of the body politic coincides with the reuniting of the Latin literary family. First the ancient Latin poets Virgil and Statius are brought together; then their successors, Dante, Guido Guinizzelli, Bonagiunta da Lucca, and Arnaut Daniel: all vernacular "Latin" writers instrumental in the rebirth of literary language during the twelfth and thirteenth centuries.[7] In this setting the theme of "rebirth" takes on a far more extensive meaning than heretofore implied. More than the rise of a new vernacular Latinity, more than the regeneration of individuals or communities, it refers first and foremost to the nature and function of all human art: "qui la morta poesì resurga" ("here let dead poetry rise again," 1, 7), Dante intones in the canticle's opening verses. From this phrase it may be inferred that the descent into Hell entailed the progressive demise of poetry. Poetry "died" by becoming implicated in crimes against morality (lust), nature (sodomy), and the social order (schism). Poetry "died," moreover, by being pushed to the limits of its expressive powers, faced with the daunting task of capturing the horror of an ugly, soulless, truly "dead" world. In *Purgatorio*, this degenerative trajectory is inverted. Poetry, the imagination, and indeed all the arts, come back to life. They "rise again" in the service of the restoration of values such as beauty, truth, morality, and community. But most of all they are "reborn" by becoming regenerative tools, instruments of salvation, torches that illumine, sparks that kindle other sparks.

The shift is signalled already in canto 2, where the harsh cacophony of Hell gives way to the sweet harmony of sacred song: "*In exitu Isräel de Aegypto*" ("When Israel went out of Egypt," 2, 46; Psalm 113).[8] Sung by souls who are themselves embarked on an exodal journey, crossing over from the world of the living into the promised land of Purgatory, Psalm 113 is but the first of a great many biblical and liturgical texts that will be heard as Dante and Virgil make their way towards the mountain's summit. To mention only a few, the *Miserere* (Psalm 50) is chanted "a verso a verso" ("verse by verse") in canto 5, 24; in canto 8, 13, the Compline hymn *Te lucis ante* is sung as part of a twilight mass; the *Te Deum laudamus* rings out as the pilgrim passes through Peter's gate (9, 140); Dante-poet translates and glosses the Lord's Prayer in the opening seven tercets of canto 11; and the Beatitudes are intoned on every terrace as an antidote to the sin to which they correspond. No less importantly, biblical materials form the backbone of Purgatory's re-education program. Every terrace, whether in the form of bas reliefs (pride), disembodied voices (envy), ecstatic visions (wrath), running spirits (sloth), prostrate souls (avarice), voices in a tree (gluttony), or singing (lust), accomplishes its restorative work by presenting its denizens with a battery of examples to be imitated and counter-examples to be shunned. Biblical episodes – the lead one always involving the Virgin Mary, the rest culled equally from the two testaments and from pagan literary sources – are thereby assembled into a balanced program that, seconded by physical punishments, strips away sin and restores the "God-ward" pull of love.

The surfeit of sacred materials in Dante's second canticle does not indicate a rejection of secular and/or pagan poetry and art. On the contrary, the sacred and secular are considered complementary: hence the inclusion of non-biblical literary *exempla* within Purgatory's educational image-bank; and hence Virgil's continuing adequacy as a guide. Moreover, unlike Paradise or Hell, Purgatory is everywhere populated with this-worldly creators: musicians like Casella, illuminators like Oderisi da Gubbio, poets like Sordello, Statius, and Bonagiunta. Their very abundance suggests that Dante viewed

art as an ennobling pursuit: a pursuit with a built-in transcendental potential (very much like dreaming). Their current state of spiritual imperfection,
however, underscores the fact that, no matter how ennobling, art alone is
not enough. In order to achieve true nobility and completeness, in order to
fulfill their potential to promote a social and spiritual rebirth, art works and
artists (and, for that matter, dreams) must find their point of anchorage in the
artistry of the sacred Word. Otherwise, they can lose their way with tragic
consequences.

The best example of art's powers and limitations is Dante's guide. In cantos 21 and 22 the Latin poet Statius, author of the *Thebaid* and *Achilleid*,
testifies to the salvific power of Virgil's poetry. Statius declares that it was
by misreading book 3 of the *Aeneid* that he was cured of the sin of prodigality (22, 37–45). "Misreading" because where Virgil had denounced the
avarice of humankind, exclaiming "quid non mortalia pectora cogis,/ auri
sacra fames!" ("to what do you not drive the appetite of mortals, O accursed
hunger of gold!," *Aeneid* 3, 56–57), Statius heard a call to curb his excess
spending. He then goes on to recount that his poetic apprenticeship coincided
with his conversion to Christianity, thanks to Virgil's fourth *Eclogue*:

> ... Tu prima m'invïasti
>   verso Parnaso a ber ne le sue grotte,
>   e prima appresso Dio m'alluminasti.
> Facesti come quei che va di notte,
>   che porta il lume dietro e sé non giova,
>   ma dopo sé fe le persone dotte,
> quando dicesti: "Secol si rinova;
>   torna giustizia e primo tempo umano,
>   e progenïe scende da ciel nova."
> Per te poeta fui, per te cristiano.
>   (*Purgatorio* 22, 64–73)

(You it was who first sent me toward Parnassus to drink in its caves, and you
who first did light me on to God. You were like one who goes by night and
carries the light behind him and profits not himself, but makes those wise who
follow him, when you said, "The ages are renewed: Justice returns and the first
age of man, and a new progeny descends from heaven." Through you I was a
poet, through you a Christian.)

Dante concocted the tale of Statius' conversion to Christianity in order to
prove the point that even non-Christian poetry can spiritually enliven and
enlighten. It can remedy sin, providing models of moral rectitude. More
significant still, it can prophesy – however darkly or unintentionally – events
like the coming of Christ, and bring about the salvation of future readers. But

this salvific effect cannot ensure an author's salvation, regardless of whether he is a Christian or a pagan. As a result, the *Commedia* will insist that the divine Virgil walks in the darkness even as his creations light the way for future generations. Blind to his own message of hope, a "rebel unto God's law," he is the sole outsider of the second realm. Everyone on the mountain is homeward bound except for Virgil, condemned to exile for eternity.

Virgil's tragedy is fundamental both to the second canticle's sustained reflection on the nature of art, and to the *Commedia*'s overall structure. (It would be erroneous to imagine that Dante secretly longed to save the Latin poet.) Virgil's role was defined as transitional from the outset. As set forth by Beatrice in *Inferno* 2, his task was to lead his charge to another guide. The mission is completed at the summit of Mount Purgatory, where, fully corrected and restored, crowned and mitered, Dante-pilgrim is pronounced "libero, dritto e sano" ("free, upright and whole," 27, 140), able to follow the dictates of his own will. Until this juncture Virgil's guidance had been indispensable to the pilgrim's progress. But now that the apprenticeship has reached its term, Virgil is powerless: he can discern no further ("io per me più oltre non discerno," 27, 129). The "occhi belli" ("beautiful eyes," 27, 136) of Beatrice are required if the journey is to proceed. And proceed it must.

The shift from Virgil's once "discerning gaze" to Beatrice's "beautiful eyes" crowns the ascent of Mount Purgatory. In a very real sense, it also stands as the central action – the *mythos*, as Aristotle would put it – of the entire *Commedia*. The transition from Virgil to Beatrice encapsulates the poem's overall movement from time to eternity, nature to the supernatural, Latin to the vernacular, and (for the *Commedia*'s author) poetic apprenticeship to poetic mastery. The transfer is effected by means of three backward glances, the first suggesting the powers of Virgil's art, the second its limitations, and the third Dante's movement beyond Virgilianism towards a new, specifically Christian, concept of literary art. With these three glances this essay reaches its conclusion.

The first occurs at the close of canto 28 when Matelda, the dancing and singing maiden who greets the pilgrim in Eden, reveals that:

> Quelli ch'anticamente poetaro
> l'età de l'oro e suo stato felice,
> forse in Parnaso esto loco sognaro.
> Qui fu innocente l'umana radice;
> qui primavera sempre e ogne frutto;
> nettare è questo di che ciascun dice.
> (*Purgatorio* 28, 139–44)

(They who in olden times sang of the Age of Gold and its happy state perhaps in Parnassus dreamed of this place. Here the root of mankind was innocent; here is always spring, and every fruit; this is the nectar of which each tells.)

The Earthly Paradise, as it turns out, is not only the seedbed of the universe, but also the poetic signbed. It is the true Parnassus, a dream fulfilled, a global source manual for poets in which everything sings out in rhyme and unison, a living sacred hymn (a psalm) crafted by God. Matelda asserts that such was the model towards which Virgil had unwittingly reached out in the form of a poetic dream when composing his *Georgics* and *Eclogues*. The disclosure causes a smile to flash back and forth between Dante, Virgil, and Statius (28, 145–47). And understandably so. Ever since Plato, poets had been denounced as traffickers in lies: "dreamers" in the negative sense. But in a universe such as Dante's, where God himself is a poet, even blatant "lies" or "dreams" like the pagan myth of the Golden Age point to and participate in a sacred truth.[9]

If the first backward glance emphasized the continuity between human and divine artistry, the second (which comes in canto 29, 55) proposes a qualification noted earlier in this essay: namely, that while poetic "lies" or "dreams" may indeed lead you to the Garden's edge, they cannot help you to cross over into Eden proper, unless illumined by the Christian Truth. The message is imparted by means of an apocalyptic pageant – a "Triumph," to be precise.[10] Preceded by an immense candelabra that paints the heavens with the colours of the rainbow, the whole of the Bible parades before the poets' eyes book by book. Scripture's triumph confirms what the programmatic use of biblical materials in cantos 1–27 had already implied: that, despite (or, indeed, *because*) of its humble style, the Holy Book is the only absolute source of literary authority, the only absolute literary model. Its authority is so great that it relegates all other books to a position at its own margins. At best, they may find their prophetic promise fulfilled in the Book of Books (the case, for instance, of the Hebrew Testament and of the *Aeneid*, which Dante viewed as a sort of pagan Book of Exodus). At worst, they may find themselves replete with empty promises.

The disclosure drives a subtle wedge between Dante and Virgil. Viewing the spectacle from within the Garden, the former feels "d'ammirazion pieno" ("full of wonder," 29, 55), while the latter, standing outside, appears "carco di stupor non meno" ("no less charged with stupor," 29, 57; my translation). A pointed contrast lurks beneath the syntactical parity implied between the two terms of comparison: Dante is "full," Virgil is "burdened"; Dante admires, Virgil is stupefied; Dante is about to be included in the spectacle, Virgil is being left behind. Virgil's exclusion – which is at once spatial, historical, and hermeneutic – comes into sharper focus in a subsequent description of the triumphal chariot at the procession's crux. "Non che Roma di carro così bello/rallegrasse Affricano, o vero Augusto" ("Not only did Rome never gladden an Africanus or an Augustus with a chariot so splendid"), Dante writes, adding that "quel del Sol saria pover con ello" ("even that of the sun would be poor to it," 29, 115–17). The biblical spectacle exhausts even the most lavish terms of comparison drawn from ancient history and myth. It thereby elicits a stupor blending wonderment with incomprehension, admiration with disbelief.

What in the Edenic pageant eludes the discernment of Virgil and, by extension, of the civilization that he represents? The answer comes in the course of a third and final backward gaze. It can be summed up in two words: Beatrice and Christ. Two words that in a sense are one, since the apocalyptic pageant celebrates the advent not of Beatrice *and* Christ, but of Beatrice *as* Christ. Dante's identification of his beloved from the *Vita nuova* with the Son of God may startle the modern reader. It both should and should not. It should because Dante is making a strong, even outrageous, claim about his beloved. Beatrice, after all, is no canonized saint; she is simply the dedicatee of a body of youthful love poems. It should not startle inasmuch as Christian typological thought makes such claims and connections tenable, founded as it is on the conviction that, beneath the apparently random surfaces of human history, there lies a deeper providential logic: a divine rationality or *logos* incarnate in Jesus Christ. This *logos* so thoroughly shapes all historical events and human experiences that everything and everyone, no matter how humble or exalted, participates in its unfolding. Like a sort of glue, it binds the past, present, and future together into an intelligible whole: a whole saturated with forward and backward interconnections pivoting around the Christ-event. "There is neither Jew nor Greek," reads a noted passage from Galatians 3:28, "there is neither slave nor free, there is neither male nor female; for you are all one in Christ Jesus." To live fully the Christian life is to participate in these interconnections; it is to "become" Christ. Yet such a metamorphosis does not entail relinquishing one's individuality, historicity, or gender. Rather one becomes a Christ-*type*, a double being, at once "Christ" and someone else.

Dante's Beatrice is such a being. When she walked the streets of thirteenth-century Florence, the typological links to Christ were hidden to all except a young poet. He alone could read a deeper meaning into signs like the mysterious nines that accompanied her earthly existence. At the summit of Mount Purgatory, those signs are made public. Beatrice is revealed for what she "truly" is and was: as a kind of personalized Messiah, as the Christ-event in Dante's biography, as the proof that poetry can lead to salvation. As Christ is to human history, so Beatrice is to Dante. The connection is spelled out in an elaborate succession scene. Three Latin verses mark Beatrice's second coming. The first, "*Veni, sponsa, de Libano*" ("come from Lebanon, my bride," *Purgatorio* 30, 11), cited from the Songs of Songs, looks forward to the arrival of a woman: a woman, conventionally allegorized as the church, coming to be crowned. The second inverts this implicit allegory, identifying Beatrice not with the bride, but with the bridegroom: according to the standard allegoresis, Jesus Christ. Shouted out by the blessed throng gathered in Eden at the moment of Beatrice's epiphany, it reshapes the mocking cry heard as Christ enters Jerusalem to be crucified, "*Benedictus qui venit in nomine Domini*" ("Blessed is he who comes in the name of the Lord," Matthew 21:9), into a more direct, but no less masculine, cry of celebration: "*Benedictus qui venis!*" ("Blessed are *you* [i.e., a male] who come!" *Purgatorio* 30, 19).

This shift from feminine to masculine, from bride to bridegroom, may seem audacious enough. But Dante adds to it a full Latin verse cited from *Aeneid* 6, whose meaning as well as gender it reverses: "*Manibus*, oh, *date lilïa plenis!*" ("oh, let me scatter lilies with full hand!" *Purgatorio* 30, 21). Pronounced at the moment of greatest sadness in Virgil's text, the moment at which the tragic price to be paid to found Rome has come most fully into view, the verse had originally referred to the scattering of funerary lilies over the corpse of the young Marcellus. Because Marcellus was the most promising of the Romans, the bravest, the best, and the most honorable, Virgil makes of his premature death a symbol of the cruel and fruitless sacrifices that history imposes upon humankind. Dante has his reader revisit this verse from the perspective of the Crucifixion, showing how Christ's fruitful sacrifice at Golgotha transmutes irony into allegory, classical tragedy into Christian comedy, Virgilian despair into Dantean hope. Beatrice returns from the dead to what were once the funerary flowers of Marcellus. These are now revealed as the eternal lilies of the Virgin Mary: flowers which signify not meaningless loss, but the resurrection of the dead for all eternity. For Virgil, history often seems little more than a nightmare; for Dante, it can only be a joyous pageant.

Such is the context within which the pilgrim-poet glances back at Virgil one last time: "volsimi a la sinistra col respitto/col quale il fantolin corre a la mamma/quando ha paura o quando elli è afflitto" ("I turned to the left with the confidence of a little child that runs to his mother when he is frightened or in distress," 30, 43–45). But Virgil is gone. In the place of the guide who had led Dante all the way from Hell to Eden, appears Beatrice. Beatrice who will name him for the first and only time in the entire *Commedia*. Beatrice who will guide him on his journey through the heavens. Beatrice who embodies both his poetic beginnings and his destiny as the founder of a new vernacular poetics, a Christian poetics fusing the exalted with the humble, the ancient with the modern. The circle is closed. The time has come to begin anew.

NOTES

1 Medieval science, following Aristotle, viewed the sublunar world as fundamentally different from the heavens. Whereas the latter were perfect, regular, and perpetual, the former was characterized by its imperfection, irregularity, and temporal flux. This distinction helped scientists to explain why, for instance, the sun follows precisely the same course year after year, whereas cloud-formations do not. Belonging as they do to the lower atmosphere, clouds appear and disappear; their formations are provisional and sporadic. The same sort of mutability extends to animal and plant life. Mount Purgatory functions as a kind of ladder between these ontologically distinct domains. The Ante-Purgatory lies fully within the realm of generation and corruption and is subject to fluctuating weather and to natural events such as earthquakes. The rest of the mountain, from the gateway to the summit, is free from all forms of natural mutability (see 21, 43–72). The Garden of Eden is not only free from mutability, but also provides the pilgrims with their first direct contact with "eternity." The "breeze" that apparently blows through the Garden is produced directly by the rotation of the heavenly spheres. It is therefore perfect, regular, and perpetual (see 28, 97–114).

2 The sequence of terraces on Mount Purgatory is best considered as a sort of orderly "reverse image" of the circles of Hell. The first circle of Hell (lust) corresponds to the seventh and last terrace of Purgatory; the second circle (gluttony) to the sixth terrace; the third circle (avarice and prodigality) to the fifth terrace; the fourth (wrath and melancholy) to the fourth and third terraces; and so on. This correspondence, however, is approximate. Categories of sin such as heresy are necessarily absent from Purgatory, and the precise connection between pride and envy (purged on the first and second terraces) and sins of violence, bestiality, and fraud (punished in the seventh, eighth, and ninth circles of hell) is not always self-evident.

3 Dante's contrastive portrayal of the gates to Hell and Purgatory is modeled after Matthew 7:13–14: "Enter by the narrow gate; for the gate is wide and the way is easy, that leads to destruction, and those who enter by it are many. For the gate is narrow and the way is hard, that leads to life, and those who find it are few."

4 Medieval mythographers and mapmakers had long represented the antipodes – literally the world which lies "opposite our feet" – as a fantastic realm, inhabited by fantastic creatures. Dante rejects this tradition, stripping the antipodes of their ties to the fantastic and granting them a pivotal role in the redemption of humankind. The fantastic is relegated and, indeed, restricted by Dante to Hell.

5 "Then God said, 'Let us make man in our image, after our likeness' . . . So God created man in his own image, in the image of God he created him" (Genesis 1:26–27).

6 This cryptic prophecy has generated a wide range of interpretations. Some scholars have argued that the advent of the DXV must be identified with the second

coming of Christ; others, that the number designates a religious or political savior. The prevailing opinion, however, remains that Beatrice is prophesying the triumph of Henry VII, heir to the Roman imperial throne. Dante's immediate model for this prophecy was Revelation 13:18, where the Emperor Nero was referred to by the number 666.

7 For Dante, "Latin" does not have the same restrictive meaning that it does at present. The term refers to Latinity in all of its expressions, encompassing classical Latin, as well as the entire family of Italian dialects and vernaculars.

8 The choice of this particular psalm is strategic. Sung in full at the mass of Sunday vespers, it commemorates the typological link between the Jews' exodus and Christ's resurrection. Moreover, as Professor William Mahrt has pointed out in an unpublished manuscript, *In exitu* is the only psalm sung according to the so-called *tonus peregrinus* (the "pilgrim's melody"): its reciting note "wanders" like the pilgrims on their way to Eden.

9 In chapter II, section i of his philosophical treatise, *Convivio*, Dante had identified this power of poetry with the notion of "allegory of the poets," to be contrasted with the "allegory of the theologians." Whereas the latter is both literally and figuratively true, the former is defined by its double nature. It presents a "veritade ascosa sotto bella menzogna" (a "truth cloaked under a beautiful lie," *Convivio* II, i).

10 The Triumph was a traditional ancient Roman festivity celebrating the return of a victorious commander. Dante would have been familiar with such events thanks to descriptions provided by Roman historians. Following the precedent of Beatrice's triumph in the Garden of Eden, the Triumph would gradually emerge as a distinctive literary genre in subsequent texts such as Boccaccio's *Amorosa visione* and Petrarch's *Trionfi*.

SUGGESTED READING

Armour, Peter, *The Door of Purgatory: A Study of Multiple Symbolism in Dante's Purgatorio* (Oxford: Clarendon Press, 1983).
   Dante's Griffin and the History of the World (New York: Oxford University Press, 1989).
Auerbach, Erich, *Dante, Poet of the Secular World*, trans. R. Manheim (Chicago: University of Chicago Press, 1961).
   "Figura," in *Scenes from the Drama of European Literature* (Minneapolis: University of Minnesota Press, 1984), pp. 11–78.
Barolini, Teodolinda, *Dante's Poets: Textuality and Truth in the Comedy* (Princeton: Princeton University Press, 1984).
Cervigni, Dino, *Dante's Poetry of Dreams* (Florence: Olschki, 1986).
Fergusson, Frances, *Dante's Drama of the Mind: A Modern Reading of Purgatorio* (Princeton: Princeton University Press, 1953).
Freccero, John, "Manfred's Scar," in *Dante: The Poetics of Conversion*, edited and with an introduction by R. Jacoff (Cambridge, MA: Harvard University Press, 1986), pp. 195–208.
Hawkins, Peter S., "Transfiguring the Text: Ovid, Scripture, and the Dynamics of Allusion," *Stanford Italian Review* 5 (Autumn 1985): 115–40.

"Out upon Circumference: Discovery in Dante," in Scott D. Westrem, ed., *Discovering New Worlds: Essays on Medieval Exploration and Imagination* (New York: Garland, 1991), pp. 193–220.

Hollander, Robert, *Allegory in Dante's Commedia* (Princeton: Princeton University Press, 1969).

Studies in Dante (Ravenna: Longo, 1980).

Jacoff, Rachel, "Intertextualities in Arcadia," in R. Jacoff and J. T. Schnapp, eds., *The Poetry of Allusion: Virgil and Ovid in Dante's Commedia* (Stanford: Stanford University Press, 1991), pp. 131–44.

Le Goff, Jacques, *The Birth of Purgatory,* trans. by A. Goldhammer (Chicago: University of Chicago Press, 1984).

Lewis, C. S., "Dante's Statius," *Medium Aevum* 25 (1957): 133–39.

Mazzeo, Joseph Anthony, "Dante's Sun Symbolism," *Italica* 33 (December 1956): 243–51.

Mazzotta, Giuseppe, *Dante, Poet of the Desert: History and Allegory in the Divine Comedy* (Princeton: Princeton University Press, 1979).

Moore, Edward, *The Time References in the Divina Commedia* (London, 1887).

Studies in Dante. First Series: Scripture and Classical Authors in Dante (Oxford: Clarendon Press, 1896).

Ryan, C. J., "Virgil's Wisdom in the *Divine Comedy*," *Classica et Medievalia* 11 (1982): 1–38.

Schnapp, Jeffrey T., "Dante's Sexual Solecisms: Gender and Genre in the *Commedia*," in K. Brownlee, M. S. Brownlee, and S. J. Nichols, eds., *The New Medievalism* (Baltimore: The Johns Hopkins University Press, 1991), pp. 201–25.

Singleton, Charles, *Dante's Commedia: Elements of Structure,* Dante Studies 1 (Cambridge, MA: Harvard University Press, 1954; rpt. Baltimore: The Johns Hopkins University Press, 1977).

Journey to Beatrice, Dante Studies 2 (Cambridge, MA: Harvard University Press, 1958; rpt. Baltimore: The Johns Hopkins University Press, 1977).

"The Poet's Number at the Center," *MLN* 80 (1965): 1–10.

7

RACHEL JACOFF

Introduction to *Paradiso*

THE GOD INVENTED and gave us vision in order that we might observe the circuits of intelligence in the heaven and profit by them for the revolutions of our own thought, which are akin to them, though ours be troubled and they are unperturbed; and that, by learning to know them and acquiring the power to compute them rightly according to nature, we might reproduce the perfectly unerring revolutions of the god and reduce to settled order the wandering motions in ourselves.

(Plato, *Timaeus* 46c)

The *Paradiso* is the continuation and culmination of the earlier canticles, and at the same time a new departure. Refiguring themes, issues, images, and episodes from *Inferno* and *Purgatorio*, it nonetheless establishes a new set of conditions for both the poet and the reader. While the poet's memory has hitherto been sufficient to his task, the *Paradiso* acknowledges the gap between memory and experience in its opening lines, and, even more, the gap between both psychological categories and language itself. The agon of the poet in his attempt to negotiate this space beyond memory and speech is ever more insistently foregrounded as the poem progresses. But the poem also provides a series of investitures by figures of increasing authority, calling attention to its progressive definition as a "poema sacro," a sacred text "to which both heaven and earth have set their hand." The reader, too, is repositioned. A series of direct addresses, as well as a number of "tasks" which actively engage imaginative collaboration, implicate the reader in the work of the poem.

This strategy is clear from the opening of the second canto, with its striking challenge:

> O voi che siete in piccioletta barca,
>   desiderosi d'ascoltar, seguiti
>   dietro al mio legno, che cantando varca,
> tornate a riveder li vostri liti:
>   non vi mettete in pelago, ché forse,
>   perdendo me, rimarreste smarriti.
> L'acqua ch'io prendo già mai non si corse.
>   (*Paradiso* 2, 1–7)

(O you that are in your little bark, eager to hear, following behind my ship that singing makes her way, turn back to see again your shores. Do not commit yourselves to the open sea, for perchance, if you lost me, you would remain astray. The water which I take was never coursed before.)

To those few who have sought the "bread of angels," those readers properly equipped by their theological and philosophical learning for the voyage, Dante promises "amazement" if they follow in his wake, "holding to [his] furrow ahead of the water that turns smooth again." This mesmerizing address is rich in implications, not the least of which is the moment of self-doubt it is designed to trigger. Only a few cantos later, Dante reverses this strategy of seeming discouragement by exclaiming, "Think, reader, if this beginning went no further, how you would feel an anguished craving to know more" (Paradiso 5, 109–11). The very contradictoriness of these two addresses points to the simultaneous difficulty and appeal of the Paradiso. Indeed, none of us ever knows quite enough about Dante's sources, about his theological and philosophical learning, about the poem's historical and political positioning, to feel fully adequate to interpret it; despite centuries of glossing, conundrums remain. At the same time, the poetic vitality and imaginative beauty of the Paradiso are dazzling; its magisterial interlacing of themes and images, its conceptual and metaphorical interplay, its dialectic of constraint and freedom, offer an inexhaustible challenge and a "craving to know more." Although the Paradiso contains more didactic and doctrinal materials than the preceding canticles, it manifests – as many of the best contemporary readings insist – the Commedia's most innovative poetry. The sheer range of Dante's conceptual and poetic arsenal, and his ability to weave together disparate traditions of thought and language, work both to clarify and to complicate every subject he touches.

The trajectory of the Paradiso leads through the visible heavens to the invisible heaven (or Empyrean) in which the pilgrim will at last be granted the transformative visionary experience posited as the poem's goal. Throughout the journey Dante invites the reader to a glimpse or foretaste of blessedness, reminding us repeatedly that only our own experience can properly gloss his words: "this passing beyond humanity ['trasumanar'] cannot be set forth in words ['per verba']: therefore let the example suffice any for whom grace reserves that experience" (1, 70–72). That irrecoverable experience is a promise to which the poem often alludes in its attempt to generate a desire for the condition of blessedness.

The cosmology of the Paradiso provides both its structural and its esthetic principle, an orderliness that reflects the nature of its Creator. "All things have order among themselves, and this is the form that makes the universe

like God," announces Beatrice in the first (1, 103–26) of several cosmological discourses melding Neoplatonic, Aristotelian, and Christian themes
into a metaphorically powerful synthesis. The Aristotelian-Ptolemaic heav-
enscape of the *Paradiso* consists of nine nested concentric spheres of increasing velocity; beyond the last of these material spheres, the diaphanous and
undifferentiated Primum Mobile, is the Empyrean, the heaven of pure light
and love which is the true home of both God and the blessed. Before Dante
reaches this immaterial heaven (in canto 30), he and Beatrice traverse the
seven planetary spheres, the heaven of the fixed stars, and the Primum
Mobile. Each sphere is distinguished by its astronomical particularities, and
these in turn are correlated with the categories of the blessed that Dante
encounters within them. Since Dante attributes certain limited power to
astral influence, this linkage must be understood not only as metaphorical,
but also as literal.

The souls are not literally assigned to the spheres, but, as Beatrice explains,
they "show themselves" in the hierarchy of the spheres in order to "far
segno," to signify the nature and grade of their beatitude. Their appearances
are compared by Beatrice to the anthropomorphic language of Scripture, an
accommodation to our perceptual limits: "It is needful to speak thus to your
faculty, since only through sense perception does it apprehend that which it
afterwards makes fit for the intellect" (4, 40–42). The "condescension" of the
blessed in the spheres, like the "condescension" of Scripture that "attributes
hands and feet to God, having other meaning," justifies the poet's own procedures as well. Paradise is imaged in a series of "umbriferi prefazi," shadowy
prefaces of its imageless reality. The impossibility of directly rendering that
reality turns out to have its positive value in the ways that it liberates the
poet for "making signs" with increasing freedom from any purely mimetic
imperative. What we have instead, to borrow St. Bonaventure's apt terminology, are "shadows, echoes, and pictures . . . vestiges, images, and displays
presented to us for the contuition of God."[1]

The cosmological organization of *Paradiso*, although different from the
topography of the earlier canticles, allows for structural analogies to them.
In both *Inferno* and *Purgatorio*, for example, the first nine cantos present a
prefatory space before the entrance to the City of Dis and the first terrace of
Purgatory, both of which occur respectively in the tenth canto. Dante con-
trives a comparable partitioning in *Paradiso* by making its first nine cantos
treat the three planetary spheres (Moon, Mercury, and Venus) still touched
by earth's conical shadow, an astronomical fact given spiritual significance
by the imperfections of the souls who appear in them. The final cantos of
each canticle are similarly set apart, with the icy circle of the traitors, the
Earthly Paradise, and the Empyrean each comprising a special "set" for the

climactic encounters of each section. These divisions give each canticle a tripartite structure which replicates both the macro-structure of the whole *Commedia* and the micro-structure of the three-line verse unit (*terzina*) in which the poem is composed. These large structural homologies are combined with other more subtle and various principles of connection which we shall explore as we chart the major episodes of *Paradiso*.

The first three planetary spheres are associated, as we have seen, by their "shadowing" by the earth. Each of them is furthermore associated with particular "defects" in relation to its own astronomical qualities. These defects (inconstancy of will, vainglory, and lust) have been seen by some critics as defects of the three theological virtues (faith, hope, and charity), later extolled in the stellar heaven. In the circle of the Moon, Dante treats the phenomena of the Moon's inconstancy and its spotted surface as pretexts for larger subjects. Piccarda Donati and the Empress Constanza are the two souls Dante sees in this sphere; the reluctant inconstancy of these nuns, forcibly removed from the convent, motivates a long discourse on the nature of the vow and on the constancy of human will. Dante's extended discussion of the vow as a sacrifice of the will, the greatest of God's gifts to humans, introduces the themes of sacrifice and martyrdom which will be developed later. The "dark signs" of the Moon's differentiated surface are the source of an interlocking sequence of discourses on the subject of difference itself. The markings or spots on the Moon were a standard subject in medieval cosmology, since their very presence seemed to call into question the commonplace demarcation of the unstable sublunar world from the changelessness of the heavenly spheres. Although it is common to think of Dante as reflecting a coherent "medieval world view," the *Paradiso* frequently engages issues on which there were a variety of conflicting views. Dante's decision to discuss the moon spots at length shows his characteristic eagerness to enter into debated arenas and to take a stand on them, sometimes even a stand that he had opposed in an earlier work.

Dante begins the moon spot discussion by reiterating the position he had taken in the *Convivio*, that the rarity or density of its matter would explain the difference in the quality of light reflected through and by the Moon. Beatrice's correction of Dante takes the moon spots as the occasion to explain the idea that diverse formal principles, rather than material causation, are the true source of difference. She begins by pointing to the variegated influences of the stellar sphere, taking as axiomatic their qualitative uniqueness. Size or brightness alone cannot determine the nature or quality of astral influence, since "different virtues must needs be fruits of formal principles" (2, 70). Beatrice further argues that rarity and density of moon-matter could not by themselves account for the marks on the Moon by reference to experience and experiment. The lesson that physical phenomena require a metaphysical explanation is one that sets the agenda for the whole of the *Paradiso*. Although the discussion of the moon spots might seem otiose on first reading, it is crucial to understanding Dante's assumptions about the ways the heavens mediate the unitary light of the divine; it also establishes the proper relationship between formal and material causation, as well as that between natural philosophy and theology.

The uneven distribution of light and shadow in the Moon finds yet another correlative in the subsequent canto's discussion of the different degrees of beatitude enjoyed by the saints. Just as the spheres of the cosmos proceed "from grade to grade" (2, 122) in hierarchical order, so the souls are ordered "from threshold to threshold" (3, 82). Because gradation itself seems incompatible with the fullness of beatitude, Dante asks the first soul he meets whether the souls in the Moon desire to be in "a more exalted place, to see more, and to make yourselves more dear" (3, 65–66). The paradox of equality and hierarchy is "resolved" by the idea of the soul's conformity to divine will; "in His will is our peace," says the soul of Piccarda Donati in the lowest of the spheres. The hierarchical arrangement which assumes some souls capable of greater receptivity than others is one in which all souls are said to rejoice, with each experiencing as much beatitude as is proper to his or her merit and capacity to receive grace. Both throughout the spheres and in the final configuration of souls in the Empyrean (where they are once again envisioned hierarchically), the necessity of representation may seem in tension with the theoretical completeness of beatitude. This is not, however, the experience of the blessed themselves: "Diverse voices make sweet music, so diverse ranks in our life render sweet harmony among these wheels" (6, 124–26). Beatrice had analyzed diversity in relation to the Moon (and, by analogy, to the human body) in comparable terms: "diverse virtue makes diverse alloy with the precious body it quickens" (2, 139–40). Piccarda extends the meaning of diversity to the "social construct" of heaven itself.

The souls in the sphere of Mercury did good deeds, but did them to acquire fame rather than for their own sake. The Emperor Justinian dominates this sphere, his importance to the poem signalled by being the sole speaker for an entire canto. Justinian is Dante's idealized emperor as law-giver, the presenter of the idea of empire embodied in the "sacred sign" of the eagle. Canto 6 is the culmination of a progressively widening and authoritative political discourse which evolves across the three canticles in the sixth canto of each. Justinian's over-arching discussion of empire is glossed by canto 7, which inscribes it within the drama of salvation history. Following St. Anselm's *Cur deus homo* (*Why God Became Man*), Dante defines the Incarnation as the event which fills the void created between man and God as a consequence of original sin. The play on the word *voto* (meaning both "void" and "vow") earlier in *Paradiso* 3 (28–30, and 56–57) receives retrospective meaning from this canto's unfolding of Christ's sacrifice as the paradigm for all such acts. This most doctrinal of cantos concludes with an argument for the resurrection of the flesh based on the "direct creation" (by God) of the bodies of our first parents, pointing ahead to the discussion of the glorified body in canto 14, and to the majestic analysis of Creation in canto 29.

In the sphere of Venus, Dante first encounters the soul of Charles Martel, heir to the thrones of Naples, Provence, and Hungary, who had died young before fulfilling his promise. The contrast between Charles and his brother Robert prompts a discussion of heredity, the role of stellar influence, and the diversity of roles necessary to civic society. The theme of "diversity," which we saw proposed in the discussion first of moon spots and then of degrees of beatitude, reappears here in an argument that "men below live in diverse ways for diverse duties." Since Venus is the planet which appears both "before and after" in relation to the sun, it fittingly contains a sequence of "before and after" conversion stories: Cunizza, a wife of Bath become oracular; Folco de Marseille, a poet and lover who renounced both poetry and earthly love to become a militant bishop; and Rahab the harlot, who was saved for her role in aiding Joshua, a type of Christ, and became herself a type of the church. Cunizza and Folco recall their former erotic errancy without pain, for their blessedness is beyond guilt: "Here we do not repent, we smile."

Throughout these opening cantos there is a gradual effacement of the human form. In the circle of the Moon, Dante sees faint outlines of the human form, first taking them for mirror images ("specchiati sembianti"). In Mercury and Venus the souls are concealed by their own luminosity, nesting in their light and signalling their joy by increasing radiance. Once Dante and Beatrice pass beyond the earth's shadow into the upper planetary spheres, the souls remain pure effulgences, "sempiternal flames," but they are constellated in choral cultural emblems: the wise in the circle of the Sun form two circles, making a double crown around Dante and Beatrice; in Mars, the holy warriors form a Greek Cross on the ruddy ground of the planet; in Jupiter, the just rulers reconfigure themselves to form a heraldic eagle; and in Saturn, the contemplatives appear as lights moving up and down upon a golden ladder.

In the double circles of the *sapienti*, the teachers of the church, Dante predominantly honors two kinds of theologians, those most associated with intellective theology, led by St. Thomas, and those associated with affective theology, led by St. Bonaventure. Yet these circles also include unexpected figures. Thomas closes his circular catalogue with Siger of Brabant, a noted Latin Averroist whose work he had attacked in life, while Bonaventure concludes his with Joachim of Flora, to whom he likewise had been opposed. The presence of Siger and Joachim argues for Dante's breadth of theological sympathies and curiosity; they remind us, as does much else in the poem, that medieval theology was as much a site of contest as of concord. These catalogues of *sapienti* also contain two biblical figures: Solomon, celebrated as one who asked for pertinent kingly wisdom, and Nathan, a prophet whose major act was the disciplining of a king. Solomon anticipates the kings in the heaven of Justice, and signals Dante's determination to valorize wisdom in relation to the active as well as the speculative life. Nathan and Joachim ("who was endowed with prophetic spirit") are figures suggestive of the poet's own increasingly prophetic voice.

The two groupings of *sapienti* in the circle of the Sun are one component of a series of "doublings" that inform these cantos. The sun's double motion on its daily and its yearly path becomes the model for other pairs in equipoise, with the repetition of the phrase "l'uno e l'altro" underlining the theme of reciprocity. Canto 10 opens with a densely compact astronomical *incipit* celebrating the double motion of the Trinity (procession and spiration) and the equinoctal crossing that marks the signature of its triune creator. The intricately analogical construction of these cantos operates on several levels, from the lexical to the thematic, with the parallel narratives of St. Francis and St. Dominic also structured to conform to the pattern of equipoise. The Dominican Thomas praises Francis who was "seraphic in ardor," while the Franciscan Bonaventure praises Dominic who was "cherubic in splendor." The complexity of these remarkable cantos has been the subject of some of the best recent work on Dante.

The striking chiastic opening figure of canto 14, "Dal centro al cerchio, e sì dal cerchio al centro" ("From the center to the rim and so from the rim to the center"), is echoed in subsequent chiastic constructions such as "Quell'uno e due e tre che sempre vive/e regna sempre in tre e 'n due e 'n uno" ("That One and Two and Three which ever lives and ever reigns in Three and Two and One," 14, 28–29). In its symmetrical inversion of sequence (ab:ba) chiasmus is a figure which mimes circularity. Although it pervades the *Paradiso*, it features prominently in this canto where it also informs Solomon's speech on the condition of the glorified body at the end of time. Solomon analyzes the condition of the lucent blessed in a causal sequence that moves from brightness to ardor, vision, and grace, and then reverses the sequence in his description of the coming metamorphosis of the blessed when they will be reunited with their glorified bodies. This discussion recapitulates a theme dear to St. Bernard, the longing of the blessed for their bodies. The eruption of this longing reaches its apogee in the exclamation of the blessed in response to Solomon's speech, and in the claim that their desire is "perhaps not only for themselves, but also for their mothers, for their fathers, and for the others who were dear before they became sempiternal flames." The profoundly endearing "domesticity" of this moment, to use Umberto Bosco's word,[2] not only humanizes an abstract discourse, but also prepares us for the next episode.

Dante's own parents never appear in the poem, but its next speaker is the poem's consummate father-figure, Dante's great-great-grandfather, his "root," Cacciaguida: crusader, knight, and martyr. Dante's meeting with his heroic ancestor rewrites Aeneas' underworld encounter with Anchises in the key of Christian comedy. The cantos of Mars contain the apotheosis of the Florentine theme that began with Dante's encounter with Ciacco in *Inferno* 6; Cacciaguida speaks of the city's idyllic phase and of its degeneration into factionalism, finally and clearly announcing its impending perfidy to Dante. Although the *Inferno* is filled with garbled and ominous prophecies of Dante's exile, Cacciaguida's definitive version spells out its devastating consequences: "You shall leave everything beloved most dearly" (*Paradiso* 17, 55–56). This fearful event of Dante's "future life," however, becomes the precondition for a greater future as Cacciaguida solemnly invests Dante with the task of writing the poem that will "infuture" ("s'infutura," 17, 98) him for those, like ourselves, "who shall call these times ancient" (17, 120). Cacciaguida's injunction to "make manifest all that you have seen" endows the poem as well as the journey with sacral authority. The consequences of this investiture scene are evident in the change in generic terminology with which Dante subsequently refers to his poem. While the poem is called a *commedia* twice in *Inferno*, it will be called a "sacred poem" in cantos 23 and 25. Dante's "staging" of his own authority in the Cacciaguida episode is based on the precedents of St. Paul and Aeneas, both of whom are invoked here, reminding us that Dante began his journey asking how he would be allowed to go to the underworld since he was neither Aeneas nor Paul (*Inferno* 2, 32). Virgil's narration of the "three blessed ladies" in *Inferno* 2 established the journey's divine sanction. Only here in *Paradiso* 17 does the poem itself receive comparable legitimacy.

The holy warriors of the circle of Mars give way to the just rulers of the circle of Jupiter. Here the souls first configure themselves in a divine skywriting that spells out a sentence of Scripture ("Love Justice, you who rule the earth"). They proceed to form an "M" which turns into a heraldic eagle, refiguring the "sacrosancto segno" of Justinian's earlier narrative of empire. This circle is the setting for a nagging question about God's justice: how can those who have no access to Christian truth be punished for their invincible ignorance? This question haunts the poem, particularly with relation to Virgil who is excluded from its system of salvation despite his efficacy as Dante's guide. The eagle puts the question in spatial terms, asking how the "man born on the banks of the Indus" can be held responsible for not knowing Christ, given the geographical impossibility of Christ's salvific message reaching him. The poem, of course, has always put the question in temporal terms, making us ask how those, like Virgil, born before Christ can be punished for not having known him. Having raised it so directly, the eagle surprises us by its refusal to respond to the question. Dante seems to be side-stepping an issue that his poem has accentuated – until the following canto where a real surprise awaits us. Among the six rulers in the eye and eyebrow of the eagle is Ripheus, a character briefly named in the *Aeneid*. Dante asks, as indeed any reader would, "How can this be?" Like the improbable presence of Cato on the shores of Purgatory, the startling presence of Ripheus in the heaven of Justice makes us think about how Dante read his classical sources and how he rewrites them. Ripheus is a sign of God's inscrutability, but also of the poet's freedom. Virgil had called Ripheus "most just," but Dante's tale of Ripheus abhorring the "stench of paganism" is pure invention. Catholic theology did allow for "baptism by desire," but no one other than Dante would have selected Ripheus as an example of it.

In the highest of the planetary spheres, Saturn, Dante varies the customary entrance ritual of remarking on Beatrice's smile and the music of the spheres. Beatrice withholds her smile and the music of the spheres is silent since Dante is not yet "ready" for such overpowering experiences. The contemplatives Dante meets here are the reformer Peter Damian, who inveighs against clerical corruption, and the founder of Western monasticism, St. Benedict, who decries the degeneration of his order. The golden ladder which marks this sphere is a traditional symbol of the contemplative life; Dante follows it upward in an instantaneous transition to the following sphere, the circle of the fixed stars, where he enters into the "glorious stars" of his natal constellation of Gemini.

Dante's extensive stay in the stellar heaven (from the end of canto 22 to the end of canto 27) is framed by two glances back to earth, the "little threshing floor that makes us all so fierce." Canto 23 presents the symbolic "triumph" of Christ and Mary with all the blessed in one of the most metaphorically dense sequences in the poem. The affective language and kaleidoscopic images of this canto create the first of several prefaces to the final vision. Dante sees a symbolic version of Christ's Advent and Ascension, followed by a version of Mary's Annunciation, Assumption, and Coronation. The intensely maternal language of this canto, with its opening extended simile of Beatrice as a nurturing mother-bird and its concluding images of the blessed flames reaching towards Mary as infants reach out after they have been fed, reinforces the importance of Mary in particular, and female mediation in general, in the poem.

Dante's interlocutors in the starry heaven are the three apostles (Peter, James, and John) who were privileged witnesses to the Transfiguration. Each apostle examines Dante on one of the three theological virtues; Dante's dense answers to the apostles compress theology, Scripture, philosophy, and experience into a set of responses that are both unique and generic. This heaven is also the site of the poem's climactic denunciation of the corrupt papacy, a thunderous invective delivered by none other than the first pope, St. Peter:

> Quelli ch'usurpa in terra il luogo mio,
> il luogo mio, il luogo mio che vaca
> ne la presenza del Figliuol di Dio,
> fatt'ha del cimitero mio cloaca
> del sangue e de la puzza.
> (*Paradiso* 27, 22–26)

(He who usurps my place, my place, my place, which in the sight of the Son of God is vacant, has made my burial-ground a sewer of blood and of stench.)

The apostles, the founding fathers of Christianity, give way to the last soul Dante encounters, the first man and father of us all. Adam defines the Fall as the primal act of transgression ("trapassar il segno"), and explains the nature of Edenic language in terms that significantly revise Dante's earlier theories about the subject in the *De vulgari eloquentia*.

The next sphere, the Primum Mobile, offers no human interlocutors. Instead of encountering radiant souls, Dante sees a hypnotic geometrical figure, an infinitesimally small and infinitely bright point of light surrounded by nine whirling circles representing the angelic hierarchies. The relationship between this vision and the structure of the nine earth-centered spheres through which Dante has just passed is one of "model" ("l'essemplo") and "copy" ("l'essemplare"). Dante strains to understand how the two figures relate; if we were to diagram them, they would look identical, although in the model (the vision of the angelic hierarchies) the smallest circle would be the one closest to God, while in the geocentric "copy" the opposite would be true. Beatrice substitutes the variable of velocity for that of size in order to account for the relationship between the innermost angelic choir and the outermost material sphere. In Dante's cosmology the angels are the movers of the spheres, their velocity a sign of their vision of God and the love that attends their intellection. The two universes, model and copy, are both governed by the "point on which the heavens and all nature depend" (28, 41–42).

This sequence has recently been a particular favorite of physicists and poets, for some of whom it seems to take precedence over the final vision as the poem's quintessential epiphanic moment. James Merrill, for example, has spoken of "the hallucinatory wonder of this little point," imagining it "partly as a model of electrons whirling round the atomic nucleus . . . partly an abstracted solar system."[3]

The Primum Mobile is the "maggior corpo" ("greatest body") of the material heavens, its velocity a function of its desire for the Empyrean which itself is immaterial, a heaven of "pure light, light intellectual full of love, love of true good full of joy, joy that transcends every sweetness" (30, 40–42). Dante's entrance into the Empyrean is presented as a transition from time to eternity. After a temporary blinding by a swath of light prepares him for a new order of vision, his first sight is of a river flowing between two banks "painted with marvelous spring," with "living sparks" coming and going between the river and its blossoming banks. This jewel-like spring landscape is an adumbration, a "shadowy preface of its truth." It turns into its "reality" as Dante undergoes an occular baptism, drinking with his eyes from the linear river of light; as he does so, the line ("sua lunghezza") becomes a circle ("tonda"), and the flowers and sparks become the sight of the blessed and the angels ministering to them. This unveiling (Dante speaks of it as an unmasking) is the first of several climactic moments in the final cantos. It is accompanied by a triple rhyme on the word "vidi" ("I saw," 30, 95, 97, 99), the only word in the whole poem other than "Cristo" which Dante rhymes on itself.

Dante sees the blessed here not as effulgences or sempiternal flames, but in their "white robes," in their glorified bodies "as they will be at the Last Judgment." This vision was promised to him by St. Benedict when Dante asked if he could see the saint concealed by his own radiance in the lineaments of his human form "con imagine scoverta" ("with your uncovered shape"): "Brother, your high desire shall be fullfilled" ("s'adempierà") where are fulfilled ("s'adempion") all others and my own." The repeated verb in Benedict's response almost contains the word "empireo" within itself. The vision of "the assembly of the white robes" also recalls Dante's definition of his profoundest hope in canto 25, where he speaks of the resurrection in the Book of Revelation's language of the "white robes" of the blessed. Dante's claim to see the blessed as they will be at the end of time is not only heterodox, but also problematic within the coordinates of his fiction; since the amphitheater of the blessed is envisioned as awaiting completion ("few souls are now wanted there"), he both does and does not see it as it will be at the Last Judgment. The reappearance of the body in its particularity (old and young, male and female) and implied historicity at this most ethereal point in the poem is an extraordinary sign of Dante's incarnational intuitions and desires.

The Empyrean is also the site of Dante's farewell to Beatrice, who returns to the "throne her merits have allotted to her" (31, 69), giving way to St. Bernard as Dante's final guide. Although Virgil had prepared Dante for Beatrice's coming, there had been no warning that she herself would be replaced. Dante's praise of Beatrice, "she who imparadises [his] mind," has been extravagant throughout the *Paradiso*. His ascent through the spheres is coordinate with her increasing radiance and beauty, until at last hyperbole defeats itself: "The beauty I behold transcends measure not only beyond our reach, but I truly believe that He alone who made it can enjoy it all" (30, 19–21). Dante's last address to Beatrice, his first to her in the familiar "tu" form, is a prayer of thanksgiving for her salvific role in his life. There is no single allegorical equivalent that can serve as an adequate gloss for Beatrice. She is a type of Christ, but also of Mary and of the church. She is Dante's instructor, guide, and lure. Her beauty, and the emotions it generates, create a powerful link between love and knowledge, an eroticization of knowledge that energizes the poet's enamored mind ("mente innamorata," 27, 88).

There are many reasons why St. Bernard serves as Dante's final guide. The miraculous prayer to the Virgin in canto 33 reminds us of Bernard's own intense Marian piety, while his role in assisting Dante's final vision clearly relates to his own eminence as theologian of mystic union. There are other reasons, too, for Dante to turn to Bernard. His writings offer a counter-motion to Dante's, insofar as he finds an erotic language to render theological experience while Dante, in his treatment of Beatrice, theologizes what began as an erotic experience. Dante's commitment to scholastic intellectuality, his insistence that intellection precedes love, is balanced by the presence of Bernard, one of the great poets of the affective tradition. Dante also shared Bernard's conviction of the soul's incomplete beatitude before reunion with the body. Furthermore, Bernard's tender meditation on Christ's humanity as a lure for man's love for God offers a Christological gloss on Dante's construction of the figure of Beatrice. In the twentieth sermon on the Song of Songs, Bernard says: "Whatever form it takes this image [of Christ's humanity] must bind the soul with the love of virtue and expel carnal vices, eliminate temptations and quiet desires." God became man "to recapture the affections of carnal men who were unable to love in any other way, by first drawing them to the salutary love of his own humanity and then gradually raising them to a spiritual love."[4] It is precisely in this function that Beatrice is most Christ-like.

Dante's approach to the final vision is staged sequentially, with the pilgrim gradually becoming a more adequate perceiver. While the object of his perception remains the same, it appears under different aspects: "Not because more than one simple semblance was in the Living Light wherein I was gazing, which ever is such as it was before; but through my sight, which was growing strong in me as I looked, one sole appearance, even as I changed, was altering itself to me" (33, 109–13). The philosophical vision of the *totum simul*, binding together "substances and accidents and their relations," gives way to a geometrical and Trinitarian image of "three circles of three colors and one magnitude." Dante's Trinity is seen in its inner relation, with the marvelous addition to orthodoxy of its "smiling upon itself" (33, 126). The pilgrim strains to perceive the mystery of Incarnation, how the image is fitted to the circle, the mystery celebrated in the canto's opening prayer to the Virgin and now yearned for. As Dante tells us what he cannot do, comparing himself to a geometer attempting to square a circle, a syntactical sleight suggests that he has already done so. What cannot happen has already happened: his mind has been smitten by a flash, and "already" his desire and will are revolving in the circular motion of the cosmic dance. Whatever the vision was, it takes place between the lines.

The last canto points in a number of directions, allowing readers to respond to its claims in different ways. Some critics focus on the lines preparatory to Dante's description of the vision which communicate the evanescence and fragility of the experience. "As he who dreaming sees, after the dream the passion remains imprinted and the rest returns not to the mind; such am I, for my vision almost wholly fades away, yet does the sweetness that was born of it still drop within my heart. Thus is the snow unsealed by the sun; thus in the wind, on the light leaves, the Sibyl's oracle was lost." This sequence of images (which includes the last, and in some ways the most potent, of the poem's many Virgilian allusions) communicates the limits of language as well as of memory. It is the culmination, too, of a whole series of images of erasure and impermanence characteristic of the *Paradiso*. Others are drawn to the initial bookish vision of all that is scattered throughout the universe "bound with love in one volume," finding it an inevitable correlative of the poem's own synthesizing achievement. The oscillation between these two compelling figures – one of dissolution and the other of preserved inclusion – constitutes the *Paradiso*'s particular and paradoxical beauty.

Paradox, in fact, is constitutive of the *Paradiso* both theologically and poetically. Dante gravitates towards the central paradoxical formulations of Christian theology and explores them in a variety of ways. For example, two crucial questions raised in the opening cantos create fictional equivalents or versions of central theological concerns. Dante, following St. Paul in 2 Corinthians 12, wonders whether his journey is "in the body or out of it." Upon entering the Moon he reformulates this doubt in more scholastic terms, "answering" the question of whether two bodies can occupy the same space by appealing to the principle of the Incarnation as another oxymoron which will ultimately be understood axiomatically, however incomprehensible or illogical it may be:

> If I was body (and here we conceive not how one bulk [the moon] could brook another [Dante in the body] which must be if body enters body), the more should longing enkindle us to see that Essence wherein we behold how our nature and God united themselves. There that which we hold by faith shall be seen, not demonstrated, but known of itself like the first truth that man believes.
>
> (*Paradiso* 2, 31–43)

Dante participates here in the tradition which celebrated the "incomprehensible" and "incredible" nature of the central paradoxical mysteries of Christian faith. If the question of how two bodies can occupy one space links Dante's journey with the theology of the Incarnation, the second question, whether one body can occupy more than one space, also has both representational and theological import. Dante's fiction that the souls appear in the spheres and yet are in the Empyrean recalls a persistent theological debate about how Christ can be both in heaven and present in the consecrated Host. Just as with the blessed, both things were said to be true in a suspension of natural law. When Dante enters the Empyrean, he defines it as the site of just such suspension: "where God governs without intermediary, natural law in no way prevails" (30, 122–23).

The suspension of natural law informs not only the theology but also the linguistic practices and poetic freedoms of the *Paradiso*. These freedoms are evident in a variety of "effects," such as Dante's increasingly arbitrary manipulation of natural imagery in supernatural terms. Natural phenomena are invoked, but often in unnatural ways. We are asked to imagine birds molting and exchanging feathers, or a snow storm in which the flakes drift upward, or a perpetual springtime "which nightly Aries does not despoil" (28, 116); we are invited to rearrange the stars in order to create new constellations (13, 1–21). The transformation of the natural into the supernatural is related to other freedoms that distinguish the verbal texture of this canticle with its abundant play on sounds, repetitions, puns, rhymes, and etymologies. "Much is granted to our faculties there that is not granted here" (1, 55–56), says Beatrice as she and Dante are about to begin their ascent. Just as the pilgrim is empowered by and moved towards the visionary experience, so the poet – despite all protestations of inadequacy – is unusually experimental and daring with language itself. The unprecedented number of neologisms gives the impression of the poet shaping, even sculpting, his language. Many of the neologisms proclaim the poet's freedom to refigure grammar: nouns, adjectives, adverbs, and even numbers are converted into verbs that stretch to communicate extraordinary states of being or of activity appropriate to the paradisal condition or to the divine. Many of these verbs use the prefix "in" to suggest the permeability of normal boundaries; others use the prefix "tras" (hapaxes such as "trasumanar," "trasmodare," "trasvolare") as a marker of the excess, the going beyond, associated with paradisal privilege.

But the prefix "tras" also has an *in malo* aspect, insofar as transgression or its threat is always a possibility. "Trapassar il segno," "going beyond the mark," is, as we have seen, Adam's marvelously generic term for the Fall. Many times we are reminded of the potential for trespass in the poet's activity as well. The potentially transgressive nature of Dante's claims has become a major topic in contemporary readings of the poem, perhaps as a way to complicate and energize a discourse that had become monolithically pious in the wake of dominant theologizing readings. But there is no doubt that Dante is aware of the dangers inherent in his ambitions and claims, and that he would have to communicate that awareness in order to avoid the truly transgressive potential of claiming to speak for God.

If we look back from the *Paradiso*'s conclusion to its opening *terzina*, we notice it posits the end point of the journey that it inaugurates, proclaiming the divine glory that both shines through and is reflected back through the universe.

> La gloria di colui che tutto move
> per l'universo penetra, e resplende
> in una parte più e meno altrove.
>
> (1, 1–3)

(The glory of the All-Mover penetrates through the universe and reglows in one part more, and in another less.)

The two verbs "penetra" and "risplende" imply the contrapuntal movements of Creator and creature, the outpouring of the unitary divine light into the multiplicity of creation, and the return of the creature to its Creator. The pilgrim's ascent to the divine is therefore a return to his origins, and origins are a recurrent subject throughout the *Paradiso*. The origins of empire are presented in Justinian's overview in canto 6, while those of Florence and of Dante himself are treated in the sphere of Mars. The heaven of the fixed stars treats the origins of the church and of man, while in the Primum Mobile, the place where time originates, the subject is the universe itself. This preoccupation with beginnings is also reflected in the way the origins of the Franciscan and Dominican orders, Benedictine monasticism, and the church itself are treated. Dante creates a sense of moving backward in time by presenting the key figures of the church and human history in reverse chronology: Francis and Dominic, Peter Damian, Benedict, Peter, the other apostles, and finally Adam.

We can observe a second contrapuntal feature in the poem's juxtaposition of cosmology and history. While the cosmological orderliness informs the journey with increasing beauty and joyfulness, the *Paradiso* is not only an exercise in harmonious celebration. The cosmic order is continuously traversed by the realities of historical violence, even historical despair, which flash before us in anecdotes, biographies, diatribes, and reflections. Saintly lives such as those of Francis, Dominic, Peter Damian, and Benedict are invoked as emblems of reformative energies, only to give way to stories of their ultimate inability to transform permanently the structures by which the world might be set aright. The cumulative effect of these and other similar declamations of failure and degeneration provides a negative counter-thrust to the pilgrim's increasingly elating ascent. The two charges, positive and negative, alternate with compressed manic-depressive power in canto 27, where St. Peter's thunderous explosion against the corrupt papacy that has turned his seat into a sewer follows upon a rapturous description of the "smile of the universe." Although Dante's theology of history insists on redemption in and through time, the *Paradiso* makes us aware of the corrosive effects of time in its narratives of good origins turning to bad effects, or of failed efforts such as that of Henry VII, "who will come to set Italy straight before she is ready" (30, 137–38).

Writing about the *Paradiso* it is tempting to list all the moments when the poem engages us in its process of making meaning. Space prevents such a catalogue, but let me close with an example of the poem's invitation to our own imaginative collaboration. Several times we are asked to envision the great patterns formed by the movements of the heavenly bodies across time and in "outer space." In the first canto, Dante delineates the equinoctal setting of the action by translating it into a geometrical pattern (four circles and three crosses) that our notes may diagram, but that none of us could ever actually see. We are asked to perform a mental version of time-lapse photography in order to translate these temporal motions into spatial forms. Similarly, Dante invites us later to look up at the point where the ecliptic crosses the celestial equator at the equinox, the Chi in the sky that is its Creator's stamp. Like so many of the *Paradiso*'s sights, this one can only be seen in the mind's eye. Dante asks the reader not only to look up at this point, but to "gaze lovingly ['vagheggiar'] at that Master's art who within Himself so loves it that His eye never turns from it." The beautiful verb "vagheggiar" is the same one Dante uses to describe the fond gaze of the joyful Creator ("lieto fattore," *Purgatorio* 16, 89) of the human soul. Dante's idea of the Creator is suffused by the sense of the happiness of the act of creation (repeatedly associated with the adjective "lieto") and with the loving contemplation of its result. Something of this joyful energy also suffuses the poet's creation as well.

The *Paradiso* oscillates between statements of its daring originality and confessions of its impossibility, of the ineffability of its vision and of the inadequacies of language to render it. The simultaneous sense of victory and defeat within which the poem comes into being contributes to its paradoxical effects, generating the haunting pathos that subtends the poem's astonishing accomplishment.

NOTES

1 *Itinerarium mentis in Deum*, trans. Philotheus Boehner, *Journey of the Mind to God* (St. Bonavenure, NY: Franciscan Institute, 1956), 2, 13, p. 61.
2 Umberto Bosco and Giovanni Reggio, *La Divina Commedia, Paradiso* (Florence: Le Monnier, 1979), commentary to canto 14, p. 225.
3 James Merrill, "Divine Poem," in J. D. McClatchy, ed., *Recitative: Prose by James Merrill* (San Francisco: North Point Press, 1986), p. 91. Cf. Mark A. Peterson, "Dante and the 3-sphere," *American Journal of Physics* 47, no. 12 (December 1979): 1031–35.
4 "On the Song of Songs 1," in *The Works of Bernard of Clairvaux*, II, trans. Kilian Walsh (Kalamazoo, MI: Cistercian Publications, 1977), p. 152.

SUGGESTED READING

Barolini, Teodolinda, *The Undivine Comedy* (Princeton: Princeton University Press, 1992).
Brownlee, Kevin, "Dante's Poetics of Transfiguration: The Case of Ovid," *Literature and Belief* 5 (1985): 13–29.
Chiarenza, Marguerite, "The Imageless Vision," *Dante Studies* 90 (1972): 77–92.
Chiavacci Leonardi, Anna, "'Le bianche stole': il tema della resurrezione nel *Paradiso*," in Giovanni Barblan, ed., *Dante e la Bibbia* (Florence: Olschki, 1988).
Durling, Robert M., and Ronald L. Martinez, *Time and the Crystal: Studies in Dante's Rime Petrose* (Berkeley: University of California Press, 1990), esp. pp. 224–58.
Ferrante, Joan M., "Words and Images in Dante's *Paradiso*: Reflections of the Divine," in Aldo S. Bernardo and Anthony L. Pellegrini, eds., *Dante, Petrarch, Boccaccio* (Binghamton, NY: Medieval and Renaissance Texts and Studies, 1983), pp. 115–32.
Foster, Kenelm, "The Celebration of Order: *Paradiso* X," *Dante Studies* 90 (1972): 109–24.
"Dante's Vision of God," in *The Two Dantes and Other Studies* (London: Darton, Longman and Todd, 1977).

Freccero, John, "An Introduction to the *Paradiso*," in *Dante: The Poetics of Conversion*, edited and with an introduction by R. Jacoff (Cambridge, MA: Harvard University Press, 1986), pp. 209–20.

"*Paradiso* x: The Dance of the Stars," in ibid., pp. 221–44.

Hawkins, Peter, "'By Gradual Scale Sublimed': Dante's Benedict and Contemplative Ascent," in Timothy Gregory Verdon, ed., *Monasticism and the Arts* (Syracuse, NY: Syracuse University Press, 1984), pp. 255–69.

Jacoff, Rachel, "The Post-Palinodic Smile: *Paradiso* VIII and IX," *Dante Studies* 98 (1980): 111–22.

"Sacrifice and Empire: Thematic Analogies in San Vitale and the *Paradiso*," in *Renaissance Studies in Honor of Craig Hugh Smyth* (Florence: Giunti, 1985), pp. 317–31.

Kleiner, John, "The Eclipses in the *Paradiso*," *Stanford Italian Review* 9 (1991): 5–32.

Lansing, Richard, "Piccarda and the Poetics of Paradox: A Reading of *Paradiso* III," *Dante Studies* 105 (1987): 63–74.

Mazzeo, Joseph Anthony, *Structure and Thought in the Paradiso* (Ithaca, NY: Cornell University Press, 1958).

Mazzotta, Giuseppe, "Order and Transgression in the *Divine Comedy*," in W. Ginsberg, ed., *Ideas of Order in the Middle Ages* (Binghamton, NY: Center for Medieval and Early Renaissance Studies, 1990), pp. 1–21.

Merrill, James, "Divine Poem," in J. D. McClatchy, ed., *Recitative: Prose by James Merrill* (San Francisco: North Point Press, 1986), pp. 87–95.

Murtagh, Daniel, "'Figurando il Paradiso': The Signs that Render Dante's Heaven," *PMLA* 90 (March 1975): 277–84.

Schnapp, Jeffrey T., *The Transfiguration of History at the Center of Dante's Paradise* (Princeton: Princeton University Press, 1986).

8

PETER S. HAWKINS

Dante and the Bible

Underwriting the entire world in which Dante lived is a single book, the Bible. Believed to be authored by a God who chose human scribes to speak his word, it had an authority quite beyond any other text. For this reason it was the most studied book in the Middle Ages, both the primer on which the young clerk learned his alphabet, and the "sacred page" that dominated every branch of higher learning. Not that the power of the Scriptures was limited to school or to the literate. As the holy book of the church, it not only informed liturgy and preaching, art and architecture, but also constituted a vast and complex symbolic network that was intelligible, on whatever level, to all classes of society. Far more than Latin, the Bible itself was the universal "language" of Christian culture.

It is not surprising, then, that when Dante's writings are considered as a whole, the Christian Scriptures should be the source of more reference and allusion than any other work: by one count there are 575 citations of the Bible in Dante, compared with 395 to Aristotle and 192 to Virgil.[1] Calculations of this sort, however, do not suggest the degree to which Dante absorbed the world of the Bible. This is most notably true in the *Commedia*, where the Old and New Testaments, both in Latin and in vernacular translation, so permeate his language as almost to become one with it. Sometimes the poet will quote the Bible or openly draw attention to its relevance; far more often, however, he will allow its presence to go unannounced, relying on the reader to catch the biblical resonance and make something of it.

A case in point is the very first line of the *Commedia*, coming immediately before Dante tells the reader of his terrifying experience in the dark wood and of his resolve to recall it "because of the good that I found there." Without apparent resort to any other text or authority – indeed, in a line that comes to personalize him as readily as his own name – he begins, "Nel mezzo del cammin di nostra vita." Here the poet opens his work by telling time: he is "in the middle of the journey of our life." When this line comes later to be annotated, commentators will remind the reader that the journey through the afterlife is set during Holy Week of 1300, that the poet was born in 1265, and therefore that he is thirty-five years old. But none of this additional information is necessary for one who remembers that the span of "our life" is already a known quantity: as stated in Psalm 89 (90):10, "the days of our years are seventy years."

Nor is this verse from the Psalms the only biblical text at play here, for in Dante's recollection of the events that took place for him "in the middle of the journey of our life," he also echoes King Hezekiah in Isaiah 38:10, whose song of thanksgiving is written down in the prophet's book to commemorate a rescue from mortal illness: "I said: in the middle of my days I shall go to the gates of hell." In this biblical passage we find a great deal more than a commonplace allusion to life's three score and ten; instead, we have a scriptural subtext for Dante's larger effort in the *Commedia*. Opening his own story of salvation from the powers of death, he appropriates the parallel experience of Hezekiah, a man saved by God's intervention from the "pit of destruction," who afterwards looks back and writes about his deliverance. In his influential commentary on this passage, St. Jerome noted that while a good man dies at the end of his days, the sinner comes to the gates of Hell in the midst of his life. Dante's losing his way "nel mezzo del cammin," therefore, is a confession of his spiritual lostness, a tacit admission from the very outset that he was (to quote Jerome's gloss on Isaiah 38:10) "in the shadow of errors that lead to hell."[2]

The opening line of the *Commedia* reveals in miniature the biblical matrix of Dante's imagination. He assumes the psalm's estimation of our lifespan, draws not only upon a single sentence, but also upon a narrative moment in the Book of Isaiah, and then adapts for his own purposes an ancient exegetical tradition regarding what it means to face Hell in the middle of one's days. Does it follow, then, that Dante was consciously deploying all these texts, patristic as well as biblical, when he sat down to begin the poem? Probably not. More likely he was writing out of a fund of scriptural metaphor and narrative so deeply assimilated as to be second nature – more a mother tongue than a foreign language deliberately acquired. In this regard he was no doubt like most of his contemporaries, whose experience of Scripture came primarily from the whole sensorium of medieval culture and not from study; who heard and saw the Bible rather than read it.

But unlike the vast majority of laymen in the Middle Ages, Dante seems also to have studied the Scriptures according to the major interpretive traditions of his time and place.[3] In the *Convivio* (II, xxii, 7), he speaks of consoling himself after the death of Beatrice by going to the "schools of the religious and the disputations of the philosophers," that is, to the convent schools established by the Dominicans at Santa Maria Novella and by the Franciscans at Santa Croce. In both environments he would have been exposed not only to the *lectio divina* that was a traditional part of monastic life, but also to lectures on the "sacred page" that were the final stage of theological study. Although the academic procedures of the two convents would no doubt have been similar – with an emphasis on parallel passages and chains of citation rather than on the text itself as a literary unit – the exegetical atmosphere of each was quite distinct. From the Dominicans he would have received the Thomistic methodology of the *Summa*, whereby the words of Scripture (along with citations of Aristotle and the church Fathers) serve to substantiate or dispute theological points. This technique is amply demonstrated throughout the *Paradiso*, and nowhere more strikingly than in the discourse of St. Thomas himself in *Paradiso* 13. At the Franciscan convent at Santa Croce – under the influence of such Spiritualists as Pietro di Giovanni Olivi (1248–98) and Ubertino da Casale (1259–1325) – Dante would have found a preoccupation with the Book of the Apocalypse and its relevance to contemporary history that he later refigured in the closing cantos of the *Purgatorio*.

By the year 1300, biblical scholars had access to many variant versions of St. Jerome's Latin (Vulgate) Bible, the most recent and important of which was the early thirteenth-century recension prepared at the University of Paris. This *exemplar Parisiensis* was a compact, one-volume edition of the Scriptures popular not only with university students but also with the preaching orders. Although full of textual errors that subsequently inspired the production of *correctoria*, the Paris text normalized the order of the sacred books and (thanks to Stephen Langton, d. 1228) made chapter divisions virtually the same as today's. Medieval Bibles typically presented the sacred text within a network of commentary, with citations both from the Church Fathers and more recent exegetes filling the margins of the page and running between the lines. With the text literally surrounded by interpretation, there was no unmediated encounter with it; to read the Bible was to encounter a cloud of diverse witnesses to its truth. In addition to the twelfth-century *Glossa Ordinaria*, the standard (and largely patristic) commentary on the Vulgate, a scholar also had other aids to biblical study: concordances, dictionaries, glossaries, and commentaries on individual books of Scripture.

While it is thought that Dante largely made use of the Paris text of the Vulgate (although there are other versions to be found in his writings), it is not known if he owned such a Bible himself. It is more likely that, whether in Florence or during the subsequent years of exile when he was actually at work on the *Commedia*, he relied on whatever manuscripts or scholarly resources were available to him, either in ecclesiastical libraries or through the private collections of the lords he served at Verona and Ravenna. (The cathedral library in Verona, for instance, was one of the finest in Italy.) Nor should we underestimate the degree to which the Scriptures he had at his disposal came to him through memory, and in particular through a constant exposure to the liturgy, with its biblical readings, hymns, prayers, and sequences. The Scriptures Dante uses most often come precisely from those books that are privileged by the worship of the church: the Gospels, the Psalms, and the Epistles of Paul. (Genesis, Proverbs, and Isaiah are also important sources, but for the prose treatises and epistles rather than for the *Commedia*.) That many of Dante's recollections of the Bible appear in Italian does not necessarily mean that he was using preexisting translations presently unknown to us. It is more likely that he himself turned the Scripture into the vernacular, "which is understood by the educated and the uneducated alike" (*Convivio* I, vii, 12), thereby joining his own literary efforts to those of the popular preaching orders. At the same time it must be said that some of his most personally daring appropriations of the Vulgate occur precisely in his Latin epistles (especially numbers 7 and 8), where one sees as vividly as anywhere else the degree to which Dante made the Bible his own.

The poet's use of Scripture varies in importance and technique from work to work, with the most striking difference seen in the contrast between his prose treatises and the *Commedia*. Both the *Convivio* and the *Monarchia*, for instance, are extremely rich in their use of medieval exegesis, showing real skill in the maneuver of the "sacred page" to advance an argument or bolster a claim. While the *Commedia* is certainly capable of doing likewise, demonstrating (in the *Paradiso* especially) a mastery of the various traditions of biblical interpretation, the poem characteristically makes use of the Scripture less as a source of proof texts than as a divine "pretext" for its own story.

This diversity of approach can be seen in the quite different ways Dante handles the Gospel account of the Transfiguration. In *Convivio* II, i, 5, it serves to illustrate the moral sense of Scripture: because Christ went up the mountain with only three of his twelve disciples, "we should have few companions in matters that touch us most closely." Dante refers to the episode again in *Monarchia* III, ix, 11, but this time for a quite different purpose: Peter's "hasty and unconsidered presumptuousness" on the mountain top becomes a way of arguing that when it comes to temporal responsibilities, it is the empire and not the church that should hold sway. In *Purgatorio* 32, 73–85, however, the entire biblical episode is conjured up not in order to substantiate a particular point, but rather to provide a lens through which to consider the identity of Dante and the mystery into which he is being called:

> . . . un splendor mi squarciò 'l velo
> del sonno, e un chiamar: "Surgi: che fai?"
> Quali a veder de' fioretti del melo
> che del suo pome li angeli fa ghiotti
> e perpetüe nozze fa nel cielo,
> Pietro e Giovanni e Iacopo condotti
> e vinti, ritornaro a la parola
> da la qual furon maggior sonni rotti,
> e videro scemata loro scuola
> così di Moïsè come d'Elia,
> e al maestro suo cangiata stola;
> tal torna' io.

(A splendor rent the veil of my sleep, and a call, "Arise, what are you doing?" As when brought to see some of the blossoms of the apple tree that makes the angels greedy of its fruit and holds perpetual marriage feasts in Heaven, Peter and John and James were overpowered, and came to themselves again at the word by which deeper slumbers were broken, and saw their company diminished alike by Moses and Elias, and their Master's raiment changed, so I came to myself.)

Invoked in the course of a densely scriptural simile that also pulls together allusions from the Song of Songs, the Apocalypse, and other New Testament texts, the Transfiguration functions in this canto to associate Dante with the disciples Peter, James, and John; to connect Beatrice typologically with Christ; and to ground the events of this poetic narrative in a complex tradition of allegorical and mystical interpretation.[4] But instead of following the lead of medieval commentary in its move from narrative to abstraction – that is, from the particularities of character and event to generic statements about the need for secrecy or the role of empire – biblical story is used here to generate narrative. Nor should it be forgotten that the three disciples mentioned in this simile will later engage Dante in person throughout *Paradiso* 24–26, suggesting thereby how Scripture moves in the *Commedia* from recollected text to dramatized encounter, from citation to scenario.

Not all uses of Scripture in the *Commedia*, of course, are so straightforward or so extensive. A substantial biblical text, with many implications for the poem, can be called up by a single word (as when "miserere" in *Purgatorio* 5, 24 signals Psalm 50 (51) "verse by verse") or by a bare phrase (as when "et coram patre" in *Paradiso* 11, 62 recalls Matthew 10:32–33). It can also be made present in any number of ways: exact or near-quotation, paraphrase, allusion, echo. Yet the sheer number of citations (or lack thereof) does not necessarily convey the extent of Dante's involvement in any given case. Although the Book of Exodus (33:19) is cited only once in the *Commedia* (*Paradiso* 25, 55–56), the paradigm of Israel's escape from the bondage of Egypt – an Old Testament event with a New Testament interpretation – provides one of the deep structures of the entire poem. Likewise with the Apocalypse: while cited only eight times, both the book itself and the exegetical traditions grown up around it offer a massive subtext for the last cantos of the *Purgatorio*, as well as informing the more general sense of apocalyptic crisis that impels the *Commedia* with increasing intensity.

If simple enumeration of biblical references is not in itself definitive, it is nonetheless instructive to note patterns within the three canticles. Given Dante's overt dependence on classical sources in the *Inferno*, as well as the rejection of God exemplified in those who have lost the "good of the intellect" (*Inferno* 1, 18), it comes as no surprise that Hell should include the fewest direct citations of Scripture. (When they occur, however, they do so with a kind of density, as in cantos 19, 23, and 33.) Nor is it difficult to see why in *Paradiso* biblical allusion is far more common than actual citation. The blessed have become so completely one with God's word as to assimilate it to their own speech, to pass beyond the mediation of the Scriptures and into the reality they signify – to be "ingodded" (to recall the neologism "indiarsi" which Dante invents in *Paradiso* 4, 28 to describe the state of beatitude). Where the Bible plays its most important role in the poem, however, is in the middle space of the *Purgatorio*, with its thirty direct citations and roughly forty allusions. In this realm of time and change, the souls have not yet reached an eternal destination. They remain *in via*, as needy of guidance and instruction as those who still live on earth. Small wonder, then, that in the second canticle Dante should pay such sustained attention to God's Book, showing the power of its transforming word among the penitents and thereby suggesting its importance for the living.

It is in the *Purgatorio*, moreover, that Dante stages a series of "meetings" with the Bible, the first of which takes place in canto 2 almost as soon as the "dead poetry" of Hell has been left behind. It is there that Dante compares himself (and his poem) to a boat that courses over better waters now that the infernal ocean has been left behind (*Purgatorio* 1, 1–6). It is not, however, the "little bark" of the poet's genius that we actually see, but rather a vessel filled with a hundred souls, ferried to the shores of Purgatory by an angel's "eternal wings" ("l'etterne penne," 2, 35):

> Da poppa stava il celestial nocchiero,
> tal che parea beato per iscripto;
> e più di cento spirti entro sediero.

"*In exitu Isräel de Aegypto*"
cantavan tutti insieme ad una voce
con quanto di quel salmo è poscia scripto.
(*Purgatorio* 2, 43–48)

(At the stern stood the celestial steersman, such, that blessedness seemed to
be inscribed upon him; and within sat more than a hundred spirits. "*In exitu
Israel de Aegypto*" all of them were singing with one voice, with the rest of the
psalm as it is written.)

The descent into Hell ended with the confused gibberish of Nimrod ("Raphèl
maì amècche zabì almi," *Inferno* 31, 67) and the wordless slobbering of Satan
(34, 55–60). Here, by contrast, is a fresh beginning for language: an infusion
of God's word sailing into the sea of poetic discourse. With its Latin words
cutting their way into Dante's vernacular, the Scripture makes its formal
entrance into the *Commedia*, "beato per iscripto." For as the souls of the
redeemed sing as with one voice the incipit of Psalm 113 (114), along with
"the rest of the psalm as it is written," they bring with them the poem's
first exact citation of the Vulgate. It is not just any song of redemption that
they sing: rather, Dante places in their mouths a celebration of the Exodus
of Israel from Egypt that from the time of the early Fathers had served
Christian exegetes as the textbook example of the four interpretive senses of
Scripture. According to this reading, the historical event of the Exodus (the
literal sense of the psalm) at once signifies Christ's spiritual deliverance from
death (the allegorical), a release from the bondage of sin (the moral), and
the expectation of future glory (the anagogical). By placing this particular
text in the foreground of the *Purgatorio*, Dante both claims the Exodus
as a prefigurement of his own journey of conversion, and joins his literary
enterprise to the exegetical traditions of the church. The inscription of "*In
exitu Israel de Aegypto*" into his narrative in effect launches the *Purgatorio*
as self-consciously biblical poetry.

It also begins a program of scriptural and liturgical reference that structures the seven terraces of purgation. On the terrace of pride (*Purgatorio*
10–12), for instance, Dante sees numerous examples of biblical (as well as
pagan) figures who either enjoin the virtue of humility or demonstrate the
wages of arrogance. As if in illustration of how the Middle Ages "stori-
ated" (10, 73) the text of Scripture in the visual arts, Dante first presents
a program of bas reliefs that "tells" biblical narrative in the fashion of a
carving, a painting, or a manuscript illumination. In the first of these, a
portrait of Mary and the archangel Gabriel at the Annunciation, the poet
deliberately emphasizes the scripted nature of such visual representation

by having the silent image seem to speak the words of the Vulgate (Luke 1:28–38):

> Giurato si sarìa ch'el dicesse "*Ave!*";
>   perché iv'era imaginata quella
>   ch'ad aprir l'alto amor volse la chiave;
> e avea in atto impressa esta favella
>   "*Ecce ancilla Dei,*" propriamente
>   come figura in cera si suggella.
>
> (Purgatorio 10, 40–45)

(One would have sworn that he was saying "*Ave!*"; for there she was imaged who turned the key to open supreme love, and these words were imprinted in her attitude: "*Ecce ancilla Dei,*" as expressly as a figure is stamped on wax.)

Yet another kind of figural art is incorporated in canto 12, where the pavement running along the terrace of pride resembles a church floor sculpted with the images of those buried underneath. On the unfolding "page" of that pavement Dante reads the examples of punished arrogance, beginning with the fall of Satan (12, 25–27) and concluding with "Troy in ashes and caverns" (12, 61–63). Although the scriptural example comes first, as if to indicate its priority not only in time but in importance, the images on the pavement (as on the walls of the terrace) freely combine the biblical tradition with the "scriptures of the pagans." Both function as visual texts to transform the souls who study their collected witness.

Purgatorio, then, describes a process in which the penitents working their way along the terraces are in effect being rewritten by the "storied" art work they see; their spiritual development takes place in response to narrative. Dante underscores their active participation in this metamorphosis not only by having the souls sing psalms or hymns or the prayers of the church, but also by having them paraphrase the word of God in their own language. Thus at the beginning of canto 11 (1–24), coming after the experience of the bas relief murals and before that of the figured pavement, he hears them praying the Pater Noster. But rather than repeating the Latin of this venerable text as it appears in the Vulgate Gospel of Matthew (6:9–13) or in the liturgy of the church, the prayer is said in Italian, in what is not so much a translation of the words of Christ as a scholastic gloss on them. Dante says that the souls are "praying good speed for themselves" (*Purgatorio* 11, 25). Yet instead of reciting sacred text, they are recreating it in the hybrid idiom of Aristotle and Aquinas – not as the *Summa* might, in metaphor-free prose, but in the *terza rima* of Dante's poetry.

O padre nostro, che ne' cieli stai,
  non circumscritto, ma per più amore
  ch' ai primi effetti di là sù tu hai,
  laudato sia 'l tuo nome e 'l tuo valore
  da ogne creatura, com'è degno
  di render grazie al tuo dolce vapore.
                    (*Purgatorio* 11, 1–6)

("Our father, who art in Heaven, not circumscribed, but through the greater
love Thou hast for Thy first works on high,
  Praised be Thy name and Thy worth by every creature, as it is meet to render
thanks to Thy sweet effluence.")

This translation of the Vulgate into the vernacular, together with the theological elaboration upon the scriptural text, can also be seen throughout the
Purgatorio in Dante's working with the Beatitudes. These revered sayings of
Christ, taken from the Sermon on the Mount in Matthew 5:3–12 (cf. Luke
6:20–24), are delivered by an angel at the exit to each terrace, thereby signalling that a given capital sin has been purged away and a corresponding
virtue attained. In all cases but one, the Beatitude is indicated by a single Latin
word or catchphrase, with the listener supplying the rest of the familiar saying even as he or she is meant to complete it in practice. After the purgation
of pride, for instance, Dante notes that "'*Beati pauperes spiritu*' was sung
so sweetly as no words could tell" (*Purgatorio* 12, 110–11). Here only the
initial phrase of the first Beatitude is given, but in keeping with the common
liturgical practice of versicle and response, the proclamation "Blessed are the
poor in spirit" is meant to elicit the remainder of the verse, "for theirs is the
kingdom of heaven." Dante repeats this simple citation of the Vulgate once
again on the seventh and last terrace of the mountain ("he sang '*Beati mundo
corde*'" 27, 8), but otherwise he varies his practice. Sometimes Vulgate quotation dissolves into the vernacular, as on the terrace of sloth when the angel
"moved his feathers and fanned us, declaring '*Qui lugent*' to be blessed, for
they shall have their souls possessed of consolation" (19, 49–51). Elsewhere
the Latin is dropped entirely, as on the terrace of gluttony where the angel
does not so much translate the Vulgate's "Blessed are those who hunger and
thirst after righteousness" as paraphrase it almost beyond recognition:

E senti' dir: "Beati cui alluma
  tanto di grazia, che l'amor del gusto
  nel petto lor troppo disir non fuma,
  esurïendo sempre quanto è giusto!"
                    (*Purgatorio* 24, 151–54)

(And I heard say, "Blessed are they who are so illumined by grace that the love of taste kindles not too great desire in their breasts, and who hunger always so far as is just.")

This absorption of the Vulgate into the poet's vernacular shows on a minutely linguistic level the larger effort of the *Commedia* to rewrite the Bible. Normally in Dante, rewriting also means refutation and revision, a "looking again" at an ancient text that most often entails a correction of its pagan limitations (as with the *Aeneid*), or an attempt to surpass its technical achievement (as with the *Metamorphoses*). With the Scripture, however, the poet was dealing with God's own Book: "For though there be many writers of the divine word, there is but one who dictates it, God, who was pleased to reveal himself to us by using many pens" (*Monarchia* III, iv, 11, cf. *Paradiso* 29, 40–41). To speak of the poet's "revision" of the Bible, therefore, means his attempt to see it again and to see it anew.

A fresh look at Scripture is quite literally what the poet offers the reader in *Purgatorio* 29. At the Edenic summit of the mountain, a flash of light from the east ushers in a procession of allegorical figures. It begins with a file of twenty-four old men walking two by two. Behind them come four winged animals who escort a splendid griffin-drawn chariot. Following this ensemble there is yet another file of elders: first a pair of old men, then a quartet of males who appear "of lowly aspect," and finally a single old man with eyes closed. Once all these figures take their place, the canto ends. The stage is now set for the advent of Beatrice in *Purgatorio* 30.

Drawing on a rich store of imagery found first in the prophet Ezekiel and then in the revelation to St. John the Divine, this elaborate and quasi-liturgical procession not only rehearses visionary moments in both testaments, but gives us a vision of the Bible itself. For what Dante sees assembled before him is the word of God made allegorical flesh; it is the canon of Scripture unfolding in time, from the Alpha of Genesis to the Omega of the Apocalypse. To begin, the twenty-four elders stand for the books of the Hebrew Scriptures, as they were enumerated by St. Jerome in his prologue to the Vulgate. The four winged animals who come next in line are a traditional representation of the Gospels, while the company that follows upon the chariot symbolizes the rest of the New Testament: the Pauline epistles and the Acts of the Apostles paired together, the four Catholic epistles (Peter, James, John, and Jude) walking behind them, and the revelation to St. John the Divine at the very end, as the canon's last word.

In the spirit of John's Apocalypse, Dante does not explain his vision or (aside from strong iconographic clues) make these attributions directly. Nor has the commentary tradition been of one mind about it: in the fourteenth and fifteenth centuries, for instance, there were other candidates for the figures towards the end of the procession, with the four men "of lowly aspect" identified as the great doctors of the church (Augustine, Jerome, Ambrose, and Gregory the Great), and the single old man with his eyes shut glossed either as Moses or Bernard of Clairvaux. Nonetheless, what has come to be the received reading of the procession interprets it as Dante's presentation of the books of the Old and New Testaments, a massive pageant of scriptural revelation no longer experienced in the fragmentary form of biblical citation and allusion, but taken as a unity – as God's *bibliotheca*.

Often missed, however, is the subtle way in which this vision of the Bible reflects the poet's engagement in controversy over the extent of the canon and the internal arrangement of the sacred text. For in choosing to follow Jerome's by no means undisputed limitation of the Hebrew Scriptures to twenty-four books, Dante was eliminating those "deuterocanonical" works which the church included within its Latin Bible (and which he does not scruple to cite elsewhere in the *Commedia*). Likewise, in having the Acts of the Apostles and the Pauline epistles walk next to one another in procession, he seems to settle an early thirteenth-century disagreement between Stephen Langton and the editors of the Paris text quite simply by mooting it. Whereas Langton arranged the sequence of New Testament books that subsequently became canonical – Acts, Pauline epistles, Catholic epistles – the University of Paris reversed this order by having the letters of Peter, James, John, and Jude follow directly upon Acts and therefore precede Paul.[5] Dante settles this academic dispute not by choosing one authority over the other, but by rendering the choice unnecessary. In his processional order of biblical books, the Catholic epistles follow directly behind both Acts *and* the Pauline corpus.

Elsewhere in *Purgatorio* 29 he does not hesitate to make a choice. In the course of describing the winged animals that represent the Gospels, he tells his readers that if more detail is necessary they should read Ezekiel, "and such as you shall find them on his pages, such were they here, except that, as to the wings, John is with me, and differs from him" (29, 103–05). At first glance there is nothing surprising here. The poet acknowledges dependence on his Old Testament source (Ezekiel 1:4) but sides with a New Testament appropriation (Apocalypse 4:8). With one testament believed to fulfill the other, it is easy to see that six wings might be a more authoritative count than four. Except that what the poet actually says here is a good deal more astounding. It is not, as one might expect, "I am with John" – that is, following in a tradition, acknowledging the greater claim of the "last" book in the New Testament – but "Giovanni è meco," "John is with me." If Ezekiel's vision has been supplanted by John's, then the truth of the latter is quite simply certified by Dante's pronouncement. The poet chooses between scriptural accounts not by appealing to higher authority or exegetical precedent or any other strategy available to the master of the "sacred page"; rather, he judges between witnesses strictly on the basis of what he saw. The authority of first-hand account lies with him; he has the last word.

So powerful is the force of Dante's repeated claims to vision, it is easy to forget that the enormous authority of his work is largely his own creation. As a layman, he had no particular standing in the church; as an exile, he had no base of political power. And yet despite his essential marginality as a "party of one" – the earthly fate predicted for him in *Paradiso* 17, 69 – his conviction of a divine call resounds throughout his writings; it enables the poet to take every license. In the *Commedia*, of course, self-doubt about his calling is expressed early on by the pilgrim: "I am not Aeneas, I am not Paul" (*Inferno*, 2, 32); but his hesitation is soon overcome once assurance is given that heaven is behind the venture. This wavering of the pilgrim might conceivably be taken as a sign of humility on the author's part; yet it is also undoubtedly a strategy intended to link Dante's fears with those of Moses, Isaiah, Jeremiah, and Ezekiel – all prophets who initially doubted their fitness for the call that God had given them.

One way to view the *Commedia*, in fact, is as an extended call narrative, a story about the making of a prophet. Dante worries at first that he is neither Aeneas nor Paul, and yet after receiving the news that heaven has intervened on his behalf, he comes gradually to learn that he has been rescued from the dark wood for a purpose beyond himself. Beatrice tells him in *Purgatorio* 32, 103–05 that the visions afforded him are "for the profit of the world that lives ill"; therefore when he returns from the journey, he is meant (like John the Divine in Apocalypse 1:11) to write down what he sees. Later in *Paradiso*, after first identifying himself with Paul in his rapture to the third heaven (*Paradiso* 1, 73–75, cf. 2 Corinthians 12:2–4), Dante is told by Cacciaguida to make manifest all that he has beheld, to let his cry be as the wind upon the mountain top, like the prophet's voice in Isaiah 40:9 (*Paradiso* 17, 133–35). Finally, no less an authority than Peter himself commissions Dante to tell the whole story when he returns below: "open your mouth and do not hide what I hide not" (27, 65–66).

By this late point in the narrative, Dante's vocation has been reinforced by the validation of almost one hundred cantos. And yet it has in reality been full blown within the text at least from the time of *Inferno* 19 when the voice of the pilgrim merges with that of the poet in assuming apostolic authority. In a canto that begins with the poet's tirade against a corrupt papacy – "O Simon mago, o miseri seguaci" ("O Simon Magus! O you his wretched followers," *Inferno* 19, 1) – the pilgrim is also licensed to speak no less boldly. Likened to a friar who hears the last confession of an assassin, he holds back for a moment in fear of madness before delivering a scathing prophetic judgment on the church to the soul of Pope Nicholas III:

> Deh, or mi dì: quanto tesoro volle
> Nostro Segnore in prima da san Pietro
>   ch' ei ponesse le chiavi in sua balìa?
>   Certo non chiese se non "Viemmi retro."
> Né Pier né li altri tolsero a Matia
>   oro od argento, quando fu sortito
>   al loco che perdé l'anima ria.
> Pero ti sta, ché tu se' ben punito.
>
> (*Inferno* 19, 90–97)

("Pray now tell me how much treasure did our Lord require of Peter before he put the keys into his keeping? Surely he asked nothing save: 'Follow me.' Nor did Peter or the others take gold or silver of Matthias when he was chosen for the office which the guilty soul had lost. Therefore stay right here, for you are justly punished.")

In an extended diatribe (19, 90–117) that cites Matthew and Acts, Isaiah and the Apocalypse, the pilgrim shows all the assurance of a preacher who knows his Scripture by heart; who also knows that the church has abandoned the Gospel not only for silver and gold, but for vain inventions and "junk" ("ciance," *Paradiso* 29, 110; Cf. *Paradiso* 11, 133–35). Ordained to deliver the word of God by no other authority than his baptism, he dares to appropriate for himself the boldness of apostolic speech, making himself in effect a successor to Peter.

The actual succession that Dante claims, both for himself and his poem, is found in *Paradiso* 25, 64–78. In the course of an examination on the theological virtues – an exam conducted by the three apostolic witnesses to the Transfiguration – Dante is asked by James about the nature of Christian hope and how he came to know it. His definition comes straight from the *Sentences* of Peter Lombard (III, xxvi, 1), but his actual knowledge is an inheritance from Scripture. It was David, the "supreme singer" (*Paradiso* 25, 72) of the Psalter, who first instilled hope in him with a specific text, Psalm 9:11 (10), here rendered in Italian: "Sperino in te . . . /coloro che sanno il nome tuo" ("Let them hope in Thee who know Thy name"). Afterwards, and following the testamental sequence of Scripture, he recalls that it was James himself who made him hopeful, adding the testimony of his epistle to the prior "instilling" of David's psalm. Then, after acknowledging his debt to what is described earlier as the "plenteous rain of the Holy Spirit which is poured over the old and over the new parchments" (*Paradiso* 24, 91–93),

Dante places himself in the path of this ever-flowing stream. Having received the abundance of the Scriptures, he tells James that he is "full, and pour again your shower upon others" ("io son pieno,/ e in altrui vostra pioggia repluo," 25, 77–78). Standing in the line of biblical authorities, and receiving from them the Spirit's inspiration, he proposes himself as a vessel of election. It is as if a third testament will flow from his pen.

In one sense, the giving away of the Bible's gifts is the duty of any believer, just as the virtue of hope is something meant to be shared. The whole burden of the *Commedia*, however, is that Dante is not simply a Christian Everyman, but someone who has been uniquely allowed to go in the flesh "from Egypt to Jerusalem" in order to write what he sees, to tell what he hears – in order, that is, to produce a poem he will not scruple to call "sacred." Indeed, at the very beginning of *Paradiso* 25, before having the pilgrim position himself at the end of a biblical line, Dante speaks unabashedly about himself as a writer and about the identity of his work. If it should ever come that he is able to return to Florence as "poeta" (25, 8), to receive a crown at the font of his baptism, it will be because of the efficacy of the word he has written, because of "the sacred poem to which heaven and earth have so set hand" (25, 1–2). In the *Monarchia* Dante had said that the divine author of Scripture delights in using many pens (III, iv, 11); here he makes it plain that one of them has been held by him. Appropriating for his own enterprise the doctrine of biblical inspiration, according to which "prophecy came not by the will of man at any time: but the holy men of God spoke inspired by the Holy Ghost" (2 Peter 1:21), Dante asks the reader to see him as the earthly partner in a sacred collaboration. He is God's scribe.

These claims are also reinforced by the Epistle to Can Grande, which suggests that the *Commedia* should be read according to the fourfold interpretation reserved for Scripture alone. Indeed, the text used to explicate the multiplicity of the poem's "senses" or levels of meaning is none other than Psalm 113 (114), "In Exitu Israel de Aegypto," the same stock example often chosen by the masters of the "sacred page" to demonstrate the principles of biblical exegesis. The implication is that, like God, Dante writes not only in metaphors, but also in events: the journey he describes in his "sacred poem" is as historical as the Exodus itself. His word is gospel.

The profusion of illustrated manuscripts and commentaries that began to appear almost immediately after its completion suggests the extent to which the *Commedia* was treated like Scripture early on, despite some clerical objections to its unorthodoxies (the Limbo of virtuous pagans, for instance). And yet, also from the beginning, the precise nature of that likeness has been in dispute. Dante's own son, Pietro Alighieri, said that the literal level of the poem was like a biblical figure of speech: the journey through the afterlife should be interpreted, therefore, as if it were on the same level as the Scripture's talk about the "arm of God."[6] Thus the reality of the poem lies not in the letter, but in what it conceals: to take it otherwise would be to turn his father into a madman. But if Pietro emphasizes the poetic component of the "poema sacro," another early fourteenth-century commentator, Guido da Pisa, stresses the sacred calling of both poet and poem: his Dante was "the pen of the Holy Spirit with which the Spirit speedily wrote for us the punishment of the damned and the glory of the blessed."[7]

This divergence among the first readers of the poem has continued until the present, with ongoing critical disagreement over what it means to call Dante a "prophet," or a mystic, or someone who imitated God's way of writing. These matters are never likely to be settled as long as Dante is treated seriously and on his own complex terms. For one of the achievements of the *Commedia* is precisely its dialectic between human poetry and divine text, between fiction and truth. Despite the clarity of its distinctions, the "sacred poem" insists on the blurring of lines. In its lexicon, "scrittura" means both Scripture and writing.

To an extent unexampled in European literature, Dante reimagined the world of the Bible and turned its sacred *figura* into his own literary "fulfillment." What this entailed most obviously was the transformation of biblical character, narrative, and typology into the vernacular of his imagination: his reinvention of the Exodus, for instance, or his re-presentation of the apostle Paul in his own self. One can also speak of how the *Commedia* revives the first-person discourse of biblical prophecy and apocalyptic, or note Dante's aspiration to be another psalmist, "the supreme singer of the Supreme Leader" (*Paradiso* 25, 72). In all these ways the poet rewrites Scripture precisely by continuing to write it – if not as a third testament, then as a sacred poem that is fully aware of itself as a work of literature. Imitating God's Book in its straightforward assertions of "I saw" and "It came to pass," Dante nonetheless produces a text that insists on its own artfulness and its human authorship, on the inescapably literary medium of the poet's divine vocation. For the *Commedia*'s "Write what you see" is at once a command to an apostle and the behest of the muse. It comes as the word of the Lord "for profit of the world that lives ill" (*Purgatorio* 32, 103), while never ceasing to be the work of one who turned God's profit to a poet's pleasure.

NOTES

1 Aldo Manetti, "Dante e la Bibbia," *Bollettino della Civica Biblioteca* (Bergamo, 1984), p. 122.
2 St. Jerome, *Commentarium in Esaiam liber xi*, Corpus Christianorum series latina, 73 (Turnholt: Brepols, 1963), p. 446.

3 Charles T. Davis, "Education in Dante's Florence," in *Dante's Italy* (Philadelphia: University of Pennsylvania Press, 1984), pp. 137–65.

4 For the importance of the Transfiguration in Dante, see Jeffrey T. Schnapp, *The Transfiguration of History at the Center of Dante's Paradise* (Princeton: Princeton University Press, 1986), pp. 92–120.

5 C. Spicq, *Esquisse d'une histoire de l'exégèse latine au moyen âge* (Paris: Vrin, 1944), p. 162.

6 Pietro Alighieri, *Super Dantis ipsius genitorius Comoediam commentarium*, ed. V. Nannucci (Florence: G. Piatti, 1845), I, pp. 4–8.

7 Guido da Pisa, *Commentary on Dante's Inferno*, ed. Vincent Cioffari (Albany: State University of New York Press, 1974), p. 4.

SUGGESTED READING

Barblan, Giovanni, ed., *Dante e la Bibbia* (Florence: Olschki, 1988).

De Lubac, Henri, S. J., *Medieval Exegesis,* trans. Mark Sebanc (Grand Rapids, MI: Wm. B. Eerdmans, 1998).

Dronke, Peter, *Dante and Medieval Latin Traditions* (Cambridge: Cambridge University Press, 1986).

Hawkins, Peter S., *Dante's Testaments: Essays in Scriptural Imagination* (Stanford: Stanford University Press, 1999).

Kleinhenz, Christopher, "Biblical Citation in Dante's *Divine Comedy,*" *Annali d'italianistica* 8 (1990): 346–59.

Lampe, G. W. H., ed., *Cambridge History of the Bible,* II, *The West, from the Fathers to the Reformation* (Cambridge: Cambridge University Press, 1969).

Lourdaux, W., and D. Verhelst, eds., *The Bible and Medieval Culture* (Louvain: Louvai University Press, 1979).

Manetti, Aldo, "Dante e la Bibbia," *Bollettino della Civica Biblioteca* (Bergamo, 1984): 100–28.

Nardi, Bruno, "Dante Profeta," in Paolo Mezzantini, ed., *Dante e la cultura medievale,* 2nd edn. (Bari: Laterza, 1983), pp. 265–326.

Ocker, Christopher, *Biblical Poetics Before Reformation and Humanism* (Cambridge: Cambridge University Press, 2002).

Penna, Angelo, "Bibbia," in U. Bosco, ed., *Enciclopedia dantesca,* 6 vols. (Rome: Istituto dell'Enciclopedia Italiana, 1970–78), 1:626–29.

Petrucci, Armando, *Writers and Readers in Medieval Italy: Studies in the History of Written Culture,* ed. and trans. Charles M. Radding (New Haven: Yale University Press, 1995).

Riché, Pierre, and Guy Lobrichon, eds., *Le Moyen Age et la Bible,* Bible de Tous les Temps, 4 (Paris: Beauchesne, 1984).

Singleton, Charles S., *Dante's Commedia: Elements of Structure* (Baltimore: The Johns Hopkins University Press, 1977).

Smalley, Beryl, *The Study of the Bible in the Middle Ages* (Notre Dame, IN: University of Notre Dame Press, 1964; rpt 1951).

Swanson, R. N., *Religion and Devotion in Europe, c. 1215–1515,* Cambridge Medieval Textbooks (Cambridge: Cambridge University Press, 1995).

Truijen, Vincent, "Scrittura," in *Enciclopedia dantesca,* V, pp. 93–102.

9

KEVIN BROWNLEE

Dante and the classical poets

Introduction: mimesis and literary models

Although all medieval literature in the romance vernaculars may be characterized – even defined – as a sustained, dynamic response to the classical canon, Dante's *Divina Commedia* is an altogether exceptional case. For, in a variety of fundamental ways, the entire *Commedia* is built on a series of extended encounters with four Latin poets: Virgil, Statius, Lucan, and Ovid. The *Commedia*'s plot line figures these encounters in four principal (and interrelated) manners. First, Dante-protagonist meets and interacts with all four poets, who are characters in his poem. Second, Dante-protagonist undergoes (and/or witnesses) a series of key experiences that are visibly modelled on narrative events from the *Aeneid*, the *Thebaid*, the *Pharsalia*, and the *Metamorphoses*. The most important, frequent, and systematic instances of this process involve two alternatives: either Dante-protagonist functions as a new, Christian, Aeneas, modeled on the single protagonist of Virgil's epic; or he functions as a corrected version of one of the many protagonists of Ovid's multi-narrative epic. Third, Dante-protagonist encounters characters from the four Latin epic poems, who serve both to link the *Commedia* to these authoritative model texts, and to figure their mimetic status within the poetic economy of Dante's work. Certain of these key characters also function as metonymic representations of their "source texts" and are used to comment on them, either implicitly or explicitly. The two most striking instances of this are the group of four diviners (Amphiaraus, Tiresias, Aruns, and Manto) in *Inferno* 20, and the figure of Cato in *Purgatorio* 1 and 2. Fourth, Dante-author explicitly names his privileged *auctores* in various ways as part of the ongoing drama of the writing of the *Commedia*, which is such an essential element in that first-person narrative. Important instances occur in *Inferno* 25, 94–102 when Dante-author apostrophizes Lucan and Ovid, and in *Paradiso* 15, 26 when he introduces Cacciaguida with a Virgilian reference that identifies the Latin poet as "nostra maggior musa." In both of these instances, authorial naming functions to establish a problematic distance between Dante-*poeta* and his classical models. This process is related to the explicit discussions of the *auctores*' texts that take place at the level of the *Commedia*'s plot: Virgil on the *Aeneid* in *Inferno* 13 and 20, and *Purgatorio* 6; Statius on the *Aeneid*, the fourth *Eclogue*, and (more briefly) the *Thebaid* in *Purgatorio* 21–22; Matelda on (primarily) the *Metamorphoses* in *Purgatorio* 28, 139–44. Linked to these authorial namings are the more or less visible citations, in Latin or in Italian, of passages from the *Commedia*'s four key model classical texts.

In the case of each of Dante's principal Latin poetic models, therefore, a double mimesis is involved: the *Commedia* represents both the poet and his text. At the same time, I suggest, the *Commedia* programmatically inscribes various tensions between each classical author and his poetic corpus. What emerges is a split, a differentiation, between *auctor* and text in terms of the Christian poetics of Dante's work. We have in each case a profound (and ultimately unresolvable) ambivalence on the part of Dante-author towards his four classical model authors that results in a variety of mimetic oppositions. The present essay will explore in some detail both the *Commedia*'s double mimesis of its major Latin models in terms of author versus text, and the different ambivalencies built into this mimesis.

First, a few preliminary remarks are necessary. The most fundamental reason for the profound ambivalence that characterizes Dante's relationship to and representation of his master *poetae* is quite simply that he uses these classical models to articulate Christian truth. And this basic fact of the poetics of the *Commedia* is directly linked to the poem's own claims to the literal-historical truth of the narrative events that constitute its plot, resulting in two key hermeneutic assumptions. First, Dante reads the four Latin epics as if they were history, that is, the record of real events in the past (*historia*), rather than either verisimilar or visibly invented fictions (*argumentum* or *fabula*). Their truth status means that the Latin epic poems can be read as directly linked to, and significant for, Christian salvation history, as *scriptura paganorum*. This hermeneutic approach to the classical corpus is, of course, employed by other medieval writers, but Dante's use of it is virtually unique in its rigor, consistency, and complexity. Second, Dante is thereby able to read his Latin poets figuratively. While both these basic hermeneutic constructs had been employed by earlier medieval writers to varying degrees, Dante developed – and exploited – them in hitherto untried ways.

In both contexts, Dante's theological politics play a particularly important role. By privileging the Roman empire within Christian salvation history, the *Commedia* presents Virgil and the *Aeneid* as the fundamental point of departure with regard to its own political vision, against which the other three *auctores* are meant to be read. The pro-Virgilian stance of Statius (most explicitly, at the end of the *Thebaid*), and the anti-Virgilian stance of Lucan (as an anti-imperial, pro-republican poet), are thus directly relevant to the *Commedia*'s mimesis of these two poets. Ovid seems to involve something qualitatively different.

A final preliminary point: each of the four key classical models is treated differently within the mimesis of the *Commedia*, as authorial character, as privileged text, and in terms of the relation between the two.

Dante's Virgil and Dante's *Aeneid*

Virgil's function as character is multiple: it involves two major components, each of which undergoes a dynamic development over the course of the poem. First and foremost, he is Dante's authoritative guide through Hell and up the mountain of Purgatory. Second, Virgil is the real, historical author of the *Aeneid*, the *Eclogues*, and the *Georgics*. Both these aspects of Virgil's character involve a fundamental ambiguity. As Dante's guide, Virgil is both immensely authoritative and fundamentally limited: he can lead Dante out of Hell and up to the Garden of Eden, but he himself is condemned to return to Limbo. As Dante's author, Virgil's ambivalence is even more pointed. For the fact of his personal damnation contrasts most strikingly with the Christian salvific power attributed by the *Commedia* to the *Aeneid* and the fourth *Eclogue*.

At the same time, the text of the *Aeneid*, especially book 6, provides a privileged model for Dante's otherworldly journey, most obviously in the *Inferno*, but also – and more surprisingly – in the *Paradiso*. Here again, a dynamic development takes place with regard to the function of the *Aeneid* as textual model. And here again, an unrelenting ambivalence is at issue.

Virgil's initial appearance in *Inferno* 1 establishes both his authority as Dante's guide, and his limitations in terms of Christian truth. He is presented as the supreme "poeta" for whom Dante-protagonist has particular reverence (1, 85). After saving Dante from the *lupa* he proleptically describes the salvific journey on which he will lead his charge, but his description, however, simultaneously involves the limits of Virgil's power: his absolute exclusion from God's elect (1, 125). *Inferno* 2 reconfirms and elaborates Virgil's authority to be Dante's guide by deriving it ultimately from the Virgin Mary, mediated by St. Lucy and by Beatrice. At the same time, Dante-protagonist is presented as a new Christian Aeneas by means of the famous double denial that serves to epitomize his sense of unworthiness to undertake the journey: "I am not Aeneas, I am not Paul" (2, 32).

The beginning of the otherworldly journey proper in *Inferno* 3 initiates the programmatic function both of Virgil as Dante's authoritative guide, and of *Aeneid* 6 as the privileged textual model for Dante's infernal descent. In both cases, the significant and systematic differences between the Italian poem and its Latin model work to highlight the former's Christian spiritual dimension. This is evident in each of the encounters with major characters and places from Aeneas' journey (most often presented as obstacles to be overcome), beginning with the liminal river Acheron and the infernal ferryman Charon in *Inferno* 3, 78–129 (cf. *Aeneid* 6, 295–330).

Inferno 4 may be seen as an epitome of this process in that the *locus amoenus* of Dante's Limbo is clearly modeled on the Elysian Fields from *Aeneid* 6. Here we encounter the virtuous pagan poets, who have, in effect, achieved paradise on their own terms, which means, by definition, not on those of the Christian God. The built-in limitations of the highest pagan poetic achievement are thus graphically illustrated, even as this achievement is celebrated. This is Virgil the character's permanent abode within Dante's Christian poetic universe. Here we have the second (and much more elaborate) statement at the level of plot (and again, by Virgil himself) of the ultimate failure of the classical poets in Christian terms, the reason for their damnation, and for Virgil's own permanent place in this ironically (tragically) privileged infernal location: the lack of baptism (*Inferno* 4, 34–42). To this absolute difference between Dante and the classical poets in terms of Christian faith is contrasted the shared poetic identity to which Dante-author aspires, as the "bella scola" of the classical poets honor Dante-protagonist by including him among their number (4, 100–05). It is in this context that Virgil's authoritative status is re-emphasized as he is addressed by the others as "l'altissimo poeta" (4, 80).

Over the course of the journey through Upper Hell, Virgil's authority is repeatedly foregrounded in his many successful confrontations with guardian figures. By contrast, Virgil's limits (in authority, in knowledge, and in faith) are strikingly dramatized before the Gates of Dis in *Inferno* 8, 82–*Inferno* 9, 106, the entry at once to Lower Hell in general, and to the sixth circle in particular. Here Virgil not only is unable to effect an entrance for himself and his charge, but doubts the divine promise of his success (*Inferno* 9, 7–9). It is important to note that the density of references to *Aeneid* 6 falls off sharply from this point on in the *Inferno*, and with a certain logic, since the Virgilian Aeneas does not enter Tartarus. *Aeneid* 6 as model is thus most visible and most relevant only for the *Commedia*'s Upper Hell, a fact underscored by the uniquely Christian status of the sixth circle (heresy), which thus functions as a kind of theological boundary vis-à-vis the literal journey of Aeneas as recounted in Virgil's text.

By contrast, Lower Hell provides the *cantica*'s two most visibly self-conscious treatments of the *Aeneid* as text, involving explicit citation at the level of the Dantean plot in order to valorize the Virgilian *scriptura*. The encounter with Pier della Vigna in *Inferno* 13 (overtly modeled on *Aeneid* 3, 22–48) dramatically demonstrates the *Aeneid*'s literal truth. The encounter with Manto in *Inferno* 20 dramatically stages the "corrective rewriting" of a key passage from the *Aeneid* (10, 198–200) in order to protect the Virgilian epic from any taint of "divination." At the same time, Lower Hell continues the strikingly bipartite representation of Virgil the character, in his capacity (and in his efficacy) as guide.

In the *Purgatorio* a fundamentally different situation obtains with regard to the status both of Virgil as character and of the *Aeneid* as text. First of all, this is new and uniquely Christian poetic territory, and *Aeneid* 6 can thus no longer function as a putatively historical model for Dante-protagonist's purgatorial journey. Second, the purgatorial Virgil is portrayed from the outset as having no direct knowledge of the place, in striking contradistinction to the infernal Virgil's past experience of Hell. A new – and fundamental – limitation for Virgil the character is thus explicitly introduced at the entrance to the second realm, though he continues to function as an active guide in moral (and philosophical) terms throughout the ascent of the purgatorial mountain. The climax of this role comes as Virgil successfully encourages Dante-protagonist to cross through the fiery wall on the seventh terrace (*Purgatorio* 27, 20–54), thus completing the ascent. In the liminal space at the final step (27, 125), Virgil explicitly announces the successful completion of his role as Dante's guide, affirming his own efficacy, while simultaneously articulating his geographic and spiritual limit. Virgil's final gesture as guide is therefore to crown and miter Dante over himself (27, 140–42).

Virgil, the character, is thus no more than a silent witness to the entrance into the Earthly Paradise (*Purgatorio* 28) and the biblical pageant (*Purgatorio* 29). The actual moment of his disappearance from the poem as a character simultaneously foregrounds the continuing presence of the text of the *Aeneid* in the *Commedia*, since the poignant dramatization of Virgil's damnation, his return to the Limbo that is his eternal Dantean abode, takes place in large part by means of a complex rewriting of a key scene from *Aeneid* 4, which underscores the fundamental difference between the *Commedia*'s mimesis of Virgil the character and its representation of his text. When Dante-protagonist sees Beatrice for the first time, his intense affective reaction is so powerfully mediated by the Virgilian subtext that the scene is presented as a recasting of that moment in *Aeneid* 4 when Dido begins to realize that she has fallen in love with the Trojan hero. In the following narrative sequence – arguably the most dramatic in the entire *Commedia* – Dante-protagonist confidently turns toward his beloved guide and discovers that Virgil has vanished. Yet even as the "altissimo poeta" disappears as character, his text remains, functioning, indeed, as the very means of articulating the character's disappearance. At the same time, the Virgilian text – as correctively reread by the *Commedia* – continues to provide a model for the ongoing personal salvation history of Dante-protagonist.

Dante-poet's recuperative reading of the *Aeneid* allows it to serve as a textual model in the *Purgatorio* almost from the beginning, though its status as literal-historical model for the *Commedia* ended with *Inferno* 34. Various key moments of Dante-protagonist's purgatorial journey are thus meant to be read figuratively against subtexts from the *Aeneid*, though this process is almost wholly restricted to the Ante-Purgatory, highlighted by the encounter with the scarred Manfred (*Purgatorio* 3, 108–12). In addition, the Virgilian Elysian Fields serve in part as textual models for both the Valley of the Princes (*Purgatorio* 7–8) and the Earthly Paradise (in *Purgatorio* 28–33). On the purgatorial terraces, the text of the *Aeneid* functions in a somewhat different way, providing *exempla* (both positive and negative) which are an integral part of the divine mechanism of purgation.

At the level of plot, there are two explicit treatments of the status of the *Aeneid* in the *Purgatorio*. The first takes place in the Ante-Purgatory (*Purgatorio* 6, 28–48), as Dante-protagonist questions Virgil on the truth of the *Aeneid* as "doctrine" wih regard to the efficacy of prayer in the Palinurus episode (*Aeneid* 6, 376). In contradistinction to the infernal Virgil's "correction" of the *Aeneid* in *Inferno* 20, the purgatorial Virgil here asserts that incorrect reading is at fault, and that his writing ("scrittura") is true in a Christian context (*Purgatorio* 6, 34).

The second overt appearance of the Virgilian textual corpus in the *Purgatorio*'s plot accords it a kind of absolute value in Christian terms, and most strikingly differentiates it from the *Commedia*'s mimesis of Virgil the character. This is the progressive revelation of the Christian salvific value of the Virgilian text in the life of the character Statius. Initially, Statius explains that the *Aeneid* was the source of his poetic inspiration, in the *Commedia*'s only direct naming of the Virgilian epic by its title (*Purgatorio* 21, 97–8). Next, Statius presents his reading of *Aeneid* 3, 56–57 as having effected his "moral" conversion, away from the prodigality that would have condemned him to hell (*Purgatorio* 22, 37–45). Finally, Statius presents his conversion to Christianity (22, 64–73) as having resulted from his reading of *Eclogue* 4, 5–7.

The presence and the function of the *Aeneid* in the *Paradiso*, after the character Virgil has definitively disappeared from Dante's poem, is directly related to this absolute contrast between the author's damnation and the salvific value of his text. For Dante-poet's mimesis of this most purely Christian realm is effected at several key moments by references to the *Aeneid*. This process involves, however, a newly ambivalent – even critical – treatment of the Virgilian text from the perspective of the new Christian poetics of the *Paradiso*.

The third canticle stages its single most important presentation of Dante-protagonist as a new Aeneas in the heaven of Mars, where Cacciaguida's initial greeting to his great-great-grandson is introduced by an extended comparison which, in a moment virtually unique in the *Commedia*, explicitly establishes and valorizes the Virgilian model, at the same time as it suggests that model's limitations: "With like affection did the shade of Anchises stretch forward (if our greatest Muse merits belief) when in Elysium he perceived his son" (*Paradiso* 15, 25–27). On the one hand, the central event of Aeneas' underworld journey – the meeting with his father that begins in *Aeneid* 6, 684–88 – underwrites the central encounter of Dante-protagonist not in Hell but in Paradise. On the other hand, a significant qualification is suggested with regard to the truth-value of Virgil as author.

This ambivalent status of the salvific text of Dante's *Aeneid* in the *Paradiso* is also at issue in the heaven of Jupiter when we are presented with the saved soul of Ripheus in the eyebrow of the eagle (*Paradiso* 20, 68; 100–04; 118–29). This minor character from Virgil's epic, described as the "iustissimus" of the Trojans (*Aeneid* 2, 426–28), exemplifies the ultimate mystery of salvation in terms of the *Paradiso*'s extended grappling with the interrelated theological problems of grace, redemption, free will, and divine foreknowledge. At the same time, the saved Ripheus (for whose salvation no other source than Dante exists) functions as a kind of extreme contrast with the damned Virgil, whose fate is thus made to seem the more poignant in retrospect.

The final Virgilian textual reference in *Paradiso* 33, 64–66 measures the distance between the *Commedia* and the *Aeneid*, emblematizing the *Paradiso*'s new critical attitude towards its privileged classical model, while simultaneously reinscribing that model as essential to the Dantean project. Dante-poet cites the example of the Cumean Sibyl whose prophetic writings on leaves are irrevocably scattered by the lightest breeze, and thus lost (*Aeneid* 3, 443–52), in order to articulate the double failure of his own memory and of his own speech before the experience of the final beatific vision. This final use of the Virgilian Sybil thus figures the ultimate limitations of the new Dantean Christian poetic discourse of the *Paradiso*.

The saved Statius and the infernal *Thebaid*

Within the overall mimetic strategy of the *Commedia*, Statius the character and the text of the *Thebaid* are presented in terms of – and in contradistinction to – Virgil the character and the text of the *Aeneid*. A striking construct of reversal is at issue: Virgil is damned, but his text is salvific; Statius is saved, but his text seems not to have Christian salvific value. In addition, Dante's Statius as character is fundamentally mediated by Virgil at the level of plot, just as he represents himself as fundamentally mediated by – and dependent upon – Virgil as poet.

Statius the character first enters the poem in the wake of the earthquake that shakes Mount Purgatory as Dante and Virgil are leaving the fifth terrace (*Purgatorio* 20, 127–51). His initial appearance (21, 7–13) is introduced by an explicit Christological comparison (Luke 24:13–16) and he quickly explains, in response to Virgil's questioning, that the earthquake had signaled the completion of his purgation. This event – unique in the second canticle – gives Statius a special status in terms of Dante's theological poetics as he identifies himself by name with an autobiographical sketch of his poetic career on earth (21, 82–102) as author of the *Thebaid* and the uncompleted *Achilleid*, stressing his absolute dependence on Virgil's *Aeneid* with regard to classical poetic inspiration and formation. The canto ends as Statius, having discovered that his interlocutor is his poetic father, Virgil, attempts to embrace him in a clear re-enactment of Aeneas' failed embrace of Anchises in *Aeneid* 6, 700–2.

After the three poets ascend together to the sixth terrace at the beginning of *Purgatorio* 22, Virgil explains how Juvenal, arriving in Limbo, brought him news of Statius' esteem (thus dramatizing the concluding tribute to Virgil in *Thebaid* 12, 816–17), before proceeding to questions on the nature of Statius' sin and conversion. The ensuing discussion involves the *Commedia*'s most explicit treatment of the *Thebaid*, characterized in "tragic" terms as singing "le crude armi/de la doppia trestizia di Giocasta" (*Purgatorio* 22, 55–56), as Virgil begins by asserting the absence of a Christian dimension in the *Thebaid* (*Purgatorio* 22, 58–60), with particular reference to the two Statian addresses to Clio, Muse of History (*Thebaid* 1, 41 and 10, 630–31). Statius' response that his reading of the fourth *Eclogue* saved him sums up his double debt to Virgil which is also the very essence of his identity as a character in Dante's poem: "Per te poeta fui, per te cristiano" (*Purgatorio* 22, 73). In his Dantean autobiography, Statius claims that he was baptized before that point in the *Thebaid* (7, 424–25) where he led "i Greci a' fiumi/ di Tebe poetando" (*Purgatorio* 22, 88–89). The non-baptismal significance of the Theban rivers in the Statian epic contrasts dramatically with the Dantean

Statius' metaphoric baptism in the river (cf. the "fiume" of *Inferno* 1, 80), that is, the text of the Dantean Virgil.

After the disappearance of Virgil, Statius plays a minimal but formally important role at the level of plot. Led by Matelda, he accompanies Dante-protagonist through the Earthly Paradise (*Purgatorio* 32, 29) until they arrive at the river Eunoe where they are both invited to drink, and where Statius the character is mentioned for the last time (33, 134). The fact that Statius thus explicitly undergoes these key plot events up to the very end of the *Purgatorio* serves to give a final and definitive emphasis to his radical difference from Virgil. This, then, presents the Dantean Statius as a Christian *poeta*, who is at the same time fundamentally dependent on Virgil both for his poetic and for his spiritual achievement. This Statius figure is thus an inscribed model who authorizes the new vernacular Christian Dante-*poeta* in the process of defining himself over the course of the *Commedia*'s story of Dante-protagonist.

Yet a radical difference obtains between the Dantean Statius and the *Commedia*'s use of the Statian epic, differentiating it from the *Aeneid* in the most important terms. For within the *Commedia* as a whole, the dominant function of the *Thebaid* as the epic of destructive civil war *par excellence* is to serve as a metaphoric textual model for Hell itself. Indeed, the city of Thebes from Statius' epic underlies – literarily and morally – Dante's City of Dis, as Ronald Martinez has shown. In this context it is particularly significant that Ulysses and Ugolino – the two most imposing sinners of the eighth and ninth circles – are presented in Theban terms.

In the ninth circle, the initial presentation of the Guelf count Ugolino della Gherardesca gnawing the head of the Ghibelline archbishop Ruggieri degli Ubaldini involves a striking Theban simile: "Not otherwise did Tydeus gnaw the temples of Menalippus" (*Inferno* 32, 130–32). The Statian subtext (*Thebaid* 8, 739–62) contains an emblematic image of the relentless circularity of Theban history: in what can be seen from a Christian perspective as a kind of non-conversion, the moment of death here simply replicates (even epitomizes) the individual "Theban" life, and leads to a new and more fierce round of the war.

Of equal importance to the Theban character of Dante's Hell is the direct link between the *Thebaid* and the *Inferno* suggested by the presence of Capaneus in the third round of the seventh circle, reserved for the violent against God. The defiant blasphemer against Jupiter in *Thebaid* 10 becomes the unrepentant blasphemer against the Christian God in *Inferno* 14. It is as if the Jovian thunderbolt that punished Capaneus' challenge to divine authority before the walls of Thebes led directly to Capaneus' transportation to Dante's Christian Hell. A similar kind of direct, physical link between the Statian landscape of Thebes and the Dantean landscape of Hell is suggested by the second of the Seven Against Thebes encountered in the *Inferno*, Amphiaraus. The Argive seer (*vates*) is swallowed up by the earth and sent directly to the underworld in *Thebaid* 7, 690–823 and 8, 1–210. It is this moment of passage from Theban earth to Christian Hell that Virgil uses to identify the diviner to Dante-pilgrim (*Inferno* 20, 31–36).

The poetics of Dante's *Inferno* thus involve a Christian recontextualization of Statius' Thebes as the epitome and emblem of human history without Christ – which is also, quite literally, the state of the damned: an endlessly repeated cycle of violence and suffering with no redemptive value or power.

Lucan, Cato, and the *Pharsalia*

The *Commedia* explicitly represents the poet Lucan only twice, and in two contrasting but complementary ways. First, as character, he is encountered by Dante-protagonist in Limbo, where he appears as the final member of the "bella scola," explicitly designated as such, "L'ultimo Lucano" (*Inferno* 4, 90). While this epithet obviously implies historical chronology, there is also perhaps the suggestion of a maximum distance from Virgil.

Second, Lucan is represented as author in the famous apostrophe by Dante-author at the point in the seventh bolgia just before the second metamorphosis (i.e., the one in which Francesco and Buoso exchange forms as man and as serpent). In this context, Dante initially addresses Lucan in a way which simultaneously presents the *Pharsalia* as literally true, and characterizes it as mimetically inadequate, as involving, even at its most spectacular moments, a profoundly limited poetic discourse. The Dantean imperative, "Let Lucan be silent . . . and let him wait to hear what now comes forth" (*Inferno* 25, 94–96), clearly presents the Roman poet as a classical model who is surpassed by Dante's Christian poetics. Significantly, the two specific Lucanian textual *loci* here evoked involve metamorphosis as *historia*, literally true but with no transcendent dimension. We have a kind of miniature taxonomy with two extreme cases, both involving Cato's Roman soldiers in their march across the snake-invested Libyan desert. The purely natural (and literally fatal) Lucanian transformation of the human body contrasts (as we shall see) both with Ovidian "supernatural" metamorphosis and with Dante's Christian poetics of transfiguration. It is also in accord with the *Pharsalia*'s anti-Virgilian, anti-imperial presentation of history in terms of the operations of a non-transcendent, cyclical Fortune.

The various events in the *Inferno* which involve characters from the *Pharsalia* reveal the same basic negative Dantean interpretation of Lucan's epic. In each case, however, there is also a specific Christian recontextualization of the Lucanian model character entailing a strategic partial misreading. Thus in the fourth bolgia, the diviner who represents the *Pharsalia* is Aruns, portrayed as having had, on earth, a literally unobstructed view of the stars and sea from the cave in which he lived (*Inferno* 20, 46–51). This is an ironic inversion of the Lucanian *vates* who, in *Pharsalia* 1, 584–638, clearly foresaw the disastrous outcome of the Roman civil war, but in horror refused to reveal it in open terms, purposefully covering his prophecy with pseudo-Sibylline ambiguities ("tegens ambage," 1, 638). The prophetic dimension of Lucan's epic as a whole is thus put into question. Similarly, Dante's version of Lucan's Curio is punished in the realm of the schismatics, adding spiritual consequences to Lucan's (implicitly incomplete) historical narrative, but this time in a way which seems to problematize Dante's own imperial politics.

The most extreme example of Dante's rewriting of Lucan's text in the *Inferno* involves Virgil's explanation of his knowledge of Lower Hell. His story of having been conjured by the Lucanian witch Erichtho who forced him to bring a spirit up from Giudecca, the lowest division of the ninth circle, appears to be a purely Dantean invention (*Inferno* 9, 22–30). On the one hand, this recalls the episode in *Pharsalia* 6, 507–830 in which Erichtho, at the request of Pompey's son Sextus, conjures the soul of a recently killed Pompeian soldier so that Sextus can learn the outcome of the battle of Pharsalia. On the other hand, Dante's guide, Virgil, here echoes the claim of Aeneas' guide, the Sibyl, to have been led through Tartarus by Hecate and thus to have full knowledge of the Virgilian "Lower Hell" (*Aeneid* 6, 564–65). Dante's rewriting of the Lucanian scene "recuperates" the witch Erichtho by making her necessary to the Dantean Virgil's status as guide: she thus functions in accord with the Christian providence that controls the advancement of the *Commedia*'s plot line. At the same time, the Lucanian Erichtho is both marginalized and subordinated to a higher power. In this sense Dante's rewriting of Erichtho also undoes Lucan's subversion of the original Virgilian model.

The figure of the saved Cato in *Purgatorio* 1 dramatically refigures the *Inferno*'s programmatically negative reading of the *Pharsalia*. Indeed, Dante's figural rewriting of the hero of Lucan's epic offers a positive mimesis of the *Pharsalia* as a whole, now correctively misread from the Dantean Christian perspective. In this context, it is important to stress the ways in which the saved Cato's presence in Purgatory seems to violate flamboyantly the *Commedia*'s own ground rules: he is a pagan, a suicide, and an arch-enemy of Caesar. This "violation" has indeed been carefully prepared by Cato's absence from the two infernal places where one would most expect to find him: among the virtuous pagans in Limbo, where the sign of Cato's absence is the named presence of his wife Marzïa (*Inferno* 4, 128); among the suicides in the seventh circle, where the sign of his absence is the evocation of his name (for the first time in the *Commedia*) to describe the burning sand of the third *girone* (*Inferno* 14, 13–14).

Dante both emphasizes Cato's Lucanian origin and supplies him with a Christian figural dimension. His long beard and hair simultaneously evoke the signs of his mourning for the Roman civil war in *Pharsalia* 2, 372–76 and the iconography of Moses the lawgiver (cf. the Virgilian Cato in *Aeneid* 8, 670). His suicide is presented by Virgil as a Christological self-sacrifice for *libertà*, and is directly linked to his salvation (*Purgatorio* 1, 71–75). Finally, the absolute difference between the saved Cato and the damned Virgil is explicitly established in terms of the dramatic contrast between the former's correct and the latter's imperfect understanding of Marzïa's status as exemplary virtuous pagan wife (1, 78–93). In addition, this saved Dantean Cato plays an active role in the salvific journey of Dante-protagonist, and is thus essential to the narrative logic of the advancing plot line, effecting Dante's first purgatorial baptism, and then initiating the actual purgatorial ascent with his condemnation of Casella's song.

Dante's Cato is thus both saved and salvific, and as such he represents a radically corrective misreading of the *Pharsalia* on the *Commedia*'s Christian terms. He is figurally linked both to Moses and to Christ, while at the same time incarnating Roman civic virtue in a republican context. Dante uses this figure of Cato to undermine and to correct both the *Pharsalia*'s pessimistic Stoic view of history, and its anti-imperial polemic. At the same time, this Dantean Cato functions to supplement the *Commedia*'s Christianized Roman political ideal by suggesting a paradoxical fusion of the Virgilian *imperium* and the Lucanian republic.

The *Commedia*'s mimesis of Lucan as both damned (*Inferno* 4) and poetically limited (*Inferno* 25) thus contrasts dramatically with its mimesis of the *Pharsalia* in the person of Cato. Yet the *Commedia*'s positive reading of Cato also inscribes a new set of tensions vis-à-vis its reading of the *Pharsalia* as a whole, which, unlike either the salvific *Aeneid* or the non-salvific *Thebaid*, remains, on the *Commedia*'s Christian hermeneutic terms, the most unresolvably ambivalent and problematic of Dante's classical model texts.

The special case of Ovid and his *Metamorphoses*

Ovid's status in the *Commedia* is exceptional, in terms of his mimesis as character, as author, and as text. Ovid as character is only minimally present in Dante's poem, and in the two instances where he is explicitly named he is linked with Lucan (*Inferno* 4, 90; 25, 94–102). This linkage, however, underscores the differences between these two poets from Dante's point of view, and, indeed, the fundamental difference between the Dantean Ovid on the one hand, and the other three Dantean *poetae* on the other. First, there is the unique status of the *Metamorphoses* as history (or non-history) vis-à-vis the other three Latin epics: Dante's treatment of them as literally true is never more than occasionally problematic. Ovid's epic is qualitatively different in its mode of representation and in its treatment of history. Indeed, with the qualified exception of the Roman historical sequence in books 14 and 15, Ovid's text is a self-conscious *fabula*, which Dante, as it were, pretends to read as *historia*. For the *Commedia* to treat the *Metamorphoses* as history involves a consistent, suggestive, and visible set of tensions and instabilities.

Second, Dante's mimesis of Ovid both as character and as author is correspondingly different. The strong coherent presences of Virgil, Statius, and Cato stand in striking contradistinction to the much more fleeting, fragmentary, multiform representation of Ovid. At the same time, the *Commedia*'s mimesis of Ovid as author is particularly ambivalent: his authority is simultaneously qualified and valorized. Third, Dante's reading of the *Metamorphoses* minimizes or even eliminates the political dimension, the theme of the divinely sanctioned Roman *imperium*. This is linked to the fact that Dante's Ovid is not read politically (or otherwise) in relation to Virgil in the way that both Statius and Lucan are. While Dante's reading of the classical poets normally makes Virgil its point of departure, Ovid functions as a kind of opposite extreme. Finally, there is the unique status of the Ovidian poetic subject matter from Dante's perspective as *theologus-poeta*: the Christian hermeneutic potential of "metamorphosis."

The *Commedia*'s most explicit representation of Ovid as author is also its most elaborate staging of his opposition to Dante-author. If the apostrophe to Lucan in *Inferno* 25, 94–96 treats the inadequate Lucanian account of metamorphosis as *historia*, the longer apostrophe to Ovid (25, 97–102) treats Ovidian metamorphosis as poetry, with a meditation on both the unique value, as well as the necessary inadequacies, of Ovidian poesis. The two examples cited from the *Metamorphoses* (Cadmus and Arethusa) involve supernatural transformation, to which Dante-poet claims both mimetic and poetic superiority. This "competition" with Ovid uses parodically the classical (Ovidian) topos of poetic rivalry, while granting a superior Christian spiritual dimension to Ovidian "supernatural" metamorphosis that makes it a negative or a positive type of Christian transfiguration. In terms of Dante's programmatic corrective readings of the *auctores*, what we have here is the claim of an improvement on Ovid: a true "conversion" (cf. "converte," 25, 97) of this particular pagan poetic model text to Christian spiritual purposes.

All of these points are elaborated in the other two passages where the truth status of Ovid's text is discussed. In *Inferno* 29, the realm of the falsifiers (where poets are not included), there is a suggestive treatment of the truth limits of Ovidian poetic discourse: the literal truth of Ovidian metamorphosis is put into question, suggestively treated as if it might be a *fabula*. Second, there is Matelda's qualified affirmation that pagan poets (and especially Ovid) figurally indicated the true Earthly Paradise when they wrote of the Golden Age (*Purgatorio* 28, 139–41).

The *Commedia*'s use of the *Metamorphoses* as text involves several different mimetic strategies. First, certain key characters from Ovid's epic appear in Dante's poem at the level of plot. There are relatively few of these and they are all found in the *Inferno*. The two most important both involve implicit Dantean commentaries on the *Metamorphoses*, which they in some sense represent. First, Dante selectively misreads the Ovidian prophet Tiresias (encountered among the diviners in *Inferno* 20, 40–45) in a way which denies the *Metamorphoses*' capacity to incarnate (or even to represent) true prophecy on its own (necessarily limited) pagan terms. The second key Ovidian character represented at the level of the *Commedia*'s plot is Myrrha (*Inferno* 30, 37–41; *Metamorphoses* 10, 298–513), whose presence among the "falsador" functions as an important aspect of the presentation of the tenth bolgia as an extended meditation by Dante on fiction-making and its attendant dangers, which is overtly linked to a meditation on Ovid's text. And, indeed, this bolgia (*Inferno* 29, 40–31, 9) involves the highest density of Ovidian references of any single geographic space in the *Inferno*. Not only does it open, as it were, under the problematic sign of Ovidian mimesis, with the initial reference to Aegina and the Myrmidons (29, 58–64), as already noted, but it contains explicit mention of two key Ovidian figures: Daedalus (29, 116) and Narcissus (30, 128). Furthermore, the mad impersonators are introduced by a complex double Ovidian simile (30, 1–27), comparing their madness to that of Athamas (*Metamorphoses* 4, 512–30) and to that of Hecuba (13, 404–571). For the taxonomic purposes of the present essay, these Ovidian references (made either by Dante-poet or by a character) involve the second major category of the *Commedia*'s use of the text of the *Metamorphoses*: that is, as part of its general representational discourse, most frequently using the Ovidian referent in a comparison or periphrasis.

I differentiate this from the third major category which involves explicit or implicit comparisons of Dante himself to various model characters from the *Metamorphoses*. The master strategy here involves a corrective Christian rewriting of both failed and successful Ovidian heroes in the person of Dante-protagonist, or Dante-poet, or both. In the *Inferno*, a particularly important double instance occurs as Dante-protagonist descends from the seventh to the eighth circle on Geryon's back. He compares his fear first to that of Phaeton (*Inferno* 17, 106–08) at the fatal moment when he let go of the reins of Apollo's chariot (*Metamorphoses* 2, 156–324; esp. 2, 178–200), then to that of Icarus (*Inferno* 17, 109–11) at the moment he felt his wings melting off (*Metamorphoses* 8, 200–35; esp. 8, 223–30). In both cases, it is the difference between the pagan Ovidian model and the Christian Dantean protagonist that is stressed: Dante is both a Phaeton made good and an Icarus *in bono*. Unlike them, he has a guide whom he obeys; where they descend to death, he ascends to life. At the same time, these infernal references to Phaeton and Icarus initiate "programs," for the two Ovidian characters will continue to function as models for Dante-protagonist in the other two canticles.

The opening invocation of the *Purgatorio* uses an Ovidian figure for Dante-poet, embarking upon his new Christian subject matter. Dante presents himself as a corrected version of the Pierides (*Purgatorio* 1, 9–12), who pridefully and unsuccessfully challenged the Muses in a poetry contest and were transformed into magpies for punishment (*Metamorphoses* 5, 294–678). Again, the Ovidian model is correctively inverted, as a figure of artistic pride is used to articulate artistic humility.

On the purgatorial terraces, there is yet a fourth mimetic status for Ovidian narratives: they are read as unproblematic histories which are morally exemplary within their original settings, and which function as *exempla* within the Christian context – indeed, as an integral part – of the mechanism of purgation. They are thus placed on the same level as the other classical, as well as biblical and hagiographic, texts from which the purgatorial examples are taken. There are, however, a disproportionately high number of Ovidian *exempla*, almost all negative.

A shift in the dominant function of Ovid's text occurs at the summit of the mountain as we encounter a series of correctively reread Ovidian models for Dante-protagonist at this particularly important juncture in the *Commedia*'s plot line. As he leaves the seventh terrace, Dante-protagonist is presented as a corrected Pyramus, with Beatrice playing the role of a corrected Thisbe (*Purgatorio* 27, 37–39; *Metamorphoses* 4, 55–166). Here again, this construct works figurally: the third-person Ovidian narrative points to, prefigures, the first-person Christian reading which at once invalidates and "completes" it. The Christian spiritual wall of fire that separates Dante from Beatrice, unlike the material wall separating Pyramus from Thisbe, will be traversed and the *Commedia*'s couple reunited. At the same time, the evocation of Pyramus at the moment of his death, hearing Thisbe's name for the last time (*Purgatorio* 27, 38), foregrounds by contrast that the name of Beatrice for Dante-Pyramus will initiate him into a "new life." The three Ovidian models for the redeemed courtly eroticism of Dante-protagonist's encounter with Matelda also involve an *in bono* version of the "tragic" Ovidian model of erotic love.

During his first encounter with Beatrice in the Earthly Paradise Dante-protagonist appears as a corrected, Christian, Narcissus. His reaction to her reproach for weeping at Virgil's disappearance includes the archetypal Narcissistic gesture of looking down and seeing his reflection in the water of Lethe. Unlike Narcissus, however, Dante both recognizes his reflection as such and turns away from it in shame (*Purgatorio* 30, 76; *Metamorphoses* 3, 413–36), to gaze instead (ultimately) upon the salvific female Other.

The final corrected Ovidian model for Dante-protagonist in Purgatory tests the limits of this figural construct as such, as well as of Ovidian mimesis more generally, while simultaneously interrogating Dante's own status as an Ovidian poet. At issue is the moment when Dante-protagonist falls asleep in the Earthly Paradise (*Purgatorio* 32, 61–69), an event cast as a contrastive rewriting of the hundred-eyed Argus fatally falling asleep to the song of Syrinx sung by Mercury (*Metamorphoses* 1, 682–721). But if Dante-protagonist's falling asleep is modeled on an Ovidian narrative, his awakening is explicitly informed by a scriptural model: the moment when the apostles Peter, John, and James are recalled to themselves by the voice of Jesus after their vision of Moses, Elias, and the transfigured Christ (Matthew 17:1–8).

This apparent interrogation of Ovidian poetic discourse does not, however, devalorize it in any definitive way within the broader context of the *Commedia*. Indeed, the juxtaposition of Argus and the Apostles, of the *Metamorphoses* and the Gospel effected by *Purgatorio* 32, 64–99, not only marks the difference between these two model Dantean texts, but also links them, conferring, paradoxically, an added prestige to the Ovidian *scriptura paganorum*. In this context, it is significant that Beatrice subsequently uses Ovidian "mythographic" language both to present the DXV prophecy and to affirm its ultimate intelligibility (*Purgatorio* 33, 40–51).

The enduring validity (and power) of Ovidian poetic discourse for Dante to articulate figurally Christian truth is most elaborately demonstrated in the *Paradiso*, the canticle characterized by the greatest number of Ovidian models which function to represent the salvific trajectory both of Dante-poet and of Dante-protagonist. The *Paradiso*'s use of these models involves four clusters which occur in four structurally significant *loci*: first, the multiple beginnings of *Paradiso* 1–3; second, the central encounter with Cacciaguida (*Paradiso* 17); third, the extended sequence which culminates in the descent of Christ (*Paradiso* 21–23); fourth, the canticle's concluding segment in the Empyrean (*Paradiso* 30–33). Furthermore, the *Metamorphoses* as textual model is particularly relevant to the poetics of the *Paradiso* as a whole, which involve transformation and transfiguration in fundamental ways, with regard both to the protagonist's experience and to the poet's language. In both of these contexts, the Ovidian narratives of metamorphosis operate as essential, yet necessarily insufficient and incomplete, figures for Christian transfiguration.

Paradiso 1 opens under the sign of Ovid. The invocation to the "buono Appollo" (1, 13) remotivates the Daphne narrative (*Metamorphoses* 1, 452–567) in an explicitly Christian poetic context, where the mark of the desired Pauline election (as "vaso," 1, 14) is the Ovidian laurel crown of the *poeta* (1, 15; 22–33). This request is made in terms of a positive misreading of the Marsyas story from *Metamorphoses* 6, 382–400. The Ovidian satyr flayed alive as punishment for his artistic presumption in challenging Apollo to a flute-playing contest is reread by Dante as a radically positive figure for Apollonian poetic inspiration (*Paradiso* 1, 19–21). A literal death in the *Metamorphoses* stands for spiritual life in the *Commedia*, and the Ovidian Marsyas thus figures the transformation of Dante-poet at the level of composition. The parallel transformation of Dante-protagonist, at the level of plot, is also figured by means of an Ovidian metamorphosis, that of Glaucus (*Metamorphoses* 13, 904–59). Here, a different reading strategy is employed, for the Ovidian Glaucus (a mortal fisherman who was transformed into a sea god as the result of eating magic grasses) offers a positive pagan metamorphosis that becomes an *exemplum* for Dante-poet's-protagonist's Christian transformation on looking into Beatrice's eyes (*Paradiso*, 1, 67–69).

In the opening lines of *Paradiso* 2, an additional Ovidian *exemplum* is used to figure Dante-poet's relationship to his readers. The successful voyage of the Ovidian Jason to Colchis and the consequent amazement of the Argonauts (*Metamorphoses* 7, 100–58) figures the future reaction of the small, select number of the *Commedia*'s proper readers as they make their way through the third canticle to the end (*Paradiso* 2, 10–18). Dante-poet is presented as a celestial Jason, and the completed *Commedia* as a Christian golden fleece: a book of parchment pages containing the truth of Christ, the *Agnus Dei*. This entire construct will be further elaborated in the hypothetical vision (25, 1–9) of the Jasonic Dante's triumphant homecoming as a *poeta* to Florence "with a different fleece" ("con altro vello," 25, 7).

The final Ovidian *exemplum* in the dense cluster that informs the opening cantos of the *Paradiso* is that of Narcissus for Dante-protagonist's first encounter with the "inhabitants" of the first celestial sphere. At issue is the inherently problematic mimetic status of Paradise as such and as poetic subject matter, as well as the inherent difficulties of perception for Dante-protagonist within that realm (*Paradiso* 3, 4–33). As Dante looks into the sphere of the Moon, he initially mistakes living beings for reflections, as Narcissus initially mistook a reflection for a living being (*Metamorphoses* 3, 416–73). The contrast between the two (*Paradiso* 3, 17–18) emphasizes their essential difference, while presenting Dante as a corrected version of the Narcissistic model. The emphasis at this point in the Narcissus program (established in *Purgatorio* 30, 76–78) is on the progressive nature of perception and intellection which proceeds from error to truth. For Narcissus, that progression is fatal; for Dante-protagonist, it is a new stage in his salvific journey.

The full revelation of Dante's exile in the central canto of the *Paradiso* is informed by a pair of Ovidian models: Dante-protagonist's initial question to Cacciaguida about his future exile (*Paradiso* 17, 1–6) is explicitly modeled on Phaeton's question concerning his true paternity (*Metamorphoses* 1, 755–61). Cacciaguida's first prophecy of Dante's future exile is made by means of a comparison with the exile of the Ovidian Hippolytus (*Paradiso* 17, 46–48; *Metamorphoses* 15, 497–505; esp. 15, 497–98). Both Dante's innocence and the injustice of his exile are simultaneously affirmed in his presentation as a new Hippolytus. The final resurrection from the dead of the Ovidian Hippolytus under the new name Virbius ("bis vir" ["twice man"]), with its suggestive Christian resonances, presents Dante's exile as a metaphoric martyrdom with Christological overtones, a kind of *imitatio Christi*, expressed in Ovidian terms. Finally, the construct reads Cacciaguida himself against the Ovidian Theseus, again presenting him as a corrective Christian father figure: instead of causing his son's death by believing ugly and noxious lies, he enhances his life by telling the unpleasant but providential truth.

Dante-protagonist's arrival in the seventh heaven, that of Saturn and the contemplatives, presents him as a corrected, Christian, Semele, thus setting in motion a program sustained over three cantos. In a strategic recall of the Ovidian model narrative, Dante-protagonist is initially compared to Ovid's Semele, who was destroyed by the revelation of Jupiter's divine being (*Paradiso* 21, 4–12; *Metamorphoses* 3, 287–315). The program culminates as Dante-protagonist undergoes a literal transformation: his experience of the Incarnate Christ (*Paradiso* 23, 28–33) – in contradistinction to Semele's fatal experience of the "unincarnated" Jupiter – makes him strong enough to bear Beatrice's smile (23, 46–48). By this point, however, negative Ovidian metamorphosis has been displaced by positive Christian transfiguration (or "transhumanization," see 1, 70). Ovid's story of failed love – and failed union – between human and divine characters thus becomes, within the global poetic discourse of the *Commedia*, a negative type of the ultimately successful (and universally redemptive) union between human and divine that is the Incarnation. In terms of the *Paradiso*'s explicit grapplings with the problem of mimesis, all of this is particularly important because the descent of Christ, Gabriel, and Mary in *Paradiso* 23 involves the only break in the mimetic mode of accommodative metaphor that characterizes the entire canticle until the protagonist's epistemological leap into the "direct" mimesis of the Empyrean that begins in *Paradiso* 30, 90.

In the Empyrean itself we find the culmination of a particularly suggestive set of programmatic Ovidian models (Narcissus, Phaeton, Icarus, and Jason), which are simultaneously validated and surpassed, shown as both necessary and inadequate for Dante's final articulation of the highest Christian theological truth in the *Commedia*'s vernacular poetic discourse. Dante's bending over the river of light (*Paradiso* 30, 85–87) recalls and makes good the key Narcissistic gesture (*Metamorphoses* 3, 406–17), while transforming its significance in both mimetic and epistemological terms. Dante-protagonist's final sight of the Virgin Mary is introduced with a complicated double simile involving sunrise in which the sun is figured as "the pole that Phaeton misguided" (*Paradiso* 31, 124–25), implicitly contrasting Dante's successful ascent with the unsuccessful end of Phaeton's ascent – a self-destructive *descent* in flames (*Metamorphoses* 2, 311–22). Dante-protagonist's journey upwards also ends "in flames," but these are the salvific Christian flames – at once metaphoric and spiritual – of the vision of the Virgin: the "pacifica oriafiamma" (*Paradiso* 31, 127). Ovid's Icarus is recalled in the final metaphoric and spiritual winged flight of Dante-protagonist (*Paradiso* 32, 145–46; *Metamorphoses* 8, 225–28; cf. *Paradiso* 33, 15). The final evocation of Ovid's Jason (*Paradiso* 33, 94–96; *Metamorphoses* 6, 721; 8, 302) valorizes the achievement of the radically innovative "impresa" (*Paradiso* 33, 95) of the *Commedia* (cf. the Argo as the first boat), and also validates the first-person poet's claim to the literal historical veracity of his narration by (paradoxically) insisting upon how much of it he has forgotten. Dante-poet's initial (and perhaps seemingly extravagant) promise to produce unprecedented *admiratio* by the end of the *Paradiso* (see 2, 17) is fulfilled by the poem's climax.

Both in terms of the Christian poetics of the *Commedia* and in terms of Dante's reading of the classical poets, Ovid's *Metamorphoses* is unique. It is a qualitatively different text from those of the other *auctores*, read by Dante in a qualitatively different way. Salvation does not result from reading the *Metamorphoses*: it is not a salvific text as are the *Aeneid* and the fourth *Eclogue* which converted the redeemed Statius. Nor are any of its key characters (treated as literally and historically real) saved as a result of Dante-poet's corrective Christian misreadings: there is no equivalent either of Cato or of Ripheus in Dante's reading of the *Metamorphoses*. Instead, Dante's Christian poetic use of model Ovidian characters involves reading them figuratively to represent his own salvific journey in the *Commedia* – both as protagonist and as poet.

SUGGESTED READING

Barolini, Teodolinda, *Dante's Poets: Textuality and Truth in the Comedy* (Princeton: Princeton University Press, 1984).

Brownlee, Kevin, "Why the Angels Speak Italian: Dante as Vernacular *Poeta* in *Paradiso* 25," *Poetics Today* 5 (1984): 597–610.

"Phaeton's Fall and Dante's Ascent," *Dante Studies* 102 (1984): 135–44.

Chiarenza, Marguerite M., "Time and Eternity in the Myths of *Paradiso* XVII," in A. S. Bernardo and A. L. Pellegrini, eds., *Dante, Petrarch, Boccaccio: Studies in the Italian Trecento in Honor of Charles S. Singleton* (Binghamton, NY: Medieval and Renaissance Texts and Studies, 1983), pp. 133–50.

Hawkins, Peter S., "Transfiguring the Text: Ovid, Scripture, and Dante's Dynamics of Allusion," *Stanford Italian Review* 5 (1985): 115–39.

Hollander, Robert, *Allegory in Dante's Commedia* (Princeton: Princeton University Press, 1969).

Il Virgilio dantesco: Tragedia nella Commedia (Florence: Olschki, 1983).

Hollander, Robert, and Albert Rossi, "Dante's Republican Treasury," *Dante Studies* 104 (1986): 59–82.

Jacoff, Rachel, "Transgression and Transcendence: Figures of Female Desire in Dante's *Commedia*," in Marina Brownlee, Kevin Brownlee, and Stephen Nichols, eds., *The New Medievalism* (Baltimore: The Johns Hopkins University Press, 1991), pp. 187–99.

Jacoff, Rachel, and Jeffrey T. Schnapp, eds., *The Poetry of Allusion: Virgil and Ovid in Dante's Commedia* (Stanford: Stanford University Press, 1991).

Martinez, Ronald, "Dante, Statius and the Earthly City," Ph.D. Diss., University of California, Santa Cruz, 1977.

Moore, Edward, *Studies in Dante. First Series. Scripture and Classical Authors in Dante* (Oxford: Clarendon Press, 1896).

Paratore, Ettore, "Lucano," III:697–702; "Ovidio," IV:225–36; "Stazio," V:419–25, in U. Bosco, ed., *Enciclopedia dantesca*, 6 vols. (Rome: Istituto dell'Enciclopedia Italiana, 1970–78).

Renucci, Paul, *Dante, disciple et juge du monde gréco-latin* (Paris: Les Belles Lettres, 1954).

Ronconi, Alessandro, "Virgilio," in *Enciclopedia dantesca*, V:1030–49.

Rossi, Albert, "*A l'Ultimo Suo: Paradiso* XXX and its Virgilian Context," *Studies in Medieval and Renaissance History*, New Series 4 (1981): 37–88.

Schnapp, Jeffrey, *The Transfiguration of History at the Center of Dante's Paradise* (Princeton: Princeton University Press, 1986).

Wetherbee, Winthrop, "*Poeta che mi guidi*: Dante, Lucan, and Virgil," in R. von Hallberg, ed., *Canons* (Chicago: University of Chicago Press, 1984), pp. 131–48.

"Dante and the *Thebaid* of Statius," in P. Cherchi and A. Mastrobuono, eds., *Lectura Dantis Newberryana*, 1 (Evanston: Northwestern University Press, 1988), pp. 71–92.

10

JOHN FRECCERO

Allegory and autobiography

Among the last words spoken by Jesus in the Gospel of John are those directed to Peter, predicting the disciple's martyrdom:

> Verily, verily, I say unto you that when you were young you girt yourself and walked wherever you wished; but when you are old you will stretch out your hands and another shall gird you and lead you where you would not go.
>
> (John 21:18)

In his commentary, St. Augustine explains that these verses mark the passage in Peter's life from youthful self-reliance to humility, from the sin of presumption to confession and contrition. In middle age (for Peter is neither young nor old), he is called upon to demonstrate his love by caring for the Lord's sheep and by being willing to accept crucifixion.[1]

The conversion from presumption to humility is also the theme of Dante's descent into Hell, which likewise takes place in middle age: "nel mezzo del cammin di nostra vita." The landscape of the prologue scene borrows several details from book 7 of Augustine's *Confessions*, where philosophical presumption is distinguished from confession: "it is one thing, from a wooded mountain top, to see the land of peace and quite another to reach it, when one's way is beset by the lion and the dragon."[2] It is likely that casting off the rope girdle halfway through the *Inferno* signifies a surrender of self-reliance analogous to Peter's, while the rush with which the pilgrim is girt at the beginning of the *Purgatorio* is a traditional emblem of humility ("umile pianta").

If one attempts to read these episodes simply as autobiographical anecdotes, they are bound to seem enigmatic, raising more questions about Dante's life than they answer. So, for example, some early commentators felt compelled to gloss them with biographical details invented for the occasion, identifying the rope girdle as part of the Franciscan habit and suggesting that Dante may once have wanted to become a Franciscan. Such inventions are unnecessary, however, once we recognize that, whatever the events in

Dante's life to which such episodes supposedly allude, they have been represented in the text in terms of a biblical figure of conversion. The passage from the Gospel of John authorizes us to read Dante's verses, "io avea una corda intorno cinta," not as a description of his dress, but rather as an emblem of his spiritual state: he was guilty of the same presumption of which Christ accused Peter and of which Augustine accused himself. Unlike modern biographies, which seek to establish above all the uniqueness of their subject, Christian biographies stress conformity to a biblical pattern, even at the expense of originality. When it comes to plot, such biographies, like Tolstoy's happy families, are all alike.

Casting off the rope is meant to attract Geryon, "the filthy image of fraud." This image seems to have no direct biblical precedent, but is reminiscent, if only by contrast, of ancient allegories of transcendence represented in terms of flight. Its spiral path is a clear indication that the monster is of celestial derivation, since the planets, sun, and moon all move in a spiral. Several studies have suggested that ancient allegories of flight, extending back to Plato, underlie the voyage of Ulysses as Dante recounts it.[3] The same may perhaps be said of the voyage on Geryon. In any case, along with biblical themes, ancient philosophical allegories of the ascent of the soul constitute another source for the figures or paradigms that the poet uses to represent the events of his life in general terms. Autobiography is represented schematically in Dante's poem by this synthesis of Platonic allegory with traditional biblical motifs, just as it was in St. Augustine's *Confessions*.

For all of its originality, Geryon's meaning in terms of the poet's biography is not difficult to decipher. Although the monster is fearsome, it is strangely docile, grudgingly responsive to Virgil's commands. This apparent inconsistency illustrates a familiar paradox of confessional literature: adversity and evil turn out retrospectively to have been of spiritual help even when they seemed most threatening. Dante's reaction to his exile embodies this paradox. In the *Convivio*, he bitterly complains of the injustice done to him, while in the *Commedia* he seems to regard his exile as having been necessary for his salvation, irrespective of the culpability of those who condemned him. The contrast between the slow, spiral descent of Geryon, and its almost instantaneous departure after its mission is accomplished, suggests a momentary, providential constraint of the forces of evil for the benefit of the pilgrim. Like Antaeus bending gently with the voyagers in his hand and then snapping back into place, Geryon participates in a "command performance" to speed the pilgrim on his way.

This providential intervention is a response to the submissiveness of the pilgrim, who will now be "led where he would not go." On this voyage, he is to be simply a passenger, rather than a Ulysses, and Virgil is there to sustain him. The self-reliance of Ulysses was interpreted by Dante (and by Augustine before him) as a form of presumption of which the young Dante – especially the Dante of the *Convivio* – might himself have been guilty. The voyage on Geryon functions as an ironic parody of the Homeric journey, a critique of the presumption of youth from the perspective of middle age.

Whatever the moral intent, Geryon is exquisitely literary; its various motifs form a patchwork whose seams Dante scarcely bothers to conceal. Elements of the monster's composition are drawn from the Apocalypse, or perhaps from the lunar dragon of the astrologers (from which the dragon of the Apocalypse probably derives). Scholars have suggested various classical sources for the image as well, notably from Virgil and Solinus. Apart from its thematic function, however, its literally central position in the *Inferno*, and the elaborate address to the reader introducing it, suggest that it was also meant to stand for the poet's own prodigious imagination. Throughout the story, the progress of the pilgrim is, at the same time, the progress of the poem. Here too, perhaps, Geryon is both theme and, like Ariosto's "hippogryph," a self-conscious emblem of the poet's creative act. Ariosto's fantastic steed is obviously a descendant of Pegasus, said to have sprung from Medusa's blood. That chthonic origin would qualify Pegasus as an ancestor of Geryon as well.[4]

The flight on Geryon seems to call forth as its antithesis the ship of Ulysses, a "navicella dell'ingegno" sailing to disaster. Both Geryon and Ulysses are recalled in the course of the poem: Ulysses is referred to twice in the *Purgatorio* and once in the *Paradiso*, while Virgil refers back to this flight as his claim to the pilgrim's continued faith in his guidance, even through purgatorial fire. His reminder to Dante, "Did I not guide you safely on the back of Geryon?" (*Purgatorio* 27, 23) recalls Exodus 19:4: "you saw how I bore you up on eagle's wings."

The flight of Geryon is described with navigational imagery, while the navigation of Ulysses is described, with a memorable phrase, in terms of flight: "il folle volo." This symmetrical opposition is reinforced by antitypes. The successful flight of Geryon evokes allusions to Icarus and Phaeton, while Ulysses is introduced by a comparison to the successful flight of Elijah. This parallelism suggests that the two journeys exist on the same level of signification, as dramatic representations of opposing attempts to reach the absolute. Because the voyage is also a figure for the writing of the poem (as is clear from the invocations to the second and last canticles, as well as from the narrative logic that makes of the journey's end the poem's beginning), the contrast between Ulysses and Geryon is also a contrast between literary genres.

The Homeric story had been interpreted since antiquity as an allegory of the soul's education. The disastrous conclusion of the story, in Dante's revised version, amounts to a Christian critique of philosophical presumption: specifically, of the claim that anyone could accomplish such a journey without a guide. The flight on Geryon, on the other hand, is providentially guided, like God's eagle in Exodus. It is a descent that precedes an ascent, in keeping with the Augustinian admonition, "Descend, so that you may ascend." Moreover, it takes place in the inner space of Hell, which may be said to stand for the interior distance of a descent within the self. Once more, Augustine comes to mind: "Noli foras ire; in te ipsum redi" ("do not go outside; enter within yourself").⁵ This inner dimension is totally lacking in Ulysses' account of his journey. He may be thought of as the archetypal explorer in outer space, describing his feat with the same understatement, *litotes*, used by American astronauts when they landed on the moon ("one small step for man . . ."). This voyage, and all other such voyages, are the stuff of epic. In contrast, Dante's journey on the Geryon of his own experience is a descent into himself. Such a turning inward is distinctly confessional.

The bizarre vehicle of Dante's descent into Malebolge is neither ship nor chariot in the tradition of Neoplatonic allegory, although it bears a grotesque resemblance to those flights of the soul; the surly beast might be compared to the horse veering to the left in the allegory of the *Phaedrus*, while the navigational imagery in Geryon's flight, like the flight imagery in Ulysses' navigation, is reminiscent of allusions to flights of the soul in Plotinus, Ambrose, or Augustine, where the means of escape from this world are compared to horses, chariots, ships, and wings.⁶ However, it is Providence, rather than a charioteer, who reins in Geryon, and it is fraud, rather than passions, that must be dominated. This flight does not take place in an interior void, but rather in the course of Dante's life, reinterpreted from the perspective of Hell. Geryon adds to the Neoplatonic tradition a political dimension of meaning. One is enjoined not simply to escape the hypocrisy and fraud of human society, as Plotinus had urged, but to understand it from within and so transcend it. This is the social significance of Virgil's warning: "a te convien tenere altro viaggio" (*Inferno* 1, 91).

Understanding in the *Inferno* is a process that might be characterized as hyperbolic doubt systematically applied to the values of contemporary society. Each encounter in Hell amounts to the ironic undercutting of the values enunciated by the separate characters. Even when those values seem perfectly defensible from a human point of view, as is the case, for example, with the humanistic aspirations expressed by Brunetto Latini in canto 15, the values are undermined by the fact of being championed by the damned. An incidental phrase meant as polite qualification, Brunetto's "se ben m'accorsi nella vita bella," becomes charged with irony as the infernal context exposes it to the obvious and therefore cruel rejoinder: if his discernment were acute, why would he be *here* – "siete voi qui, Ser Brunetto?" (15, 30).

This corrosive irony gives the *Inferno* its negative quality; not only is this canticle devoid of redemptive possibilities, it seems devoid of all affirmation as well. The goal of the descent is to reach the zero-point from which the climb of the *Purgatorio* can begin. In order to do this, it is necessary first to strip away all the illusory values with which we ordinarily comfort ourselves. In Plato's myth, the star-soul had to shed all its layers of materiality in order to return to its celestial home; in the Christian myth, it is sin, rather than matter, that weighs down the soul. Before any ascent can begin, it is necessary to go through Hell simply to reach the cave ("natural burella") which Plato assumed to be the point of departure. Christian ascent begins, not from a point zero, but rather from a point minus one. In the poem, that point is described in the prologue scene: the landscape is derived from what Augustine called "the region of unlikeness."[7]

The primary destruction that must take place in this mythic representation of biography is the destruction of the poet's former self. If Plato's myth of education is the account of *morphosis*, the formation of the soul, then the story of a conversion is a *meta*-morphosis, in which an illusory self must be destroyed before a new soul can take its place. One of the ways in which this destruction takes place in the poem is through a series of ironic autocitations, in which Dante undercuts his own previous work. The most obvious of these is his citation of his own earlier love poetry, placed in the mouth of Francesca da Rimini, who was ill-served by the theory of "love and the gentle heart." But it is perhaps the canto of Ulysses that constitutes Dante's most important and most critical autocitation.

According to a hypothesis first advanced by Bruno Nardi,[8] there is a certain parallelism between the attempt of Ulysses to reach the absolute and Dante's attempt, in the *Convivio*, to outline a guide to happiness through the pursuit of secular philosophy. Both attempts were doomed to failure. The parallel between this failure and the experience of Augustine was first pointed out by Giorgio Padoan,[9] who showed how Augustine, in the *De beata vita*, outlined the disastrous course of his life, including his search for happiness through secular philosophy, in terms of a tedious allegory based on the voyage of Ulysses. He suggested that the episode of Ulysses in the *Inferno* is biographical in the same way that Augustine's prologue to the *De beata vita* was biographical: that is, an allegorical outline of an experience of which the literal elements are suppressed. The voyage of the *Divina*

Commedia begins where the shipwreck of Ulysses ends, with the survival of a metaphoric shipwreck (*Inferno* 1, 23). The survival, "come altrui piacque," marks the difference between Dante's own epic presumption and his novelistic conversion.

We can only speculate about the details of Dante's experience, for the text provides us only with figures such as these. In a sense, no experience can be conveyed except by a figure, since, according to a medieval maxim, what is individual is ineffable. Allegory and other figures serve to generalize experience so that it can be communicated, as Dante says with the simile of Glaucus in the *Paradiso*: "Trasumanar significar *per verba*/non si poria; però l'essemplo basti/a cui esperienza grazia serba" (1, 70–72).

One would expect heavenly vision to be ineffable, of course, but there are good institutional reasons for expressing even penitential sentiments in general terms. Confession requires the translation of individual experience into general terms in order to affirm the equality of all sinners in the sight of God, no matter how imaginative their transgressions. Thus Augustine, in his *Confessions*, chooses to illustrate the nature of sin by confessing that as a boy he stole some pears from a neighbor's orchard. Had he been writing "confessions" in the modern sense, he might have dwelt upon any number of actions in his life that even today strike us as reprehensible. He might have gone into greater detail, for instance, about how, because of his mother's fear of scandal, he rejected his mistress, taking their son from her and sending her back to Africa. That gesture tells us more about Augustine as a young man, more perhaps than we might want to know, than it does about the humdrum sinfulness of Everyman.

The theft of forbidden fruit in Augustine's text was obviously meant to recall the sin of Adam and Eve. At the level of anecdote, any of his readers might have been guilty of such a sin; in an allegorical sense they in fact were, through the sin of the first parents. At the other pole of the drama of salvation stands the fig tree of the conversion in book 8 of the *Confessions*. It would also appear to be the recounting of an historical event – Augustine weeping under the fig tree and the voices of children singing "tolle, lege" – yet the scene recalls the calling out of Nathanael from under the fig tree in the first chapter of the Gospel of John. Whether or not Augustine actually ever wept under a fig tree, the episode is an allusion to the call for the conversion of the Jews at the beginning of the Gospel. For all of its apparent historicity, Augustine's conversion is a re-enactment of the paradigm for all conversion.

There is no symbolic theft involved in Dante's confession. Unlike Augustine's, his drama of self-appropriation is accomplished without transgression or parental interdiction. It takes place in the Earthly Paradise, when

Virgil dismisses him with a secular blessing and Beatrice calls him by name. Whatever the nature of his guilt, it is represented here in erotic terms, but inscribed within a penitential context – Beatrice was once the occasion of his sin and is now its judge – as if to suggest that Eros is here redeemed rather than condemned. The return of Beatrice, in contrast with the banishment of Augustine's mistress or of Rousseau's Marianne,[10] marks the return of an Eros now domesticated and transformed into that amalgam of Christian and cosmic love which is distinctively Dantesque. This insistence on the recuperability of his erotic past distinguishes Dante's confession from virtually all others in the Christian tradition.

The confession itself is completely generic, with schematic allusions to the drama of salvation. There is a tree whose fruit must not be eaten, and a tree, perhaps even a fig tree, under which repentance takes place. These are elements of an elaborately stylized dumb show, revealing almost nothing of the concrete details of Dante's life. On the other hand, because of her previous appearance in the *Vita nuova*, Beatrice seems to be more than simply an allegorical figure. Her literary existence outside the confines of the *Purgatorio* confers a certain reality upon her, just as reality is conferred upon Virgil. In both cases, intertextuality counterfeits a history, about which we would otherwise know nothing.

To return to the general outline of autobiographical allegory in the *Inferno*, it may be said that the descent itself, and particularly the figure of Geryon which epitomizes it, are allegorical motifs claiming no existence outside the text. They structure elements of Dante's experience in such a way that an account of his life has at the same time a moral significance for "nostra vita." The protagonist of the story is at once Dante Alighieri and, as Charles Singleton pointed out, "whichever man," meaning by that phrase not the abstract "everyman" of morality plays, but rather an historical individual, elected by grace.[11] If we were to ask about the "truth" of such an account, in the everyday, biographical sense, the answer would certainly not be found in these allegorical motifs – rope, dragon, abyss – but rather in the existential realities underlying them.

We have said that Geryon introduces a social dimension into the tradition of Neoplatonic allegories, inasmuch as it suggests that the corruption of society can serve as a vehicle for plumbing the depths and then transcending them. Similarly, the central cantos of the *Inferno* embody a social and political critique unlike anything in Augustine's *Confessions*. Specific details of Dante's personal life elude us, as Augustine's do not, since they are represented – sometimes, perhaps, masked – by allegorical figures. Dante's public battles, however, are more readily accessible to interpretation.

The "veil" of allegory seems most transparent in the central cantos of the *Inferno*. Luigi Pirandello once suggested that the so-called "comedy of the devils" in the circle of barratry should be understood autobiographically, as Dante's grotesque indictment of the political corruption of his day, especially of the Black Guelfs, and also as his defense against a trumped-up charge of barratry brought against him during his absence.[12] This, for Pirandello, is the significance of the episode in which the pilgrim is nearly "tarred with the same brush" as the barrators. In these cantos, Dante uses the weapon of farce, rather than moral indignation, to refute the charges brought against him by his enemies.

Pirandello's observations may be adapted to apply to the flight on Geryon and other mysterious and apparently irreducible autobiographical details. The description of the crowds in Rome during the Jubilee year suggests perhaps an association between Dante's flight and his embassy to Rome to avert the entry of Charles of Valois into Florence. The duplicity of the pope might aptly be represented by a duplicitous Geryon, while the imagery of Antichrist that is used to describe the monster is consistent with traditional descriptions of a corrupt papacy.[13] Finally, Dante's defense for the smashing of the baptismal font would seem to be a New Testament version of his defense, in his letter to the Italian cardinals, for having laid hands on the Ark; that is, for having, as a layman, interfered in ecclesiastical matters, as did Uzzah, who was struck dead for his pains.[14] The meaning of such a clearly symbolic action – to smash the font, literally, would have been impossible without a wrecking crew – and of others like it can be derived from reading the events of Dante's public career in the biblical figures and patterns by which he has represented them.

As for the rest, the personal details that we would expect in autobiography, the text is mute. Dante's realism, his ability to endow traditional allegorical motifs with realistic substance (as did Augustine before him, with similar protestations about the historicity of his account), should not obscure for us the extent to which the particulars of Dante's life escape us.

Dante's journey is neither a poetic fiction nor a historical account; it is exemplary and allegorical. Like Augustine's life, it was meant to be both autobiographical and emblematic, a synthesis of the particular circumstances of an individual's life with paradigms of salvation history drawn from the Bible. It is what A. C. Charity has called "applied typology,"[15] meaning by that phrase the manifestation in Dante's life of the redemptive pattern of biblical history. In the following pages, we attempt to discuss the sense in which Dante's narrative may be thought of as theological allegory, and the degree to which its theological quality may be acknowledged even in a purely secular reading.

Allegory of poets, allegory of theologians

Just before Geryon appears, the narrator anticipates the reader's incredulity by insisting that he is telling the truth, even if it would seem to be a lie – "quel ver c'ha faccia di menzogna" (*Inferno* 16, 124). This remark amounts to distinguishing a fiction from a fraud: his story is the truth with the face of a lie, while fraud, Geryon, has the face of truth ("la faccia d'uom giusto"), hiding a lie, or at least the tail of a scorpion.

The contrast between a fraudulent lie and a fiction, a lie *secundum quid*, is reminiscent of Augustine's defense of poetic fiction in his *Contra mendacium*, where he remarks that "fictive narrations with true significations" are to be found in the Bible as well as in secular literature.[16] The episode of Geryon is just such a poetic fiction.[17] The narrator swears to the truth of his account by "le note di questa comedìa," which is perhaps an arch way of attributing a purely verbal reality to the monster. If this central part of the journey can be characterized as a fiction, then we may be justified in thinking of the whole journey in that way. The *Epistle to Can Grande* gives us some encouragement, since it uses the adverb "fictive" in order to describe the poem's *forma tractandi*. In spite of some complications which we shall have to discuss, the poem could then be said to conform to the definition of the "allegory of poets" given in the *Convivio*: "truth hidden under a beautiful lie."[18]

We shall see that the "allegory of poets" may be interpreted broadly to mean all of the figures and tropes a poet must employ in order to express his intended meaning. Because the meaning is intended, theologians sometimes referred to this kind of allegory as "allegory of the letter." Like the fictive narrations mentioned by Augustine, it is to be found in the Bible, as well as in secular literature. Beyond this kind of allegory, however, there is another kind, not in the writer's control, called the "allegory of theologians," which appears only in the Bible and was thought to be divinely inspired. From a modern, naturalistic point of view, it might be said that the allegory of theologians was sometimes a way of interpreting a text in spite of the author's intended meaning, as a way of superimposing a Christian significance anachronistically on an Old Testament text. This significance might also be referred to as the "allegory of the spirit," or, simply, the spiritual sense.

Obviously, the fact that both poets and theologians used the word "allegory" has led to considerable confusion, especially among Dante's interpreters. Most of the confusion has to do with the meaning of the word "literal." For poets, "literal" means what the words say, even if what they say is clearly a fable or a fiction. "Allegory" is what such fables or fictions mean: hence Dante's definition of allegory as truth hidden beneath a beautiful lie. For theologians, on the other hand, concerned with the historical authority of the Bible, the "letter" is thought of as the history of the Jews: the people, facts, and events of the Old Testament, rather than the mode in which the words convey that history. "Littera *gesta* docet," according to the mnemonic jingle of the Schools, "the letter teaches us *what happened.*" This is why the literal level is always true: no matter how poetically recounted, the events of the Old Testament did in fact take place. Such an assertion has nothing whatever to do with whether the words conveying those events are figurative or realistic.

An example will help to make this clear. Since the Bible is written in human language, it may be subjected to the same analysis as the writings of a human author. Thus, in a purely poetic analysis of Exodus 19:4, "You saw how I bore you up on eagles' wings," what the poets would call the letter is the figurative language, having to do with eagles and wings, while the allegorical sense has to do with what is signified by that figure, the events of Exodus. For the theologian, on the other hand, the letter lies beyond the words, in the historical fact: God leading the Jews out of Egypt into the desert. The metaphoric or figurative language conveying this literal meaning (wings and the eagle in the present instance) is simply rhetoric, what Thomas Aquinas calls "allegory of the letter."[19] Any meaning clearly intended by a human author is from a theological standpoint necessarily a *literal* meaning, even if conveyed by a most elaborate allegory of poets. No human author living in the time of Moses, however, could have foreseen what theological allegory would make of Exodus: for the theologian, the events of Exodus signify our redemption, wrought by Christ. The allegory of theologians is therefore an allegory *in factis*, not *in verbis*; it is not a way of writing at all, since the literal events were thought to exist quite apart from the words that commemorated them. It was, rather, the retrospective interpretation of the events of Jewish history in order to read in (or *into*) them the coming of Christ.

Theological allegory may be thought of as *meta*-allegory, in which the reality signified by the words of the text – say, Moses, or the river Jordan – is in turn taken as a sign to be further allegorized – Moses "means" John the Baptist, and Jordan "means" baptism – without any compromise of historicity. Taken together, all the persons and events of the Old Testament signify the coming of Christ. Put most simply, allegory in this sense is the relationship of the Old Testament to the New.

Only in a text of which God is the author can things both *mean* and *be*. From such a perspective, Joshua, for example, would not only *be* the man who led the Jews across the Jordan, he would also *mean* Jesus, whose name is the same as Joshua in Aramaic. Joshua existed, which is what is meant by the truth of the literal level, but he also functions as a figure for Christ. For this reason, he may be said to be a "shadow-bearing preface" of his own truth (*Paradiso* 30, 78).

The Old Testament is not the only repository for such signs; theological allegory looks at all reality as though it were so many signs written into a book, of which God is the author. This is what Augustine meant when he said that men use signs to point to things, but only God can use things to point to other things. It is as though there were no "thing-in-itself," but only signs in the "book" of the universe. Dante makes this point in the heaven of Jupiter, where presumably historical individuals, some mentioned only in secular texts, function as signs, semiotic sparks spelling out a biblical text. This suggests that the Bible could be considered the divinely inspired translation of God's anterior "book," historical *gesta*, into human language.

Moses and the Jews really existed and the events of Exodus took place, irrespective of whether the history was recounted in descriptive prose or allegorical poetry. The literal level of the Book of Exodus is the same as the literal level of Psalm 113 (114), "In Exitu Israel de Aegypto," in spite of the fact that the words of the psalm could scarcely be more figurative, with the sea and the river personified and the mountains and hills compared to rams and sheep. The author of the *Epistle to Can Grande* certainly speaks as a theologian rather than a poet when he ignores the lyrical prosopopaeia, the "bella menzogna" of Psalm 113 (114), telling us simply that "the letter [of the first verse] presents us with the departure of the children of Israel from Egypt in the time of Moses." The truth-value of the psalm and that of the Book of Exodus are exactly the same, for it is the truth of history, not of words. "Realism" and "lyricism" are part of the poet's craft; to a theologian defending the truth of the literal level, they are irrelevant.

The theological meaning allegorically signified by the verses beginning "In Exitu Israel de Aegypto" is, according to the epistle, "our redemption, wrought by Christ." Here too, it is clear that the author speaks as a theologian, since the meaning he ascribes to the verse is recoverable only by accepting on faith the authoritative interpretation given to the Exodus by St. Paul: "we were all with Moses, under the cloud and in the sea."[20] This significance, not discernible in the words of the text or even in the events they signify, could be read into those verses only by a Christian. In fact, theological allegory was virtually synonymous with the Christ-event: "quid *credas* allegoria." The New Testament was thought to be not so much a separate revelation, as the definitive ending of the revelation begun with the Old Testament, the fulfillment of its promise. If the letter of biblical allegory is the history of the Jews, then the spirit, the allegorical sense, is the coming of Christ.

The coming of Christ was believed to have been an event in time which transcended time, a *kairotic* moment which could be repeated in the soul of every Christian until the end of time. Thus, the advent of Christ was believed to be threefold: once, in the past, when He appeared among us in human form; again, in the present, in the soul of the convert or regenerate sinner; finally, at the end of time, in the Second Coming. It follows that the spiritual or allegorical sense, which is essentially the coming of Christ, is also threefold: the historical or allegorical sense as it is recounted in the New Testament; the moral or tropological sense (*quid agas*), meaning the applicability of those events to us now; and the anagogic sense (*quo tendas*), referring to the Second Coming and the end of time. The four levels of biblical allegory are more easily remembered as one plus three, meaning the history of the Old Testament interpreted by the threefold revelation, past, present, and future, of the New.

The word "historical" means *literal* when it applies to the history of the Jews, but it is also used to describe the first of the spiritual senses, meaning the historical coming of Christ. The ambiguity can be the source of some confusion, but it can also serve as a reminder that theological allegory is essentially the juxtaposition of two sets of events, two histories, rather than a rhetorical figure. As for the word "allegory," in its theological acceptance, it too can give rise to some confusion, as the epistle points out. "Allegory" in the strict sense means the second of the four levels of meaning, the historical coming of Christ. But "allegory" broadly speaking, in the theological sense, is synonymous with "spiritual" or "mystical," meaning all of the theological senses put together, the past, present, and future allegorical interpretations of the Old Testament.

Theological allegory may be said to be a reading of the Old Testament as if its plot were the Incarnation. However, there are other interpretive contexts in which the same allegorical principles have been applied. "Old Testament typology," for example, is the relationship of providential events in the history of the Jews to subsequent moments of their history, without reference to the coming of the Messiah. The same principles have also been invoked to establish connections between separate moments in the New Testament, without reference to the Old. Finally, just as the principles of poetic allegory were often applied to the interpretation of biblical texts, so theological principles have from time to time been applied to the interpretation of secular literature. Because of both its subject matter and its allegorical mode, the *Divina Commedia* in particular has been subjected to methods of interpretation that seem more appropriate to the Bible than to a literary work. What is more, many of the bitter disputes about literal truth in Scripture, fundamentalists against latitudinarians, have been recapitulated in the history of Dante criticism, often without the participants being aware of it.

If some interpreters have granted a quasi-biblical status to Dante's work, it is because the text seems to demand it by claiming to be prophetic and divinely inspired. The most obvious way to deal with such a claim is to accept it uncritically, and to attribute the poem's genesis to a vision, or to delusion. No critic has been so "fundamentalist" as to maintain that the entire text, complete with Virgilian echoes and autocitations, was dictated in *terza rima* to the poet/scribe. What has been suggested, however, is that the vision of Beatrice which Dante claimed to have had at the end of the *Vita nuova* was somehow the inspiration for this very different literary text.[21]

The appeal to divine revelation (or hallucination) in the interpretation of a text has a way of ending all discussion. Source hunting is greatly simplified, and one need no longer be puzzled about whom Dante put where and why if he did so on such unimpeachable authority. The theory breaks down, however, when we try to determine which parts of the poem should be considered intrinsic to his vision, and which are simply literary elaboration. Few critics have difficulty accepting Dante's claim that he saw God, for example, but it is evident that not even the poet expects us to believe in Geryon. If, on the other hand, we suppose that Dante's vision is not localized in the text, then it is no more relevant to this poem than Paul's vision is to his letters: such experiences may enhance the prophetic authority of the visionary among believers, but if they are not in the text, they have little to do with literary interpretation.

A more sophisticated way of dealing with the theological claim is to consider it a literary device, an attempt to imitate Scripture rather than to provide an account of a religious experience. Leo Spitzer perhaps anticipated this formalist approach to the poem when he attempted to understand Dante's impassioned addresses to the reader not as a claim to prophetic witness, as Erich Auerbach had argued, but rather esthetically, as a way for the poem to create its own audience.[22] By far the most influential formalist interpretation of the poem, however, is the work of Charles Singleton, for whom Dante's realism seemed to imitate, perhaps even rival, "God's way of writing."[23]

According to Singleton, Dante must have intended his allegory to be biblical, since he presented the poem's literal level as true, rather than as a "bella menzogna," and only the Bible could make such a claim. Singleton associated the extraordinary realism of Dante's poem with Scripture's claim to truth, construing the allegory of theologians to be, among other things, a superlative way of writing. The elegance of Singleton's argument masked its essential flaw: it blurred the distinction between what *seems* real and what really happened, between poetry and history, as distinguished by Aristotle in the

Poetics. Singleton's tone was ironic and deliberately provocative, intended to challenge *dantisti* who were diffident about using theology or biblical exegesis to interpret Dante's text. Nevertheless, his argument soon became canonical and led to a certain confusion about the meaning of theological allegory and its applicability to the poem.

The dramatic and mimetic power of Dante's story made it seem too *real* to Singleton for it to be classified as one more poetic allegory "of this for that," in which the literal level is a lie, so he associated it with biblical allegory, in which the letter is supposed to be true. This, said Singleton, is the allegory of "this *and* that." What made this shift possible was the ambiguity of the word "literal." In poetry, the literal level is the fiction, while in theology, it is the historical event. Thus, to say that Dante's fiction is theological allegory is to say that it is not fiction, but fact. Singleton attempted to avoid the obvious contradiction by suggesting that Dante was only *pretending* to be describing historical events: "[the] fiction is that the fiction is not a fiction." This is true, but trivial; such irony might be used to describe any fiction whatever.

The mimetic power of Dante's verses tells us nothing about their historicity, nor would historical truth, if it could be ascertained, make the text more profound or even more interesting. On the contrary, according to Aristotle, poetry is more philosophical and more significant than history because it deals with universals, which may be merely possible, rather than with particulars, however true. History makes particular statements that are subject to external criteria of truth or falsity, whereas poetry expresses universals and is judged by its coherence, or by what Northrop Frye called the "centripetal aspect of verbal structure."[24] Never was there a verbal structure more centripetal than Dante's poem, as Singleton, more than anyone else, has helped us understand. Its apparent substantiality does not imply historical truth, however, any more than figurality, in the psalm of exodus, precludes it.

No human author could possibly write theological allegory and still have any idea of its significance. It was precisely the point of theological allegory to take meaning out of the hands of an author and place it under the control of an exegetical tradition. So, for example, the Song of Songs was said to be about the relation of Christ to His Church, and Virgil's fourth *Eclogue* was about the coming of the Messiah, no matter *what* the words seemed to say. For theologians, the measure of all meaning, even in ancient literature, was the Bible, as interpreted by the New Testament. Whether the words of the Old Testament relate a fiction, such as the Song of Songs, or the realities of Jewish history, such as the Exodus, only God could make those elements *mean* the coming of Christ.

There remains the question of whether a human author can *imitate* theological allegory as Singleton suggests, by imitating reality. In fact, mimesis has the opposite effect, short-circuiting allegory and transforming it into irony. Instead of reaching out for meaning allegorically, realism turns significance back on itself by repeatedly affirming and then denying its own status as fiction. In Dante's terms, we might say that realism is alternately truth with the face of a lie, and a fraud that looks like the truth. Mimetic representation reaches ironic impasse rather than significance; it is a Geryon incapable of flight, a chimera with its tail in its mouth.

By its very nature, mimetic representation constantly affirms and simultaneously denies its identity with the original it seeks to reproduce. No matter how closely it resembles its model, we remain aware that it is merely a copy. Dante alludes to its inherent instability when he describes the reliefs on the terrace of pride in the *Purgatorio*. They are so lifelike that they defy interpretation by the pilgrim's two senses ("Faceva dir l'un 'No,' l'altro 'Sì, canta,'" *Purgatorio* 10, 60), leaving him unable to decide whether he is perceiving reality or its representation. The continual oscillation between the affirmation and denial of presence ("No . . . Sì, canta") is the same irony that we find expressed in Singleton's repetitive formula ("[the] fiction is that the fiction is not a fiction"). In spite of its mimetic virtuosity, "visibile parlare" remains difficult to interpret. It perplexes precisely because it is so lifelike, more like cinema than iconography.

It may be remarked in passing that if mimesis can provoke the uneasiness we associate with irony, it is also true that our failure to perceive irony may lead us to mistake it for mimesis. Thus Auerbach, in his famous essay on mimesis in *Inferno* 10, unwittingly revealed himself to be a victim of infernal irony when he perceived in the dazzlingly cerebral verses spoken by Cavalcante only "a direct experience of life which overwhelms everything else."[25] Praise for Dante's realism in this encounter masked Auerbach's impatience with the theological import of the father's lament. Far from indicating the biblical nature of the allegory, "mimesis" here indicates that even the most learned of Dante's critics reached an interpretive dead end.

Because he was anxious to account for the poem's extraordinary realism, Singleton associated it with the allegory of the Bible, and sought to distinguish both from the purely literary allegory of poetry. We have, however, seen that what distinguishes the allegory of theologians from the allegory of poets is not verisimilitude, but the fact that it is expressed in things and events, rather than words. Beyond the words of the Bible, there was said to be another allegorical significance, inherent in things signified by the written text, a "deep structure" of meaning independent of any scribal intention. This significance was thought to be part of God's plan for the entire cosmos, the text imagined by Augustine as inscribed on "the parchment of the heavens," without letters and without words.[26]

In reality, of course, this ideal allegory was nothing other than the church's interpretation of the Bible, particularly of the Old Testament, hypostatized as though it had an autonomous existence and were the source of the written text, rather than its spectral projection. Its "deep structure" was simply the virtual image of surface structure, a reduplication that created the illusion of origin: Derrida would describe it as a form of "archiécriture."[27] It is in the nature of allegory that it can make no claim to literal truth and that its significance is open to conflicting interpretations. For the believer, however, the illusion that the Bible derived from God's book, when in fact it was its source, had the effect of conferring ontological reality with significance. In such a perfectly intelligible universe, where things are as meaningful as words, the promise of allegory is already fulfilled by the presence of its Maker.

In the *Paradiso*, the end term of both the journey and the poem are represented by the vision of the Trinity in the form of a book, made up not of words, but of things: "sustanze e accidenti e lor costume" (33, 88). This divine text obviously belongs in the same tradition as Augustine's cosmic parchment, and has been studied in that way, most prominently by E. R. Curtius.[28] Nevertheless, Dante's representation of God's book is distinctively his own. Just as the inscription on the gates of Hell is written in *terza rima*, as though there were no distinction between what he saw and what we read, so the vision of God as a book corresponds to the closure of the text we hold in our hands, despite the protestations of its fragility and dispersion. Dante asserts that God's book is his transcendent source, that he is merely God's humble scribe. It might equally well be said, however, that God's book is the idealized reflection of Dante's own text, serving to justify his prophetic (not to say Promethean) claim. He imitated the Bible by aspiring to its authority, not by copying its style.

Theology and literary structure

We have seen that the allegory of theologians is analogous to poetic allegory, except that it was believed to be inherent in things, rather than merely expressed in words. The same might be said of the general relationship of theology to poetry. The two systems are analogous, except that theology claims to reflect spiritual reality rather than create it. From a modern point of view, theology would seem to be a form of collective poetry which attempts to bestow existence on the perfection to which it aspires, much as St. Anselm's ontological argument tried to confer substantiality on a syllogism. The doctrine of the Incarnation would seem the ultimate sanction for granting reality to verbal structures, since it was itself described in the Gospel of John as the *Word* made flesh.

Once theology is recognized as a verbal system, rather than a religion, its affinity to poetry becomes clear. Both use what Kenneth Burke calls the "logic of perfection" to reach totality and closure.[29] Because of this affinity, theologians often used linguistic analogies to describe the spiritual world. According to Burke, it is possible to reverse the process; that is, to reduce theology to "logology" in order to show how theological principles were in fact derived from verbal systems. The interchangeability of theological and poetic coherence is particularly apparent in the works of Augustine, for whom the mystery of time, the relationship of signs to significance in the Eucharist, the creation of the universe, and the inner life of the Trinity, were all to be understood according to verbal and poetic models. Divine Justice was like a poem with variable meter, death was like phonemic silence, even God's relationship to the world was thought of as the embodiment of a speech act, the incarnation of a proffered word. The fact that this verbal system was "made flesh" seemed to Augustine to distinguish it from Platonism, which he thought of as an equally logocentric system.

A form of logological analysis will help us to understand the theological claim of Dante's poem in terms of narrative principles. Only a believer could accept the truth of theological allegory, since it entails a belief in the possibility of death and resurrection. Yet an analogous act of faith is required to take seriously the claim that autobiographical narrative is a faithful and definitive portrait of an author's former self. The apparent absurdity of theological allegory is much like the narrative absurdity which we accept each time we are presented with a story that purports to be the true and final portrait of a protagonist who has become narrator and judge of his own story. Spiritual death and resurrection constitute not only the theme of such a narrative, but also the logical condition for its existence, since it cannot begin without a separation of the protagonist from the author, nor end without a return. Singleton is correct to say that Dante's allegory is biblical, but it is not the poem's mimetic power that so qualifies it. It is, rather, its narrative structure, identical to the narrative structure of the Old Testament in the Christian reading, or of any retrospective reading of one's own history, thematically represented as a conversion.[30]

Our discussion of theological allegory has stressed its diachronicity as the juxtaposition of two sets of historical events, rather than a trope. This corresponds exactly to the diachronicity of narrative structure, the "then" of experience reinterpreted in the "now" of the story. It might be argued that narrative diachronicity stands for the "conversion" of the Old Testament into the New, or for the experience of personal conversion. It might equally well be argued, however, that narrative diachronicity creates the illusion of retrospective reinterpretation, that there is no conversion unless and until the story is told. Whether the diachronism of conversion corresponds to an experience or is an illusion created by the narrative, however, it is the source of the irony that is pervasive in the *Inferno*. Infernal irony is a dramatization of the conflict inherent in autobiography, the clash between the naive perspective of a former self, and the retrospective correction superimposed upon it from the ending of the story.

To some exegetes, it seemed that the first words of the Gospel of John referred back to the first words of Genesis. Universal history might be understood as the unfolding of God's word back to its own origin, from the Creation to the Incarnation. It was like a sentence, beginning with the intention of a speaker whose word is gradually unfolded until it has been completely uttered and "made flesh." An analogous circularity exists in the unfolding of autobiography. Beginning with what Burke would call a narrative tautology ("I am I"), a negative is introduced ("I was not always so") in order to be refined away ("therefore I am I").[31] Reconciling the diachronic linearity of the story with this circular return to the beginning is the narrative equivalent of squaring the circle.

The Incarnation is not only the final theme of the *Paradiso*, but also the moment that, from the standpoint of narrative logic, makes the poem possible. The transformation of the omniscient, disembodied voice of the narrator into the voice of the pilgrim, speaking in the present tense – "cotal son io" – may be thought of as a novelistic incarnation, the coming together of an intelligible "word" with the "flesh" of individual experience. The geometrical paradox to which Dante alludes corresponds to a narrative paradox: the closing of a narrative circle which is at the same time squared by the linear temporality of the journey.

NOTES

1 *Tractatus* 123 on John 21:18 in *Patrologia Latina* 35 (1966). For a contemporary view of the passage and discussions of its meaning, see Rudolf Bultmann, *The Gospel of John: A Commentary*, trans. G. R. Beasley-Murray (Oxford: Blackwell, 1971), p. 713.

2 *Confessions* 7, 21.

3 See, among many others, Maria Corti, "On the Metaphors of Sailing, Flight, and Tongues of Fire in the episode of Ulysses (*Inf.* 26)," *Stanford Italian Review* 9 (1990): 33.

4 See A. Ascoli, *Ariosto's Bitter Harmony* (Princeton: Princeton University Press, 1987), p. 251.

5 For Dante's use of these Augustinian themes, see the first chapter ("Allegory") of Charles S. Singleton, *Dante's Commedia: Elements of Structure*, Dante Studies 1 (Cambridge, MA: Harvard University Press, 1954), esp. p. 7.

6 Pierre Courcelle, *Recherches sur les Confessions de St. Augustin* (Paris: E. de Boccard, 1950), esp. pp. 111ff.

7 *Confessions*, 6, 10, 16. Courcelle compiled a repertory of citations of Plato's "region of unlikeness" from *Statesman* 272 to André Gide in *Les Confessions de St. Augustin dans la tradition littéraire* (Paris: Etudes Augustiniennes, 1963), pp. 623ff.

8 Bruno Nardi, "La tragedia d'Ulisse," in *Dante e la cultura medievale: Nuovi saggi di filosofia dantesca*, 2nd edn. (Bari: Laterza, 1949), pp. 153–65. See also David Thompson, *Dante's Epic Journeys* (Baltimore: The Johns Hopkins University Press, 1974).

9 Giorgio Padoan, "Ulisse 'fandi fictor' e le vie della sapienza," *Studi danteschi* 37 (1960): 21–61.

10 The conclusion of book 2 of Rousseau's *Confessions* relates Jean-Jacques's theft of a piece of ribbon to give to Marianne, a servant girl, whom he then publicly accuses of having stolen it. The episode is obviously an imitation of Augustine's theft of pears, but with a difference: the triviality of Augustine's theft was meant to suggest that any of his readers would be capable of such an act, whereas Rousseau's virtuosity consists in transforming banal pilfering into a truly reprehensible crime.

11 *Journey to Beatrice*, Dante Studies 2 (Cambridge, MA: Harvard University Press, 1958), p. 5.

12 "La commedia dei diavoli," in *Saggi, poesie e scritti vari*, ed. Manlio Lo Vecchio-Musti, (Milan: Mondadori, 1960). Leo Spitzer is more skeptical: "Farcical Elements in *Inferno* XXI–XXIII," rpt. most recently in *Representative Essays*, ed. Alban K. Forcione *et al.* (Stanford: Stanford University Press, 1988), p. 172.

13 See John B. Friedman, "Antichrist and the Iconography of Dante's Geryon," *Journal of the Warburg and Courtauld Institutes* 35 (1972): 108–22.

14 *Epistola* 32, 9, referring to 2 Samuel 6:6.

15 A. C. Charity, *Events and their Afterlife* (Cambridge: Cambridge University Press, 1966), p. 35.

16 *Contra mendacium*, 13, 28, quoted by Busnelli and Vandelli in their commentary on *Convivio* II, i, 5 (Florence: Le Monnier, 1968), I, p. 98.

17 See the remarks of T. Barolini, *Dante's Poets: Textuality and Truth in the Comedy* (Princeton: Princeton University Press), p. 213. On the question of narrative truth, see Ruth Morse, *Truth and Convention in the Middle Ages: Rhetoric, Representation and Reality* (Cambridge: Cambridge University Press, 1991), who does not, however, discuss Geryon.

18 There is a serious lacuna at *Convivio* II, i, 4, emended with discussion by Busnelli and Vandelli who include a useful appendix. For an accurate translation and explanation, see Christopher Ryan, trans., *The Banquet*, Stanford French and Italian Studies, 61 (Saratoga: Anma Libri, 1989), pp. 42–43 and note.

19 See P. Synave, "La doctrine de St. Thomas d'Aquin sur le sens littéral des Ecritures," *Revue Biblique* 35 (1926): 40–65.

20 For the applicability of the theme to the *Purgatorio*, see Charles S. Singleton, "In Exitu Israel de Aegypto," rpt. in J. Freccero, ed., *Dante: Twentieth Century Views* (Englewood Cliffs: Prentice-Hall, 1965), p. 102.

21 Perhaps the most consistent exponent of such a theory was Bruno Nardi, who returned repeatedly to his idea of Dante as visionary prophet: "Dante profeta," in *Dante e la cultura medievale*, p. 265.

22 Spitzer, "The Addresses to the Reader in the *Commedia*," in Forcione *et al., Representative Essays*, p. 178; Erich Auerbach, "Dante's Addresses to the Reader," *Romance Philology* 7 (1954): 268–78.

23 Singleton, "Appendix: Two Kinds of Allegory," in *Dante's Commedia: Elements of Structure*, p. 84.

24 Northrop Frye, *The Great Code* (New York: Harcourt Brace Jovanovich, 1982), pp. 60ff.

25 Erich Auerbach, "Farinata and Cavalcante," in *Mimesis*, trans. W. R. Trask (Princeton: Princeton University Press, 1953), pp. 174–202.

26 *Confessions*, 13, 15, with reference to Apocalypse 6:14 and Psalms 103:2.

27 Jacques Derrida, *De la grammatologie* (Paris: Editions de Minuit, 1967), p. 103.

28 E. R. Curtius, "The Book as Symbol," in *European Literature and the Latin Middle Ages*, trans. W. R. Trask (New York: Pantheon, 1953), p. 302.

29 Kenneth Burke, *The Rhetoric of Religion: Studies in Logology* (Berkeley: University of California Press, 1961), on which see J. Freccero, "Burke on Logology," in H. White and M. Brose, eds., *Representing Kenneth Burke*, English Institute Essays (Baltimore: The Johns Hopkins University Press, 1982).

30 Narrative diachronicity is incompatible with a Joachistic theory of a third testament to come. However congenial triadic speculation may be for models of becoming (Hegel), the idea of conversion requires duality, just as *terza rima* requires duality in order to begin or end.

31 Burke, *Rhetoric*, p. 183.

II

JOAN FERRANTE

A poetics of chaos and harmony

That Dante presents Hell as a realm of chaos and confusion, and Paradise as one of harmony and union, a reader of the *Commedia* recognizes in the first reading. The astonishing variety of settings and of infernal guards in Hell, the rapid shifts from one of the many damned souls to another, their hostility to Dante and to their companions, all contrast sharply with Paradise, where the heavens seem to differ only in intensity of light and joy, where the souls come to meet and to share their joy with Dante, and the movement from one soul to another seems slow and dignified. Purgatory is transitional, with fewer changes in setting, guards who instruct rather than control, souls fixed only temporarily where Dante sees them, trying to be helpful to him and to each other. Perhaps because it is transitional, Purgatory is more given to formal and visual patterns which fix it in the mind if not in reality.

These large differences are suggested by the action of the plot, but are reinforced by a whole range of formal elements. I shall consider a number of these here: the length of individual cantos, the relative proportions of narrative and speech, enjambment, and the varieties of rhyme and of rhyme sounds within and beyond *terza rima*. In each case, the question I put to the poem gave me the expected answer, but sometimes in unexpected ways. I came to see that the apparent increase in the poet's control over formal techniques as he proceeds is an illusion carefully created by Dante, that he exercises as much control and skill to craft the chaos of Hell as the harmony of Paradise.

The three canticles are symmetrical, with thirty-three cantos each, except that *Inferno* has one more, an introduction to the whole poem, which prevents it from having the numerologically significant thirty-three, and gives Dante the ideal total of one hundred. Within that larger symmetry, however, there is considerable variety in the length of lines per canto, and in the differences in length between cantos (see charts 1 and 2). The differences, as one would expect, are the greatest in *Inferno*, contributing to the sense of chaos;

Chart 1 *Number of lines per canto*

	Inferno	Purgatorio	Paradiso
1	136	136	142
2	142	133	148
3	136	145	130
4	151	139	142
5	142	136	139
6	115	151	142
7	130	136	148
8	130	139	148
9	133	145	142
10	136	139	148
11	115	142	139
12	139	136	145
13	151	154	142
14	142	151	139
15	124	145	148
16	136	145	154
17	136	139	142
18	136	145	136
19	133	145	148
20	130	151	148
21	139	136	142
22	151	154	154
23	148	133	139
24	151	154	154
25	151	139	139
26	142	148	142
27	136	142	148
28	142	148	139
29	139	154	145
30	148	145	148
31	145	145	142
32	139	160	151
33	157	145	145
34	139		

Note: There is a range of 42 lines between the longest and shortest canto of *Inferno* (115 to 157 lines), of 27 lines in *Purgatorio* (133 to 160), 24 lines in *Paradiso* (130 to 154); the greatest difference in length between one canto and the next is *Inferno* 5 to 6 (27 lines), with frequent large leaps (from 12 to 24 lines), whereas the largest leap in *Paradiso* is 18 lines, with most between 3 and 6, and in *Purgatorio*, the largest differences are 21 and 18 lines, all occurring, like the 15-line leaps, within set patterns. There is a clear movement towards greater unity as well as greater length in *Paradiso*: 21 cantos number between 142 and 148 lines, making that span the norm for the poem (only 4 cantos in *Paradiso* are longer, only 7 shorter, while in *Purgatorio*, 8 are longer, 12 shorter, and in *Inferno*, 6 are longer and 21 are shorter). There are 11 different canto lengths in *Inferno* (6 recurring only once or twice), 9 in *Purgatorio* (1 nine times, 4 only once or twice), and 8 in *Paradiso* (2 nine times, and only 3 once, evenly distributed through the canticle [see chart 2]).

Chart 2 *Frequency of canto lengths*

Number of lines	*Inferno*	*Purgatorio*	*Paradiso*
115	2	0	0
124	1	0	0
130	3	0	1
133	2	2	0
136	7	5	1
139	5	5	6
142	5	2	9
145	1	9	3
148	2	2	9
151	5	3	1
154	0	4	3
157	1	0	0
160	0	1	0

Chart 3 *Symmetrical patterns in the structure of* Purgatorio

Ante-Purgatory	Dream	Sins	Dream	Sins	Dream	Earthly Paradise
Cato	eagle	pride	siren	avarice	Lia	Matelda
drama of		envy		gluttony		procession
serpent and		wrath		lust		drama of chariot
angels		sloth				

Terraces of *Purgatorio*

angel	examples of virtues	souls	examples of vices	angel

Terrace of avarice and prodigality

angel	soul	examples	soul	examples	soul	angel
	pope		king		poet	

Note: Enrico De'negri suggested the structure for the terraces of Purgatory, "Tema e iconografia del *Purgatorio*," *Romanic Review* 49 (1958): 81–104. I extended it to the canticle.

the smallest in *Paradiso*, reinforcing the sense of unity. In *Purgatorio*, on the other hand, the differences are frequently used to establish patterns. Singleton pointed out one pattern of seven cantos in the middle of the canticle, with Virgil's discussion of love as the motivation of all action, good and bad, at its center (see chart 1); I would extend this pattern to the two cantos which immediately precede and follow this group, and note that Dante sets off the whole pattern with the two largest leaps in the canticle (twenty-one lines), perhaps registering his excitement at the appearance of the poet, Statius, and then of his friend, Forese. The same three significant line numbers that occur, as Singleton pointed out, at the center (139, 145 = 10, and 151 = 7) with one other, 136 (= 10), also occur in a similar pattern in the Ante-Purgatory, centered on the political canto 6 and its fierce attack on Italy and Florence, set off by leaps of fifteen lines.[1] At the end of the canticle, there is a similar rise and drop of fifteen lines on either side of canto 32, the longest in the poem (160 lines), which describes the action of the griffin and the relations between church and empire, a subject of prime importance to the poet. The longest canto in *Inferno* is 33, the canto of Ugolino, the traitor, the arch symbol of the damned who all in some way betray society and destroy themselves and those around them. In *Paradiso*, the longest cantos (three of 154 lines) include descriptions of a state of innocence in the polis (the old Florence, canto 16), in the church (the beginnings of monasticism, canto 22), and in the individual (Dante's statement of faith to St. Peter, canto 24).

The same sorts of distinctions are found in the distribution of descriptive narrative, dialogue, and long speeches: in *Inferno*, there is greater difference in the number that fall into one category or another, more cantos that are both narrative and dialogue, and generally shorter speeches within the dialogue; in *Purgatorio* there is more balance between the number of cantos dominated by long speeches, dialogue, or narrative, but still a considerable number (ten) that are divided; while in *Paradiso*, only two cantos are divided, and the number dominated by long speeches is more than double that of *Inferno* (see chart 4). Except for Virgil, who speaks at length in two cantos (canto 11 on the categories of sin, and canto 20 correcting himself on the origin of Mantova), the long speeches of *Inferno* are delivered by major sinners: Ulysses (fifty-three lines), Guido da Montefeltro (sixty-nine lines), and Ugolino (seventy-two lines); others who leave a strong impression on the reader, like Francesca, Brunetto Latini, and Pier della Vigna, do not in fact speak at length. The long speeches in *Purgatorio* are given by statesmen and women, and epic poets: Virgil (in canto 17, again on the division of sins), Guido del Duca, Marco Lombardo, Hugh Capet, Statius, and Matelda. The only non-epic poet to speak at length is Sordello, who was concerned with the responsibilities of European rulers; other vernacular

Chart 4 *Distribution of types of discourse*

	Descriptive narrative	Dialogue	Long speeches	
Inferno				
cantos with margin of over 100 lines	17, 24, 25	2	at least 50 lines	11, 20, 26, 27, 33
more than 30 lines	3, 4, 9, 22, 31, 34	7, 10, 13, 15, 30		
Purgatorio				
cantos with margin of over 100 lines	6, 9, 10, 12, 29, 30, 32	5, 11, 21, 22	at least 50 lines	7, 4, 16, 17, 20, 25, 28
37 to 50 lines	2, 27	18, 23, 33		
Paradiso				
cantos with margin of over 100 lines	18	0	80–145 lines	2, 4, 5, 6, 7, 11, 12, 13, 16, 29, 32
more than 60 lines	14, 23, 30, 31, 33	8, 9, 15, 17, 19, 24, 26, 27		
30 to 50 lines	1, 10	3, 20, 21, 22		
Divided cantos:	*Inferno* 1, 5, 6, 8, 12, 14, 16, 18, 19, 21, 23, 28, 29, 32 *Purgatorio* 1, 3, 4, 8, 13, 15, 19, 24, 26, 31 *Paradiso* 25, 28			

Note: I have not included in the cantos dominated by long speeches in *Paradiso* several which would have qualified in *Inferno* or *Purgatorio* because speeches of 39 to 62 lines are not long by the standards of *Paradiso*.

poets, Bonagiunta da Lucca, Guido Guinizzelli, and Arnaut Daniel, are not permitted to say much. Beatrice, who dominates the last canto of *Purgatorio*, makes relatively short speeches (the longest is forty-eight lines) compared to *Paradiso*. There, her speeches (from 80 to 136 lines) dominate five cantos, 2, 4, 5, 7, and 29, but the only figure whose words occupy an entire canto (in all of the *Commedia*) is the Emperor Justinian (canto 6). The other major speakers are Thomas Aquinas (cantos 11 and 13), Bonaventure (canto 12), Cacciaguida (canto 16), and Bernard (canto 32): three saints (authors), and Dante's crusader ancestor, whose presence dominates three cantos.

Dante allows his characters' words to take over the poem more and more as he progresses through it, both by longer speeches and by giving them, rather than the narrator, the first or last word of a canto. Sixteen of the cantos in *Paradiso* end with a spoken word, with Beatrice having the last word in six, Cacciaguida in three, Thomas in two, Bonaventure, Adam, Justinian, the eagle, and Charles Martel in one each. Five cantos begin with a character speaking: Beatrice twice, Justinian, Bernard, and "tutto paradiso" once each. Bernard's opening words in canto 33 complete the sentence Dante had begun at the end of the previous canto. Four of the cantos in *Purgatorio* begin with a spoken voice: souls praying, Guido del Duca, the nymphs in the Earthly Paradise, and Beatrice continuing from the previous canto (as Dante notes [31, 1, 4], saying she began again without a pause, though his words create a pause). Fifteen cantos end with a character speaking, seven a minor character: two women (Pia and Sapia), an excommunicated prince (Manfred), a pope (Hadrian), an illuminator (Oderisi), and the two poets who make long speeches (Sordello and Statius) are permitted to have the last word. In *Inferno*, only three cantos begin with someone speaking: Pluto, and Virgil describing the monsters, Geryon and Lucifer. Eleven cantos end with a spoken word: five times souls command our attention – the anonymous suicide and Ulysses both describing their chilling ends, Vanni Fucci attacking Dante, Bertran de Born defining his punishment, Capocchio boasting of his gifts – and the deceptive offer of the pilgrim Dante to avenge Ugolino ends one canto, while Virgil's words of assurance, direction, or correction end five.

Transitions from one canto to another are, as one would expect, sharper in *Inferno*, where there are clear endings or new beginnings fourteen times, while six cantos look ahead to the next at their end, and fourteen carry over the action or comment on it. In *Purgatorio*, Dante begins to extend the divisions well beyond cantos to whole sections of the mountain: only six cantos here have distinct endings or changes of section. The extensions are even greater in *Paradiso*, where one heaven can take up four cantos, and all but four of the cantos are continuous in setting or scene.[2] In addition, two characters come back to speak to Dante after others have spoken, Thomas Aquinas after a break of one canto, and Peter after a break of two, which seems to extend those sections. Forese had also resumed a conversation with Dante after Bonagiunta's, but within the next canto (*Purgatorio* 24), and of course Farinata continued to speak to Dante after Cavalcanti's brief interruption in the same canto (*Inferno* 10).

The extension beyond cantos that begins in *Purgatorio* and intensifies in *Paradiso* is echoed on a smaller scale by enjambment. A device that in *Inferno* Dante uses mainly for surprise or shock, to unsettle the reader, is used in the other canticles primarily to extend the thought further and further beyond the line. Enjambment occurs much less frequently in *Inferno* where each line tends to be a unit even when it is intimately connected to another. The primary effect of enjambment in *Inferno* is to force the reader to rethink a previous notion, or to take in an uncomfortable new thought, for example, "Mal dar e mal tener lo mondo pulcro/ha tolto lor" (7, 58–59), where "lo mondo pulcro" seems to be the object of "dar" and "tener," seducing us into making the same error the misers and prodigals made, until we come to the next line and discover it is the object of "ha tolto," what they have lost not what they gave and held. Enjambments in *Inferno* are often emphasized by alliteration: "infin che 'l Veltro/verrà" (1, 101–02); "coloro/che corrono" (15, 121–22); "grazie/grandi" (18, 134–35); "l'imagine perversa/parea" (25, 77–78); "qual mozzo/mostrasse" (28, 19–20).

The enjambments in *Inferno* are usually between noun and modifier, subject and verb, transitive verb and object, participle and auxiliary; occasionally a line ends with "quando" or "forse," but only once, I believe, with a pronoun subject ("ch'ello/non s'apparecchi," 22, 92–93). In *Purgatorio*, Dante ends more lines with pronouns, as well as articles and an occasional preposition, creating a greater sense of suspension and drawing the thought out: "ch'io/non potea" (*Purgatorio* 28, 23–24), "ne la/via" (17, 55–56). Although enjambment is occasionally used to startle in *Purgatorio* ("O è preparazion che ne l'abisso/del tuo consiglio," 6, 121–22, where we expect the abyss to be Hell, rather than divine counsel), it is most often used as it will be in *Paradiso*, to extend the thought, to lengthen the poetic unit beyond the line, ultimately to the *terzina* (and further in *Paradiso*):

> E io a lui: "I' mi son un che, quando
> Amor mi spira, noto, e a quel modo
> ch'e' ditta dentro vo significando."
> (*Purgatorio* 24, 52–54)

The presence of other poets, particularly Sordello and Statius, seems to move Dante to a greater use of enjambment (cantos 6 and 7, 21 and 22), as does the departure of Virgil: "Virgilio n'avea lasciati scemi/di sé" (30, 49–50). As he did in *Inferno* but proportionally less frequently, Dante sometimes uses alliteration to emphasize the surprise: "io stavo/stupido" (*Purgatorio* 4, 58–59); "passo/possibile" (11, 50–51); "vita nova/virtualmente" (30, 115–16); "poco/più" (33, 5–6); "mosse/me" (33, 14–15).

While the instances of strict enjambment in *Purgatorio* number in the tens and twenties per canto, and are usually fewer than fifteen per canto in *Inferno*, they rise to the thirties, forties, and fifties in *Paradiso*. The line is no longer a sufficient unit for Dante's thought here, and even the *terzina* must occasionally be extended. Names are divided ("Alberto/è di Cologna," *Paradiso* 10, 98–99; "Bonaventura/da Bagnoregio,'" 12, 127–28), as are Latin phrases ("superinfusa/gratia Dei," 15, 28–29, even one of great sanctity, "Ave,/ Maria," 3, 121–22), numbers (cinquecento cinquanta/e trenta fiate," 16, 37–38), and most startling, a word ("differente-/mente," 24, 16–17), as though the end of the line had no significance (despite the rhyme, but even the rhyme is subject to extension in *Paradiso*, see below). This is not to say that enjambment is not still used to startle ("là entro si tranquilla/Raab," 9, 115–16), but its primary purpose in *Paradiso* is to destroy the boundary of the poetic line, sometimes with perfect symmetry, noun/verb . . . verb/noun:

> Né per ambage, in che la gente folle
> già s'inviscava pria che fosse anciso
> l'Agnel di Dio che le peccata tolle.
> (*Paradiso* 17, 31–33)

The extension of the poetic unit begins at the beginning of the canticle ("Nel ciel che più de la sua luce prende/fu' io, e vidi cose che ridire/né sa né può chi di là sù discende," 1, 4–6) and continues throughout, extending often beyond the *terzina*, as in 14, 118–23, where a "come/così" construction makes a unit of two *terzine*, and enjambment connects the lines within them.

The unusual Latin enjambments in *Paradiso* – there is one in *Purgatorio*, "Beati/pacifici" (17, 68–69), less startling because of the way it continues "che son sanz' ira mala" – are typical of the way Dante uses Latin in the canticle. Not only are there more Latin words in the text in *Paradiso*, but they are more at home in it, part of the Italian sentence and rhyme scheme, rather than a distinct quote as they usually are in *Purgatorio*. In *Paradiso*, Dante seems to be moving towards a kind of universal language, incorporating Latin, Greek, Hebrew, and French elements, as well as Italian words he creates. In *Inferno*, on the other hand, language usually gets in the way of communication. There is little Latin in *Inferno*,[3] but there are dialect words, which emphasize the isolation and limited vision of the damned ("sipa," 18, 61; "co," 20, 76; "otta," 21, 112; "mo," 23, 7 and 27, 20; "issa," 23, 7; and "Istra ten va; più non t'adizzo," 27, 21), and gibberish, which points up their inability to interact rationally (Pluto's "Pape Satàn, pape Satàn aleppe," 7, 1; Nembrot's "Raphèl maì amècche zabì almi," 31, 67). Even the souls who speak elegantly, like Francesca, Farinata, and Ulysses, attempt to deceive with their words, the worst abuse of speech.

Purgatorio, in contrast, makes a successful effort to reclaim speech, to use it for prayer and guidance, compassion and love, to overcome, by ignoring, the obstacles to understanding in different languages. Here Latin, French, Provençal, and Italian are still distinct languages, but they are all "ours": the

Italian-born, French-dwelling, Provençal poet, Sordello, says of Virgil: "he showed what *our* tongue could do" ("mostrò ciò che potea la lingua nostra," *Purgatorio* 7, 17). Hugh Capet and Dante use "Frenchisms," "giuggia" (20, 48) and "alluminar" (11, 81), and Arnaut Daniel speaks in his native Provençal for eight lines within the Italian rhyme scheme (26, 140–47). Latin is scattered throughout the canticle, mainly citations from the Bible, beginning with "*In exitu Isräel de Aegypto*" (2, 46), and one from the *Aeneid*, "*Manibus oh date liliä plenis!*" (30, 21). Pope Hadrian identifies himself using Latin, presumably as suitable to the dignity of his position ("scias quod ego fui successor Petri," 19, 99), and Dante echoes the elevated spirit of the procession with the gratuitous "ad vocem tanti senis" (30, 17). The loss of Virgil also inspires Latin from Dante, "Virgilio dolcissimo *patre*" (30, 50, rhyming with "matre"; my emphasis).

Like "patre," the Latin words in *Paradiso* seem to be an integral part of Dante's thought. He speaks of "latino" in this canticle as the equivalent of clarity, of the highest level of discourse (*Paradiso* 3, 63; 10, 120; 12, 144; and 17, 35), and he uses Latin precisely, as in 1, 70: "trasumanar significar *per verba*/non si poria," where he means, I think, it cannot be done in *Latin* words; cf. "necesse" and "esse" in 3, 77 and 79, which carry a weight of scholastic thought (cf. 13, 98–100), and the "velle" of 33, 143, with the full theological meaning of the "will." Dante also incorporates a few words from God's language, Hebrew, into a Latin hymn ("sabaoth" and "malacoth," 7, 1–3), which, because the first alliterates ("Osanna, sanctus Deus sabaoth") and the second rhymes, do not seem alien. Dante adopts Greek words, "archimandrita" (11, 99), and "latria" (21, 111), and makes one up, "teodia" (25, 73), from *theos*, apparently by analogy with *salmodia*, but all of them sit well within the Italian text.

The *Commedia* has many neologisms, the exact number depending on who is counting, but everyone finds twice as many in *Paradiso* as in the other canticles. Most of them are verbs, made from other verbs, or nouns, or numbers, or adjectives, or pronouns, all an attempt to describe an action which cannot be adequately described with the available vocabulary. This is particularly evident in *Paradiso*, where words like "imparadisa," "inciela," "ingigliarsi," "sempiterni," and particularly "inmii," "intuassi," "inlei," and "inluia," approximate the deep union of souls with heaven or with each other. The most interesting made-up words in *Purgatorio* describe the mountain or the setting: it "dislakes" itself ("si dislaga," 3, 15), that is, rises from the sea towards heaven but with the added sense of leaving the sea behind; it "disevils" ("dismala," 13, 3) those who climb it; the third step at the gate "amasses" itself ("s'ammassiccia," 9, 100) over the others, as satisfaction must loom larger than contrition and confession. The best-known neologism in *Inferno* is "contrapasso," the Aristotelian name Bertran de Born gives to the relation of his punishment to his sin (28, 142), but a number of others are worth noting. Virgil refuses to beautify words to describe the misers and prodigals ("parole non ci *appulcro*," 7, 60); the tears of the old man of Crete "derock" themselves down through Hell ("lor corso in questa valle si *diroccia*," 14, 115); one simoniac pope speaks of another who preceded him "simonizing" ("simoneggiando," 19, 74); Virgil tells Dante to "unbed" himself ("omai convien che tu così ti *spoltre*," 24, 46), and the ice of Cocytus is so thick that it would not "creak" if a mountain fell on it ("non avria . . . fatto *cricchi*," 32, 30; my emphasis), an onomatopoeic coinage.

Many of these neologisms are also rhyme words, bringing them all the more to the reader's attention. Dante's rhymes are the last, and perhaps the most important, of the formal elements to be discussed. I will not talk about *terza rima* per se, since the scheme of three interlocking rhymes and their relation to the Trinity is by now a truism. I will, instead, look at the variations of *terza rima*, the use of equivocal and "core" rhymes within a rhyme group, and the extension of a group by fourth and fifth rhymes, or by alliteration, assonance, and consonance, which connect it to other rhymes outside it. Dante uses equivocal rhymes, the same word with different meanings, in all three canticles, with decreasing frequency (about thirty-five in *Inferno*, twenty-six in *Purgatorio* [not counting the two repeated rhymes, "per ammenda" and "me"], and twenty-two in *Paradiso* [not counting "vidi" or "Cristo"]). In *Paradiso*, Dante seems to move instead towards the unity of repeated rhymes, "vidi" as the sole rhyme word in one group, "Cristo" in four (always meaning the same thing except when "Christ" is repeated within the line by false followers who negate his meaning, *Paradiso* 19, 106); there are no repeated rhymes in *Inferno*. Seven equivocal rhymes are repeated in *Inferno* ("volto," "ombra," "volse," "legge," "anche," "piglio," "porta"), four in *Purgatorio* ("sue," "parte," "sole," "volto"), one in *Paradiso* ("parte"); three occur in all three canticles ("volto," "porta," "parte"), six in two of the three ("volte," "legge," "noi" in *Inferno* and *Purgatorio*; "porti" in *Inferno* and *Paradiso*; "punto" and "lievi/levi" [spelled differently but the same word] in *Purgatorio* and *Paradiso*). This means that of the eighty-three equivocal rhymes I have identified, forty-two are never repeated: fifteen occur only in *Paradiso*, twelve in *Purgatorio*, and fifteen in *Inferno*.

As one might expect, Dante uses the equivocal rhymes differently in different canticles. In *Inferno*, the same sound with different meaning contributes to a sense of confusion, while in *Paradiso*, and frequently in *Purgatorio*, the apparently different meanings turn out, on closer study, to be related if not identical. "Parte" means "political party" and "physical direction" in *Inferno* 10, 47 and 49, Farinata's party, opposed by Dante's, which was able to return from all directions as Farinata's was not; in *Purgatorio* 10, 8, 12, it is both noun and verb, but both refer to the apparent motion of the rock (moving on both "sides," one side "departing"); in *Paradiso*, too, both verb and noun refer to the same thing, the place in heaven in which the two motions of the sun meet, revealing the art of God whose eye never departs from it (10, 8, 12). "Legge" means "law" and "reads" in *Inferno* 5, 56, 58, the law by which Semiramis "made her libido licit," the ruler abusing the laws she should protect, about whom one reads, and in 19, 83, 85, a pope without law will be a new Jason of whom one reads in Maccabees, the repetition of the rhyme with the same meanings making an unflattering comparison of the pope with the scandalous queen; in *Purgatorio* 26, 83, 85, it is the lustful souls, who did not observe human law, in whom one "reads" (literally in the words they speak) the name of Pasiphae, the arch example of their sin. "Porti" means "harbors" and "carries": in *Inferno* 3, 91, 93, Dante must go to different harbors carried by a different boat, Charon tells him; in *Paradiso* 1, 112, 114, all natures move to different harbors, determined by the instinct which carries them, both motivation and destination inspired by God.

Equivocal rhymes are a demonstration of skill, but they can also reveal the dangers in human cleverness. The greatest concentration of equivocal rhymes in *Inferno* is in canto 24, where Dante begins the metamorphosis that will lead him to challenge Ovid and Lucan; there are five equivocal rhymes, two in the opening simile about confused perception. Three equivocal rhymes are found in the cantos of the blasphemers (canto 14) and the heretics (canto 10), where thought is particularly confused; in the latter, all three occur without an intervening rhyme and in the same grammatical form, both nouns or verbs, rather than verb and noun as is usually the case. In contrast, in *Purgatorio*, human cleverness is positive: "arte" is Virgil's "art" which got them through the "narrow" ways (27, 130, 132); "versi," like "arte," is an equivocal rhyme only in *Purgatorio* (29, 40, 42), where the muses must "pour out" what Dante needs for his "verses."

Equivocal rhymes combine harmony of sound with confusion in meaning, punning. I shall return shortly to harmony of sound, which is characteristic of all the remaining types of rhyme to be discussed, after a few words about other puns in the poem. They occur in all three canticles, with the expected differences. In *Inferno*, they point up a distortion of thought: "cherci," "chercuti," "querci" (7, 38–40), the tonsured clerics whose vision is distorted by their greed; "baratti," "baratro" (11, 60, 69), and "baratta" (21, 63), barrators, the chasm in which they throw themselves (and the state), and the strife they cause; "parlasia" (20, 16), the paralysis which is caused by the false seers' abuse of their gifts (including speech). In *Purgatorio*, the puns are more complex: even Sapia's play on her name, "savia non fui avvegna che Sapìa/fossi chiamata" (13, 109–10) has a double edge, since the rhyme changes the accent on the name so that it suggests "pious," which she was no more than she was "wise"; when Oderisi talks about the vanity of pride in human powers, he says how briefly it lasts on the peak ("in su la *cima* dura," 11, 92), and two lines later mentions *Cima*bue who thought he excelled, but has been eclipsed or driven from the peak by Giotto; and the next canto begins with Dante walking with another of the proud souls, like oxen in a yoke, "come *buoi* che vanno a *giogo*," the words recalling the names of the two painters just discussed. The most striking pun in *Purgatorio* is the visual "OMO" that can be read in the face of a man (23, 32), the same word, in the form "uom," that emerges from the acrostic on pride (12, 25–63), another kind of visual pun. In *Paradiso*, the puns suggest deeper meanings and connections or reinforce the lesson: in canto 3, the equivocal rhyme "voto," the "vow" which is "empty" (3, 28, 30) is repeated within a line ("fuor negletti/li nostri *voti*, e *voti* in alcun canto," 3, 57); the "M" from which the eagle rises in Jove comes from earth ("terram") and turns into a symbol of monarchy, the manifestation of divine justice on earth, a kind of visual pun; "s'indonna," which rhymes with "donna," (7, 13, 11), and "donnea" ("La Grazia, che donnea/con la tua mente," 24, 118–19), and its obverse, "La mente innamorata, che donnea/con la mia donna," 27, 88–89), all pun on the word "lady" who is the source of the power over Dante in "indonna," the inspiration of the "courting" in the second "donnea," and implicitly the source of Dante's divine grace as well. Finally, the angels are the subject of a series of puns in canto 28: they are grouped in trios, because of the Trinity, and as he describes them Dante incorporates the word for three in several rhyme words: "*termin*onno" (28, 105), "sempi*terna*" 28, 116), "in*terna*" (28, 120), and "*tri*pudi" (28, 124).

Many of the puns occur in rhyming words, which calls added attention to them, just as equivocal rhymes can be accentuated because they are also core rhymes (in *Inferno*, never in *Paradiso*): "ombra," "arte," "anche," "tempo," "entro." "Core rhyme" is the name I give to rhyme groups in which one of the rhyme words is contained within the other two as if it were their core. This device connects the three rhymes even more closely and focuses attention on the "core" word. Dante uses core rhymes throughout the *Commedia*: 189 in *Inferno*, 187 in *Purgatorio*, 183 in *Paradiso*, according to my count, while partial cores (in which the word is contained in only one of the other two rhymes) occur 91 times in *Inferno*, 139 in *Purgatorio*, and 127 in *Paradiso*, increasing the sense of harmonious sound that becomes more and more characteristic of the last two canticles.

Within the core rhymes Dante has a number of variations, not only equivocal rhymes, but also rhymes which pare down to, or build up from, the core: "ribelli," "belli," "elli" (*Inferno* 3, 38–42), the rebel angels, containing their former beauty, and within that the assertion of self that pitted them against God; "arte," "parte," "diparte" (*Purgatorio* 9, 71–75), Dante enhancing his "art" as they reach a "place" where an opening "parts" the wall, that is, when they reach the gate of Purgatory where Dante formally reverses the process that brought him to the center of evil and of sin within himself and begins to climb towards salvation, using a core rhyme that builds up. Paring down is not necessarily a function of Hell or Ante-Purgatory, indeed the movement from "melode," the music Dante hears from the martyrs which contains "lode," the praise which he can hear, "ode," but not yet fully understand (*Paradiso* 14, 122–26), is a paring down that is required by the limitations of the living human, a necessary lesson in Paradise.[4] Fewer core rhymes build up, and those that do occur only after Dante reaches the gate of Purgatory. The core word may also be set between the two that build up from it: "arte" between "parte" and "diparte" (*Inferno* 4, 71–75), where the art Virgil adorns both separates and unites the distance between Dante and the classical poets, and the distinction that sets them apart from the other noble pagans; in *Paradiso* 6, 101–05, the political art of the Ghibellines lies between their party and the separation of the eagle from justice; in 29, 50–54, the angelic art Dante is witnessing lies between the part of the angels who rebelled, and the eternal circling of those who did not, who never depart from circling.

Thus far, I have been concerned with variations within the three rhymes. I will conclude with a look at Dante's extensions of *terza rima* beyond those three words, either by adding a fourth or fifth rhyme to the three, or by connecting them to other groups by alliteration or assonance. The four- and five-rhyme groups occur most often in *Paradiso* (thirty perfect four-rhymes, six imperfect, and two five-rhymes), least in *Purgatorio* (seventeen perfect four-rhymes, no imperfects, no fives); *Inferno* has twenty perfect fours, three imperfects, and one five-rhyme. What distinguishes these rhymes in *Inferno* from those in *Paradiso*, besides the smaller number, is that though they use four or five words, they never have fewer than three rhymed words; in *Paradiso*, however, the four-rhymes may involve only two different words (this also occurs twice in *Purgatorio*), or even one word, and the five-rhyme may involve only three. Thus while the added rhymed word or words reinforce(s) the rhymed sound in *Inferno*, they create greater unity only in *Purgatorio* and *Paradiso*. Since this technique is self-explanatory, I shall simply give some examples, first of perfect four-rhymes in *Inferno*: "a poco a poco/loco/fioco" (1, 59–63); "ratto/tratto/disfatto fatto" (6, 38–42); "quatto quatto/ratto/patto" (21, 89–93); and one which involves four distinct words, "tutti muti/venuti/aiuti" (33, 65–69), which is followed directly by "ad uno ad uno/ciascuno/digiuno" (33, 71–75); the one five-rhyme is "aguta/a muta a muta/aiuta aiuta" (14, 53–57); and an imperfect four-rhyme is "molto/volto/volte volto" (1, 32–36).

The repeated word comes in the middle four times in the seventeen four-rhymes in *Purgatorio*, only three of twenty in *Inferno* but ten of thirty, a third of those, in *Paradiso*. As in *Purgatorio* (1, 98–102), the first four-rhyme has the repeated word in the middle: "dintorno/giorno a giorno/addorno" (*Paradiso* 1, 59–63), Dante's first perception of heavenly light, which is perhaps echoed in the four-rhyme at his first sight of the rose (30, 110–14), "addorno/intorno intorno/ritorno". One four-rhyme in *Paradiso* involves four words, though the first two are intimately connected, "io e mio/pio/disio" (19, 11–15), while three are based on two words or the equivalent, "luce/da luce a luce/produce" (2, 143–47), "voglia/di soglia in soglia/invoglia" (3, 80–84), "aduna/lacuna/ad una ad una" (33, 20–24), which is also a core rhyme (cf. 9, 53–57; 33, 116–20). One four-rhyme is all one word, "Cristo" (19, 104–08). The five-rhymes are "cotanto/canto/santo santo santo" (26, 65–69), the one instance of a triple repetition in the *Commedia*, and "doglia/soglia in soglia/foglia in foglia" (32, 11–15). Imperfect four-rhymes include "mille miglia/assotiglia/maraviglia" (19, 80–84), and "Indi/bindi/quinci e quindi" (29, 101–05).

The movement towards greater harmony of sound to which the four-rhymes, particularly those formed from two words or from core rhymes, contribute is furthered in *Paradiso* by a variety of poetic techniques: inner rhyme, alliteration, and the connection of rhyme words by alliteration, assonance, and consonance. All these techniques are practiced in the other canticles as well, but they come together, beginning in the middle of *Purgatorio*, with increasing intensity, building to a climax of sound in the latter part of *Paradiso*, whereas in *Inferno* the connection of rhyme sounds beyond *terza rima* is sporadic, patches of sound in twos and threes, emphasizing a particular moment of horror or pain.

The dominant sound effects in *Inferno* are harsh and disturbing. What remains in the ear are the onomatopoeic "s" sounds, the hissing of flames or blood (cantos 13, 26), the harsh rhymes in the circle of misers and prodigals ("eppe," "occia," "abbia," "upo," "ucca," "iddi," "oppa," "ozzi," "uffa," "ocche," "ozza," "ezzo," 7, 1–130), or of the flatterers (18, 101ff.), or scattered through the cantos of the barrators (cantos 21, 22, and 23, 1–18), or the thieves (24 and 25), and the "rime aspre e chiocce" Dante pretends not to have when he describes the circle of the traitors ("uco," "occe," "abbo," "ebe," "icchi," "accia," "ecchi," "azzi," "ezzo," "occa," "eschi," "uca," "ecca," canto 32). The reader is struck by the contrasts of soft, romantic sound with the harshness of reality in the canto of Francesca, the sad lament of "n" sounds and diphthongs in: "e come i gru van cantando lor lai/faccendo in aere di se lunga riga/ . . . traendo guai" (5, 46–48); Francesca's sweet-sounding tale, climaxing in the desired kiss, "quando leggemmo il disiato riso" (5, 133) which is quickly subverted by the reality of that kiss, the hard "b" sounds of "la bocca mi basciò" (5, 136), just as Dante's sympathetic faint, the softly fading, "io venni men così com'io morisse" (5, 141) is contrasted with the hard sound of the body falling "e caddi come corpo morto cade" (5, 142).

The hissing "s" sounds of canto 13, which take over strings of rhyme, do not let us forget that the sound is coming from the wound in the tree: "schiante," "sangue bruno," "scerpi," rhyming with "sterpi," and "serpi," followed by "arso sia," which climaxes two lines of "s"s: "'se state fossimo anime di serpi.'/Com d'un stizzo verde ch'arso sia"; the "s" sounds continue in the rhymes from 59–64 ("volsi," "si soavi," "tolsi," "offizio," "polsi," "ospizio"). The rhyme may emphasize the shocking aspect of what is described, as in the metamorphosis of the thief, Agnel, where the horror of the fusion of two beings into one is intensified by the core rhyme "uno," connected by assonance to "due" and the rhyme sound "uti":

> "Ohmè, Agnel, come ti muti!
> Vedi che già non se' né due né uno."
> Già eran li due capi un divenuti,
> quando n'apparver due figure miste
> in una faccia, ov' eran due perduti.
> (*Inferno*, 25, 68–72)

The plight of Ugolino's children, offering themselves to satisfy their father's hunger, is emphasized by the rhymes in "ti" ("isti," "uti," the closely related "edi," "orti," "enti," broken only by the significant core rhyme "uno"), which underline the distance between the father whose sin has involved supposedly innocent sons, and the sons who offer themselves to save him.

In *Purgatorio*, the sound effects are gentler, more comforting. We begin to get longer strings of connected rhymes and sounds, as in the meeting between Dante and Casella: "trarresi avante/per abbracciarmi . . . affetto/che mosse me . . . somigliante/ . . . aspetto/ . . . avvinsi/ . . . con esse al petto./ Di maraviglia . . . mi dipinsi;/ . . . sorrise e si ritrasse,/ . . . oltre mi pinsi./ Soavemente disse ch'io posasse;/ . . . e pregai/che, per parlarmi, un poco s'arrestasse" (2, 76–87), where "a," "s," "p," and "r" bind the rhyme words and reinforce them through the passage. This, in increasing intensity, is characteristic of later *Purgatorio* and of *Paradiso*. As they approach the gate of Purgatory, Dante connects the rhyme sounds by assonance and consonance, occasionally reinforcing them with alliteration: "orto," "ore," "unto," "orno" (9, 41–54), sometimes alliterating with "d" or soft "g": "giunto," "dintorno," "digiunto," "giorno," "dormia," "addorno" (9, 49–54). In 10, 52–67, in the examples of humility, the rhyme words with one exception are connected by "s": "imposta," "presso," "disposta," "stesso," "santa," "commesso," ("quanta"), "sensi," "si canta," "incensi," "naso," "fensi," "vaso," "salmista," "caso," "vista." The beginnings of lines as well as the ends may be connected by alliteration, as in *Purgatorio* 19, 79–84, with "v"s and "p"s: "Se voi venite . . . /e volete trovar . . . /le vostre destre . . . /Così pregò 'l poeta . . . /poco . . . /nel parlare." Rhymes may be repeated within the line, as in 23, 13: "O *dol*ce padre, che è quel ch'i' odo?" where the first sounds are also the rhyme word. Rhyme sounds that suggest first- and second-person pronouns, with echoes within the lines, lend excitement to the passage in which Virgil asks Statius about his conversion to Christianity: "ar*mi*," "a*sta*," "a*sti*," "o*tte*" (22, 53–69); "teco li tasta/non par che ti facesse . . . ti stenebraron sì che tu drizzasti/ . . . Ed elli a lui: tu prima m'inviasti/ . . . e prima appresso Dio m'alluminasti," climaxing in "per te poeta fui, per te cristiano" (22, 58–73). Sounds of the first-person pronoun, "ma," "mi," along with intense alliteration (and enjambment), heighten the excitement of Dante's encounter with Guido Guinizelli in 26, 95–99, along with the alliteration of "d" sounds (110–13), and of "p"s and "c"s, combined with a series of *o* rhymes (123–35).

In *Paradiso*, Dante does not introduce new sound effects, but he intensifies their use so that they come to dominate the canticle: repetition of words and sounds, long series of alliterated rhyme words or rhyme phrases, inner rhyme, rhymes linked by alliteration, assonance, or consonance (as many as two-thirds of the rhymes in a canto),[5] alliteration of the beginning and end of a line, or the end of one line and the beginning of the next, diphthong rhymes. It is the piling up of these effects, often in combination with core and equivocal or four-rhymes, that makes the sound of *Paradiso* unique. A kind of frenzied joy is evoked in *Paradiso*, particularly by the use of "i"s, as in canto 5, 119–23 when Justinian first offers to satisfy Dante's curiosity: "disii/ . . . chiarirti . . . ti sazia/ . . . di quelli spirti pii/ . . . / . . . Di, di/ . . . credi come a dii." The "i" sounds in this passage are reinforced by the rhyme sounds from lines 103 to 127: "ori," "ia," "izia," "esti," "oni," "azia," "ii," "idi," "aggi"; every rhyme contains "i." In canto 20, when Dante describes the songs of the living lights in the eagle, he uses "i" once again, but in combination with "u," and "l," and various secondary alliterations:

però che tutte quelle vive lu*ci*,	v	
vie più *lu*cendo, cominciaron canti	v	cc
da mia memoria lab*ili* e caduci.	mm	c
O dolce amor, che di riso t'ammanti,	am	am
quanto parevi ardente in que' flai*lli*,		
ch'avieno spirto sol di pensier santi!	ss	ps
Poscia che i cari e *lu*cidi lap*illi*	p	
ond' io vidi ingemmato il sesto *lu*me	s	
puoser si*le*nzio a *li* ange*li*ci squ*illi*.	p s	s

(*Paradiso* 20, 10–18)

Although he claims that his memory cannot hold the songs, he captures something of their effect in his sounds.

While the poetic effects evoke the harmony of Paradise, they also reinforce Dante's lessons. In the heaven of the Moon, Beatrice introduces the sense of difference within sameness that runs through the canticle when she explains about difference in creation using repetition ("diversa," "avviva," "viva," and "vita," "lieta" and "letizia," "formal" and "conforme"), alliteration (of "v," "l," and "d"), equivocal rhymes ("lega" and "luce"), and a four-rhyme ("luce/da luce a luce/produce"). When the souls of Venus first offer themselves to Dante's pleasure, a series of pronoun-related rhymes, including "noi" and "essa," and rhymes ending in "ti" or "te" (*Paradiso* 8, 31–39), subtly suggest the fusion of beings through love that will be intensified by the neologisms of the next canto, "s'io m'intuassi, come tu t'inmii" (9, 81). In the heaven of the Sun, where Dante first sees the figure of the Trinity in circles of souls and describes the Trinity in the circular "Quell'uno e due e tre che sempre vive/e regna sempre in tre e 'n due e 'n uno," he also makes close connections in sound between beginnings and ends of lines: "del padre corse . . . morte/la porta . . . diserra/e dinanzi . . . corte/*et coram patre*," which brings us back to the beginning of the pattern (11, 59–62). When in the Empyrean Dante describes Beatrice's smile for the last time, he claims to be conquered more than any comic or tragic poet by a point in his theme, a "punto," the word associated in this realm with God; he alliterates the key rhymes, "tema," "tragedo," "trema," and though he says that the memory of her smile takes him out of himself, he does so in words which keep the self at the center of the experience, "lo ri*me*mbrar del dolce riso/la *me*nte *mia* da *me* *me*desmo *mi* s*ce*ma" (30, 26–27). The first sight of Beatrice and the last is contained in the alliterating "v" words, "vidi," "viso," "vita," "vista" (30, 28–29), which associate her with Dante's first sight of the rose later in the canto ("vidi," "visibil," "vedere," 30, 94ff.).

Shortly before the end, Dante addresses God in a *terzina* which builds on a two-word phrase Bernard had addressed to the Virgin: "*In te* misericordia, *in te* pietate,/ *in te* magnificenza, *in te* s'aduna" (33, 19–20), and applies it to God, so that it reveals the essential oneness and circularity of God, always coming back on itself (while subtly emphasizing the intimate connection between God and the Virgin):

> O luce etterna che sola *in te* sidi
> sola *t'in*tendi, e da *te* *in*telletta
> e *in*ten*den*te *te* ami e arridi!
> (*Paradiso* 33, 124–26)

This is, for me, the supreme example of the way Dante uses sound to impress a meaning on our subliminal minds, saying more with the sound than he says with the substance of the words.

All the material I have considered here suggests that Dante was a consummate poet at every stage of the poem, that all the techniques were available to him from the beginning and used as the setting demanded. There is no question that in the *Paradiso* Dante achieves the highest peak of technical success, using rhyme and all the other ways of connecting words by sound to enhance, and sometimes to carry, his meaning, to induce in us a sense of heavenly harmony that cannot be described. But this does not mean that he has greater control over his material, or that his skills as a poet have developed in the course of the poem. While this may be so, it is not necessarily the case, since all the techniques Dante uses to such effect in *Paradiso* are present in *Purgatorio* and even in *Inferno*, but they are used, in *Inferno* particularly, in very different ways and to very different ends. The same technique, equivocal rhyme and enjambment, can contribute to the confusion of Hell and the harmony of Heaven; that the cantos are of wildly varying lengths in *Inferno* means only that Hell is a realm of chaos, where order would be out of place, not that Dante was less in control of canto lengths when he wrote *Inferno*. With all the chaos and all the apparent variety, Hell is finally much more a realm of sameness, of aggressive selfishness with different trappings, while Paradise, with all the harmony, is, poetically, the realm of greatest variety. It is the diverse voices in *Paradiso* that create its sweet harmony.

NOTES

1 This kind of symmetry and balance is characteristic only of *Purgatorio*, and is also to be found in the symmetrical patterns in the structure of the canticle and of each terrace (see chart 3).

2 Clear endings or new beginnings in *Inferno*: cantos 1, 2, 3, 4, 5, 12, 17, 18, 19, 20, 23, 27, 31, 33; endings that look ahead: cantos 6, 7, 9, 10, 11, 16. Distinct endings in *Purgatorio*: cantos 1, 12, 13, 14, 24, 27. Non-continuous cantos in *Paradiso*: 7, 9, 20, 29. Barolini discusses transitions and endings in an appendix of *The Undivine Comedy*; she finds only eleven cantos in *Inferno* which have no clear transition, whereas *Paradiso*, in reverse, has clear transitional endings in eleven. Though we classify beginnings and endings differently, our findings are similar.

3 The Latin consists of a few phrases spoken by Virgil, "sub Iulio" (1, 70), and "Vexilla regis prodeunt inferni" (34, 1, which parodies a hymn), Brunetto Latini ("ab antico," 15, 62, part of his snobbery about the pure Florentines), Guido da Montefeltro ("quare," 27, 72, a suggestion perhaps of his logical but flawed view), and Dante ("Miserere" to Virgil, 1, 65, a cry for help, and "suo loco," 18, 6, as he begins to describe the careful plan of the Malebolge).

4 Similarly, "scala," the stairway or ladder of contemplation, moves to "cala," the descent which accommodates the human "ala," wing or capacity, *Paradiso* 22, and *Purgatorio* 3, where the worst ascent on earth seems a stairway compared to the foot of the cliff in Purgatory, which must slope downward for Dante and Virgil who climb without wings.

5 Canto 29 has the largest number of rhymes linked by consonance or assonance that I have found, 96 of the 145 lines, or 66 percent, if my count is correct, and that does not include some 20 more linked by alliteration. Bernard's description of the rose in canto 31 is also filled with linked rhymes, 89 of 151, or 59 percent, as well as nearly identical but non-rhyming rhymes ("scanno/scanni, Agusta/aggiusta/gusto/gusta"), nearly identical rhymes ("discese/distese, vetusto/venusto, chiavi/clavi"), the identical Cristo rhyme, a five-rhyme and a four-rhyme.

SUGGESTED READING

Baldelli, Ignazio, "Rima," in U. Bosco, ed., *Enciclopedia dantesca* (Rome: Istituto dell'Enciclopedia Italiana, 1970–78), IV, pp. 930–49.

Barolini, Teodolinda, *The Undivine Comedy* (Princeton: Princeton University Press, 1992).

Bianchi, Dante, "Rima e verso nella *Divina Commedia*," *Rendiconti dell'Istituto Lombardo, Accademia di Scienze e Lettere* 95 (1961): 126–40.

Di Pretoro, P. A., "Innovazioni lessicali nella *Commedia*," *Rendiconti delle Sedute dell'Accademia Nazionale dei Lincei* 35 (1970): 263–97.

de Salvio, Alfonso, *The Rhyme Words in the Divina Commedia* (Paris: Champion, 1929).

Ferrante, Joan M., "Words and Images in Dante's *Paradiso*: Reflections of the Divine," in Aldo S. Bernardo and Anthony L. Pellegrini, eds., *Dante, Petrarch, Boccaccio:*

Studies in the Italian Trecento in Honor of Charles S. Singleton (Binghamton, NY: Medieval and Renaissance Texts and Studies, 1983), pp. 115–32.

Dante's Beatrice: Priest of an Androgynous God (Binghamton, NY: Center for Medieval and Renaissance Texts and Studies, 1992).

Malagoli, Luigi, *Linguaggio e poesia nella Divina Commedia* (Genoa: Briano, 1949).

Migliorini, Bruni, "Gallicismi," in *Enciclopedia dantesca*, III, pp. 90–91. "Latinismi," in ibid., III, pp. 588–91.

Parodi, Ernesto, "La rima e i vocaboli in rima nella *Divina Commedia*," in *Lingua e letteratura* (Venice: Pozza, 1957), II, pp. 203–84.

"La rima nella *Divina Commedia*," in *Poesia e storia nella Divina Commedia* (Vincenza: Pozza, 1965), pp. 53–67.

Schildgen, Brenda, "Dante's Neologisms in the *Paradiso* and the Latin Rhetorical Tradition," *Dante Studies* 107 (1989): 101–19.

Wlassics, Tibor, *Interpretazioni di prosodia dantesca* (Rome: Signorelli, 1972).

"Note sull'anadiplosi nella *Commedia*," in *Dante narratore* (Florence: Olschki, 1975).

12

A. N. WILLIAMS

The theology of the *Comedy*

The *Comedy* is a poem of ends. Its central question is one of the central questions of all Christian theology: what is humanity's end and how do we attain to it? Unlike most theological treatises, however, the poem begins from this end, with two of the traditionally named Four Last Things: Heaven and Hell. Inasmuch as the location of the *Comedy*'s characters in either one of these realms or in Purgatory presupposes a determination regarding salvation, a third of the Last Things is anticipated, namely judgment, although this has not formally been rendered in the time of the poem. The first of the Last Things, death, is also presupposed for the majority of the figures in the poem, with the exception of the demons and angels, the pilgrim himself, and the few proleptically damned of whom the pilgrim hears in *Inferno*. These Last Things, conventionally among the final subjects treated in a systematic theology, are the point from which the *Comedy* begins: in the middle of the pilgrim's life, but beyond the final moral determination of his human characters. The end of the narrative of the shades' earthly lives becomes the basis for a theological exploration of the end of human life as the vision of God.

The immediate prompt for the entire poem is however Dante's own end: it is out of concern for what may become of him that Virgil is asked to guide the pilgrim through the world of the shades so that he may not be lost, at risk as he apparently is. By the end of *Paradiso*, when the pilgrim has 'seen' the blessed Trinity, it is clear that his own salvation is assured: if it is rare that any human being should see God and live, it is unthinkable, within the parameters of Christian theology, that anyone who has attained to the vision of God that belongs to the blessed alone should subsequently perish. As we are frequently reminded throughout the poem, however, Beatrice's mission to save Dante from suffering the ultimate consequence of middle-aged folly unfolds into Dante's mission – and here the roles of pilgrim and poet collapse into each other – to speak of what he has seen, for the benefit of others. The readers of the poem are thus taken into the poem to become

201

pilgrims themselves, and on Dante's salvation hinges our own – thus, at least, the poem.

The extent to which salvation depends on human decisions and human actions – whether the choice to believe rather than not, or to live a life of virtue or of vice – has been sharply contested in the history of Christian theology, yet the conviction that human beings can affect their own, and even others', salvation, is the dominant theological idea in the *Comedy*. The relation of divine judgment and human acts was little disputed before the fourth or fifth century: the ready assumption was that virtue would be rewarded and vice punished in the Age to Come, and that human beings are free to choose whether they will live virtuously or not. The late fourth-century debate between Augustine of Hippo and the monk Pelagius forced the questions surrounding these assumptions into the open, and from that time onwards the question of the relation of human freedom and divine grace, between human action and divine determination, became one of the thorniest for Christian theology; there is no theological consensus on this point, no single view that can be identified as "generically" Christian. Augustine's own view of the matter shifted in the course of his life, though the moderate position of his middle years was subsequently vindicated at the second Council of Orange in 529. Both the original debate between Augustine and Pelagius and this later decree of a local council were largely forgotten or ignored until the High Middle Ages, and the intervening period saw the default establishment of the view many now assume to be incontestably Christian: that God rewards with eternal life those who live rightly and punishes with eternal damnation those who do not. The difficulty with this picture, perennially popular though it is, is that it compromises divine sovereignty, making human beings largely the arbiters of their own destiny.

By the mid-thirteenth century, the acts of the Council of Orange had been rediscovered, and with them came a renewed theological insistence on the priority of divine grace: fallen human nature requires both the healing grace infused at baptism and the sanctifying grace given throughout a Christian's life, if anyone is to do the good, much less acquire the good habits which are called virtues. By the time the Western church had reacquainted itself with the vexatious question of the relation of human freedom and divine grace, and the equally troublesome issue of the relation of both to the salvation of the individual, however, other developments had occurred (such as the gradual codification of belief in Purgatory), yielding the distinctive brew of issues and preoccupations with individual salvation that is medieval Western Christianity. The *Comedy* represents its author's wrestling with this complex of questions bequeathed him by the theological tradition and stands as perhaps the single most notable example of Western Christianity's reflection on the salvation of the individual in any genre, theological or literary.

However much the detail of the poem concerns individuals, though, Dante places the question of redemption where any medieval theologian would have placed it, firmly in the shadow of the cross, and in so doing reveals a distinctively medieval concern with divine justice. Christian theology had always asserted God was just, of course, but in the Middle Ages this concern became systematically significant in a way it had never been before. Now justice was viewed not only as an attribute of God, but a logic determining the shape of redemption. The classic statement of this theology is that of Anselm of Canterbury (who is mentioned fleetingly in *Paradiso* 12, 137): the sin of Adam and Eve at the Fall was a grave offense against God and justice required that satisfaction be made for it. On this reasoning, God could not simply forgive humankind for sin, because doing so would be contrary to his very nature as just. Because the "debt" owed to God was owed by humanity, satisfaction had to be made by a human being, but because it was owed to God, it was infinite and could therefore only be "paid" by another infinite being; hence logic indicated that the one person capable of making satisfaction for the debt of sin was Christ, because he alone was both human and divine. Satisfaction, in the form of Christ's death on the cross, was the Anselmian answer to the question posed by the title of his work on the subject, *Cur Deus homo?*, literally "Why the God-Man?" Anselm's answer to the question was that God became human in order to make satisfaction through his death for the debt owing since the Fall. Although this theology never attained the status of official dogma, Anselm's theory became widely accepted in the Western church as an account of the relation between Christ's death on the cross and the salvation of the faithful, and it is this theory of salvation that Dante privileges by putting it in the mouth of Beatrice (*Paradiso* 7, 25–45). However, in this version of the satisfaction theory divine love comes rather more to the fore than it does in Anselm's treatise. While Beatrice concurs that any other means of solving the problem created by humankind's rebellion would have been unsatisfactory (*Paradiso* 7, 118–19), her emphasis is not so much on the logical necessity of the scheme as on the vastness of God's love: "for God showed greater generosity/in giving his own self that man might be able to rise,/ than if he simply pardoned" (*Paradiso* 7, 115–17). Here Dante seems to have softened the sharp logic of Anselm's theory with an insight from the theory of salvation associated with Peter Abelard, who saw Christ's death on the cross as the ultimate sign of God's love (this is the so-called "moral influence" theory of atonement).

The vision of Christ's two natures, divine and human, together with the vision of the Trinity, constitutes the poem's literary and theological peak, yet the concluding vision in one sense stands in marked contrast to the matter of the rest of the poem. Although the telos of the *Comedy* is identical with the telos of human existence as Dante understood it, namely the vision of God, the poem is in an important sense more human than divine. The theological convictions which inform it, and the debates on technical (for the most part minor) theological aporias which figure in some of its cantos, are overwhelmingly concerned with the doctrine of creation, and especially with theological anthropology, that is, the Christian account of what it means to be human. The theological humanity of the poem – its prevailing concern with the relation of the body to the soul, the nature of the soul as intellectual and volitional, the freedom of the will and human responsibility for right action in consequence of this freedom, the human habits known as virtues and vices, human actions and how they are judged – is intimately linked to the humanity of its poetic device: the theological issues are explored entirely in the context of human encounters and human conversations. The figures whose lives and thoughts embody and voice the *Comedy*'s theology are precisely not stock figures, personifications or abstractions, and, for the most part, are not mythological. Their real humanity itself points to a preoccupation with the human and the historical as the realms in which we encounter God: Dante's poem is chiefly concerned, not with theories of the good in the abstract, but with human salvation, explored on the occasion of particular human beings.

Accordingly, what some of the *Comedy*'s commentators have seen as the tension between earthly and otherworldly concerns in the poem – or, more starkly, between politics and theology – might alternatively be seen as the necessary relation assumed by its author between behavior in this life and one's fate in the next. It is the conviction of this intrinsic connection that is both the poem's fundamental premise and its impetus. Underlying all these presuppositions is a virtue ethic, that is, an account of the good that seeks in the first instance to discern it by looking to the virtue (or lack of it) in ethical agents. So the souls in Hell and Purgatory are punished for their vices, while those in Purgatory are purified from vices and encouraged to acquire the virtues which are their opposite through being reminded of particular persons who possessed these virtues in abundance. The adoption of what is broadly speaking a virtue ethic approach correlates with the poem's personalism: this series of personal encounters and dialogues befits a discussion of virtue and its relation to salvation, for virtues can no more be saved than vices damned; that is the crucial distinction between a virtuous person and the personification of a virtue. It is of course possible to reflect on human acts and character from a virtue ethic perspective without considering particular persons who possess virtues or vices – both Aristotle and Aquinas did so – but it is the distinctive characteristic of virtues that they exist only in persons possessing them and it is only there, in persons, that they are "visible." They are thus less abstract than hypothetical cases, and someone who wished to reflect on the way in which virtues manifest the character of good persons and vices manifest the absence of good character might do well to do precisely as Dante did, considering the question on the occasion of particular historical persons.

Because the poem's theology is prosecuted through personal encounters, it has more in common with the dialogical form of the philosophical treatises in antiquity, such as those of Plato and Augustine, than with the many theological treatises of the High Middle Ages. The latter were, however, ultimately rooted in the heated exchanges of the theological schools and, because the pursuit of the logical and ethical questions in the *Comedy* occurs within the framework of human dialogues, the poem could be said to provide a literary counterpart to the forms of academic theology in the Middle Ages. Whether in one of the universities which came to dominate higher education, in a cathedral school, or in the *studium* of an order (such as the Franciscan and Dominican ones in Florence which Dante frequented), medieval theology reflected classroom practices of both lecturing and disputation. The textbooks of medieval theology, the *summae*, were orderly collections of *quaestiones*, explorations of problems posed by authoritative theological pronouncements (for example, from the writings of the church Fathers) which seemed to contradict one another. A *quaestio* could also reflect a classroom debate, however. A trained teacher of theology in a university, a master, might select a set of propositions which his students then argued, learning in the process both the substance of Christian doctrine, and also its methods of reasoning, a tradition which Dante explicitly invokes in *Paradiso* 24, 46–51. What are often referred to as his theology "examinations" in *Paradiso* 24–26 seem to reflect no more than the usual learning exercise of a medieval university, rather than any kind of qualifying test – there is no sense that Dante risks expulsion from Paradise if he fails to give the "right" answer, any more than a student in a modern university would be expelled for giving an inexact or incomplete answer in class. Along with the disputations held regularly in universities, the *quaestiones* provided an opportunity for dialogic learning, and, even if some of these events tended undoubtedly to become dry, pro forma performances, the medieval school of higher education was, to a far greater extent than a modern university, a place of verbal interaction, and not merely of one-sided instruction. The conversations of the *Comedy*, although rarely as combative as a debate proper, reflect the question-and-answer format of medieval theology and theological education, not in the manner of a catechism, where a definitive and necessarily simple answer is given to a question, but in the manner of the *quaestio*, where an answer must be given along with objections to, and further questions about, this answer. Dante-pilgrim pursues his questions, if not in the manner of a debater poking holes in an argument, then at least as one pursuing hard questions out of a sincere desire to know the truth (*Purgatorio* 6, 28–33; *Paradiso* 4, 10–12), and in *Paradiso* Beatrice's role often resembles that of a master in a medieval theological debate, providing both correction and expert answers to a student's questions.

Unlike a medieval *summa*, however, the *Comedy* can avoid giving definitive answers to every question it raises. Among the largest of these dodged questions is the rationale for the salvation of some of the poem's characters and the damnation of others. Dante's boldness in peopling Purgatory, Heaven, and perhaps worst of all, Hell, not with fictional characters or stock personifications, but with his personal acquaintances, might be explained away by appeal to the poem's standing as the record of a vision; if this were the case, Dante could effectively shrug off his impudence in claiming his political enemies were literally damned by pointing to the supernatural origin of his information. The poem is not, however, unambiguously the record of a divinely given vision and the very grounds for dispute on this point underscores his daring: he declines to claim the surest ground for the determinations of divine judgment recorded in his poem.

If the poem shows Dante's audacity, though, it also shows the subtlety of his moral vision: it is easier to pronounce judgment on tidy abstractions than on the welter of inculpating and exonerating detail that is the stuff of individual lives. That subtlety is evident particularly in the judgments made on the final destiny of the figures who people the *Comedy*, the sometimes baffling logic that rescues the latest of late repentants (such as Buonconte da Montefeltro in *Purgatorio* 5) but consigns the virtuous pagan like Virgil to the endless grey hopelessness of Limbo, to which he is condemned for no reason other than his lack of faith (*Purgatorio* 7, 8). To understand this logic the modern reader must broaden her conception of virtue and vice, extending beyond the judgment of acts to the judgment of thought and disposition.

The notion that dispositions of the mind (such as prudence and wisdom) count as virtues, and, conversely, that their absence is morally culpable, goes back to Aristotle (though Aristotle himself is excluded from salvation, *Inferno* 4, 131); his *Ethics*, which Dante knew well, was incorporated into a fully Christian system in Aquinas' *Summa theologiae*. However, long before the rediscovery of Aristotle in the Middle Ages, Christianity had stressed the significance of belief in a way other religions did not. For the early church, right belief (which is what "orthodoxy" literally means) mattered because belief was the sole distinguishing mark of a Christian; for a religion which eschewed all distinctions of race, nationality, class, or sex, the identity of the community, as of its individual members, was determined solely by subscription to a set of views, which came to be summarized and enshrined in creeds, as their formal parameters were decreed by the councils of the early church. Orthodoxy, therefore, functioned as the tie that bound the individual not only to God or to the truth, but to a community. By the High Middle Ages, the patristic emphasis on right belief had been married to the Aristotelian system of ethics which included intellectual virtues, with the result that faith was now classified as a virtue, numbering with hope and charity as the highest of all, the theological (*Purgatorio* 7, 35 and the "examinations" of *Paradiso* 24–26).

Right belief (orthodoxy) and right action (orthopraxis) were conceived of, not only as goods independent of each other, but also as interrelated. The assumption was not only that one should practice what one preaches, but that a dissolute life was the prime sign of imperfectly held beliefs. The point in the *Comedy* where this link between belief and life is made with unmistakable clarity is the otherwise odd appearance among those condemned in Hell for heresy of the "Epicureans." Strictly speaking, heresy is a deviation from Christian belief and, as such, no pagan philosophy could count as one. Dante's exemplar of Epicureanism is however no ancient philosopher, but a near-contemporary whose life bears little sign of adherence to Epicurean philosophy in any formal sense: Farinata, member of a rival Florentine political faction who was posthumously excommunicated for heresy (*Inferno* 10). He numbers among the heresiarchs because of his supposed denial of life after death, a view which Dante takes to be the equivalent of Epicurus' denial of the immortality of the soul (technically, the two are distinct, if related, but Dante seems either unaware of the distinction or unconcerned by it).

That Dante should choose this belief as the exemplum of heresy, and that its spokesperson should be, not Epicurus himself, but a man who in all likelihood had no knowledge of Epicurean philosophy per se, reveals much about the overarching theological presuppositions of his poem. Denial of life after death would, in the first place, invalidate the immediate premise of the *Comedy* and stands in contradiction to the virtues of faith and hope, belief and trust in God's will to draw all creation to himself. More significantly from Dante's perspective, the absence of life beyond the death of the body would imply the denial both of justice and of the very purpose of human existence: the denial of justice because the ill-doers who all too often escape punishment in their earthly lives would escape any censure whatsoever, and denial of the purpose of human existence because the only conceivable fitting end for humanity for a medieval Christian was the vision of God granted to the blessed in Heaven. The choice of unbelief in the afterlife, over myriad other heresies which from a theological perspective would seem much more serious (such as denial of the Trinity or the divinity of Christ), signals Dante's purposes in the poem, both artistic and theological, as well as the link, of which he was so deeply convinced, between this life and the next. The fact that the poem is not presented as a picture of what Dante's own life after death will be, but as the experience of one still in the body (of which we are reminded by the contrast between the pilgrim's corporeity and the shades' lack of it, e.g., *Inferno* 8, 27 and 12, 28; *Purgatorio* 3, 88–93 and 21, 133–36), that many of those he encounters were personal acquaintances or close relations of such acquaintances, and the repeated enjoinders to the pilgrim to remember that he has messages to carry back to the world of the living, all serve to underscore the intimate link of life before and after death. The worlds of Heaven, Purgatory and Hell are precisely not remote from this world, as divine justice is not a far-off threat for the vicious, or salvation the merely pious hope of those who trust in divine mercy.

The question of salvation would appear to hinge on the individual soul's relation to God and the choices it makes during earthly life, on a rightly ordered will in other words, but the *Comedy* provides a constant, if in one sense ironic, reminder of the centrality of embodiment to any anthropology that can be called Christian. Christianity has of late apparently acquired a reputation for being hostile to the notion of the goodness of the body (a view with which Augustine is often, and inexplicably, associated), but in its doctrine of creation (in virtue of which all matter exists explicitly by the will of God), its doctrine of the Incarnation (the assertion that God became human), its sacramental theology (which indicates how grace is received via the body), and its doctrine of the resurrection (identifying salvation with the eternal maintenance of our embodied state), Christianity is in an important sense deeply materialistic. By setting the *Comedy* after the death of almost all its protagonists but before the final resurrection, Dante might be said to have skirted as closely as possible the danger of allowing his readers to forget these facts, for apart from the Virgin Mary he is the only human character in the poem who really has a body: the others are shades, living in a peculiar state in which their souls are separated from their bodies – and there is good theological reason to maintain that no such existence is possible on a Christian account. The significance of the gradual development of the doctrine of Purgatory in the Middle Ages is not simply that by Dante's time the conviction had developed that the prayers of the living availed in hastening the purification of the departed, but, more fundamentally, that it was possible to envisage any kind of personal existence for the dead in advance of the general resurrection.

While belief in the resurrection of the body had always been a key element of Christian theology, there was before the Middle Ages no clear consensus about what happened to individuals between their own death and the general resurrection. While it was widely held that God does not allow souls to die, it was also firmly held Christian belief that a human being is not to be equated with a soul alone, but that each of us is a composite of a soul and a body. If having a body is essential to being human, there should be no possibility of personal existence between the physical death of the individual and the general resurrection; on the other hand, if physical death means the at least temporary end of the person as a psychosomatic unity, one would be admitting that the soul dies along with the body. The evolution of the schema we see in the *Comedy*, where the disembodied know some form of shadowy personal existence in advance of the resurrection, represents one solution to this problem.

That Dante should have adopted this view is in itself unremarkable, given its ecclesiastical entrenchment by his time, but the personalism of the poem constantly reminds the reader of the shades' real existence as thinking, and dialogical, subjects, even as the poet inserts regular reminders of the shades' lack of material bodies. Dante follows the dominant Western tradition regarding the origins of the human soul (what is called creationism: the notion that each human soul is created by God, destined for union with a particular human body, and infused by God into the embryo before birth [*Purgatorio* 25, 67–75]), as well as the complex Aristotelian and Thomistic categorization of vegetative and intellective souls (*Purgatorio* 25, 52–66).

The persistence of the soul after bodily death, the view often termed immortality, is Christian teaching only in a highly qualified way, as we have noted. Properly speaking, the immortality of the soul is a Platonic doctrine which stipulates an intrinsic life to the soul such that it cannot perish, a view whose logical presupposition is the preexistence of souls: they no more go out of existence than they came into it. The Christian view is a little different: the soul owes its coming into existence to God, and is therefore never not dependent on God for its life.[1] Dante followed the conventional wisdom regarding the soul's direct creation by God, its persistence after the death of the body, and rejection of its preexistence, but deals with the question of immortality only obliquely: the judgment on individual souls prior to the final and general judgment points to their necessary relation to God's purpose and will, even if Dante sometimes writes as if they possessed some form of intrinsic immortality. An intimation of his recognition of a more precisely Christian view is evident in Beatrice's speech in *Paradiso* 7, 142–46, where she connects the soul's direct creation by God and the divine desire that this soul exist to the conclusion of the resurrection as a logical deduction: the one who desired the human creature so ardently would be irrational if he wished it then to perish.[2] Here is one of the many signs that the poem might aptly have been entitled "The Triumph of Divine Love."

The theology underlying the notion of the human person as a psychosomatic unity is both Aristotelian and biblical, though its detail certainly owes more to the former. Aristotle's notion that all material entities are composed of matter and form (hylomorphism) provided the medieval theologians with a gloss on the standard Christian conviction of the body as essential to the human person: now the soul was taken to be the form of the matter that is the body. The significance of adopting this bit of Aristotelian substance metaphysics (see *Purgatorio* 18, 49–54) is less that pagan philosophy has subverted a peculiarly Christian anthropology as that philosophy has been co-opted to underscore a deeply Christian view of the inseparability of body and soul: hylomorphism does not describe the constitution of things which happen to coexist, but which could exist self-sufficiently and distinct from each other. The form of a table separated from the matter from which it is made is not an imperfect or unusual table, but no table at all, as far as Aristotle and his followers were concerned. If Dante is willing, following medieval convention, to envisage a temporary disembodied existence for the human soul between death and the resurrection, the affirmation of hylomorphism in his anthropology nevertheless reinforces the Christian definition of the human person as a psychosomatic unity, as well as the Christian assertion of an ultimate reunion of body and soul at the resurrection (*Paradiso* 14, 43–45).

Part of the impetus to assert an interim existence came from the development of the notion of Purgatory. The ideas that some of those who will ultimately be blessed must undergo purification (known in the Christian tradition since at least Clement of Alexandria in the second century), and the notion that prayer for the departed can alleviate their pains, were quick to appeal to the faithful, but these sensibilities represented no more than theological opinions or the development of popular piety. Another powerful formative force in the doctrine was the notion of the need to make satisfaction for sin, the significance of which we have already seen in the poem's operative theory of salvation. Although Christ's death on the cross makes amends for the general offense of the Fall, individuals must still do penance for their actual sins, hence the notion that one is purified from the sullying effects of sin by undergoing purgatorial punishment. The pains of Purgatory are therefore simultaneously penal and remedial. Omberto Aldobrandeschi most succinctly voices the penal element of his punishment in Purgatory: "Until God has been satisfied, I bear/this burden here among the dead because/I did not bear this load among the living" (11, 70–72). The trials of Purgatory purify those who undergo them, but they also constitute a kind of coin which enables the sinner to repay a debt owed to God. The conversations of Purgatory display also the medieval conviction that there was more than one way to pay these debts incurred by sin. Indulgences granted by the pope could lessen the time one spent (as those granted for the Jubilee Year of 1300, *Purgatorio* 2, 98–99), as could the sincere prayer of a righteous person still on earth (*Purgatorio* 23, 85–90).

These "allowances" are in Dante's Purgatory curiously unlegalistic in their effect. One of the striking differences between Hell and Purgatory in the *Comedy* is not only that in Hell there is no hope whereas Purgatory is entirely built on hope, or that Hell's population is damned and that of Purgatory saved, if currently suffering. The fundamental difference is that Hell is non-volitional and, in that sense, a violation of what Dante regards as most human, while Purgatory is entirely volitional, and, in that sense, the souls in the middle canticle could be seen as the most fully human of any in the poem. Although the length of punishment of the souls in the first cornice appears to be proportionate to the seriousness of their sin (*Purgatorio* 10, 136–39), elsewhere it appears that souls ascend from one level to another – or indeed, from Purgatory to Heaven – in accordance with their own will (*Purgatorio* 21, 61–66). Heaven, in contrast, is peopled by those who cannot choose to sin, and to the modern mind this absence of choice looks like a violation of human freedom, as well as of the poem's own theological logic. On this point, Dante leans on an Augustinian distinction: true freedom consists, not in having the choice to sin or not sin (*posse non peccare*), but in the freedom that is not being able to sin at all (*non posse peccare*). The highest freedom consists in whole-heartedly loving rightly, not in thrashing about in agonies of indecision about whether or not to do the good. Here is another respect in which the poem celebrates the primacy of love.

The purification of Purgatory consists above all in the restoration of the will damaged at the Fall (*Purgatorio* 17, 91–124), so that instead of loving wrongly – as Paolo and Francesca do, for example – the purified saint becomes able to love rightly. Virtue and vice are both prompted by love of some sort, whether rightly or wrongly ordered (*Purgatorio* 17, 103–05; *Paradiso* 26, 62–63). To love rightly, that is, to love God above all else and other things as lesser goods (*Purgatorio* 17, 97–98), is the soul's true end; the soul was created to love (*Purgatorio* 18, 19) and love is the seed of all virtue (*Purgatorio* 17, 104). This preoccupation with rightly ordered love reflects the deeply Augustinian flavour of the poem's theology, although Augustine himself receives only passing mention in the poem (*Paradiso* 10, 120 and 32, 35). Dante's conception of Purgatory thus links his anthropology, hamartology (theology of sin), and virtue theory into a coherent whole, showing how the nature that deviated at the Fall can once again be pointed towards its true end, Heaven.

However essential the body is to human identity, it is nevertheless not our distinguishing mark, for other animals also have bodies (as well as certain sorts of souls). What distinguishes us from the other animals, but likens us to the angels (from whom we differ with respect to embodiment), is not the possession of any soul whatsoever, but a rational soul, the seat of a mind and a will. Here Dante leans on an ancient Christian tradition, but one whose root he probably knew as Augustine. In this view, intellect and will, the two constitutive faculties of the human soul, correspond both to the faculties of the one divine nature and, analogically, to the second and third Persons of the Trinity (the Word as the divine intellect and the Spirit as will or love). Theological meditation (which one could reasonably view as a form of constructive play) on the dynamic interrelation of these two was passed from Augustine to Anselm to Aquinas and so to Dante.[3] Dante concurs with Augustine in holding that knowledge logically precedes love (see, e.g., *Paradiso* 29, 139–40) and with Aquinas in maintaining that the "content" of beatific vision is an act of the intellect (*Paradiso* 28, 109–11). However, his focus on salvation and the will's role in affecting it reflects a shift from these earlier thinkers, who granted precedent to the intellect (one must think something before one can will it), to later medieval theologians, who accorded primacy to the will (and so are known as voluntarists): it is freedom which makes us like God (*Paradiso* 7, 79–80), and it is because sin impairs the freedom of the will that it is so serious, erecting a barrier between ourselves and God. Likewise, one can only grasp the theological technicalities (such as the rationale for the crucifixion) if the intellect has "matured within the flame of love" (*Paradiso* 7, 60), love being the highest expression of the will. It is for this reason that the human being who stands closest in heaven to the divine Trinity is the Blessed Virgin Mary, who is "the noonday torch of charity" (*Paradiso* 33, 10–11).

This insistence on the primacy of love and its precondition, human freedom, stands in a tensive relation in the *Comedy* to Dante's characteristically medieval fascination with divine predestination, and worse (from a theological perspective), fate and the stars. The fact that each canticle ends with "stars" need not be taken as having any sort of theological significance, especially given the vigorous disavowal of their controlling influence in *Purgatorio* 16, 70–81. Nor, despite the apparent similarity to the modern mind, is the Christian notion of predestination equatable with the pagan one of fate. To a medieval, the crucial distinction between the two would have been that one was attributed to the will of a wise and just supreme God, the other to arbitrary forces or capricious "deities" unworthy of the name.

What is from a theological perspective much more difficult is to reconcile the affirmation of human freedom that is necessary to preserve human merit (*Purgatorio* 18, 43–45) with the apparent determinism of grace (*Paradiso* 32, 55–66), and Dante engages in a constant balancing act in the *Comedy* to hold the two together. The conundrum with which he is wrestling is ancient, famously connected to the name of Augustine, but figuring significantly in the works of much earlier writers, such as Origen. One of the distinctive marks of the shape the issue takes in the *Comedy* is that the positioning of the issue is typically in relation to love. Thus in the pilgrim's exchange with Virgil in *Purgatorio* 18, Dante queries how, if love is merely an automatic response to the stimuli of attractive things, the soul could ever be said to have merit. Virgil explains (61–66) that while the freedom that is the condition of love is in itself neither good nor bad, true assent entails the assistance of the power of judgment and it is by the rectitude of our judgments about what we love that we are deemed meritorious or not. We cannot help having appetites (nor that the heavens nudge them into motion, *Purgatorio* 16, 73), but we always have the power to curb or direct them rightly (*Purgatorio* 18, 70–72).

It would seem, then, that one's ultimate destiny, one's place in the geography of Heaven and Hell, depended entirely on the sum of choices made by individuals, but Dante tries to hold together human freedom with divine redemption and grace. God bestows his grace directly, at his own good pleasure, and this gift of grace constitutes an eternal law which orders Heaven; Dante throws up his hands in the attempt to reconcile these divergent theological data of grace and freedom: "here fact alone must be enough" (*Paradiso* 32, 55–66). If the appeal to the inscrutability of divine decree seems intellectually unsatisfying, Dante offers two sorts of mollification to the restless mind that will not cease from questions. The first comes from Piccarda Donati, the first of the blessed he encounters in Heaven, whose chronological placement in the journey reflects her geographical placement farthest from the heavenly throne. Piccarda's utter contentment with a lot that in a less perfected soul might have occasioned grumbling rebukes the reader who protests "How can this uneven distribution of grace be fair?" Second, though neither the poet nor any of the guides can explain the logic of this justice, the fact that it accords with God's wisdom is enough to settle the matter: fair it must be, even if finite intellects cannot see how (*Paradiso* 3, 130–42 and 21, 91–96).

Because Dante declares divine judgment to be ultimately inscrutable, there is little point in extrapolating from the placement of theologians in Heaven to determinations about which theology the poet himself regarded as superior. It is sometimes claimed that the Thomism of the poem has been exaggerated, the evidence for this being the higher placement of another theologian, Bernard of Clairvaux, than Aquinas in the heavenly hierarchy. The immediate flaw in such reasoning lies in the fact that although Dante certainly regards truth and holiness as interrelated – so that a notoriously wicked person could not possibly write true theology – no one is saved by their originality of mind. The teachings of the Bible and the church suffice for salvation (*Paradiso* 5, 76–79; cf. 24, 91–96), so where the doctors of the church differ over theologoumena (theological views on issues not dogmatically defined by official ecclesiastical pronouncement), these constitute no more than pious or learned opinions, interesting in themselves perhaps, but not salvifically significant. Thus, when Gregory the Great arrives in Heaven, he discovers that his angelology was wrong and that of his predecessor, the Pseudo-Dionysius, was right – and he smiles as he sees his mistake (*Paradiso* 28, 133–35). In Heaven, the answers to all theological questions will be revealed, as far as human beings are able to comprehend them, and in perfected souls there will be joy sheerly in contemplating the truth, without pride or dismay at who was right and who was wrong on earth.

The ordering of both Heaven and Hell emphasizes the primacy, not of thought, but of love: Paolo and Francesca love wrongly and are damned for doing so (*Inferno* 5), but their sin is judged as less serious than those whose self-regard leads them to betray those they should honor and love, who are doomed to an eternity not of fire, but of ice. Conversely, Piccarda and Costanza, who loved God enough to become brides of Christ but not enough to remain constant to their vow when forced into marriage, float in the outer circles of heaven, while Bernard of Clairvaux, theologically most notable for his sermons on the Bible's great love poem, the Song of Songs, stands closer to the throne of grace than any other theologian, including those on whom Dante's own theological reasoning is much more directly, and often, dependent.

The Song is a dialogue of a lover, his beloved and a chorus who celebrate their love, just as *Paradiso* is a theological conversation rooted in its speakers' love for the one who is the subject of their discourse, and this dialogue of the characters in the *Comedy* is one of the many expressions of the doctrine of the communion of saints in the poem. At the most elementary level, the prayers of the living for the departed, alluded to in the middle canticle, is one expression of this interconnectedness which the doctrine expresses. The social and communal dimension of human existence is attested also in the poem by the sheer fact that no one, whether in Hell, Purgatory, or Heaven, is alone. We are saved on the basis of individual merit, our personal degree of virtue or vice, but the blessed are not saved for solitude, nor the damned allowed to escape the company they have chosen for themselves.

In the depths of Hell, the earthly enemies Ugolino and Ruggieri keep their gruesome society eternally, and even Lucifer knows no splendid solitude (*Inferno* 33–34). The society of Purgatory and Heaven is happier, of course, but no less inevitable. Although the souls in Purgatory are each amending their own sinful ways, they are cast together in unlikely companies, spanning continents and centuries, of sinners of similar weaknesses. Unlike the shades in Hell, however, here past sin creates no enmity, no barrier to fellowship, and perhaps the loudest sign of this communion of the imperfect is their song.

Purgatory is not only a school for sinners, but a schola for choristers. Choral singing, in itself a deeply social form of music-making, becomes doubly so on the holy mountain, because the songs are those of the church: ancient liturgical canticles such as the Te Deum (9, 140), parts of the proper of the mass, such as the Gloria and the Agnus Dei (20, 136 and 16, 19), office hymns such as the Te Lucis Ante Terminum (8, 13), as well as countless psalms. No one in Purgatory sings her own tune, and this communal chanting of the community's songs in itself signifies that holiness is being worked here, the barriers created by self-love being worn down by the sounds of many voices in concert. If the harmony of song is sometimes punctuated by the roar of shouting as a shade ascends, it is only a musical concord that is broken: the spontaneous shouts of joy over the blessing enjoyed by another show that in Purgatory there is no envy or back-biting, much less the quarrelling of the sinners in Hell, who cannot stanch their rancor even though there can be no possible point to it.

The songs of the faithful fill the courts of Heaven, too (e.g., the Regina Coeli in 23, 128, the Te Deum in 24, 113 and the Gloria in 27, 1), but that "place" which is none other than the mind of God (*Paradiso* 27, 109–10) renders a richer sensory experience than either of the other two realms: Heaven is a feast of light and sound and, perhaps most surprisingly of all, dance. At first, the dancing of the saints might seem strange, given the ambivalence of religion to dance, sensuous as it can be. However, if the Bible attests to the power of dance to bewitch and lead astray (as in the story of Salome recounted in Matthew 14:6–12, or the Israelites dancing before the golden calf in Exodus 32), dance is also an expression of religious joy: such as the dancing of Miriam and her attendants after the drowning of Pharaoh's army in the Red Sea (Exodus 15:20) and, above all, King David's un-self-conscious dancing before the ark, which fills his wife Michal with disdain (2 Samuel 6:14–16), an incident which Dante uses as an example of humility in one of the marble friezes adorning the sides of Mount Purgatory (10, 64–69). In Heaven the seductive associations of dance are gone, and instead dance represents the joyous activity of the saints acting in bodily concert, even though they have as yet no real bodies. Their whirling, unlike the ceaseless turbulence of the winds of *Inferno* 5, is neither disordered nor destructive; it continues for all eternity, yet it is not pointless: its end is no less than the celebration of fraternal love and the love of God.

In making Heaven into a great theological ball, Dante has modified in a daring, albeit biblical, way the standard account of the activity of Heaven. For centuries, Christian theology had portrayed human engagement with God as a form of sight: contemplation was the rubric that covered the activities today variously designated as theology and prayer. To contemplate God was to apprehend something of the truth about God, as far as the finite human intellect was capable, but also simply to gaze on the "face" of the beloved. While Dante by no means abandons the visual imagery of the tradition, he adds to it the less purely cerebral element of the human body's participation in the joy of love. The two sides of contemplation hold together both the discursive and non-discursive aspects of theological meditation, and this synthesis of movement and stillness seems echoed by Dante's choice of round dances as a way of epitomizing the activity of the blessed. As in the discursive reasoning of medieval school theology, there is movement, yet this is not the linear progression from premises to conclusions, but the circling motion of meditation (*Paradiso* 29, 54), whose end is the activity itself, centering upon the object of reflection and devotion, holding the mind's gaze there in the fullness of love. While the dialogues of the blessed are up to a point validly construed as conversations in which the pilgrim seeks answers, or "examinations" in which he demonstrates his grasp of theological truths, they can equally well be interpreted as sheerly doxological, their purpose being to praise God by dwelling on the truths of the faith. The wordy encounters of Heaven are broken off, not by the resumption of punishment or the renewed outbreak of old hatreds as in Hell, nor by haste to return to the urgent task of scrubbing off the stain of sin as in Purgatory, but by the desire to rejoin the joyous circling around the divine mystery that is the business of Heaven, a circling that echoes the dynamic relation of the Persons of the Trinity themselves.[4] The round is danced to a song without words, for the summit of the *Comedy* is Dante's own vision of the Trinity and the Incarnation, which even the poet has no words to describe: "From that point on, what I could see was greater/than speech could show" (*Paradiso* 33, 55–56).

NOTES

1 Justin Martyr explicitly denies that the soul is immortal in the Platonic sense (*Dialogue with Trypho* v). Tertullian is willing to call it immortal, though he insists it came into being by God's will, and excoriates Platonists whose doctrine of the soul effectively places it in a paradise with God (*On the Soul* 24). In the first chapter

of Gregory of Nyssa's *On the Soul and the Resurrection*, both the views that the soul has an existence distinct from the body and that all that exists, exists only by divine will, are affirmed.

2 The one exception to the "rule" of the resurrection is the suicides, who never regain their bodies, which is for them the core of their eternal punishment, *Inferno* 13, 103–06.

3 It is elaborated in greatest detail in Augustine's *De Trinitate*, but versions of it can also be found in Anselm's *Monologion* and Aquinas' *Summa theologiae*, 1.27–34.

4 This is the notion of perichoresis (which derives from the Greek words *peri*, meaning around, and *choreuo*, to dance): the Persons of the Trinity are united in their common activity and their mutual indwelling.

SUGGESTED READING

Boyde, Patrick, *Dante Philomythes and Philosopher: Man in the Cosmos* (Cambridge: Cambridge University Press, 1981).

Cunliffe-Jones, Hubert, with Benjamin Drewery, eds. *A History of Christian Doctrine* (Philadelphia: Fortress Press, 1978).

Foster, Kenelm, *The Two Dantes and Other Studies* (London: Darton, Longman, and Todd, 1977).

Gilson, Etienne, *The Spirit of Mediæval Philosophy*, trans. A. H. C. Downes (Notre Dame, IN: University of Notre Dame Press, 1936).

Dante the Philosopher, trans. David Moore (London: Sheed and Ward, 1948).

Knowles, David, *The Evolution of Medieval Thought*, 2nd edn., ed. D. E. Luscombe and C. N. L. Brooke (London: Longman, 1988).

Le Goff, Jacques, *The Birth of Purgatory*, trans. Arthur Goldhammer (London: Scolar Press, 1981).

Marenbon, John, *Later Medieval Philosophy (1150–1350): An Introduction* (London: Routledge, 1987).

13

PIERO BOITANI

The poetry and poetics of the creation

In the *Commedia*, Dante first mentions the creation at the very beginning, when the protagonist has put the dark wood behind him and finds himself at the foot of the hill of virtue, where he is stopped by the leopard of lust. We are immediately given the hour of the day and season of the events about to unfold: a spring morning with the sun in the constellation of Aries, i.e., the spring equinox, precisely the time of year when, according to medieval tradition, God had created the universe: when the sun "was mounting with those stars which were with it when Divine Love first set in motion those fair things." For one moment, as the sun of this first spring lightens the landscape, the terror which had seized Dante in the dark wood seems to give way to hope. Dante clearly feels nostalgia for the Beginning as some essential aspect of his own self: a feeling which is both sensual and intellectual. The idea of the beginning of all things allows him, imaginatively, to see and enjoy the sun and stars as "cose *belle*" (*fair* things), and not simply "good," as Genesis has it. This first firmament possesses a *pulchritudo* of intimate and pristine aesthetics, like the dawn and the aura which the "things" shed on everything surrounding them.

What this introductory canto of the *Inferno* is also doing is attributing the Creation to divine love, in an operation which is both poetic and evangelical. Dante is possibly thinking of Thomas Aquinas' commentary on Aristotle's *Metaphysics*, where he states that the poet Hesiod, "before the time of the philosophers," had placed love as "principium rerum."[1] The act of Creation is then envisaged by Dante, following Aristotle, as a first, primordial ("di prima") impulse to the movement imparted by the Prime Mover to the celestial bodies, setting time and space in motion. The verb "mosse" in line 40 is a precise philosophical term which, followed by "cose belle," is also perceived as an effortless gesture, as if God had given a flick at some slender circle of light which, however, supported the entire weight of gravity of the universe. Genesis' "Fiat lux," "fiat firmamentum," and "fiant luminaria" are thus translated from words into one silent, luminous, touch, reflected by the light of the sun and the stars.

It is difficult, then, to maintain that Dante has no specific poetics of Creation when these verses begin the wonderful rainbow which is completed in the very last line of *Paradiso*: "l'amor che move il sole e le altre stelle." Here, the "desire and will" that Dante speaks of three lines before the end are finally fulfilled by the vision of God, and are directed by that same "love which moves the sun and the other stars"; here Dante himself becomes, with the "cose belle" of *Inferno* I, an object of the Creation.

The rapt poetry of the Creation is to return, as we shall see, in the *Paradiso*, but Dante is too subtle and complex a thinker to remain infatuated by "fair things." Immediately after their creation, God turned his hand to something else: to the gates of Hell and the reign of eternal pain (*Inferno* 3, 1–9). The modern world tends to take a dim view of this duality in a God of love; for Dante, however, there is no ambiguity: it is indeed the "divine power," the Father, the Supreme Wisdom, the Son, and the Holy Ghost, defined as First Love, which have produced these gates, in a display of both immense power and infinite wisdom and love. Wisdom, because the moral economy of the universe needs a place or state to contain the evil of the primordial past and all the evil to come, and love, because this confinement of evil is a supreme good. The poetics of Creation as awed admiration of "fair things" is complemented, then, by Creation as an expression of unfathomable Justice producing terrifying things, fair only in the sense of "justified." In other words, the theology and poetics of Creation justify the poetry of both the *Inferno* and the *Paradiso*.

Dante is fascinated by the creation of all things eternal. In the *Purgatorio*, the reign of the human and the beautiful, between the horror of the *Inferno* and the sublimity of *Paradiso*, he twice speaks of the creation of the immortal soul. The two passages are strictly interlinked, but their underlying poetics are fundamentally different. In the first, *Purgatorio* 16, 85–90, the deftness and delicacy of God's movements are transmitted to the soul, here conceived as a young girl, crying and laughing in turn, the "simple soul" which turns in delight to whatever catches its eye. It issues "from [God's] hand" effortlessly, a bubble materializing on the divine palm, or a spark released for some dance or game. But the Creator's loving glance was fixed on "her" even before her creation: "with pleasure and delight He looks at her and contemplates her as if mirroring Himself in her, who is his own image."[2] This divine "fondness" (*vagheggiare*) is a response to the soul's ineffable beauty, its *vaghezza*, and its simplicity: simple, innocent, and pure to the point of knowing nothing: the *tabula rasa* evoked by Aristotle and Aquinas.[3]

Having caught a glimpse of God's hand and his delighted and loving glance, we now learn that he is a joyous ("lieto") maker, moving the soul of each individual as, in *Inferno* 1 and *Paradiso* 33, he moves the sun and the other stars. The delight God feels in creating the human soul is clearly an essential aspect for Dante, who returns to it in *Purgatorio* 25, and again in Bernard's words, almost at the end of the poem.[4] Nothing so stirs divine joy as the creation of a human soul, which then reverberates with the same joy, unconsciously recognizing a spontaneous desire to turn back to the father/mother figure who "dandles" or "cuddles" it ("trastulla"). The soul naturally desires happiness, Aristotle would say, and if it fails to turn to its Maker for this happiness, it tries the taste of "a trifling good," and rushes to the pleasures of the flesh (*Purgatorio* 18, 19–21). In other words, the principle of happiness governing Aristotelian ethics is replaced by the pleasure principle which Freud perceives as governing the mechanisms of the psyche.

What interests me, however, is more the poetry of the passage. The central image, of the soul as a young child, may be remotely inspired by Proverbs (8:30), where Wisdom describes how it was conceived by God before the Beginning and amused itself by playing in his presence. At the end of his life, the Emperor Hadrian wrote a childlike lyric which is quoted in the *Historia Augusta*: "Animula vagula, blandula." Hadrian's soul is like a playful small girl, wandering about and charming, the body's guest and companion, but ready to leave off all play and fly, naked, stiff, and pale, towards bare, bleak spaces. If Dante had been aware of the emperor's melancholy lines he might have conceived this passage in *Purgatorio* 16 as Wisdom speaking out in joyous counterpoint to it.[5] He probably was not, however. Perhaps we should read his passage, then, as sudden empathy with the concrete, referential actions of a child who cries and laughs as she plays. The memory of this simple spontaneity then fused with his perennial aspiration towards primordial innocence: the soul before original sin.

In actual fact the process of Dante's inspiration is here much more complex. In the *Convivio* (IV, xii), to describe the soul following first the lesser, then the greater good, he had used the image of the *parvuli*, the small boys, reaching first for an apple, then some small bird, then, when they grow up, a woman and a horse. At this point, association would have led him to his soul-child image. The idea was not unknown in the Middle Ages, however: in the *Passio Petri et Marcellini*, for example, the souls are elegantly dressed young women, and in three cases at least, the *Dormition of the Virgin* in the Byzantine mosaics (of the Norman period) in the church of Santa Maria dell'Ammiraglio in Palermo, and in the mosaics of Santa Maria in Trastevere and Santa Maria Maggiore in Rome, the soul is represented as a child.[6]

The theological tradition goes back to Origen and his *Commentary* and *Homilies* on the Song of Songs, and thence to Guillaume de Saint Thierry's *Commentary* and Bernard's *Sermones in Cantica*: the Bride as the perfect soul, ardently desiring her Bridegroom, the Word, and being desired by him in return. When Origen speaks of God "creat[ing] man in his own image; male and female created he them" (Genesis 1:27), he maintains that the verse can be interpreted allegorically, as the creation of the inner man uniting the spirit (male) and the soul (female). Wherever they find concord and consent, they increase and multiply, generating "good motions," thoughts and reflections with which to "replenish the earth." The soul, however, "is conjoined and, as it were, coupled with the spirit, and can occasionally sink to the level of bodily pleasures, tainting itself with bodily adultery," in which case it can neither increase nor multiply. The "first Creation" which Origen reads in Genesis 1:26–27 posits a "primordial existence" for man, namely "the being according to the creator's image." It is this element created "according to the creator's image" that Origen interprets as the soul.

The soul, then, occupies centre stage in Origen's theology, so often revisited in the Middle Ages: created by God in his own image, with the spirit it forms part of Paul's "inner man." Though it can be diverted towards earthly matters, it is also the Bride seeking the Bridegroom. Every created soul is naturally small, and can only grow with experience and the gradual knowledge of God. The image of the children thus emerges quite naturally, reinforced and directed by the echo of the Gospel in which Jesus invites the disciples to "suffer little children to come unto [him], for theirs is the kingdom of heaven." Combining various passages in Matthew (18:2–5), Luke (18:17), and the First Letter of Paul to the Corinthians (13:11; 3:1–2), Origen traces a great circle, departing from God's creation of the human soul, to his image, as a woman, and returning to the Logos as the desired Bridegroom of the Child-Bride. Within this circular rhythm there is both the moment in which the soul can turn aside from its divine end, and, equally, the possibility to become as a child and enter the kingdom of God, which is also a child.[7]

It is this sort of theological conception which forms the backdrop to Dante's lines in *Purgatorio* 16, where we find exactly this same circle, going from Creation to its return towards the Maker, and the Creator's love for his creature, which is equally returned: a strictly human trajectory against the cosmic backdrop of the Beginning and the End. If we then ask ourselves what the poet adds to the theologian, the answer will certainly center on the weeping, smiling, playing child, the simple soul, and the *trastulla* that, as it were, entertains the soul, but which is also connected to the power of speaking, singing, and poetry:[8] all expressions with connotations of the nature, activities and *language of or about children*. From the *Convivio* on, this is then the poetry of the *parvuli*, the poetics of a writer who becomes an evangelical child.

At the same time, at the centre of such a poetics lies, on the subject's side of things, the *vagheggiare* Dante attributes to the creating God, a loving contemplation, an enraptured love of the first things. It is significant that this *vagheggiare* will, in the *Paradiso* (26, 82–84), be ascribed to the soul of Adam, the first which God ever created, and again, by virtue of syntactical ambiguity, to God himself. *Vagheggiare* (the verb courtly poetry employs for human eros) is also the very aim of what I would call the "theological aesthetics" of Dante. When he ascends to the fourth heaven, the heaven of the Sun and the *Sapientes*, he invites his readers to lift up their eyes with him to the lofty wheels (of the celestial equator and of the ecliptic) and direct them where the motion of the one strikes the other: there they should begin to "vagheggiar" the art of that Master who so loves it in his heart that his eye never leaves it (*Paradiso* 10, 7–12).

The object of such a "vagheggiar" is the *art* of God, in other words the created universe, the cosmos in which we live and which Dante portrays in his poem: lifting his eyes, the reader will encounter not only God's art, but also the poet's. While man's loving contemplation of the work of the divine Maker corresponds to the love which he bears to it within himself, Dante immediately afterwards returns to the *reader*'s pleasure in following him: "Stay now, reader, on your bench, thinking over this of which you have a foretaste, and you shall have much *delight* before you are tired." And he finally points to himself, the scribe who writes down God's art: "I have set the food before you, now feed yourself, for the theme of which I am made the scribe bends to itself all my care" (*Paradiso* 10, 22–27). "Quella matera ond'io son fatto scriba": this, finally, is the object of the readers' *vagheggiare*: lift your eyes *with me*: Dante places his poetry – his own creation – as the intermediary between God and humankind.

Of quite a different nature is the language Dante uses to describe the creation of the intellectual soul in *Purgatorio* 25, 67–78. Here he is keen to distinguish between the generation of the vegetative and sensitive souls on the one hand, and the creation of the rational soul on the other: to demonstrate how the human foetus "from animal becomes a child." The whole passage, like the parallel one in *Convivio* IV, xxi, attests that Dante's source on this subject is not only Aristotle's *De generatione animalium*, but also Albert the Great's *De natura et origine animae*. In other words, here he is speaking not "as a child," but as a scholar and philosopher; and the register is sustained until the point when Statius, now his Christian mouthpiece, turns to the question of the creation of the intellectual soul. At the very moment where the Aristotelian influence shows how "the articulation of the brain is perfected in the foetus," a subtle but swift change occurs in Dante's imagination. The Aristotelian Prime Mover ("motor primo") turns to the human embryo in a way which is equally Aristotelian,[9] but simultaneously Christian, on account of both its turning (for Aristotle it would be immobile), and, above all, its joyousness: "lieto" (glad) once again, almost as if it were now contemplating with love (*vagheggiando*, so to speak) the work of art which nature has generated in the foetus.

From this Aristotelian-Christian sequence the directly biblical inspiration of the "second" Creation follows:[10] "e spira spirito novo": as the climax to the entire process, the divine breath breathes an immortal soul into the embryo. But Dante stays with Genesis for a second only: this new spirit, "full of virtue," attracts into its substance what is already active in the vegetative-sensitive soul, fusing with it, according to Albert, to become "one single soul," living, like the being in Genesis, and sentient, but also possessing the supreme capacity for contemplation: "che vive e sente e sé in sé rigira." It "turns" on itself, revolving like a wheel, contemplating not only the truth, but also, as Dante states in the *Convivio* (IV, ii), its own contemplation, "and the beauty of it, turning about itself and with itself falling in love, for the beauty of its first view." Here the soul falls in love not only with God, the main object of its *trastulla* in *Purgatorio* 16, but above all with itself and its own thought.

The passage ends with another leap. Here, Dante uses the famous analogy of the heat of the sun which, joined to the juice that pours from the vine, becomes wine. Dante's sureness of poetic foot – in all senses – has no problem in dealing with exactly how the spiritual embeds in the corporeal, however, and foregrounds the dizzying distance between the celestial, immaterial heat of the sun and the earthly, filtering humours of the vine, at the same time indicating the inevitable and perfect encounter between the two (corporeal) elements, which infallibly produces a new substance, wine. This marvelous and most natural metamorphosis needs no Cicero or medieval philosopher to explain it: the *nous* of a farmer will do just as well – or, equally, the biblical knowledge of the average Christian, who will immediately think of the marriage of Cana, where the earthly element of water is transformed into wine, the "sign" of the Eucharist, and remember Christ's statement that "I am the true vine, and my Father the husbandman" (John 2:1–12; 15:1–11). And so, after a most learned kind of poetry, honed by the technicalities of Aristotle and Albert, the confutation of Averroes and the inspiration of the Bible, Ciceronian satisfaction, cosmic exultation, and contemplative pleasure all reach their perfect *kairòs* in wine: not the refined toast of poets, but the liquid drunk in Tuscany, the Veneto, and Romagna. The complete soul of man is no longer a child caught between laughter and tears, but a simple, thick, aromatic and inebriating wine. Philosophy and theology create their own poetics: that of the winemaker after that of the child.

The leap in register from *Purgatorio* to *Paradiso* is near paralyzing for the reader. It is no simple return to the cosmic nostalgia of *Inferno* 1, or to the philosophical discourse on the creation of the human soul in *Purgatorio*. *Paradiso* is not for the philosophically faint-hearted: it gives a Neoplatonic reading of the Scriptures which makes no concessions to the uninformed. This is poetry for the few who "reached out early for the angels' bread," and who can "put forth [their] vessel on the salt depths, holding [Dante's] furrow before the water returns smooth again": for the few who have fed on divine wisdom and the Word which is Christ. This type of poetry had never been heard before: the result of an agon, a struggle with the philosophical, theological, and not least verbal raw materials, creating an unprecedented effect of wonder on his readers.[11] In a word, this is a new, unique, and sublime form of poetry.

It is beyond my present scope to give a detailed analysis of the poetics of Creation in the *Paradiso*. I intend to concentrate on two seminal passages, in cantos 19 and 29, and call other lines to witness where relevant. Canto 19 is part of the long, extraordinary sequence of the Eagle, which extends from 18 to 20. Now in the sixth heaven, the sphere of Jupiter, the pilgrim watches, amazed, as the head and neck of an eagle are picked out in fiery sparks, and begin to explicate the mysteries of divine justice. Throughout the episode comprising *Paradiso* 18–20, Dante returns continuously to the theme of poetry and art which was announced in *Paradiso* 17 by the last motion of Cacciaguida, "an artist among the heavenly singers." He creates a scale of *poietai* from the supreme Painter and Architect of the universe down to David, "singer of the Holy Spirit," and then to the "buon cantor" who closes canto 20, afterwards reascending to the unique and extraordinary voice of Dante Alighieri, *poietes* of Paradise and the *Paradiso*.

The image of the Divine Architect in canto 19 (40–45), which interests us here, is absolute. This is the geometer "turning his compass about the bounds of the world," filling it with any number of things, manifest and hidden, but without infusing them with his own "valore – his power as the creating Father – to avoid making his idea and word (the Son) appear "infinitely exceeding" with respect to the created world. In just two *terzine*, the Creation is evoked in all its theological and philosophical complexity (with the whole structure of the universe, in which all things visible and invisible are contained, in discrete order), with the great biblical image (Proverbs 8:27–29) of the compass as a beguilingly visual introduction which "encompasses" the reader and stuns him into acceptance of the difficult cosmic ride ahead. This is Dante's rewriting of the beginning of Genesis and John's Gospel:

> Poi cominciò: "Colui che volse il sesto
> a lo stremo del mondo, e dentro ad esso
> distinse tanto occulto e manifesto,
> non poté suo valor sì fare impresso
> in tutto l'universo, che 'l suo verbo
> non rimanesse in infinito eccesso . . ."

(Then it began: "He that turned his compass about the bounds of the world, and within it devised so variously things hidden and manifest, could not make his power to be so impressed on the whole universe that his Word should not remain in infinite excess . . .") (*Paradiso* 19, 40–45)

At the human level of *poiein* there is, in *Paradiso* 18–25, no higher "maker" than David, traditionally considered the author of the Psalms. Here he is actually the "singer of the Holy Ghost" (20, 38), and "the sovereign singer of the sovereign Lord" (25, 72). Dante acknowledges David's inspiration as coming directly from God; he also recognizes that David's "tëodia" (25, 73) was a fundamental human experience for himself, in that it was the means by which hope was "first distilled in [his] heart." *Theody*: a hymn to God, a song in his honour, the monotheist's equivalent of the Greek ode to winning athletes, and to the gods; the highest lyrical model which the *Paradiso* enacts as narration (18, 82–87).

The challenge is met head on in the Eagle sequence, as evinced in two passages from *Paradiso* 18 and 19, in which Dante as poet demonstrates full self-awareness of both his attempt and his success. The first invokes the "Pegasean" Muse to illumine the human painter, and enable him to represent the letters and words formed by the spirits of the just *as he conceived them*. The Author is certainly God: but the Writer is equally certainly Dante, and the Muse confers glory and long life on *human* genius, which in its turn, jointly, confers fame on the cities and kingdoms of the world (19, 7–9).

Dante, of course, is perfectly aware to what extent the Muse's power is displayed in the present cantos: at the beginning of *Paradiso* 19 (7–9) he states proudly that what he is about to relate of the Eagle was never sung by any voice, written by any pen, nor conceived by any imagination. His poetry is, then, totally new. No models can exist for an imagination which, to celebrate divine justice and attack the knotty problem of pagan salvation, reinvents the eagle of Ezekiel and John, fleshing it out into a unity and, simultaneously, plurality of movements and arabesques, in a flash of gold on silver, and a display of fire, water, sun, birds. This is the poetry and poetics of Creation *as Justice*, as in *Inferno* 3: but, as the delicate, purified, blissful murmur of contemplation, wholly different.

Let me now skip to *Paradiso* 29, my other major text on the Creation. This is a canto which predicates being in its primeval forms, and which moves through time and space to hover over out-of-time and outside-space; which moves constantly from the instant to eternity, from the "points" to the celestial waters and on to the final dizzying height and breadth. It is, also, a canto which is boldly re-scripting Scripture, rewriting the Hebrew-Christian Genesis and the Prologue of John's Gospel in the Greek-Latin-scholastic language of the Platonists and the Aristotelians, roundly dismissing any anthropomorphism in favor of metaphysics and the categories of thought. Leaving aside the general structure of *Paradiso* 29, I shall here concentrate on precisely these themes.

It is in fact in this canto that Dante's long consideration of the divine Creation finally ends: a meditation which is not without reason, since creation by God of all that exists represents the central foundation, the intellectual pivot of a religious understanding of the cosmos. This canto contains all his impassioned analysis of the theme in passages which encompass a number of philosophical traditions and hover at the threshold of the ontologically unutterable. As soon as Beatrice starts speaking in the opening lines of *Paradiso* 29, she moves to the absolutes of beyond-time, beyond-space. She leaps towards the eternity which is God's, beyond any need and any desire to increase: "not to gain any good for himself." For the pure pleasure of it, and according to his desire ("come i piacque"), "the Eternal Love unfolded himself in new loves." God's only aim is to multiply existence into new, self-conscious lives, "that his splendour, shining back, might say *Subsisto.*" This Latin verb which Beatrice uses includes not mere existence, of course, but the whole and complete state of Being, a scholastic echo of the *Ego sum qui sum* through which God reveals his being to Moses, concealing it in absolute mystery (Exodus 3:14).

The creation of the angels – which constitutes Beatrice's first theme here – is a reflection of light, an opening out of Love into new loves, a blossoming and "breaking," as the last lines of the canto will have it, of the Eternal Goodness into "so many mirrors," "remaining in itself one as before." This, of course, is the Neoplatonism of Pseudo-Dionysius the Areopagite, but with an aesthetic consistency lacking in its models: a powerful affirmation of being requiring no divine hand (unlike, for example, *Purgatorio* 16), nor, surprisingly,

John's Logos or Word.[12] When Goethe's wretched Faust attempts to translate the *incipit* of the Fourth Gospel, "In the beginning was the Word," he tries out four different expressions to render into modern thought-systems the *Verbum* which was already an adaptation, via *Logos*, of the Hebrew *dabhar*: *Wort, Sinn, Kraft*, and *Tat*. Dante, for his part, is having nothing of semantic speculations: he goes confidently to tradition and in the place of Word, Sense, Might and Action consecrates Love: supreme Eros and Charity, which, as such, was never inactive, but had always ("né prima né poscia," since time only came into existence after the Creation) proceeded as a "discorrer di Dio sovra quest'acque," as God's moving over the face of "these" waters.

I intend to stop here for the moment and examine Dante's moves more closely. When, in the Bible, God creates the heaven and the earth, the earth is "without form, and void," and darkness is "upon the face of the deep." The Spirit of God "moves" (in the Vulgate, *ferebatur*) "upon the face of the waters." God then says, "Let there be light." Immediately afterwards, he divides light from dark, which he calls day and night: "and the evening and the morning were the first day." Dante eliminates all this. He also considerably alters the one biblical phrase he quotes, "and the Spirit of God moved upon the face of the waters." In the first place, the waters become "*these* waters." Following a tradition gaining considerable currency in the thirteenth century, he takes them as the waters above the firmament, those of the ninth heaven above the stars, in the Crystalline or Primum Mobile. Beatrice and Dante are now above the same primeval waters over which the divine Spirit of the Beginning moved: *these* waters; and from this giddy height Beatrice (i.e., Dante) dares to re-script the Holy Scriptures.

Secondly, Dante boldly cuts across centuries of controversy over the expression "Spirit of God" by simply attributing the action to God himself. Lastly, he eliminates the neutral form of the verb *ferebatur* of the Vulgate, ignores the *incubabat* and *fovebat* (i.e., the incubating and brooding which are the origins of Milton's version), and, jettisoning the various connotations of *volitabat* and *irruebat*, opts for a verb which is simultaneously powerful and delicate, *discorrer*, the signifier of movement which is in the English noun and verb "course." In both classical and medieval Latin *discurrere* also stands for the orator's exploring the ramifications of an argument (as in "discourse"). The former would agree with the opening of Eternal Love into new loves; the latter would refer indirectly to the action of God's word, which is fundamental to Genesis and John but notably absent from *Paradiso* 29.

In the Vulgate the spirit of God is carried or proceeds (*ferebatur*) above the waters. A tradition going from Augustine to Thomas Aquinas, and aptly summarized by Peter Lombard, interprets this as the will of the creator which "passes above" the matter it wishes to shape.[13] Dante, who was certainly at home within this tradition, is thus describing the action whereby the supreme Agent-Artisan-Artist is preparing to give shape to shapeless matter, to the *res fabricandae*, the things to be created.

In short, Dante's is a complete rewriting of Genesis. In the Bible, Creation continues for six full days. But Dante subverts this, too, replacing the temporal sequence by the single moment. The Divine Being "raggiò insieme tutto sanza distinzione in essordire" and "senza intervallo": i.e., the Creation of the universe was both simultaneous and instantaneous. The point is that Dante – who knows perfectly well the troubles which the opening chapter of the Bible creates for the philosopher and the theologian[14] – rejects the anthropomorphic imaginary which dominates the account in Genesis and so many other myths of creation to start a philosophical *mythos* of his own. Dante is not interested in the single creatures, species, or types (trees, fish, reptiles, etc.), but the prime essences, created directly, immediately,[15] by God, which Dante then collects under philosophy's capital letters of Form and Matter, and analyzes within the context of the equally upper-case categories of Act and Potency.

To grasp the fascination (and indeed value) of these capitals it will perhaps be sufficient just to review, briefly, their meaning within the philosophical tradition. Here "form" indicates the basic, necessary, essence or substance of the things which possess matter; the cause or *raison d'être* whereby a thing is what it is; and then the act or actuality of the thing itself, the beginning and end of its becoming. "Matter" can be taken as both the subject (i.e., that which "lies below") and the potency: the raw, amorphous, passive, receptive material of which all things are composed.[16] Aristotle identifies matter with potency: "all things produced by both nature and art possess matter since the possibility each has of being or not being in itself, for each, constitutes its matter."[17]

So when, in lines 22ff. of *Paradiso* 29, Dante orders the creation of the universe into these categories, he is moving to the heart of the matter, the substance of things. Form and matter: each in absolute, singular, purity, or united: that is to say, pure form (or pure act), angelic intelligence; pure matter (or pure potency), prime matter; and form-and-matter together, a compound of both, the heavens. The three things together take the place of the biblical heaven and earth, constituting the object of the Big Bang, and the foundations of the universe. The instant had been announced in *Paradiso* 7, when the long and fascinating argument of Plato's *Timaeus* had been filtered through Boethius' *Consolation*, so that to the Bible's *bonum* ("and God saw that it was good") was then added the Greek *kalon* (*pulchrum*) to achieve the perfect *kalokagathon*:[18]

> La divina *bontà*, che da sé sperne
> ogne livore, ardendo in sé, sfavilla
> sì che dispiega le *bellezze* eterne.

(The divine *Goodness*, which spurns all envy from itself, burning within itself so sparkles that it displays its eternal *beauties*.)   (*Paradiso* 7, 64–6)

At Dante's objection that the elements – air, fire, water, and earth – and their compounds are corruptible although created by God, Beatrice had at that point answered that the angels and heavens were created "as whole beings," while the elements and compounds "are informed by created virtue," and thus receive their form from a created force between God and themselves: the influence of the heavens. The same idea, the same imagery (luminous rays, mirrors, and splendour), and the same vocabulary (love, goodness, one-and-many, substance, potencies, act, and contingencies) are all used by Thomas Aquinas in *Paradiso* 13 (52–66), in the magnificent lines in which he distinguishes between direct and indirect divine Creation, before going on to describe generation:

> Ciò che non more e ciò che può morire
> non è se non splendor di quella idea
> che parturisce, amando, il nostro Sire;
> ché quella viva luce che sì mea
> dal suo lucente, che non si disuna
> da lui né dall'amor ch'a lor s'intrea,
> per sua bontate il suo raggiare aduna,
> quasi specchiato, in nove sussistenze,
> etternalmente rimanendosi una.
> Quindi discende all'ultime potenze
> giù d'atto in atto, tanto divenendo
> che più non fa che brevi contingenze;
> e queste contingenze essere intendo
> le cose generate, che produce
> con seme e sanza seme il ciel movendo.

(That which dies not and that which can die are nothing but the splendour of that Idea which our Sire, in Loving, begets; for that living Light which so streams from its shining source that it is not parted from it nor from the Love which with them makes the Three, of its own goodness gathers its beams, as it were mirrored, in nine subsistences, remaining forever one. Thence it descends to the last potencies, passing down from act to act and becoming such that it makes nothing more than brief contingencies; and by these contingencies I mean things generated with or without seed, which the heavens by their motion produce.)

At the same time, there is a significant difference between *Paradiso* 7 and 13 on the one hand, and *Paradiso* 29 on the other: the former are in the present tense, the latter in the past. The first two describe and explain the creative act as it *always* is in the universe, from substances, "subsistences," to generated things; the third, the creative act *in principio*, that out-of-time instant from which time began: constant and continuous creation, as it were, and primitive creation and order.

This is why the Beginning was simultaneous and instantaneous creation, "like three arrows from a three-stringed bow:" a radiant bursting out of all things, like a ray of light shining in transparent glass, amber, or crystal (for our medieval ancestors, light propagated instantly). The double image is one and three, like the Creator and the three original substances (angels, matter, heavens): three-string bow and three arrows; ray, glass, amber, and crystal. In both cases it takes place at astounding speed, echoing the moving over the waters, while the effulgence of the second mirrors the splendor and primordial brightness of the angels. Dante invents a Beginning of absolute Light which only in this aspect recalls the biblical *Fiat lux*.

Being was created with its structure: the "order" which arranges it according to hierarchical degree, and the "construct," the construction in which the degrees are interrelated: at the top, then, the substances in which the pure act was produced, created as pure forms, i.e., the angelic intelligences; at the base, pure potency, formless prime matter; in between, potency and act, tied in the heavens by an indissoluble knot.

We would be wrong to imagine any gap in time between the creation of the angels, and of the heavens and prime matter, the mistake made by Jerome, the prince of the Latin Fathers: the Bible itself – "the writers of the Holy Spirit" – states the opposite,[19] and reason also proves it: it is implausible for the angels, the heavenly movers, to have passed a considerable period in a state of imperfection, that is, without lending movement to all the rest as their function and hence their perfection requires. Beatrice is here lightly rapping the knuckles of Jerome and a number of others. But while noting that for her as for Dante human logic and the Scriptures are considered at no variance, we also have to note that "this truth" declared here obliquely places Dante the poet on the same level as the writers of the Holy Spirit. Scripture and its rewriting have a similar status and inspiration: indeed, the rewritten Word knows better than the original (which in no canonical book gives us a blow-by-blow account of the creation of the angels!) "where and when these loving spirits were created."

One might well ask, at this point, what kind of creation poetry Dante is bent on fashioning in the *Paradiso*. His passage on the Creation in canto 29, with the exception of the memory of the angels, faithfully follows Book II, *Distinctio* II of Peter Lombard's *Sententiae*: the sequence, allusions, problem of time, and reference to Jerome are almost identical.[20] But Dante is far more daring: Peter quotes Genesis, Ecclesiasticus, the Book of Wisdom, the Psalms, Job, and Isaiah; Dante injects the Hebrew prophets and Hebrew wisdom with Greek wisdom in the shape of Platonic images and Aristotelian concepts. In doing this he is, of course, following a time-honored Christian technique, but in a much more advanced form than his predecessors, be they Church Fathers, twelfth-century Platonists, or scholastics. What sort of poetry is this, which uses imagery and concepts of the kind? One very reasonable definition, well beyond Croce's distinction between "poetry" and "non-poetry," is: "philomythic." But this immediately requires, while not exactly begging, another question: why does a passage like this still exert such a singular attraction on the averagely cultivated reader who is no philosophy specialist? Because, Patrick Boyde maintains, "difficult concepts are conveyed through metaphor in such a way that they capture the imagination even when they are imperfectly understood."[21] I would absolutely agree, but would also add a comment inspired by the passage in which Aquinas glosses Aristotle's *Metaphysics* on the question of the philosopher and the *philomythes*. Taking wonder as the start of all philosophy, Aristotle maintained that the mythically inclined (the poet, the *philomythes*) is in a sense also a philosopher, since myths deal with wonder-ful things. Aquinas reverses the terms, stating that the philosopher is in a sense *philomythes*, the quality proper to the poet. The first authors, he says, who dealt with the principles of things in a "mythical" manner are called *poetae theologizantes*, "as was Perseus, and some others, who were the Seven Sages."[22] Dante thus emerges as a *poeta theologizans*, who treats *de principiis rerum poetice et fabulariter*: a "metaphysical" poet in the original, Aristotelian, sense.

Seven hundred years on, however, the expressions take on a rather different significance. The whole *Commedia* reads as *fabula*, and not only in the sense of a fiction containing innumerable other fictions, but because it is now a myth of Western consciousness and the modern imagination. It is not simply the journey through the three realms, Virgil, Beatrice, and the various characters encountered which comprise the *fabulae* and *mythoi*, but also, for us, Dante's whole system of logic and philosophical lexis, underpinning both the individual passages and the whole structure of the poem.

It is not a question of the extraordinary imagery – Boyde's "metaphor" – which Dante employs to illustrate his concepts: Love unfolding like a flower, the triple-strung bow, the three arrows, or the ray shining inside glass, amber, or crystal. While totally necessary, they would not explain the work's aesthetic reception *today*. What conquers the modern reader is the dissonant echo of the Scriptures on the one hand, and the philosophical register on the other. The echo is "dissonant" in that it restores a significantly rewritten Word, Dante having no scruples about placing himself on the level of the writers of the Holy Spirit and making free with Genesis, the Book of Wisdom, and the Fourth Gospel to produce a new text, his own (re)Scripture. It is this echo and simultaneous transformation, text speaking to and through text, which captivates the modern reader.

When, in *Paradiso* 26, Dante is examined by St. John about charity, he answers that what prompted his love for God was both philosophical reasoning and the authority of Scripture. And by these he means first Aristotle; then the voice of the "true Author," God, who tells Moses in Exodus (33:19), "Io ti farò vedere ogne valore" (*Ego ostendam omne bonum tibi*);[23] and finally John himself, "the eagle of Christ," who began "l'alto preconio che grida l'arcano," the sublime announcement, contained in the Prologue to his Gospel, which, more than any other heralding, proclaims on earth the mystery of God (*Paradiso* 26, 25–45). This, precisely, is the poetry which the "theologizing poet" creates, and his poetics of the "sacred poem to which both heaven and earth have set their hands," now therefore going beyond David's theody (*Paradiso* 25, 1–3): Aristotle's philosophy, the Old and the New Testament. It is significant that, among the texts of the latter, Dante should choose the opening of John's Gospel, "In the beginning was the Word." For that line does not only rewrite the Creation, but has a sublime aura acknowledged by all commentators and speaks the language of Hellenic philosophy as much as that of Judaic theology.

The philosophic register on which the Creation is re-created, on the other hand, is beguiling in its use of canonical categories which effortlessly "universalize" the immense variety of individual creatures. Furthermore, it seems to me that words such as "form" and "matter," "potency" and "act," "being" and "substance," have a significance which in part differs from the present one, and differs again from the very precise meaning they had for a thirteenth-century Aristotelian. They lie, so to speak, half way between "alterity" and "modernity," are alien yet comprehensible, surprising yet expected – an ideal situation for the reception of a work of poetry. Classical statements, almost archetypes of the Western (and not only Western) mind and culture, they possess a philosophical aura which is part of our conceptual framework, in representing ideas with which our reason and our language have lived for twenty-five centuries. At the prephilosophical, prespecialist level, they work for us in the same manner as Homer's epithets for the sea or dawn, "wine dark" and "rosy fingered," while at the prephilological level they function as myths embedded in our cultural DNA, in the *logos* of our subconscious.[24]

A similarly "metaphysical" modern poet has no similarly evocative models; modern culture has replaced being with scientific becoming and a discourse of quantity. The Big Bang hardly lends itself to poetry: it has to be quantified and mathematically analyzed for the first three seconds, minutes, or million years. Democritus has won, and the barion, quark, and photon are not forms, but elementary particles of matter: *brevi contingenze*, Dante would say. As far as we know, only Lucretius was able to make poetry of them, more than two thousand years ago. When a modern poet – Rainer Maria Rilke or T. S. Eliot, for example – writes poems of being, he has to enlist the angels,[25] or situate himself at "the point of intersection of the timeless with time": Love and the "crowned knot of fire" where "the fire and the rose are one."[26]

NOTES

1 1 John 4:8: "Deus est charitas"; Thomas Aquinas, *In duodecim libros metaphysicorum Aristotelis expositio*, I, 4, 984b 29, *lect.* 5, 102 (Turin and Rome: Marietti, 1964), p. 29.

2 *L'Espositione di Bernardino Daniello da Lucca sopra la Comedia di Dante*, eds. R. Hollander, N. J. Vickers, K. Brownlee and J. Schnapp (Dartmouth, NH: University Press of New England, 1989), p. 231, *ad Purgatorio* XVI, 85–87.

3 Aristotle, *De anima* III, xiv; Thomas Aquinas, *Summa theologiae* I, q. 79, a. 2.

4 *Paradiso* 32, 61–66: "le menti tutte nel suo *lieto* aspetto/ creando" (creating all minds in his *glad* sight).

5 In "Animula," one of the *Ariel Poems*, T. S. Eliot wrote a perfect modern counterpoint to Hadrian's and Dante's lines: "Issues from the hands of God, the simple soul."

6 See *Enciclopedia dell'arte medievale*, I (Rome: Istituto dell'Enciclopedia Italiana, 1991), s.v. "anima," p. 810.

7 References in this paragraph: Origen, *Comm. in Cant.*, I, 1, 2, ed. W. A. Baehrens, *Die griechischen christlichen Schriftsteller der ersten drei Jahrhunderte* (Leipzig: Hinrichs, 1925), XXXIII; *Omelie sul Cantico dei Cantici*, I, i, 50–53; I, 3, 25–35; I, 6, 14–19 (ed. M. Simonetti, Milan: Valla-Mondadori, 1998). Origen, *Homelies sur la Genèse* I, 15 (Paris, Cerf, 1985), p. 67; Origen, *Comm. Ioann.* 20, 182; H. de Lubac, *Exégèse médiévale*, I (Paris: Aubier, 1959), pp. 207–38, and in particular p. 234 and n. 12; Origen, *Comm. Matt.* xv, 7–8 (*Origenes Matthäuserklärung*, hrsgb. E. Klostermann–E. Benz, 2e Auflage hrsgb. U. Treu, Berlin: Akademie-Verlag, 1968–76); Origen, *Comm. Matt.*, XIII, 18 (Jerome, *Comm. Matt.* III, 179).

8 "Trastulla" will be used in *Paradiso* 9, 76 of the voice of Folchetto da Marsiglia which, together with the song of the Seraphim, gives joy to Heaven, but Folchetto was also one of the most famous troubadours. The same "trastulla" is employed by Cacciaguida in *Paradiso* 15, 121–23, when he describes the Florentine women of his age, when mothers kept watch tending their children's cradles, using "the tongue that first delights ('trastulla') fathers and mothers." Note that for Dante this childish "idioma" gives delight in the first place to parents, not to children. The "trastulla" of *Purgatorio* 16, 90 is anticipated by Guido del Duca in his "del ben richiesto al vero e al trastullo" in *Purgatorio* 14, 93. An ethics and poetics of *trastullare* are therefore present as well, the latter coming close to that of *vagheggiare*.

9 Aristotle, *De generatione animalium* II, 3, 736b, according to whom the intellect does not come from nature by generation, but "from outside," "et divinum esse solum."

10 Genesis 2:7: "And the Lord God formed man out of the dust of the ground, and breathed into his nostrils the breath of life ("spiraculum vitae"); and man became a living soul ("in animam viventem")."

11 *Paradiso* 2, 1–18: in particular, "l'acqua ch'io prendo già mai non si corse," l. 7; "Que' gloriosi che passaro al Colco/ non s'ammiraron come voi farete," ll. 16–17.

12 Indirectly present, on the other hand, in *Paradiso* 13, where the same splendor attaches to the Idea "che parturisce, amando, il nostro Sire" ("which our Sire, in loving, begets"): the Son, the Word.

13 Augustine, *De Genesi contra Manichaeos*, I, vii, 12; Peter Lombard, *Sententiae in IV Libris Distinctae*, I, XII, c. 3; Thomas, *Summa theologiae* I, q. 66, I ad 2.

14 For which it will be enough to recall Augustine's discussion in the *Confessions*, Book XII, and in the *De Genesi ad litteram*, particularly in Book IV.

15 *Paradiso* 7, 67 states: "sanza mezzo."

16 Plato, *Timaeus*, 50b–d. For Aristotle, matter is subject: formless, indeterminate, unknowable; such is for him prime matter (the raw material not in the sense of bronze, wood, etc. of which an object is made, but the subject common to all materials).

17 *Metaphysics* VII, 7, 1032a 20.

18 *De consolatione philosophiae* III, m. IX, 6–8: "tu cuncta superno/ ducis ab exemplo, pulchrum pulcherrimus ipse/ mundum mente gerens." Dante had translated these lines in *Convivio* III, ii, 17: "Tutte le cose produci da lo superno essemplo, tu, bellissimo, bello mondo ne la mente portante."

19 Genesis 1:1; Ecclesiasticus 18:1.

20 *Sententiae in IV Libris Distinctae*, Tom. I, Pars II (Grottaferrata: Editiones Collegii S. Bonaventurae, 1971).

21 P. Boyde, *Dante Philomythes and Philosopher* (Cambridge, Cambridge University Press, 1981), p. 266.

22 *In duodecim libros metaphysicorum Aristotelis*, I, iii, 55.

23 Dante's translation of Exodus is Cavalcantian, from the sonnet "Vedeste, al mio parere, onne valore," which is Cavalcanti's answer to the first sonnet in Dante's own *Vita nuova*.

24 One would of course need to qualify this statement with regard to our reception of Homer, specifying that in this instance what is involved is the *mythos* in our subconscious.

25 In the second of the *Duino Elegies* Rilke maps, with a near-Dantean enchantment, Creation's first peaks (*Höhenzüge*) and first dawn-like mirrors (*Spiegel*) of creation, the angels: blossoming, being, and beauty: see *Duino Elegies and the Sonnets to Orpheus*, trans. A. Poulin, Jr (Boston: Houghton Mifflin, 1977), 'Frühe Geglückte, ihr Verwöhnten der Schöpfung," "Fortunate first ones, creation's pampered darlings."

26 T. S. Eliot, *Four Quartets*: "The Dry Salvages" v; "Little Gidding" iv and v. I wonder if Eliot's "point" might not be an echo of Dante's "punto" in *Paradiso* xxix.

SUGGESTED READING

Dronke, Peter, "L'amor che move il sole e l'altre stelle," in *The Medieval Poet and His World* (Rome: Edizioni di Storia e Letteratura, 1984).

Foster, Kenelm, "The Mind in Love," in John Freccero, ed., *Dante: A Collection of Critical Essays* (Englewood Cliffs, NJ: Prentice Hall, 1965), pp. 43–60.

Frye, Northrop, *The Great Code: The Bible and Literature* (New York and London: Harcourt, 1987).

Hawkins, Peter S., *Dante's Testaments: Essays in Scriptural Imagination* (Stanford: Stanford University Press, 1999).

Hollander, Robert, "Dante *Theologus-Poeta*," in *Studies in Dante* (Ravenna: Longo, 1980), pp. 39–89.

Moevs, Christian, *The Metaphysics of Dante's Comedy* (New York: Oxford University Press, 2005).

Nardi, Bruno, *Nel mondo di Dante* (Rome: Edizioni di Storia e Letteratura, 1944).
  Studi di filosofia medievale (Rome: Edizioni di Storia e Letteratura, 1960).

Pépin, Jean, *Théologie cosmique et théologie chrétienne* (Paris: P. U. F., 1964).

Steiner, George, *Grammars of Creation* (New Haven: Yale University Press, 2001).

Took, John, *L'etterno piacer: Aesthetic Ideas in Dante* (Oxford: Clarendon Press, 1984).

Van Wolde, Ellen, *Stories of the Beginning: Genesis 1–11 and Other Creation Stories*, trans. John Bowden (London: SCM Press, 1996).

14

JOHN M. NAJEMY

Dante and Florence

Dante's angry denunciation of Florence and the Florentines is one of the memorable themes of the *Divina Commedia*. Repeatedly in the great poem, and in several of his letters, Dante excoriated the Florentines for the violence, factionalism, and instability of their politics, for their excessive pursuit and consumption of wealth, and, worst of all, for their criminal resistance to what he considered the divinely ordained authority of the Roman emperor. Because we know so little of Dante's political views and opinions about Florence before his exile in 1302, it is tempting to use the fact of the exile and Dante's emotional reaction to it as a way of explaining his harsh critique of his own city. While there is no doubt much truth in such an approach, it is equally important to grasp the influence on Dante of the traditions of political and historical thought that emerged in Florence during the course of the thirteenth century, and in particular of the ideas associated with movements of popular opposition to the traditional dominance of the elite of upper-class families.

What little is known of Dante's political life before 1302 suggests that he played a role quite typical of those politically active Florentines who did not belong to the elite of economically powerful and influential families. The Alighieri were Guelfs, but by the 1290s Ghibellinism was a dead issue in Florence and everyone (or at least anyone who wanted any role in politics) was a Guelf. From about the mid-1290s, Dante held a number of important posts and was several times a member of the advisory boards convened by the government to give advice and support to its policies. In 1300 he served a two-month term on the chief executive magistracy of the priorate, apparently the first of his family to do so. Florentines were quite conscious of the frequency of election to the priorate as a measure of family prestige, and the fact that Dante was the first and only Alighieri to serve as prior indicates that they were not among the elite. Dante himself gained his eligibility for the priorate through membership in a non-elite but still major guild. The city's republican constitution and the popular movement that came to power in the early 1290s created the conditions for the participation in communal politics of large numbers of men like Dante: citizens who took their turn in office but who were not outspoken leaders of the various factions of the political class. The most noteworthy indication of any policy, not to say ideology, espoused by Dante in the years before his exile was his advice in one of the legislative councils against a proposal to renew military aid to Pope Boniface VIII in June 1301. Dante's view was voted down, and there is no way of knowing whether his opinion on this question had anything to do with the hostility he later expressed toward Boniface and the temporal power of the papacy.

Dante's political career coincided with the onset of a violent split among the families of the Florentine elite. Why some families ended up among the so-called Black Guelfs, whose leaders were the Donati and in particular Corso Donati, and others among the White Guelfs, headed by the Cerchi, is one of the great mysteries of Florentine history. No clear demarcation of ideology, economic interest, or class has ever been demonstrated as the cause of the split, although there are some indications that the Blacks thought of themselves as older families of more established status, and saw the Cerchi and their allies as more recent arrivals. But both the Donati and the Cerchi and most of the families allied with them were in every sense part of the urban elite: large families, and in some cases clans, with interregional and even international economic interests in banking, trade, and textile manufactures; important ties to the countryside, including sometimes extensive landed holdings; a tradition of involvement in communal politics that went back decades in some cases and a century or more in others; a perhaps even older tradition of patronage networks and neighborhood influence that often included both their corner of the city and their piece of the countryside; and, not least, some claim, real or otherwise, to association with the old aristocracy of knighthood. The fact that there were families with some or all of these characteristics on both sides of the Black–White split made (and still makes) it difficult to discern any political or historical logic in what very quickly assumed the proportions of a civil war.

It is usually claimed that Dante belonged to the party or faction of the Whites, but he was more closely tied to them in the first few years after his exile than he had been in the period of his political participation. Between early 1300 and the fall of 1301, when the Blacks finally took control, factional conflict engulfed the city. In May or June 1300, the priors tried to restore order by banishing leaders from both factions, including Corso Donati and several other Blacks, and, from the White party, three of the Cerchi and Dante's friend, the poet Guido Cavalcanti. But exactly when the decree of exile was promulgated is not clear. If it occurred after June 15, when the priorate of which Dante was a member took office, he presumably agreed to these banishments. But if it occurred before that date, Dante had nothing to do with the decision. The attempt at evenhandedness between the factions soon ended with the priors recalling the White exiles, and according to one chronicle account this happened in July, when Dante's priorate was still in office. Thus, whatever his role in sending the factional leaders into exile, Dante apparently participated in the decision to repatriate the Whites, including Cavalcanti (who, ill with malaria contracted in exile, died at the end of August). Dante was, therefore, at least in sympathy with the White Guelfs and, after the Blacks forced their way back into Florence with Charles of Valois and papal support in November 1301, the long series of condemnations and decrees of provisional and then permanent banishment that followed over the next few months included those against Dante. And for the next two years he joined the exiled Whites in the effort to reverse the results of the Black *coup d'état*. So the habit of identifying Dante as a White, even in the years before 1302, comes easily as a way of making sense of his exile. One possible interpretation of his political career and thought is thus that, belonging to the faction that lost the struggle for control of the city, finding himself exiled, and placing his hopes first in his fellow exiles and then in the grand dream of imperial peace, Dante rejected not only Florence and its politics, but the whole idea of the city as the proper and natural form of political association.

Dante himself contributes to interpretations along these lines by making his alienation from Florence an essential element of the dramatic structure of the *Commedia*. The journey to the three realms of the afterlife is given the precise historical moment of Holy Week in the year 1300. By setting the action of the poem a year and a half before the political crisis that resulted in his banishment, and in fact at the beginning of his own period of intensive involvement in politics, Dante has his pilgrim learn through a series of prophetic utterances, culminating in *Paradiso* 17, that exile awaits him. He also learns that his exile will serve higher purposes and that the meaning of his life and poetic vocation will thereafter consist in the revelation – to him and by him – of truths that become accessible precisely because of his separation from the city. In a sense the poet asserts that his own intellectual and philosophical detachment from the city is independent of its expulsion of him: in the fiction of the poem he rejects it before it rejects him. Leaving Florence behind in every sense thus becomes the necessary precondition for the vision of political and moral redemption entrusted to him for the benefit of humankind. In place of what he now sees as the selfish particularism of the city, the poet affirms the universalism of the empire.

The anti-Florentine polemic of the *Divina Commedia*, and especially of its first canticle, is severe and sustained. As Joan Ferrante shows in her study of the poem's political vision, Dante's Hell is full of Florentines, and Florence almost seems to be the model for the corrupt society displayed in the *Inferno*. But this critique nonetheless has a quite specific focus. Most of Dante's attention here is on the violent factional conflicts that lacerated the city in two distinct periods: the long struggle between the Guelfs and the Ghibellines in the mid-thirteenth century, and the civil war between the Blacks and the Whites of the years around 1300. The first mention of Florence in the *Divina Commedia* comes in canto 6 of *Inferno* in which the glutton Ciacco identifies himself to Dante as one who lived in "your city, which is so full of envy." When the pilgrim asks "what the citizens of the divided city will come to," "if any one in it is just," and "why such discord has assailed it," Ciacco prophesies the bloody events of 1300–02: the exile of the Black leaders by the Whites, the return of the Blacks engineered by Boniface, and the "heavy burdens" inflicted on the defeated party. He adds that only "two" Florentines deserve to be thought of as just (and no one pays any attention to them), and that "pride, envy, and avarice are the three sparks that inflamed" the hearts of the Florentines. Ciacco's prophecy and judgments on the Florentine leaders of Dante's time evidently create some puzzlement in the pilgrim's mind about what to think of the leaders of the earlier conflict of the Guelfs and the Ghibellines. He asks about five of them: the Ghibelline captain Farinata degli Uberti; two Guelf leaders, Tegghiaio Aldobrandi of the Adimari family and Jacopo Rusticucci; and the legendary instigators of a famous murder in 1215–16 that allegedly sparked the long civil war, Mosca dei Lamberti and a certain Arrigo (almost certainly Oddo Arrighi, or Odarigo de' Fifanti). He wants to know whether these and "the others who set their minds on doing good" are in Heaven or Hell. This is an extraordinary moment. The list of political leaders and the pilgrim's curiosity about their fate in the afterlife dramatically open up the question of how, from the vantage point of the early fourteenth century, the Guelf–Ghibelline conflict and the upper class of great families that provided the leadership of that struggle should be judged. The surprising thing about the pilgrim's question is that the issue had seemingly been settled by the definitive triumph of the Guelf cause more than a generation before 1300.

Although the murder of Buondelmonte de' Buondelmonti was probably more a symptom than the cause of this earlier division of the Florentine aristocracy, by about 1240 two loose coalitions of families vied with each other for control of the city and the government of the commune: the Ghibellines in alliance with Frederick II, who ruled the south of Italy as heir (through his mother) to the old Norman kingdom of Sicily and who, as emperor and

grandson of the Hohenstaufen Barbarossa, was attempting to bring under his control the territories of northern and central Italy (including Tuscany) that were nominally part of the empire; and the Guelfs in alliance with the papacy and a league of north-central Italian cities, both determined to resist Frederick's grand design. In the 1240s, Frederick and the Florentine Ghibellines gained the advantage in Tuscany to the extent of banishing a large number of Guelfs in 1248. But Ghibelline power in Florence suddenly collapsed in 1250 when a new government was proclaimed in October by a movement that called itself the *popolo* and declared itself formally neutral between the two parties. Two months later Frederick died, his representatives left the city, and the new popular government forcefully asserted its strength against both the Ghibellines, in disarray without their great protector, and the Guelfs, who were just beginning to return to the city. The *popolo* governed the city for a decade and did its best to reduce the power of the great families and keep their party conflicts out of the city and its government. However, when Frederick's illegitimate son Manfred got himself crowned king of Sicily (although never emperor) and revived Hohenstaufen and Ghibelline hopes throughout Italy, it became clear that the Florentine *popolo* would be as much a target of Manfred's hostility as were the Guelfs. Unavoidably, the popular government closed ranks with the Guelfs and adopted a more openly anti-Ghibelline posture. Ghibellines left the city in large numbers in 1258 and 1259 as the great conflict approached. In September of 1260 at the battle of Montaperti near Siena the Guelfs and the *popolo* suffered a catastrophic defeat at the hands of a coalition of Florentine Ghibellines (led by Farinata degli Uberti), Sienese troops, and Manfred's Hohenstaufen forces. For the next six years Florence was Ghibelline. The government of the *popolo* was dismantled, and the great Guelf families were driven into exile, their property confiscated, and their homes destroyed.

In the early and mid-1260s, large numbers of these exiled Guelfs formed the historic alliance with the papacy and the Angevins of France through which they achieved their definitive and triumphal return to power. Scores of Florentine Guelf bankers and international merchants entered into an arrangement with two successive French popes whereby the former promised to provide the financial means needed to mount an all-out war against Manfred in return for the right to collect into their own coffers the taxes that Rome imposed on the local and territorial churches of Europe. The third partner in this alliance was Charles of Anjou, brother of Louis IX of France. With papal support and Florentine loans, Charles assembled the Guelf army that wrecked the Hohenstaufen and killed Manfred at Benevento in February 1266. After a brief and unsuccessful attempt by the *popolo* to revive the constitution of 1250, the Guelfs returned in April 1267 and got their revenge: now it was the Ghibellines who were forced into exile and had their property seized and sold and their palaces destroyed. It was the end of Ghibellinism in Florence and of the Hohenstaufen cause in Italy.

For Florentines of Dante's generation, these were the tragic and heroic events that created the Florence they knew: the independent city-state free of imperial overlordship; the cornerstone of the Guelf alliance that replaced Hohenstaufen power in Italy; and the economic and financial giant of Italy and southern Europe, thanks in significant measure to the banking ties established with the papacy and the commercial privileges conceded by the Angevins in the conquered south in return for the loans that Charles and the church accepted to finance the war against Manfred. And here was Dante's pilgrim asking Ciacco whether the almost legendary chiefs on both sides of that struggle so decisive for Florence's destiny and identity were in Heaven or Hell. Ciacco's answer revealed that they were all condemned: "They are among the blackest souls, and different faults weigh them down toward the bottom; if you descend that far, there you can see them," as indeed Dante-pilgrim does. He meets Farinata among the heretics in canto 10, the two Guelf leaders among the sodomites in canto 16, and Mosca dei Lamberti (but apparently not Arrigo) among the disseminators of discord in canto 28.

It was not unusual for Florentines of Dante's time to cast the protagonists of the Buondelmonti murder in the role of villains who initiated the long civil war. And, as late as the 1280s, Farinata degli Uberti could still be thought of as an arch-enemy, as his posthumous condemnation for heresy shows. But Farinata was also remembered, as Dante recalls in canto 10, as the one Ghibelline leader who refused to contemplate the destruction of Florence ordered by Manfred (or his vicar) after Montaperti in 1260, and through this story he became something of a Florentine hero and patriot despite his Ghibellinism. The remarkable thing about Dante's condemnation of the five political leaders is that it cut across the Guelf–Ghibelline split, indicting both sides and evidently flying in the face of the conventional judgment, expressed by the pilgrim, that these were all men "who set their minds on doing good," and that two of them – Farinata and Tegghiaio, a Ghibelline and and a Guelf – "were so worthy." When the pilgrim meets the Guelfs Tegghiaio and Jacopo Rusticucci, accompanied by yet another and still more famous Guelf captain, Guido Guerra of the noble family of the Counts Guidi (which actually had members on both sides of the conflict), he tells them, "I am of your city," and immediately adds, "and always have I rehearsed and heard with affection your deeds and honored names." Like many Florentines in the generation after Florence became definitively Guelf, the pilgrim had been brought up to honor and revere these heroes of the Guelf pantheon. His political education in Hell consists largely in learning of their sad record of misrule.

Dante dramatizes his critique of the Florentine aristocracy in the encounter with Farinata degli Uberti in canto 10. Farinata first recognizes the pilgrim's Tuscan speech and, without knowing anything else about his visitor, declares that he must be "a native of that noble fatherland to which I perhaps did too much harm," an allusion to the war of 1260. The bond of language thus generates both patriotic sentiments and remorse in the proud Ghibelline. But then Farinata asks the crucial and divisive question, apparently so simple but in fact the opening to the tensions that suddenly flare between them: "Who were your ancestors?" As soon as Farinata hears the answer, he knows that the pilgrim's family was Guelf and counts them among his enemies: "They were fiercely adverse to me and to my forebears and to my party, so that twice over I scattered them." Now Farinata's loyalties and the collectivities that define them ("a me e a miei primi e a mia parte") become limited to family and party and no longer make any mention of the "nobil patria" for which, just moments earlier, he had expressed remorseful affection. And so he arrogantly boasts that he drove the Guelfs from Florence twice, in 1248 and in 1260 after the battle of Montaperti. The pilgrim responds in kind, here too initially as a partisan Guelf, telling Farinata that the Guelfs "returned from every quarter, both times," but that "yours have not learned that art well." Because Farinata died in 1264, during the period of Ghibelline rule, he learns for the first time from these words that after his death the Ghibellines were defeated and sent into exile from which they never returned. So distressing to Farinata is the news of the permanent exile of his family and party that he confesses that it "torments me more than this bed" in Hell. But he gains a measure of revenge against the pilgrim by telling him that he too would soon learn how difficult is the "art" of returning home from exile. Thus Farinata and the pilgrim re-enact in their exchange the long history of reciprocal acts of injury, revenge, and banishment that Guelfs and Ghibellines inflicted on each other from the 1240s to the 1260s.

Dante uses the Farinata episode to expose the fatal blindness of the Florentine aristocracy in its attachment to party and family at the expense of broader loyalties to city and "patria," a world in which the very mention of family names set citizen against citizen, in which fierce hatreds between rival blocs of families plunged the whole city into civil war, and in which the irrational rituals of family rivalry led men who should have been care-takers of the common good to commit the most heinous and outrageous acts of betrayal against their city, and sometimes even against their own party. Farther on down in Hell, the pilgrim meets, as we know, Mosca dei Lamberti (*Inferno* 28, 103–08) whose instigation of the Buondelmonti murder of 1215–16 "was seed of ill to the Tuscan people." And in the canto (32) of the traitors against their own relatives, country, or party, of the thirteen sinners named or referred to, no fewer than seven are members of great Florentine families, both Guelf and Ghibelline: the brothers Napoleone and Alessandro of the counts Alberti, who took opposite sides in the Guelf–Ghibelline war and ended by killing each other; Sassol Mascheroni, of the Ghibelline Toschi family, who killed a relative; Camicione de' Pazzi (another Ghibelline family) who also murdered a relative and is waiting for his kinsman Carlino, who will let himself be bribed into betraying the exiled Whites in 1302 by handing over a fortified town to the Blacks; Bocca degli Abati, who betrayed the Guelfs at Montaperti; and Gianni de' Soldanieri, who betrayed the Ghibellines in 1266 by giving his support to the popular movement that rose in opposition to the weakened Ghibelline government in the aftermath of Benevento. The betrayals cross every line and involve every party and faction, but the one thing common to all these Florentine traitors is that they belong to the elite of great families.

It is worth emphasizing that much of what at first glance seems to be Dante's polemic against Florence is actually directed against its upper class of large, rich, and politically influential families, the class that led the city into two tragic periods of civil conflict. In focusing his criticism on the misdeeds of the *grandi* and their politics of family and faction, Dante was echoing and representing the view of this class that had emerged from the experiments in a different kind of politics supported by the *popolo*, the non-elite local merchants, shopkeepers, notaries, and artisans of the guild community. This too Dante dramatizes in canto 10. Farinata, learning that his family and party had become permanent exiles, asks the pilgrim: "why is that people ['popolo'] so fierce against my kindred in all its laws?" The "popolo" in this question at some level no doubt refers to the Florentines in general, but no Florentine of the fourteenth century would have failed to see in the juxtaposition of the "popolo" and its "laws" an allusion to the governments of the *popolo* whose chief purpose was indeed to rein in the arrogance and *prepotenza* of the great families and their party organizations with the stern enforcement of laws. Nowhere is Farinata's blindness (and thus the tragedy of the entire Florentine aristocracy) so evident as in his need even to ask this question. Although he himself had recalled the "harm" he did the city, he still needs to have the pilgrim explain to him that it was "the havoc and the great slaughter, which dyed the Arbia red," that "caused such prayers to be made in our temple." If the terrible bloodshed at Montaperti made the Florentines resolutely anti-Ghibelline, the pilgrim's answer also suggests that the whole long civil war, which brought suffering to every Florentine household, gave rise to the movements of the *popolo* and "all its laws."

Governments of the *popolo* presented themselves as an alternative to regimes of the parties, with different ideas about the organization and legitimacy of power. In 1250, the *primo popolo* proclaimed a constitution in which the city was divided into twenty military-administrative subdivisions, each functioning as a *societas populi*, a company or legal corporation with the right to assemble its members, elect officers, and send representatives to the council of the rectors and standard bearers of all twenty companies. This council, together with another composed of the heads of the guilds, assumed significant functions in the government, including some role in the election of the chief executive magistracy of the commune, the *Anziani*, or Elders. For the first time in the history of the city, the legitimacy of communal government depended on the consent and representation of local and professional associations. For several years the *popolo* kept members of both the Guelf and Ghibelline parties out of important offices. It abolished the old association of knights (the *universitas militum* through which the aristocracy had directly and prominently taken part in the government of the commune before 1250), and decreed and enforced the prohibition against private or family towers higher than twenty-nine meters, both a practical and a symbolic attack on the rivalries, the control of neighborhoods, and the recourse to private violence so typical of the elite families.

In the brief interval of popular government in 1266–67, the guilds emerged as the chief institutional expression of the challenge to the elite. A number of guilds organized themselves into a federation whose governing committee of priors claimed the right to represent the interests of the member associations in communal government. This became a significant precedent for the guild movement of the 1280s and 1290s, when the guilds of a much larger federation transformed Florence's republican polity. To understand why these professional associations were able to gain such influence and power, it is necessary to have some idea of what guilds represented in terms of political theory and practice. Guilds were voluntary, self-constituted structures of authority (*universitates* in medieval legal language) that received from their own members the right to assume obligations on their behalf, to establish and enforce regulations governing professional and business activities, to guarantee agreements entered into by any member with outside parties, and to discipline members who failed to honor contracts or to observe generally recognized standards of professional conduct. Guilds preserved the good faith of their members by "rendering justice" (*ius reddere*) and functioning as courts to which outside parties could bring civil actions against their members. Each guild's court was presided over by a committee of consuls, elected by and from the membership for terms of several months. The consuls and the guild council, consisting of anywhere from a dozen to several score members, also functioned as a deliberative and legislative body which debated and voted on procedures and penalties to be implemented in the guild court, standards of production and business contracts, elections to the consulate or other guild offices, and any changes in the guild's statutes. Guilds were in effect miniature republics, their authority and jurisdiction created and guaranteed by the promises and oaths of the members themselves. They embodied a theory and practice of government that began with the assumption that self-constituted collectivities could exercise legitimate authority on the basis of their members' consent.

After a decade of Guelf–Angevin rule and an unsuccessful attempt at a reconciliation of the Guelf and Ghibelline parties in the early 1280s, the guild movement resurfaced in 1282 with the objective of transforming the constitutional bases of communal government. The chronicler Dino Compagni, who was among the leaders of this and subsequent phases of the *popolo*'s rise to power, recalls his participation in a lobbying committee that succeeded in "converting citizens" to the idea of reinstituting the priorate of the guilds, "so that they might help the merchants and guildsmen wherever necessary." At first an office of just three members from three of the economically most powerful guilds, the priorate soon expanded into a magistracy of six, for which the members of twelve guilds were eligible, and within a year became the central executive magistracy of the commune. Compagni describes the emotional atmosphere in which this transfer of power took place:

> And so much did the boldness of the *popolani* grow with [the election of] these three, seeing that they were not challenged, and so much were they encouraged by the openly expressed words of citizens who spoke of their liberty and of the injuries they had suffered, that [the new priors] boldly began to make laws and ordinances of such a sort that they would be difficult to abrogate . . . And they were called Priors of the Guilds, and they took up uninterrupted residence for their term of office in the tower of the Castagna near the Badia so as not to have to fear the threats of the powerful. (*Cronica* I, iv).

Although the elite preserved much of its power for the next decade through the skillful management of electoral politics, during these same years popular pressure resulted in the promulgation of the first anti-magnate laws, and, while it is true that they were not always or even regularly enforced, neither were they abrogated.

The potential for something more radical had been established. As in the 1250s, Florentine government in the 1280s, and even more so in the 1290s, was strongly influenced by the *popolo*'s conviction that the city's major domestic problem and threat was its still untamed elite of great families: the aristocracy's easy recourse to intimidation and violence and its contempt for all those "laws" and "ordinances" of the *popolo*. This perception was deeply rooted in the political and historical discourse of the *popolo*, and it helped bring about the installation of a new and revolutionary popular government. In a council debate on electoral policy at the end of 1292, a group of non-elite guildsmen succeeded in getting approved new procedures based, for the first time, on the idea that all twelve guilds that had nominally been part of the new constitution since 1282 would enjoy full autonomy and equality in the election, every second month, of the communal priors. The first priorate elected under this system promulgated the Ordinances of Justice in January 1293. The prologue of this famous document began by defining justice, according to Roman law, as the "constant and perpetual desire to secure to each his own right," and the first rubric declared that the security of these rights would be achieved by a formal federation of the city's guilds. Echoing the legal maxim that became the basis of many theories of representation and popular sovereignty, "that which touches all must be approved by all," the Ordinances decreed that "that is considered most perfect which consists of all its parts and is approved by the judgment of them all." Each of a now expanded group of twenty-one guilds was invited to send a syndic (a legal representative) to swear his guild's loyalty to the "good, faithful, pure society, and company" of the twenty-one guilds. Representatives of the original twelve guilds would still elect the priorate, for which only guild members regularly active in their professions or business were eligible. Most significantly, the Ordinances and the popular priorates of 1293 barred the members of at first thirty-eight and later seventy-two upper-class families from sitting on the priorate, the consulates of the guilds, and certain of the legislative councils. Magnates also had to post surety for good behavior, and were subject to harsh penalties – in the worst cases, destruction of their city homes – for crimes of violence committed against non-magnates. The list of magnate families does not, to be sure, give us a social class, but it does give us a rather large chunk of the Florentine elite. Not all great families had the misfortune to be included among the magnates. Among those who were, some were older families (a few even with titles of nobility), while others had become prominent in the aftermath of the Guelf ascendancy of the late 1260s. The first group included the Nerli, Lamberti, Cavalcanti, Uberti, Bogolesi, Fifanti, Amidei, Buondelmonti, Soldanieri, Adimari, Abati, and Donati, and in the second group we find the Frescobaldi, Bardi, Mozzi, Pulci, Franzesi, Scali, Spini, and Cerchi. The entire list is about evenly divided between Guelf families and families that had traditionally been Ghibelline.

For about two years this frontal attack on the privileges of the *grandi* dominated Florentine politics. All the chronicles agree that the charismatic leader of the movement was one Giano della Bella, himself from an old upper-class family, and remembered by Dante (*Paradiso* 16, 131–32) as the one from his family "who now sides with the *popolo*." The most detailed portrait of Giano and his policies and style comes from Compagni, who was a devoted ally and adviser but was still willing to see Giano's (and the movement's) failings. For Compagni, Giano was above all a passionate defender of justice and the laws: "a strong and spirited man [who] was so bold that he upheld those things which others let drop, and spoke of those which others hushed up, and did everything in support of justice and against the guilty." The *grandi* "abominated him and the laws" and conspired against him (*Cronica* I, xii) by planting rumors that this or that group was betraying him, to which he responded with calls for uncompromising retribution and justice that only alienated his supporters within the guild community. Compagni's account is carefully crafted to suggest that the entire movement of the second *popolo*, as the Florentines called it, shared in Giano's combination of strengths and weaknesses, and that Giano's fall in 1295 and the collapse of much of what the government of 1292–95 had achieved reopened the floodgates for the very disaster of factional strife within the upper class that governments of the *popolo* had sought repeatedly to avert. With Giano gone, Compagni says that "the city, governed with little justice, fell into new danger, because the citizens began to divide up in a contest for political offices, each one abominating the other" (I, xx). Thus he begins the story of the split between the Donati and the Cerchi that engulfed the city and led to the tragedy of 1301 that also ended his political career.

Compagni's interpretation of the crisis of 1300–02 turns on the opposition between the entire aristocracy of great families (whether Black or White, Guelf or Ghibelline) and the *popolo* in its guilds, with its notions of collective authority, consent, representation, and government by law and institutions. This interpretation takes its place within a tradition of popular political discourse and reform that goes back at least to the *primo popolo* of 1250–60, and which spawned a vigorous chronicle literature. Perhaps the best example before Compagni is the anonymous *Cronica fiorentina* (once attributed, interestingly enough, to Brunetto Latini, the chancellor of the *primo popolo* and the first Florentine theorist of good government along lines broadly compatible with the assumptions and practice of the *popolo*). The *Cronica* places great emphasis on the fratricidal conflicts of the Florentine upper class. It contains what may be the oldest extant account of the Buondelmonti murder, and it explicitly links that "original" moment of bloodletting to the subsequent history of the Florentine *grandi* and their violent ways. In concluding its description of the origins of the Donati–Cerchi feud, the *Cronica* comments that from this "was born much evil to the shame of the city and its citizens; for all the *grandi* and *popolari* of the city divided . . . in such a way that they revived the ancient hatred between the house of the Uberti and that of the Buondelmonti; on account of which all Italy has shed blood." Compagni organized the beginning of his *Cronica* with the same juxtaposition: he opens with the Buondelmonti murder, then jumps to 1280, and leaves his reader to see the obvious parallel with the onset of civil war in 1300.

Thus, by Dante's day, there was a well-established tradition of popular politics and literature whose common ground was the critique of the upper class's politics of factionalism and the expectation of some better order of things from the experiments in guild and popular government. It is impossible to think that Dante was not deeply influenced by this tradition of thought and practice. He certainly shared the *popolo*'s repudiation of the elite's politics of family and faction, but to what degree did he display any sympathy for the *popolo*'s alternative view of politics? To judge from the famous invective against "servile Italy" in *Purgatorio* 6, the answer would seem to be none at all. Here, too, it is the sorry spectacle of civil war that Dante bemoans and the imperial solution that he invokes. But with no emperor willing to take up the mission of rescuing Italy and Rome, "all the cities of Italy are full of tyrants, and every yokel who comes to play the partisan becomes a Marcellus." The name Marcellus recalls opposition to tyranny and defense of liberty, except that Dante's point seems to be that those in the Italian cities who style themselves defenders of liberty are really nothing more than promoters of their own *parte*, just another faction seeking its own advantage. Full of obvious irony, the poet addresses himself to "my Florence," which can enjoy the satisfaction of knowing that his "digression" on Italy's servitude does not concern her, "thanks to your *popolo*" and its readiness for action. This *popolo* is clearly the political movement, and Dante unleashes scorn and sarcasm against its most honored principles. Whereas others have justice in their hearts but release it slowly so as not to let laws fly without proper consideration, "your *popolo*" has its justice "ever on its lips." Whereas others decline public offices, "your *popolo*" cries out its eagerness to undertake such responsibilities without even being asked. Florence can indeed rejoice in its wealth, its peace, and its wisdom. Athens and Sparta, which made the ancient laws "and were so grown in civil arts," made only a small gesture at "right living, compared with you that make such subtle provisions that what you spin in October lasts not to mid-November." The frequent changes in laws, coinage, institutions, customs, and even in the structure and composition of the body politic, amount to little more than a futile attempt to hide Florence's real misery, "like the sick woman who cannot find repose upon the down, but with her tossing seeks to ease her pain." This is a precise denunciation of the fundamental institutions and language of the *popolo*:

its notions of justice, its ethic of citizen participation, and its emphasis on law and constitutional reform. Here Dante has gathered the characteristic terms of the *popolo*'s discourse of politics, clustered around and following the hammering repetition of "popol tuo": "giustizia," "consiglio," "comune," "leggi," "civili," "viver bene," "provedimenti," "officio," and "membre." It would seem that his rejection of all this could not be more complete.

Yet Dante's bitter parody of the Florentine *popolo*, so ready to leap into action, so lacking in prudence and caution, and overzealously committed to a rhetoric of liberty and justice that it misunderstands and misuses, must remind us in part of Dino Compagni's portrait of Giano della Bella. In Compagni's case, a critical evaluation of Giano and of the excesses of the second *popolo* tempered but did not destroy his conviction that Florentine popular government had established the foundations and structures of the only viable alternative to the aristocracy's disastrous factionalism. It would certainly be going too far to claim that Dante's view of politics was rooted in the popular movement. Although his brief reference to "a time" when the judicial records were kept safe and protected (*Purgatorio* 12, 104–05) is apparently meant to contrast the more rigorous administration of justice by the second *popolo* with the corruption of the next few years (and it is noteworthy that the specific instance of such corruption to which this passage alludes is also reported in some detail by Dino Compagni [*Cronica* I, xix]), Dante nowhere directly links his own political ideas or loyalties to the government of the second *popolo*.

But when Dante attempts, in the *Commedia* and elsewhere, to give some idea of the principles and assumptions that he considers fundamental to a properly organized society, he does so in the language of the *popolo*. In *Paradiso* 8 he has Charles Martel ask rhetorically: "sarebbe il peggio/per l'omo in terra, se non fosse cive?" ("would it be worse for man on earth if he were not a citizen?") and, after the pilgrim's quick assent to so obvious a proposition, he asks again, "E puot' elli esser, se giù non si vive/diversamente per diversi offici?" ("And can that be, unless men below live in diverse ways for diverse duties?") To illustrate his point about the diversity of duties (occupations, callings, offices), Charles Martel adds that "the roots of your works must needs be diverse, so that one is born Solon and another Xerxes, one Melchizedek and another he who flew through the air and lost his son." This list includes two "offici" that can be specifically associated with the regimes of the *popolo*: Solon is, of course, the civic legislator, and the one "who flew through the air and lost his son" is Daedalus, the representative of mechanics and artisans, of those who build and construct with their hands and their skills. This passage is not intended as a description of the typical social organization of cities. It seeks rather to explicate a fundamental principle of all human society as Dante believed it should be, and in so doing it makes use of civic and specifically popular images of society as constituted by different professional groups, including lawmakers and artisans. Other examples of this same tendency to adopt the language of the *popolo* occur in *Monarchia* I, xii, where the argument for a world ruler is supported by notions of representation and the accountability of power, and in *Convivio* IV, iv, where the "root foundation of imperial majesty" is made to derive from the need on the part of all social entities to join in federations and to form larger wholes.

The most eloquent manifestation of Dante's tenacious attachment to this popular discourse, despite his imperial convictions, must be the one and only description in the entire *Commedia* of an ideal human community: his ancestor Cacciaguida's nostalgic evocation (*Paradiso* 15 and 16) of the smaller, simpler, more virtuous Florence of the mid-twelfth century. If the Florence of Dante's day had become the worst of all places, Cacciaguida now tells us that it was once the best, and what he describes for the pilgrim is in many respects a utopia straight out of the dreams of the *popolo*. This ideal city is a small community free of the various forms of excess that Dante – and the *popolo* – associated with the competitive and transgressive behavior of overmighty families. Cacciaguida's imagined Florence "within her ancient circle . . . abode in peace, sober and chaste," a city only one-fifth the size of the metropolis of 1300 and rigorously demarcated from the surrounding countryside. Cacciaguida explains "how much better it would be" for the city to have its boundaries at Galluzzo and Trespiano (respectively, two and three miles from the city walls to the south and north) in order to avoid the "intermingling" of people from the countryside and its small towns with the population of the city itself. This is sometimes read as an attack against the "gente nuova" whom Dante had earlier blamed (*Inferno* 16, 67–75) for the decline of "cortesia e valor" and their replacement by the "orgoglio e dismisura" generated by rapid commercial growth ("i subiti guadagni"). But Dante and his contemporaries would not have associated this economic expansion, and the corruption it allegedly entailed, with the non-elite guildsmen – the local and regional traders, the shopkeepers, retailers, manufacturers for the local market, craftsmen, and artisans – who supported governments of the *popolo*. In fact, as examples of the kind of people that Florence would not have had to endure had she kept her boundaries at Galluzzo and Trespiano, Cacciaguida mentions not poor immigrant artisans, but no less than the Cerchi, who "would [still] be in the parish of Acone," and the Buondelmonti, who would still be in their ancestral home in Valdigreve. Addressing the member of the latter who was both cause and victim of the legendary original crime that split the upper-class families into two warring camps, Cacciaguida exclaims: "Many would be happy who now are sad if God had committed you to the [river] Ema the first time you came to the city!" Cacciaguida's city keeps the families that became the knightly and commercial upper class of *grandi* in their prehistory of rural simplicity and isolation. Not even the most radical *popolano* or the toughest anti-magnate law could have asked for more.

The conspicuous and excessive consumption of wealth that Cacciaguida laments in the modern city of the pilgrim – the necklaces, coronals, embroidered gowns, the girdles "more to be looked at than the person," the exaggerated dowries that "cause fear to the father" of every girl – was a phenomenon of the upper class of great families and completely alien to the frugality, thrift, and calculated moderation of the *popolo*. Compagni, too, underscores the lavish expenditures for the sake of appearance on the part of families like the Cerchi ("gran ricchi, e vestivano bene, e teneano molti famigli e cavalli, e aveano bella apparenza," *Cronica* I, xx), and like Dante he juxtaposes corrupt wealth and political factionalism in describing Florence in the same breath as both full of men "bold in arms, arrogant and contentious," and "rich with unlawful profits" (I, i). Cacciaguida's "sober and chaste" city in which men went "girt with leather and bone" and women came away from their mirrors "with unpainted face" comes out of the same critique of upper-class profligacy that led Compagni to complain that the "grandi e potenti" did not "protect the wealth of the commune, but rather sought better ways to plunder it" (I, v). In the imagined city of old, women worked as spinners "at the spindle and the distaff" and were thus producers rather than consumers of wealth. The *popolo*'s mistrust of the elite's international commerce and banking is reflected in Cacciaguida's comment that in those days women had their husbands at home, "none as yet deserted in her bed because of France." This was a world in which the nuclear household – the original social unit, according to Aristotle (and Dante), from which the city grew – prevailed to the apparent exclusion of broader ties of family, party, and clan, and yet preserved and transmitted the ideology of the city and its destiny. Here mothers kept watch over their own children and, while spinning, recounted tales of "the Trojans, and Fiesole, and Rome": the semi-historical legends and foundation stories that linked Florence's origins to the great themes of ancient myth and history, especially of Rome and its beginnings. When Cacciaguida remarks that in those days "a Cianghella or a Lapo Saltarello would have been as great a marvel as Cincinnatus and Cornelia would be now," his choice of virtuous Romans again alludes to the *popolo*'s critique of the political and economic corruption of the great families. Cincinnatus was the soldier-patriot who never let himself be tempted by riches, and Cornelia was the mother of the Gracchi, the tribunes of the plebs who led the revolutionary challenge to the senatorial aristocracy.

Cacciaguida's perfect city is a "viver di cittadini" and a "fida cittadinanza," and, before its population became mixed with immigrants from the *contado*, this "cittadinanza" was "pure down to the humblest artisan" ("pura vediesi ne l'ultimo artista"). The old Florence of Dante's imagination was thus a community of citizens exercising their *arti*: their skills and trades. Again, no fourteenth-century reader would have failed to see in those words an allusion to the community of *artefici* organized in their guilds, and thus to the image of the city, promoted by the second *popolo* of the 1290s, as constituted by the federation of its guilds. To be sure, Cacciaguida's roll-call of great old families, many of them extinct by 1300, is no list of artisans or guildsmen. These were all "alti Fiorentini," "illustri cittadini," and "così grandi come antichi." But Cacciaguida saw them all *before* they were "disfatti/per lor superbia" ("undone by their pride") and before the ruinous rivalry of family against family destroyed their sense of civic duty. Of one family he says that in that time they knew what it meant to govern ("sapeva già come/regger si vuole"), and of others that they were then good citizens ("e già era/buon cittadino Giuda e Infangato"). The force of this historical fiction of the decline of the Florentine aristocracy from the condition of good citizens of simple life who took their place within the "fida cittadinanza" to their corruption by factionalism and ostentatious wealth in the thirteenth century lies in its implicit acceptance of the *popolo*'s prescriptive and polemical definitions of good cities and good citizens. By having Cacciaguida claim that the great families had once shared in the virtues and attitudes typical of the *popolo*, Dante in effect rebukes the elite for its failure to reflect the image of the political movement that opposed it: "With these families, and with others with them, I saw Florence in such repose that she had no cause for wailing. With these families I saw her people so glorious and so just ['glorioso e giusto il popol suo'], that the lily was never set reversed upon the staff, nor made vermilion by division."

But on one fundamental issue there was complete disagreement between Dante and the *popolo*. Despite all his sympathy for the *popolo*'s critique of aristocratic misrule, and even for the moral and social elements of its vision of the good society, Dante's approach to the political problems of Florence, and of cities in general, repudiated a central assumption of the *popolo*: that each city can and should function as an autonomous, self-legitimating, and self-constituted sovereign whole. For Dante, at least in the later years of his exile, only the whole of humankind constituted a legitimate, sovereign whole. Cities were merely parts of that whole, which, in his reading of history, had to be Roman and thus could be legitimate only under the rule of this universal Rome's emperor. Dante heaped scorn on Florence and the other cities for abandoning the empire and setting up new states "as if Florentine *civilitas* were one thing, and Roman *civilitas* another" (*Epistolae* 6, 2). This, of course, is precisely what the *popolo* (in Florence and in a score of other cities) insisted on: the autonomous legitimacy of each city's *civilitas*, or, as the fourteenth-century jurist Bartolus of Sassoferrato would put it, the notion that any city responsible for making its own laws was *sibi princeps*. Governments of the *popolo* were predicated on the assumption that self-constituted collectivities (*universitates*) exercised legitimate authority and jurisdiction over their members because the latter created the whole and its authority voluntarily and by express consent. Many such wholes could, if they wished, join together and make themselves the parts of a larger whole, again if and because the parts consented to the constitution of that authority. The political discourse of the *popolo* thus accepted a multiplicity of autonomous, legitimate authorities, whether these were entities that constituted a city, or the many cities of Italy. Dante rejected this notion out of hand in the *Monarchia* (I, x) with a dictum from Aristotle's *Metaphysics*: "a plurality of authorities is an evil." And he rejected it implicitly or explicitly on nearly every page he wrote about politics.

And thus we are left with the dilemma and paradox that, although many of his deepest convictions and assumptions about Florence and the proper ordering of city life derived from the language and experience of the *popolo*, Dante nonetheless constructed his formal political theory around a premise that contradicted the fundamental and enabling proposition of the *popolo*'s program. The memory of the second *popolo* and of those, like Dino Compagni, who tried to keep it alive in Florence during the crisis of 1300–02 evidently made a deep impression on Dante. It is even possible that for a brief time in 1300 and 1301 he may have thought of himself as one of their number. In the years of his exile that moment must have seemed distant and superseded, but because the *Commedia* is in part the story of its pilgrim's political education and transformation, the poet may have wished to give that moment – brief but decisive for pilgrim and city alike – its due.

SUGGESTED READING

Aquilecchia, Giovanni, "Dante and the Florentine Chroniclers," *Bulletin of the John Rylands Library* 48 (1965): 30–55.

Astorri, Antonella, *La Mercanzia a Firenze nella prima metà del Trecento* (Florence: Olschki, 1998).

Bornstein, Daniel E., trans., *Dino Compagni's Chronicle of Florence* (Philadelphia: University of Pennsylvania Press, 1986).

Dameron, George, *Episcopal Power and Florentine Society, 1000–1320* (Cambridge, MA: Harvard University Press, 1991).

Florence and Its Church in the Age of Dante (Philadelphia: University of Pennsylvania Press, 2005).

Davidsohn, Robert, *Geschichte von Florenz*, 4 vols. (Berlin: 1896–1927; rpt. Osnabrück: Biblio Verlag, 1969). Italian translation, *Storia di Firenze*, 8 vols. (Florence: Sansoni, 1972–73).

Davis, Charles T., *Dante's Italy and Other Essays* (Philadelphia: University of Pennsylvania Press, 1984).

Del Lungo, Isidoro, *Dino Compagni e la sua* Cronica, 3 vols. (Florence: Le Monnier, 1879–87).

I Bianchi e i Neri (Milan: Hoepli, 1921).

Del Monte, Alberto, "La storiografia fiorentina dei secoli XII e XIII," *Bollettino dell' Istituto Storico Italiano per il Medio Evo* 62 (1950): 175–282.

d'Entrèves, A. P., *Dante as a Political Thinker* (Oxford: Clarendon Press, 1952).

Doren, Alfred, *Das Florentiner Zunftwesen vom 14. bis zum 16. Jahrhundert*, vol. II of his *Studien aus der Florentiner Wirtschaftsgeschichte* (1908; rpt. Aalen, Scientia Verlag, 1969). Italian translation by G. B. Klein, *Le arti fiorentine*, 2 vols. (Florence: Le Monnier, 1940).

Ferrante, Joan M., *The Political Vision of the Divine Comedy* (Princeton: Princeton University Press, 1984).

Gilson, Simon, *Dante and Renaissance Florence* (Cambridge: Cambridge University Press, 2005).

Green, Louis, *Chronicle into History: An Essay on the Interpretation of History in Fourteenth-Century Florentine Chronicles* (Cambridge: Cambridge University Press, 1972).

Hollander, Robert, and Albert L. Rossi, "Dante's Republican Treasury," *Dante Studies* 104 (1986): 59–82.

Holmes, George, *Dante* (New York: Hill and Wang, 1980).

Florence, Rome and the Origins of the Renaissance (Oxford: Clarendon Press, 1986).

Hunt, Edwin S., *The Medieval Super-Companies: A Study of the Peruzzi Company of Florence* (Cambridge: Cambridge University Press, 1994).

Hyde, J. K., "Italian Social Chronicles in the Middle Ages," *Bulletin of the John Rylands Library* 49 (1966): 107–32.

Society and Politics in Medieval Italy (New York: St. Martin's Press, 1973).

Jones, Philip, *The Italian City-State: From Commune to Signoria* (Oxford: Clarendon Press, 1997).

Lansing, Carol, *The Florentine Magnates: Lineage and Faction in a Medieval Commune* (Princeton: Princeton University Press, 1991).

Lansing, Richard, ed., *The Dante Encyclopedia* (New York: Garland, 2000).

La Roncière, Charles-M. de, *Prix et salaries à Florence au XIVe siècle (1280–1380)* (Rome: École Française de Rome, 1982).

Lesnick, Daniel R., *Preaching in Medieval Florence: The Social World of Franciscan and Dominican Spirituality* (Athens, GA: University of Georgia Press, 1989).

Maire Vigueur, Jean-Claude, *Cavaliers et citoyens: guerre, conflits et société dans l'Italie communale, XIIe–XIIIe siècles* (Paris: Ecole des Hautes Etudes en Sciences Sociales, 2003).

Martines, Lauro, *Power and Imagination: City-States in Renaissance Italy* (New York: Random House, Vintage, 1979; rpt. Baltimore: The Johns Hopkins University Press, 1988).

Najemy, John M., *Corporatism and Consensus in Florentine Electoral Politics, 1280–1400* (Chapel Hill: University of North Carolina Press, 1982).

"The Dialogue of Power in Florentine Politics," in Anthony Molho, Kurt Raaflaub, and Julia Emlen, eds., *City States in Classical Antiquity and Medieval Italy* (Stuttgart: Franz Steiner Verlag, 1991), pp. 269–88.

"Brunetto Latini's 'Politica'," *Dante Studies* 112 (1994): 33–51.

"Florence," in R. Lansing, ed., *The Dante Encyclopedia*, pp. 386–403.

Noakes, Susan, "Dino Compagni and the Vow in San Giovanni: *Inferno* XIX, 16–21," *Dante Studies* 86 (1968): 41–63.

Ottokar, Nicola, *Il Comune di Firenze alla fine del Dugento* (1926; revised edn. Turin: Giulio Einaudi, 1962).

Studi comunali e fiorentini (Florence: La Nuova Italia, 1948).

Pampaloni, Guido, "I magnati a Firenze alla fine del Dugento," *Archivio storico italiano* 129 (1971): 387–423.

Peters, Edward, "*Pars, Parte*: Dante and an Urban Contribution to Political Thought," in Harry A. Miskimin, David Herlihy, and A. L. Udovitch, eds., *The Medieval City* (New Haven: Yale University Press, 1977), pp. 113–40.

Pinto, Giuliano, *Il Libro del Biadaiolo. Carestia e annona a Firenze dalla metà del '200 al 1348* (Florence: Olschki, 1978).

Pirillo, Paolo, *Costruzione di un contado. I fiorentini e il loro territorio nel Basso Medioevo* (Florence: Le Lettere, 2001).

Quinones, Ricardo, "Foundation Sacrifice and Florentine History: Dante's Anti-Myth," *Lectura Dantis* 4 (1989): 10–19.

Raveggi, Sergio, Massimo Tarassi, Daniela Medici, and Patrizia Parenti, *Ghibellini, Guelfi e Popolo Grasso. I detentori del potere politico a Firenze nella seconda metà del Dugento* (Florence: La Nuova Italia, 1978).

Rubinstein, Nicolai, "The Beginnings of Political Thought in Florence," *Journal of the Warburg and Courtauld Institutes* 5 (1942): 198–227; rpt. in N. Rubinstein, *Studies in Italian History in the Middle Ages and the Renaissance*, I, *Political Thought and the Language of Politics. Art and Politics*, ed. Giovanni Ciappelli (Rome: Edizioni di Storia e Letteratura, 2004), pp. 1–41.

"Dante and Nobility," in Rubinstein, *Studies in Italian History*, I, pp. 165–200.

"Marsilius of Padua and Italian Political Thought of His Time," in J. R. Hale, J. R. L. Highfield, and B. Smalley, eds., *Europe in the Late Middle Ages* (Evanston: Northwestern University Press, 1965), pp. 44–75; rpt. in Rubinstein, *Studies in Italian History*, I, pp. 99–130.

Salvemini, Gaetano, *Magnati e popolani in Firenze dal 1280 al 1295* (1899; rpt. Milan: Feltrinelli, 1966).

La dignità cavalleresca nel Comune di Firenze e altri scritti (Milan: Feltrinelli, 1972).

Schiaffini, Alfredo, *Testi fiorentini del Dugento e dei primi del Trecento* (Florence: Sansoni, 1954). (The "Cronica fiorentina compilata nel secolo XIII," formerly attributed to Brunetto Latini, is on pp. 82–150.)

Schnapp, Jeffrey T., *The Transfiguration of History at the Center of Dante's Paradise* (Princeton: Princeton University Press, 1986).

Starn, Randolph, *Contrary Commonwealth: The Theme of Exile in Medieval and Renaissance Italy* (Berkeley: University of California Press, 1982).

Sznura, Franek, *L'espansione urbana di Firenze nel Dugento* (Florence: La Nuova Italia, 1975).

Villani, Giovanni, *Nuova Cronica*, 3 vols., ed. Giuseppe Porta (Parma: Ugo Guanda editore, 1990–1991).

Waley, Daniel, "The Army of the Florentine Republic from the Twelfth to the Fourteenth Century," in Nicolai Rubinstein, ed., *Florentine Studies: Politics and Society in Renaissance Florence* (Evanston: Northwestern University Press, 1968), pp. 70–108.

Zorzi, Andrea, "Politica e giustizia a Firenze al tempo degli Ordinamenti antimagnatizi," in Vanna Arrighi, ed., *Ordinamenti di giustizia fiorentini. Studi in occasione del VII centenario* (Florence: Archivio di Stato di Firenze, Ministero per i Beni Culturali e Ambientali, 1995), pp. 105–47.

15

CHARLES TILL DAVIS

Dante and the empire[1]

In his brilliant little book *Dante as a Political Thinker*, published more than fifty years ago but arguably still the most stimulating introduction to the subject in English, my old teacher Alessandro Passerin d'Entrèves assigns to Dante's theory of the empire only a limited place. D'Entrèves emphasizes Dante's preoccupation with his Florentine "patria" and the church, as well as his cultural patriotism, while denying his political nationalism. Dante was therefore, in the tradition of his family, essentially a loyal "Guelf," even if a troubled one as the *Commedia* shows (a work begun, d'Entrèves believes, after the collapse in 1313 of Emperor Henry VII's Italian expedition). Dante's "Ghibellinism," his advocacy of the imperial cause, was an important but passing phase in the evolution of his thought. His treatise on the empire, *Monarchia*, which d'Entrèves dates as *c.* 1312, was an aberration, indicating how he had been overcome by the hope that a human saviour could take away the sins of the world, forgetting the fundamental Christian idea that from within, and not from without, must mankind be redeemed and saved. D'Entrèves believes that the *Commedia* was written after the *Monarchia* and marks a return to a more orthodox view of salvation. In my view, both works reveal the central importance to Dante of the empire. There is ample evidence also in Dante's vernacular encyclopedia, the *Convivio*, that he believed men must be saved not only from within but also from without, and that the emperor is the essential agent for this task. Even if d'Entrèves's dating of *Monarchia* and the *Commedia* is correct, they seem to reveal no important change in Dante's convictions about the nature, purpose, and importance of the empire.

Already in 1304 Dante's first mention of an emperor, Frederick II, occurs in *De vulgari eloquentia*. He is obviously upset by the disintegration of the Hohenstaufen inheritance in Italy at the hands of what he regards as a multitude of contemptible princelings. Dante's first mention of the empire occurs in *Convivio* IV, written *c.* 1307. Three of his letters, *Epistolae* 5, 6, and 7, written 1310–12, hail the expedition of the emperor-elect, Henry VII, to Italy for his coronation. The date of the writing of Dante's *Monarchia* is uncertain, but, whenever it was finished, its inception was probably due to the same expedition. The longing for the restoration of a universal empire, and its necessity for the attainment of human happiness, are also a central theme of the *Commedia*.

For Dante, empire or monarchy signifies the command directing all other commands, the jurisdiction embracing and authorizing all other jurisdictions, the will uniting all other wills (*Convivio* IV, 4). Dante also occasionally uses the word "imperium" in a territorial sense, as when speaking of Italy as the "garden of the empire" (*Purgatorio* 6, 105). But the primary meaning of the word is universal authority. This authority was won by the Roman people under the republic, and then passed to the emperor or imperial office, called by Dante "imperiatus." The holder of the office, according to Dante, is chosen by God, and his choice is presently announced through German electors, though their perception of God's choice may on occasion be clouded by cupidity. The empire is intended to be the political authority regulating the "humana civilitas," which may perhaps be best translated as the civil order of mankind. "Civilitas" is a word embodying political jargon new in Dante's day.[2] "Civilitas" was a term often used by translators of, and commentators on, Aristotle in the thirteenth and fourteenth centuries to translate the Aristotelian word *politeia*, or "polity," considered under its constitutional aspect. Dante uses it more generally in many places to mean simply "polity" or "government." The greatest, or "humana civilitas," embraces the whole human family, and reaches its political fulfillment under the empire.

That empire, or rule over the entire world, comes directly through God, not through any other authority such as the pope's jurisdiction. The papal dignity is even higher than the imperial, but exists in an entirely different sphere. The emperor relies on philosophical teachings to lead men to their human goal of temporal happiness; the pope relies on theological teachings to lead men to the divine goal of salvation.

What are the limits of imperial authority? In the fourth tractate of the *Convivio*, Dante says that geographically it extends over the whole world, that is, to the banks of the great sea that Dante thought encircled the land area of the earth. Legally it is omnicompetent, though Dante says in his treatise *Monarchia* that it should not concern itself with minor and technical matters (*Monarchia* I, xiv, 4). The emperor makes and executes general laws. These laws should be directed toward the common good, otherwise, Dante says, they are not laws (II, v, 2–3). Moreover, laws, as Dante observes in the *Convivio*, extend to men's actions and not their opinions and theories, and primarily to actions involving the moral virtues. The rules of discourse, for example, the laws of mathematics, or the refinements of the shipbuilder's craft, are not subject to the emperor, but all actions that involve will and choice are.

The emperor therefore presides over the moral world. It is his duty to put the ethical teachings of philosophers, especially Aristotle, into effect. The emperor has jurisdiction over actions but not over thoughts. The master of thought, Dante believes, is Aristotle. Each needs the other, for the imperial authority without the philosophical is dangerous, and the philosophical without the imperial is weak, "not for itself but because of the confusion of the people" (*Convivio* IV, vi, 17). The purpose of law is to restrain cupidity and, as Justinian's Digest says (*Convivio* IV, vi, 17), to demonstrate equity. It is enough for young men to accept and obey this law willingly. But old men, of whom Cato is the prime example, should have equity in their hearts (IV, xxvi, 14). Augustine, quoted in this context by Dante, says there would be no need of written law if men had such equity in their hearts (IV, ix, 18). But in postlapsarian society there is need of such law and of someone – the emperor – to enforce it. The emperor is the rider of the human will (IV, ix, 10). He must control the cupidity that Aristotle says is natural to men (*Politics* I, 9) and that also finds expression in the ambitions of subordinate societies like kingdoms and cities (IV, iv, 3). Since the emperor is the supreme ruler and, as Dante says, the possessor of everything (having nothing further to desire) he should be free from cupidity and therefore able to act as the just and impartial arbiter of these disputes (*Monarchia* I, x, 1–3). According to Dante, it is Italy that needs the emperor's discipline most desperately.

The emperor's task is to restrain cupidity, a fundamental defect of men and societies according to both Aristotelian and Christian teaching. However, the emperor is not expected to formulate moral doctrine. If he does so he may go astray, as Dante believed Frederick II did, with his definition of nobility as good manners and old wealth (*Convivio* IV, iii, 6). In this theoretical sphere, Dante believed that Frederick as emperor had no more standing than anybody else, and less than an ethical philosopher like Aristotle – or even like Dante himself for that matter. Dante, in fact, after furnishing his own definition of nobility in terms of individual worth, asserts that this definition should be accepted by all kings and other rulers forthwith (IV, xvi, 1).

Ethics had been invented by the ancients when they discovered and defined the concept of moral liberty: the adherence of the will to correct rational decision. The same ethics guided men in Christian times to their human and natural felicity, defined by Aristotle as full activity according to the intellectual and moral virtues. Such virtues, Dante thought, were totally within the natural power of man, be he pagan or Christian. It was the function of the empire to facilitate and encourage their acquisition and exercise, and to restrain their opposites, unregulated passions and, especially, cupidity. The enforcement of "written reason" – that is, law – by the emperor should help inculcate in men that true liberty which comes from willing adherence to the rational choices made by individual intellects. The emperor should also support rightly constituted subordinate states – kingdoms, aristocracies, and popular regimes dedicated to liberty – and oppose perverted forms of government such as tyrannies, oligarchies, and democracies, since Dante believed with Aristotle that it is almost impossible to be a good man in a bad state. Dante claims that all governments exist for the good of their citizens and not vice versa, and that the emperor himself should be the servant of all (*Monarchia* I, xii, 12).

All these duties applied indifferently to pagan and Christian rulers. Even the virtues they should have tried to implant in their subjects were essentially the same. Like Aquinas and unlike Augustine, Dante regarded the moral virtues as valid in themselves, even though they did not suffice for salvation. They were under the aegis of lay temporal rulers, either pagan or Christian, whereas the theological virtues (faith, hope, and charity) were under the aegis of the pope. However, Dante did not draw an absolute line between these two groups of virtues. He found, for instance, spectacular examples of the theological virtue of charity not only in Christian, but also in pagan, heroes. God, Dante said, had infused divine love of their "patria" in the self-sacrificing heroes of Rome (*Convivio* IV, iv–v). This view was shared, incidentally, by two older Tuscan contemporaries, the Dominican writers on politics Tolomeo Fiadoni from Lucca, and Fra Remigio dei Girolami from Florence. The emperor too, Dante says in *Monarchia* I, xi, 13, should be moved by "caritas" in establishing justice, for "caritas" is the opposite of cupidity. And cupidity is the chief obstacle to justice (I, xi, 13).

There was no need for Dante to choose between "Augustinian" and "Aristotelian" theories of the state, for both rested on curiously similar views of human imperfection. Aristotle's conception of the natural deficiencies of man resembled Augustine's conception of man's unnatural defects after the Fall. The state is viewed by Dante both as a remedy for sin and, as Bruno Nardi suggests, as an attempt by nature to mend her faults. This eclecticism is apparent in Dante's first analysis of the empire in *Convivio* IV, iv–v.

If Dante's theory of imperial jurisdiction is both Augustinian and Aristotelian, both a remedy for sin and the polis writ large, his theory of history is profoundly Virgilian. This, too, becomes apparent in *Convivio* IV, iv–v. Here, after asserting the necessity of the imperial jurisdiction to the felicity of the human race, he invokes in favor of this assertion the Aristotelian argument that behind the various societies, household, village or neighborhood ("vicinanza"), city, kingdom, and also, Dante adds, behind that greatest of societies, the "humana civilitas," there must be a single directing will. In order to keep the subordinate societies at peace, imperial authority is essential. But in order to achieve this peace, which Dante believes is the greatest of all auxiliary goods contributing to human happiness, it is necessary that the imperial authority be Roman as well as universal. Dante's stylized view of Roman history demanded that it tell the story of a chosen people parallel to that of the Jews. Only Rome, asserts Dante, aimed at the good of the whole human race. And no people ever exhibited more gentleness in exercising, more endurance in retaining, and more subtlety in acquiring rule than the Latins (a term that Dante would use indifferently to apply to either the Romans or the Italians), just as he regarded Virgil, "the glory of the Latins" (*Purgatorio* 7, 16), as "our greatest poet" (*Paradiso* 15, 26).

Although Dante, as he tells us in *Monarchia*, had at first believed that the Roman conquests were based only on force, he came to see them as the result of divine providence which had elected so noble a people to rule the whole world forever. Had not the births of Aeneas and David occurred at the same time? Had not the birth of Christ coincided with the universal peace established by Augustus? That was the fullness of time, when the ship of human company seemed to be sailing most happily to its port. This was the apotheosis of human history, preceded by the exploits of Roman heroes. "O most holy breast of Cato," Dante exclaims, "who will presume to speak of thee?" (*Convivio* IV, v, 16).

What is Dante's authority for his belief in the divine bestowal of the gift of "imperium" on the Roman people? Virgil, and particularly the passage in *Aeneid* I where Virgil puts the assertion "To them I have given empire without end" into the mouth of Jupiter (called God by Dante). Dante also shows evidence in *Convivio* IV that he has read, or reread, *Aeneid* VI with its account of Aeneas' journey to the other world to learn the secrets of the destiny of Rome. This providential "Virgilian-Christian" component of Dante's conception of the Roman empire is manifested in an even more arresting way in *Inferno* 2, 13–33, where Dante the pilgrim corroborates the testimony of Virgil's *Aeneid* that Aeneas went (like St. Paul, Dante says) in his own body to the other world. "That journey of which you give testimony," he says, "was the cause both of Rome's victory and of the papal mantle" (*Inferno* 2, 25–27). Does Dante believe that there would have been no papacy if Rome had not been founded? Obviously, for the pope would have had no function if there had been no redemption, and for Dante there would have been no redemption if Rome's power had not been legitimate. In *Paradiso*

6, 84–90 and elsewhere he refers to the curious theory, partly borrowed from Augustine's contemporary, Orosius, that if the Roman imperium had not had legal authority over Christ, his execution would not have resulted from the decision of a legitimate judge and could not have atoned for Adam's sin.

Dante does not mention the papacy in the *Convivio*. Neither there nor in *De vulgari eloquentia* does he reveal his hostility to what he describes in *Monarchia* and the *Commedia* as clerical usurpations of temporal power. Dante's conception of the role of secular government, and especially the empire, in shaping human morality seems to have been based on his study of Aristotle, Virgil, and Augustine, and to have developed independently of the church–state pamphlet war that raged in the late thirteenth and early fourteenth centuries. But the empire for Dante was not merely a guide for secular morality; it also represented a very important piece of sacred history.

Beginning with *Convivio* iv, iv–v, Dante tries to sanctify Roman history. Although he could speak elsewhere of Rome's "false and lying gods" (*Inferno* 1, 72), he took the miracles told by Livy very seriously and made them, perhaps in imitation of the miracle stories in the Old Testament, testimonies of God's favor and his aid to the Romans. As we have seen from *Inferno* 2, Dante appears to have regarded Aeneas' journey to the other world as a miraculous historical event, making possible both Roman imperium and papal dignity. He thus establishes a close parallel between the two major earthly offices, while differentiating sharply their immediate origins and proper functions. In the *Convivio* there is not yet any indication that a close relationship between emperor and pope would bring disaster. This conviction, expressed later in Dante's denunciations of the Donation of Constantine, may have come to him during the Italian expedition of Henry VII (1311–13).

The alleged gift of the western lands of the empire by Constantine to the pope was savagely attacked by Dante in *Inferno* 19, which may have been written before Henry VII's advent, but which did not assume its final form until after 1314, since it mentions Pope Clement's death. The Donation was also discussed at length by Dante in *Monarchia*. Because of such papal usurpation of imperial powers, castigated by Dante in many passages of the *Commedia*, vice abounded and very few souls, especially in Italy, were being saved. Dante thus thought that both empire and papacy were essential to the work of salvation, but only by keeping their functions radically distinct could their effective collaboration be preserved.

As things now stood, the empire was enfeebled and had lost much of its power, while the church had sacrificed its purity to an obsession with wealth and temporal rule. Dante wanted the restoration of a strong empire and a pure, which for him meant a poor, church, a church that would only be a trustee and not the absolute proprietor of temporal things. In several crucial prophecies in the *Commedia*, he demonstrates his longing for an earthly savior – almost certainly an emperor – to restore "the good world that Rome made" (*Purgatorio* 16, 106), and probably also the poverty of the primitive church. In *Monarchia* he went so far as to claim that the emperor should escape cupidity by possessing everything, the pope and other clerics by possessing nothing, like Christ and his apostles. The emperor should realize that God had bestowed on the Roman people, and on him as their representative, the right to rule the world. His authority had been established by God's providence and was founded on human law, and not on any delegation from clerics. The church (Dante used the word "ecclesia" here, as had become customary in his time, to refer only to the clergy) should be made to realize that its one legitimate function was to imitate the life of Christ. Only in this way could the ravages of cupidity and the revolts of subordinate states, often abetted by the papacy, against the empire be controlled.

I shall mention only three of the prophecies in the *Commedia* which refer to the coming of an earthly reformer. First, Virgil in *Inferno* 1 prophesies the coming of a "Veltro," or greyhound, who will be the salvation "of humble Italy" and drive the wolf (also a symbol of Rome and appropriate for its presently corrupt state under the pope) back into Hell from whence it came. Second, in the course of the mystical procession exhibited to Dante in the Earthly Paradise, the eagle of empire swoops down and leaves its feathers (the Donation) on the chariot of the church, which promptly turns into a monster with a prostitute as its rider. Beatrice tells Dante that the imperial eagle will not remain forever without an heir, but that a savior designated under the number 515 will soon come and kill the "whore" (*Purgatorio* 33, 36–45). Third, St. Peter in *Paradiso* 27 says that his graveyard, Rome, has become a sewer, but that "that high providence which with Scipio defended for Rome the glory of the world [the imperium] will bring quick help." So, presumably, the imperium, won by republican heroes like Scipio and perfected by Augustus, will be restored by a future emperor. Perhaps he will also prepare the world for the second coming of Christ, just as Augustus prepared it for his first coming.

What a strange theory of history and politics! It rests primarily on memory and desire, memory of an alleged golden age under Augustus, a universal peace that Dante believed existed only once in human history, and desire for a savior, evidently a new Augustus, who would restore this unique and vanished order to the modern world. Can Dante, despite his frequent quotations from Aristotle, really be regarded as a political theorist at all? Not if we take a narrow view of politics and separate it from religious reform, or try to distinguish between Dante's political theorizing and his prophetic message, which is at once political and religious.

But we have not yet looked for a theory of the state in Dante's main work on government, *Monarchia*. Dante certainly begins book I in a portentous philosophical vein, announcing that he is attempting something never attempted before. He had made the same claim at the beginning of the *De vulgari eloquentia*. The new doctrine he is expounding now, however, is that of temporal monarchy, which will be of great utility for the human race. He differentiates this doctrine explicitly from that of human happiness advanced by Aristotle, which he calls definitive, and which he had used as the basis for his justification of law and political power in the *Convivio*. That encyclopedic work had been addressed to a wider audience than his *Monarchia*. In the earlier work he had said specifically that he was appealing to the "bellatores" or fighters, those with little Latin but much good sense, and not the professional classes, clerics, and lawyers, who were interested only in money. He therefore wrote the *Convivio* in the vernacular for men and women of noble heart, as he put it, those who were neither brutalized by manual labor like the peasants, nor corrupted by profit like the professional classes. They were the backbone of society.

Monarchia was obviously intended for a more highbrow audience, and in it Dante does not shrink from using abstruse philosophical argument. At the beginning of his treatise, however, he announces its purpose simply enough. He will answer three questions in its three books: first, whether universal monarchy is necessary for the well-being of mankind; second, whether the Roman people acquired it justly; and third, whether imperial authority is derived directly from God or depends on some other authority instituted by God (that is, the papacy). The first two questions had been treated in compressed form in *Convivio* IV, iv and v. The third had not been treated at all in the earlier treatise. But the novelty Dante promises is contained in the first book. It concerns the premise on which the arguments about the utility of universal monarchy are based: that premise is a grandiose conception, which Dante seems to have derived at least partly from the heretic Muslim and famous commentator on Aristotle, Averroes.

The proper function of the "humana civilitas," Dante says, is to "keep the whole capacity of the possible intellect constantly actualized, primarily for speculation, and secondarily for action" (*Monarchia* I, iv, 1). In *Monarchia* he is concerned primarily with the latter. Dante observes that this activity of the human race is ordained by nature, and different from the ends that nature had decreed for the individual, the family, the village, and the city or kingdom. It can only be achieved by a multitude of men, by the whole society of mankind, since nature does not allow for potentiality to remain unactualized. Dante observes that Averroes agrees with this opinion in his commentary on Aristotle's *De anima*. But where does the empire fit into this picture?

Dante says that it brings the most precious of auxiliary gifts to the accomplishment of humanity's goal. That gift is peace. It is "in the tranquillity of peace" that the "humana civilitas" can best fulfill its function. This function must be fulfilled somehow in any case, and no doubt lesser societies are of some help for this achievement. But only the empire can bring universal peace. Only the empire can be the proper government of the whole legal and political community of men.

Actually that doctrine may depend only very slightly on Averroes, for Averroes so far as we know had not envisaged a universal political community corresponding to the rational unity of mankind that he had suggested. Moreover, Dante certainly did not accept Averroes' view of only one possible intellect for the whole human race with its consequent denial of individual immortality. For Dante, as for Aquinas, there were as many such intellects as there were people. Moreover, in Aristotle's *Nichomachean Ethics* and Aquinas' commentary, Dante found the political dimension lacking in Averroes: the doctrine that politics was the great ordering art of men. It prescribed what acts were desirable, and even what branches of knowledge should be taught for the utility of the state, though not the content of those subjects. After this glittering and somewhat pretentious philosophical prologue, Dante quickly settles down to a discussion of the imperial role. But the prologue has the merit of moving the foundations of civil societies as far as possible from any association with the church, and grounding them in the rational nature of man.

The opening book of *Monarchia* contains much discussion about the subordinate societies useful to man and the culmination of ordered civil life in the "humana civilitas" that recalls very similar, if briefer, discussions in the *Convivio* (IV, iv). More lengthily treated in that tractate is the emperor's function as the implementer and instiller of moral philosophy. If we look carefully at book I of *Monarchia*, we also find the emperor functioning in a moral role. But Dante describes this role very generally; there is no trace of the "mirror of princes" genre here. Dante says that the emperor, dominating all things, is, or should be, free from cupidity. Since cupidity is the opposite of charity, and the emperor is free of cupidity, he should possess charity in the highest degree. Charity invigorates justice, which should inform all the emperor's legal and political judgments. Justice strengthens peace, and the consequence of the emperor's rule is moral liberty for his subjects, which can be defined in this context as willing obedience to just laws. The emperor reassumes the moral role that he had exercised in the *Convivio*, and talk of facilitating the actualization of the possible intellect fades away. It does not reappear even at the end of *Monarchia* III where the temporal felicity of the human race is defined in the same way as in the *Convivio* as the full exercise of the intellectual and moral virtues.

There is little here that modern thought would call political. Dante answers few concrete questions about the details of the imperial order he envisages. In *Epistola* 5 to the rulers and peoples of Italy, Dante, styling himself as "humilis ytalus," calls on his countrymen to rise up and greet their king. He says that the Italians should remember that they are not merely under the emperor's "imperium," but are reserved as free men, "liberi" for his "regimen" (*Epistola* 5, 19). But he neglects to explain the difference between "imperium" and "regimen," or to say whether the Italians are the sole "liberi" under the emperor's "regimen." Nor is there any mention of a king of Italy.

Dante, it would seem, hopes that the emperor will establish his capital in Rome, since in *Epistola* 11 he refers to Rome as widowed of both her husbands, the emperor as well as the pope. But it is hard to determine what he thinks the specific jurisdiction of the emperor in Rome and the papal states should be. The rest of Italy, with its variety of municipal regimes, would offer a fertile field for the emperor's attempts to favor just against perverted forms of government. But how Dante imagines this will be accomplished is not made clear. Nor is the relationship between the imperial law and that of various governments, whose own more specific regulations allegedly draw validity from it, discussed in any detail. Despite his practical experience of administration in Florence, Dante seems little interested in how governments, even the emperor's, actually work. As for Italy, Dante is obviously deeply grieved over its disorder. But besides urging Henry in *Epistola* 7 to strike first at the Hydra on the Arno, the tyrant of Tuscany, his own city of Florence, he gives little indication of how exactly an emperor should try to cure this chaos.

In *Monarchia* Dante seems eager, after a brief treatment of the philosophical and political themes in book I, to get on to the historical material in book II. It was, after all, the reading of history in Virgil and other writers that had first convinced him of the righteousness of Rome's "imperium." Book II of *Monarchia* is an expansion of *Convivio* IV, iv–v. Dante's treatment in *Monarchia* II is more detailed and gives more emphasis to the universality of Rome's mission. One way in which he expresses this universality is through a long description of Aeneas' cosmopolitan background and catholic taste in wives (one from Asia, one from Africa, and one from Europe). In addition to Virgil, Dante relies heavily on Livy (whom he read probably in Florus' epitome) and on the miraculous and semi-miraculous events he described. He also uses Cicero's *De officiis* as a source for asserting that the Romans sought the common good of their subjects as well as themselves, and established a *patrocinium* or benevolent protectorate for the world.

The picture Dante paints is uniformly glowing; he does not echo Cicero's fears that the time of benevolence has come to an end in his own late republican period, or mention, like Orosius, the dark side of the Roman conquest. He feels no need to justify the conquests according to ordinary human criteria of justice like Cicero or a sober contemporary writer on the Roman empire, Engelbert of Admont. Instead, he simply affirms that the conquests were willed by God, and God's will as expressed through his providence is by definition just. He says that he has abandoned his earlier belief that these conquests were based on force. Force was only their material cause, but their efficient cause was God. He remarks that Rome had waged a number of "duels" with other nations to discover God's will. So for him force is not only the material cause of conquest but the way to discover God's will. It is both the instrument and the sign of his providence.

Dante's sacralizing of Roman history continues with his exposition of the theory that the legitimacy of Rome's rule was affirmed by both Christ's registration in the Roman census under Augustus and his execution at the hands of the Roman governor Pilate under Tiberius. Rome thus prepared the way for the spread of Christ's gospel and participated in his expiation of man's original sin. But Rome did this while maintaining its own specifically human mission, which involved exercising supreme political jurisdiction over the human race. It was only when part of that jurisdiction was usurped by the papacy as a result of the well-intentioned but disastrous Donation of Constantine that Rome failed in its God-given vocation to guide men to the freedom of moral responsibility resulting from cultivation of those virtues that lay within their own power.

In the third book of *Monarchia* Dante attacks clerical arguments justifying what he regards as papal usurpations of imperial power and possessions. He wants the emperor to monopolize the direction of the "humana civilitas" on earth and the pope to have no political role whatever. The reform of the church will therefore have two desirable results – its purification as a church, and its removal as a competitor with the imperial power. Dante mentions only the emperor as the ruler of the "humana civilitas." A contemporary political theorist, the author of the *Quaestio de utraque potestate*, written before the *Convivio*, used the same term, but expressed the roles of the pope and emperor in a more traditional way: "Since polity [*civilitas*] is twofold, human and divine, earthly and heavenly, temporal and spiritual . . . the imperial power commands and orders the worldly and temporal polities . . . For the government of both polities God ordained two swords."[3] But Dante never said that polity was twofold, since he could not envisage collaboration between emperor and pope in governing the city of man: he thought the emperor should perform this task alone. At the same time, he did not think that the pope's position and function was dependent on the emperor's any more than the emperor's was dependent on the pope's. He seems to have disapproved both of the deposition of a pope by an emperor, and the crowning of an emperor by a pope (*Monarchia* III, x, 18–20).

Dante was not a professional jurist, though he had read in both civil and canon law. For him they were two parts of "written reason." But while civil law was the preserve of the emperor, canon law should draw primarily on the Bible, the Fathers, and the councils. Dante thought that canon law should be mainly theological in scope, and he disliked intensely the additions made to it by the thirteenth-century commentators or decretalists who envisaged a pope who governed. Dante did not. For him government belonged only to the emperor and to the subordinate officials authorized by him. The emperor should rule the "humana civilitas." The pope should point men to the polis that was Paradise.

If the emperor permits the pope to participate in government the ship of human company goes astray. But the emperor owes the pope reverence and obedience in theological matters. This is made clear by Dante in *Paradiso* 6, the great canto of the empire. There Dante meets Justinian in heaven and Justinian describes to him how Pope Agapetus had corrected a grave heresy into which the emperor had fallen. After he had accepted the pope's teaching, he was able to move against the Barbarians occupying Italy and, as Justinian put it, cut out of the laws "the superfluous and the vain" (*Paradiso*, 6, 12). Justinian also eulogizes the providential conquests of the "bird of God," the imperial eagle, but says that all the eagle did before was as nothing compared to the privilege of playing an essential role in the redemption of man. This grandiose vision of the empire and human history is the central revelation that Dante believed he was called upon to make. It was his particular originality to sacralize secular or at least imperial government without in any way clericalizing it or neglecting its natural function.

NOTES

1 I owe special thanks to my son, Frank Davis, without whose help and collaboration this essay could not have been written.
2 I follow the interpretation of Lorenzo Minio-Paluello, "Tre note alla *Monarchia*," in *Medioevo e rinascimento: studi in onore di Bruno Nardi* (Florence: Sansoni, 1955), II, pp. 503–24, esp. pp. 511–22.
3 From M. Goldast, *Monarchia*, II, p. 99, cited by Minio-Paluello, "Tre note," pp. 521–22.

SUGGESTED READING

Armour, Peter, *Dante's Griffin and the History of the World* (Oxford: Clarendon Press, 1989).

Bowsky, William M., *Henry VII in Italy: The Conflict of Empire and City-State, 1310–1313* (Lincoln, NE: University of Nebraska Press, 1960).

Dante, *Monarchy*, trans. and ed. Prue Shaw (Cambridge: Cambridge University Press, 1995).

Davis, Charles Till, *Dante and the Idea of Rome* (Oxford: Clarendon Press, 1957).
  Dante's Italy and Other Essays (Philadelphia: University of Pennsylvania Press, 1984).

d'Entrèves, Alessandro Passerin, *Dante as a Political Thinker* (Oxford: Clarendon Press, 1952).

Ercole, Francesco, *Il pensiero politico di Dante*, 2 vols. (Milan: Alpes, 1927–28).

Ferrante, Joan M. *The Political Vision of the Divine Comedy* (Princeton: Princeton University Press, 1984).

Gilson, Etienne, *Dante and Philosophy*, trans. David Moore (New York: Harper and Row, 1963).

Mancusi-Ungaro, Donna, *Dante and the Empire* (New York: Peter Lang, 1987).

Nardi, Bruno, *Saggi di filosofia dantesca*, 2nd edn. (Florence: La Nuova Italia, 1967).

Ricci, Pier Giorgio, "Impero," in U. Bosco, ed., *Enciclopedia dantesca*, 6 vols. (Rome: Istituto dell'Enciclopedia Italiana, 1970–78), III, pp. 383–93.

Russo, Vittorio, *Impero e stato di diritto: studio su Monarchia ed Epistole politiche di Dante* (Naples: Bibliopolis, 1987).

Sasso, Gennaro, *Dante, l'imperatore e Aristotele* (Rome: Istituto Storico Italiano per il Medio Evo, 2002).

Woodhouse, John, ed., *Dante and Governance* (Oxford: Clarendon Press, 1997).

16

ROBERT HOLLANDER

Dante and his commentators

No poem has ever drawn the attention of so many exegetes as has Dante's *Divina Commedia*. It is probably fair to say that any young student of poetry who was aware of what is required of a *dantista* would happily choose to remain an amateur in respect to the poem, would choose to own it privately, only as it speaks to one's own eyes and ears. Dante himself is so much richer and deeper than we who write about him are, and allow him to seem, that the defender of the uses of the commentary tradition may be expected to display a certain hesitation. That tradition is so vast that those who decide to devote themselves to the study of it tend, understandably enough, to lose sight of the poem upon which this huge and unwieldly corpus sits. Nonetheless, we should probably observe that the originary fault lies with Dante himself. For no other poet has more evidently hoped to have a commentator at his margins. (Boccaccio, rightly, was so worried that no one would ever contribute a commentary to his *Teseida* that he supplied his own; and it was probably the existence of his own marginalia which encouraged at least two later and now mainly forgotten *studiosi* to contribute theirs.)

The more than twenty addresses to the reader which we find in the *Divina Commedia* are perhaps the single most unmistakable sign that Dante has invited us to share the burden of the poem's interpretation, suggesting both that he has written it in such a way as to create a series of problems for the reader, and that these problems have solutions. I do not suggest that the text is nothing more than a series of riddles or schoolboy exercises, but that it frequently includes such, or at least things very like them. It is better to proceed by example. In *Inferno* 5, 61–62, Virgil indicates perhaps the most significant exemplar of lust among the group of seven he points out to his pupil (all of the rest are identified by name) by periphrasis, one of the most effective teaching tools available in the rhetorical foundry of the poet: "The other there is she who killed herself for love, thus breaking faith with the ashes of Sichaeus." I do not think there is a single example in the history of Dante studies of a commentator who has got this wrong. And if the reader is nonplussed (as many a young contemporary reader may be, given the condition of our Latin culture), it will not take long to find a remedy: Sichaeus, at least according to Virgil's account in the *Aeneid*, was the husband of Dido. This is she who balances on the dark and stormy air of the circle of lust. If we do not know this, the commentators do, either because they know their Virgil, or because they know the commentaries of others who preceded them.

Let us move from the "easy" end of the spectrum to the "decidedly difficult" one. In *Paradiso* 2, 7–9, Dante makes a strong claim for the inspired nature of the third canticle of his poem. What he says is this: "The water that I travel has not been coursed before; Minerva inspires me, Apollo is my guide, and nine Muses point out to me the Bears." This particular tercet is of considerable difficulty. I choose to focus on only one part of that difficulty, the last clause, "and nine Muses point out to me the Bears." By the latter is meant the constellations Ursa Major and Ursa Minor and thus, inferentially, the North Star, and thus, further and metaphorically, God or the Empyrean, the highest heaven, the "home" of God and the directing agency, as well as the destination of the poet and his poem (not all will agree with this interpretation, but it is fairly widespread). However, the real difficulty is found in the beginning of the verse: "and nine Muses." Here the commentators are in considerable disarray. What is meant? Among them one finds two major and differing opinions: either Dante is referring to the canonical nine muses or (in a tradition that perhaps begins with Bernardino Daniello [1568]) to *new* muses, as befits his subject in this Christian poem. While elements in both solutions are attractive, it seems clear that Dante expects us to notice that he has made a linguistic switch here. If he had wanted to refer to *the* nine Muses he would have said so (i.e., "*le nove Muse*" and not "*e nove muse*"). In my opinion, he is here using the phrase metaphorically (and, were I to edit this segment of the text, I would be tempted to replace the capital "M" of the current standard text with a small one). That is, he is not referring to the nine Muses of classical literature, but to the informing "muses" of his vision, the nine celestial spheres, which give shape not only to the universe, but to the *Paradiso*, leading Dante "home" to God.

I have chosen these two examples to make evident two things. First, this poet behaves in such a way as to indicate that he is frequently in evident search of a glossator; second, the commentary tradition is usually interesting but hardly always "correct." One of its greatest uses is to make our mistakes for us and in this way force us to examine them. In the last case, the reading I propose is not sanctioned anywhere in the commentaries. And it may not be correct. It is, I think, a useful counter-argument to what others have said

that is plainly wrong or else unconvincing. With that much by way of introduction, I shall proceed to a discussion of my subject, which is in three parts.

The ancient tradition (1322–1570)

Dante's earliest commentators hardly waited for him to die before dissect-
ing him. That they existed at all is remarkable. In the history of Western
literature, line-by-line glossing was reserved for sacred texts or secular texts
of unquestioned and ancient authority (for example, Aristotle among the
philosophers and Virgil among the poets). For a contemporary poet writing
in the vernacular to receive this kind of attention was (and remains) nothing less than amazing. And the activity, itself so surprising, is all the more
notable for the numbers of commentators who were drawn to the poem,
even in the first few years after Dante's death. The major figures here include
Jacopo Alighieri (Dante's eldest son), Graziolo de' Bambaglioli, Jacopo della
Lana, Guido da Pisa, the so-called "Ottimo Commentatore" (now generally believed to have been Andrea Lancia), and Pietro Alighieri (Dante's
second son). While dating these texts has proved difficult, we can say that
these were the first half-dozen major commentaries (there are several others
from this period, some edited, others still not), and that all of them were
composed, in whatever order, between *c.* 1322 and 1340, the year in which
Pietro published the first version of his *Commentarium* (he would eventually revise it at least twice). With Pietro's appearance on the scene, perhaps
because of his authority as a son of Dante and because of his command
of classical materials (his is the first commentary to show decided "prehumanist" leanings), the rash of commentary came to a temporary halt. The
next major figure to be involved is major indeed, Giovanni Boccaccio, the
first paid (by the Commune of Florence in 1373–74) lecturer on Dante. His
commentary was not finished, breaking off at *Inferno* 17, perhaps where
Boccaccio's lectures in Santo Stefano in Badia themselves were broken off by
his worsening health in the penultimate year of his life. Benvenuto da Imola
(arguably the greatest of all the early commentators and certainly the most
prolific: his text runs to five hefty volumes), who probably heard some of
Boccaccio's lectures, finished his commentary *c.* 1380. He was followed by
another remarkable commentator, Francesco da Buti (*c.* 1395). These nine
fourteenth-century commentators are more or less those referred to when
Dante scholars mention "the early commentators." The list can (and will)
be expanded as other commentaries are discovered and published. A major
and strange figure at the very beginning of the next century is Filippo Villani
(the nephew of the chronicler Giovanni Villani). As the third person
appointed to lecture on Dante by the Commune of Florence he was of the

opinion that the *Commedia* was inspired directly by the Holy Spirit, and that Dante read the classics, Virgil in particular, with a similar understanding (his twelve-page Christian allegorization of the *Aeneid* is one of the more bizarre readings of that text ever proposed). These remarks are found in the only part of his lectures that has survived, his commentary on the first canto of the poem. The next major presence in the tradition is that of John of Serravalle. This Franciscan, who rose to the ecclesiastical rank of bishop, wrote a lengthy commentary that he completed in 1416. It is often a restatement of Benvenuto (he refers to Benvenuto as his *magister* in five separate passages in the commentary); however, at times his interpretations break new ground. Since it is not held in many libraries, it has not been attended to as much as it probably should be. (The only printed edition [1891] has recently been reissued in anastatic reproduction.)

The first stage of the tradition breaks rather neatly into these two groups, 1322–40 and 1375–95 (with an important addendum in the early fifteenth century). The pause in commentary production between John of Serravalle (1416) and Cristoforo Landino (1481) serves to mark the passage from medieval to renaissance attitudes toward the poem. Where Pietro di Dante opened the way toward "humanist" readings of Dante, and where Boccaccio and Benvenuto exemplified the growing "prehumanist" tide in late fourteenth-century Italian culture, in Landino we discover the beginning of a truly "renaissance" reading of the *Commedia*. It is in his commentary, and in those of his sixteenth-century followers, that we find, for instance, the identification of the less obvious classical citations that had escaped the notice of even the few classically minded fourteenth-century commentators. Landino is paid more attention for his general allegorization of the poem (which signifies the growth of the human soul, on the heels of such readings of the *Aeneid* as were sponsored by Fulgentius and [the pseudo-] Bernard Silvester and seconded by Landino himself) than for his wonderfully acute ear for classical citation. His follower, Alessandro Vellutello (1544), continues both these traditions of exegesis, while the last of the "ancient commentators," Bernardino Daniello (1568) and Lodovico Castelvetro (1570), are more inclined to the second activity as well as a more closely literal explanation of the text.

These fourteen names (Jacopo Alighieri, Graziolo de' Bambaglioli, Jacopo della Lana, Guido da Pisa, the "Ottimo," Pietro Alighieri, Boccaccio, Benvenuto, Francesco da Buti, John of Serravalle, Landino, Vellutello, Daniello, and Castelvetro) constitute the core of the first stage of the commentary tradition. The relations among them are complex; they are more unlike than like, and it is not possible to say many things which are true of all of them. Yet what most of them do seem to share, if in varying degrees, is a desire to turn the literal sense of the *Commedia* into a stage for an allegorical understanding. And this tendency, which is largely absent from the fresher and more literally and philologically inclined Graziolo, emerges less than halfway through the first canto of the poem, with the appearance of Virgil. Admittedly, if Dante wanted us to take his Virgil as historical (as I believe he did), he was probably undermining his intention by beginning his narrative with so evidently metaphorical a landscape (dark wood, lost way, etc.). The metaphorical nature of the opening of the poem, no matter what "historical" connections we may contrive to see in it, makes their task difficult for the champions of a non-allegorical understanding of the persons and actions encountered in the poem. On the other hand, the exertions of the exegetes are so grossly inadequate and strained that we should wonder how they have held their audience as long as they have. Except for Graziolo, who identifies Virgil as "a Roman poet" (what blessings have I heaped upon his absent head when I thank him, not for what he said, banality itself, but for what he did not say), nearly every early commentator leaps to the "obvious" interpretation: Virgil is reason with a capital "R." Is he? Many continue to think so. I think they are making a crucial and non-redeemable error, that they will never read the poem to which many of them have devoted their lives, but only the potential poem which Dante graciously did not write, a poem that would have been as reducible as traditional allegorical fables and as uninteresting. The lesser Dante of the commentators has composed, as one tradition of Virgilian interpretation would interpret the *Aeneid*, an allegory, an extended metaphor, in which the Appetitive Soul (= Dante) is schooled by the Rational Soul (= Virgil) until Theology (= Beatrice) comes to take over the Rational Soul's task. If this is your idea of a good read, you will feel quite at home in the early commentaries. When an allegorically minded commentator with a certain amount of common sense (e.g., Francesco da Buti) comes upon a moment in the poem in which Virgil is acting not only not rationally but downright rashly (for instance, at several moments during cantos 21 and 22), he may admit that "here the allegory is intermittent." That the basic allegory of the poem is operative is, however, never doubted.

It is only in the twentieth century that a strong case has been made against such readings, most notably by Erich Auerbach. And even today, if one suggests in many quarters that Virgil is not Reason but Virgil, one can be assured that right-thinking *dantisti* of the old school will be present to take the offender to task. The ancient commentators have many virtues. In my opinion it would be foolish indeed to try to come to grips with the myriad difficulties of Dante's text without consulting them. They offer help with philological questions, historical references, Dante's citations of classical texts (but rarely of earlier vernacular poets), issues in medieval theology and philosophy. And in many of these matters their expertise is more pertinent, because of their greater propinquity to Dante's time, than is our own. There are, however, critical tasks that they perform less well. They generally do poorly by Dante's self-citations; they tend to seize almost any opportunity to retell pagan myths (frequently by including lengthy paraphrases of Ovid) in order to display their "classical erudition"; and they tend not to think of Dante as citing classical works in context, but rather as merely embellishing his text (as they do theirs) with bits of Latin finery. And, in my opinion, what they do worst is to insist on a simplistic allegorical formulation of passage after passage in the poem. Unfortunately, the next period of interpretation did not improve greatly on their record.

The modern tradition (1732–1945)

Between the years 1570 and 1732 not a single major commentary on the *Commedia* was published. This is not to say that there was no commentary activity, but that no text that we are likely to read today was produced. When we contrast the 162 years between Castelvetro and Venturi with the 248 years that had produced fourteen major commentaries we can intuit what a decline Dante's reputation had suffered. As Bembo had urged, most readers, in Italy and elsewhere on the continent, were pleased to consider Petrarch the Italian master of poetry and Boccaccio, of prose. Dante needed not apply.

It was the Jesuit Pompeo Venturi, styling himself the first modern commentator, who got the "Dante industry" moving again, at least with respect to the writing of commentary. He loved to make fun of his precursors and spent much time and effort on matters of detail. His philological exertions are welcome, but not always well considered, as Lombardi (1791) frequently took pains to point out. Undoubtedly considering himself (and with some reason) the *real* first modern commentator, Lombardi is vigorous in his criticisms of various of Venturi's judgments. His commentary, reprinted frequently during the nineteenth century, ruled the roost for roughly one hundred years. It was perhaps the major authority for longer than has ever been the case, even though it was soon after its time that commentary-writing began to enjoy its highest moment. Dante, who had not played a major role in discussions of literature for two centuries, suddenly became, once again, a great figure on the literary horizon; but this time he arose as a European figure, at first with the sponsorship of Blake and others in England, of Schlegel and many other major figures in Germany, and then, rediscovered by painters (Delacroix and others) and writers alike in France. The events preceding, and then following, the unification of Italy also turned Dante into a national poet. The nineteenth century developed America's Dante as well, the one discovered by Emerson and then, at Harvard in mid-century, by Longfellow, Norton, and Lowell; among the makers of fiction by Melville and Hawthorne, especially the latter; and in the twentieth century by Santayana, Pound, and T. S. Eliot, who are perhaps responsible for Dante's inclusion in "Great Books" courses in the 1930s and 1940s. He is, more than anything else, a Romantic Dante, admired by Shelley, celebrated by many men and women of letters. Throughout the nineteenth century in Italy, commentaries proliferated. The major names are Paolo Costa (1819), Gabriele Rossetti (1826), Niccolò Tommaseo (1837), Raffaele Andreoli (1856), Gregorio di Siena (1867), Brunone Bianchi (1868), A. G. De Marzo (1873), G. A. Scartazzini (1874), Giuseppe Campi (1888), Tommaso Casini (1889), Gioachino Berthier (1892), and Giacomo Poletto (1894). However, there is the Dante of the commentators, the creature of schoolchildren and their teachers, and the Dante of De Sanctis, that glorious creation (and it is a wonderful creation, if it is not one Dante himself would have recognized or liked), the Romantic poet of the great-souled damned. This public Dante has had a remarkable career among poets (Victor Hugo), painters (Dante Gabriele Rossetti), sculptors (Rodin), and even composers (Lizst). What Dante knew best how to portray, for these and other illustrious figures, was the passion of suffering. It would be foolish to claim that this vision of the *Commedia* is entirely incorrect; rather, one would better claim that the great Romantic reading of the poem seized the foreground and put it against another backdrop, as though Francesca, Pier delle Vigne, Ulysses ("to strive, to seek, to find, and not to yield," as Tennyson would restate his purpose), and Ugolino were characters in a text by Goethe at his stormiest. The "professional" *dantista* may decry the Romantic reading (and I will surely join in the chorus); however, all of us who deal professionally with the poet ought to realize that, in a real sense, we owe our jobs to the Romantic recovery of his work.

While Romanticism breathed new life into his reputation, the "new philology" in Italy, guided by Michele Barbi (1867–1941), raised philological examination of the poem to the highest level it had ever achieved. It is in the last half of the nineteenth century and in the first of the twentieth that Dante studies began to look "professional," "scientific." The ancient commentators were reprinted, concordances and *rimarii* appeared, modern commentaries approached philological problems with far better preparation than had been possible before, Italian historiography proved useful in illuminating dark corners of a poem filled with the minutiae of local and distant histories. One might argue that, had the First World War (which took a heavy psychic toll on Italy, as well as on Germany, France, and England) not occurred, the Great Age of Dante studies would have occurred (I am aware that there were graver consequences). All the elements were present.

In Italy not merely one but *two* bi-monthly publications (*Giornale dantesco* and *Bullettino della Società Dantesca*) were devoted to microanalysis of particulars of the poem; Barbi's colleagues and students were ascendant. Two aspects of the picture were askew: the Romantic reading had infiltrated the scholarly world, with the result that the next step did not occur when and where it should (in Italy); and the apparatus, perhaps fatigued in the aftermath of the First World War, was soon to find itself operating under the man who saw himself as the *Dux* called for by the poem itself. (The chapter of Dante's *Nachleben* that Mussolini [identified by several commentators as the Veltro of *Inferno* 1, unbelievable as that may seem to us] intended to create, a monument to Dante and to himself, was fortunately not completed.) In any case, the period 1918 to 1945 was not what, from the point of view of 1915, might have been expected. The Romantic reading, in the hands of another great Italian critic, Benedetto Croce, became even less moral and theological than it had been. For Croce and his followers (including the influential commentator Attilio Momigliano), Dante was the creator of esthetic excellence. The theological precisions of the poem were not to be studied closely. One celebrated what one loved in the poem and forgave Dante the rest. We might remember the title (and the intention) of Cesari's *Bellezze della Divina Commedia* (1824). This estheticized *Commedia* is still among us.

Dante today (1945–present)

The postwar years have seen two major commentary presences, first Sapegno (1955) and then Bosco/Reggio (1979). Other major twentieth-century commentators not mentioned elsewhere in these pages include Francesco Torraca (1905), C. H. Grandgent (1909), Enrico Mestica (1909), Carlo Steiner (1921), Luigi Pietrobono (1924), Isidoro Del Lungo (1926), Carlo Grabher (1934), Ernesto Trucchi (1936), Dino Provenzal (1938), Manfredi Porena (1946), Daniele Mattalia (1960), Siro A. Chimenz (1962), Giovanni Fallani (1965), Giorgio Padoan (only *Inferno* 1–8, 1967), Pasquini/Quaglio (1982), Tommaso Di Salvo (1985), Vallone/Scorrano (1985), Anna Maria Chiavacci Leonardi (1991–97), and Nicola Fosca (*Inferno*, 2003). Where Scartazzini (one of the great commentators, especially in his monumental second edition of 1900, badly bowdlerized in the version produced by Vandelli, first in 1903, and then in nine subsequent editions, with the result that the "real" Scartazzini is often unknown to the scholars who believe they are citing him) had been the essential name for the first fifty years of the century, Sapegno wore that mantle for its third quarter. (Bosco/Reggio is now perhaps the "standard" commentary, though it is also true to say that currently there is no single commentator whom most *dantisti* consider better than all others. My own choice is Francesco Mazzoni, whose published commentaries now extend to one tenth of the poem's cantos; they are voluminous and exemplary.) Outside Italy there have been two major commentaries produced in this period, those of the German Hermann Gmelin (1954), and of the French André Pézard (1965). Singleton's attempt (1970–75) to create the first major modern English commentary has met with some success, even if it is flawed by its curious detachment from the critical position of the author, as well as by its cavalier treatment of precursors and its surprising failure to deal with a number of pressing problems in the text that simply demand response. Recently two new American translations of *Inferno* and *Purgatorio* also include plenteous notes: Durling/Martinez (1996, 2003) and Hollander (2000, 2003).

A phenomenon that has been of great interest (and it is not only Americans who think so) in the postwar period is the emergence of American Dante studies. To be fair, the first movement came from Germany, or at least from the exiled German Jew, Erich Auerbach. It was he who successfully reshaped the argument about Dante's allegory. The misprision of that argument has been, in my opinion, the single most negative force hindering the development of Dante studies. What Auerbach proposed was that Dante's allegory should be thought of along the lines of theological allegory, namely as being figural rather than figurative, historical rather than metaphoric. Auerbach's work was slow to make its way to a larger public and, since he was not translated into Italian until 1963, his effect in Italy was secondary to that of Singleton (whose *Dante's* Commedia: *Elements of Structure* [1954] was translated in 1961). In the remainder of the century there was only one Italian commentary which accepted the basic precepts of this school of interpretation, that of Giuseppe Giacalone (1968 [but now see Fosca, 2003]). As for Singleton, who is generally credited as being the shaping force in the new *dantismo*, his first work, *An Essay on the Vita Nuova* (1948), and then his *Dante Studies* (two volumes, 1954; 1957), have been the central *loci* of repair, first for American, and then for other students of the poem who believe that the claims made in the *Epistle to Cangrande* (whether Dante wrote it or not, an issue which is once again hotly debated) essentially account for the mode of signifying that distinguishes the *Commedia*. This is far too vexed a subject for discussion in brief. Yet it must be said that it is probably the determinative argument among *dantisti* today. Where one stands on that question is essential, and is deemed to be so, at least by most people on either side of the question. To Singleton (who had the ill grace never to mention Auerbach's ground-breaking work on theological allegory in any of his writings) belongs the credit (or, if one is so minded, the blame) for formulating the essential argument about the nature of the problem. It does not matter that, in his own treatment of the poem (and particularly in his commentary), he does not use the technique as a Singletonian would or ought. What he did accomplish was to bring the theoretical argument into play at a time and in a way in which it could be intelligently addressed. For that reason Dante studies, and not only in America, are still in a Singletonian age.

What will the future bring us? Who can say? I would like, rather than to predict, to say what I hope will transpire. First of all, I hope that the rich resources of the most elaborate commentary tradition that exists for any poem will begin to be used more systematically and more interestingly. In the nineteenth century one tradition that grew up in Italy, that of the *Lectura Dantis*, allows the individual reader pretty much free rein in avoiding the poem's past. One unvoiced justification for such critical behavior may have been that there is so much written on Dante that no one can possibly be blamed for simply giving up on the task of being conversant with it all. All too often a *Lectura Dantis* will deal with four or five standard treatments of the canto under discussion and then go on to present the author's (often very subjective) impressions. Now that we have the Dartmouth Dante Project and other such tools at our disposal, I would hope that the commentary tradition will regain the position Guido Biagi envisioned for it (Biagi and three colleagues were responsible for the publication of a huge three-volume "commentary of commentaries" [1921–40], a work which gave copious excerpts from nearly two dozen major commentaries). The commentary tradition is an extremely useful tool, perhaps less for coming up with "answers" than for indicating the complexity of the problems which need to be addressed. Perhaps *dantisti* will increasingly come to realize that no one has ever cornered the market on being right or interesting. One never knows where the fruitful interpretation may be found. Commentators and critics who may not be considered as interpretive allies, or as particularly gifted, have their moments. There is hardly anyone from whom we cannot learn, at one time or another. Second, I also hope that the monstrously large bibliography of Dante studies will be put into better order. It should not be implausible to imagine that, for instance, the Cornell Dante Catalogue, an analytical bibliography complete up to 1920, will be brought up to date and revised in such a way as to afford a relatively secure means of finding out what has been written on nearly any problem being investigated. And last of all, I would hope that students of Dante will engage in more collaborative work. Scientists have long ago learned to work together *per necessitatem*; they understand that complex and difficult problems require collaboration. A recent example (Guido Biagi offers an older one) of what may be achieved when scholars as gifted as Umberto Bosco and Francesco Mazzoni are willing to turn their intelligence and energy to a common cause is the *Enciclopedia dantesca*, one of the monuments of modern Dante scholarship, and a model to be emulated.

SUGGESTED READING

Baranski, Zygmunt G., "Reflecting on Dante in America: 1949–1990," *Annali d'Italianistica* 8 (1990): 58–86. (A recent review of the status of current American work on Dante.)

Bosco, U., ed., *Enciclopedia dantesca*, 6 vols. (Rome: Istituto dell'Enciclopedia Italiana, 1970–78). (Of special interest are the entries dedicated to individual early commentators, most of which were prepared by Franceso Mazzoni, the leading authority on the subject. These, even for readers without Italian, will help organize the vast bibliography dedicated to the commentary tradition.)

Caesar, Michael, ed., *Dante: The Critical Heritage 1314(?)–1870* (London and New York: Routledge, 1989). (A useful introduction, followed by a sampling of 650 years of critical responses to Dante.)

The Dartmouth Dante Project. (An on-line data base of seventy-two commentaries, 1322–2006. The current address is dante.dartmouth.edu; in 2005 Dartmouth developed and implemented a new Web interface for this project.

Rigo, Paola, "Commentatori danteschi," *Dizionario critico della letteratura italina*, II (Turin: UTET, 1996), pp. 6–22.

Vallone, Aldo, *Storia della critica dantesca dal XIV al XX secolo* (Padua: Vallardi, 1981).

17

DAVID WALLACE

Dante in English

> . . . adventures and scenes more wild than any in the Pilgrim's Progress.
>
> Thomas Warton (1728–90)

The translation, imitation, and contestation of Dante in English shows no signs of abating after six hundred years. The waning of scholasticism, the Reformation, the rise of new nation-states (including Italy, Ireland, and the United States), the two World Wars, the sectarian violence of Northern Ireland, and the struggles of African-Americans have all been articulated through readings and rewritings of Dantean texts. The first part of this history is easy to narrate: the painstaking intelligence with which Chaucer, Milton, and Shelley respond to Dante is easily distinguished from the general ignorance and imaginative feebleness that prevails in the first four centuries. Thereafter things become more complicated: an American Dante comes into being; Pound and Eliot connect American, English, and continental traditions; an Irish Dante (Yeats, Joyce, Beckett, Heaney) achieves things that are beyond the grasp of the English or Americans. Interest in Dante has, if anything intensified in the last few years. This survey begins with a secure origin – Chaucer's *De Hugelino Comite de Pize* – and works forward to an imperfect, Farinata-like vision of our own immediate future.

Chaucer's decision to lift the Ugolino story from *Inferno* 33 for his *Monk's Tale* set a trend that has never been broken: the Ugolino episode has been translated into English more times than any other Dantean passage (Paolo and Francesca run a poor second). But Chaucer's "Ugolino" can hardly be called a translation; the tale is radically recontextualized and the dominant emotional register is pathos, rather than terror or revulsion. Whereas Dante finds Ugolino and the archbishop Ruggieri "frozen in one hole" (*Inferno* 32, 125), with Ugolino gnawing at the archbishop's skull, the reader of Chaucer finds no mention of Hell and no archbishop: the Ugolino story is narrated as one of many in a sequence illustrating the fall of the illustrious, including Lucifer, Adam, and the cross-dressed queen Cenobia.[1] Chaucer makes no mention of Ugolino's prophetic dream, gives his Hugelyn three children to Dante's four, and makes them infants (the eldest "scarsly fyf yeer was of age," 7, 2412). The Dantean Ugolino maintains an icy control of his emotions as he counts out the passing of the days and the deaths of his sons (*Inferno* 33,

70–72): Chaucer's monk, rather than counting upon the reader to supply an adequate emotional response, gives us emotion in such abundance that we remain spectators to a scene that seems wholly generic and unreal:

> Thus day by day this child bigan to crye,
> Til in his fadres barm adoun it lay,
> And seyde, "Farewel, fader, I moot dye!"
> And kiste his fader, and dyde the same day.
> And whan the woful fader deed it say,
> For wo his armes two he gan to byte,
> And seyde, "Allas, Fortune, and weylawey!
> Thy false wheel my wo al may I wyte."
>
> (7, 2439–46)

This stanza represents a dramatic falling-away from the poetic achievement of the Dantean original. The last two lines here remind us, however, that the declared purpose of the *Monk's Tale* is not to imitate Dante, but to "biwaille in manere of tragedie/The harm of hem that stood in heigh degree, And fillen" ("and fell," 7, 1991–92). The rubric which precedes this *Tale*, "*De Casibus Virorum Illustrium*," suggests that it is Boccaccio's Latin encyclopedism (Boccaccio wrote a work with that title) rather than Dante's vernacular poetry that is the monk's primary inspiration. The debt to Italian protohumanism is explicitly acknowledged later in the *Tale* by the monk's reference to "my maister Petrak" (2325). When Chaucer made his two extensive visits to Italy in 1372–73 and 1378, Latinate humanism was the dominant cultural force in educated circles, not Italian poetry: even the later Trecento commentaries on Dante's poem, including the one by Dante's son Pietro, were written in Latin, rather than Italian. The *Monk's Tale*, then, may be read as an attempt to introduce the new Italian proto-humanistic format to an English audience; the Ugolino story is accordingly pared down to fit into an encyclopedic sequence.

The first extended account in English of a scene from the *Commedia* seems, then, on the face of it, like an opportunity extravagantly wasted: an established Italian masterpiece is rewritten to exemplify the characteristics (and defects: the *Tale* is not popular with Chaucer's pilgrims) of a new Italian fashion. We should note, however, that Chaucer does not end his Hugelyn section without inviting us to a detailed reading of the "word" of the Dantean original:

> Whoso wol here it in a lenger wise,
> Redeth the grete poete of Ytaille
> That highte Dant, for he kan al devyse
> Fro point to point: nat a word wol he faille.
>
> (7, 2459–62)

There is no doubt that Chaucer read Italian texts "fro point to point," with extreme and meticulous care. His first encounter with the text of Dante is vividly registered by *The House of Fame*, a poem in three books that sees him travel through the heavens in the company of an otherworldly guide. Although *The House of Fame* has been described as a parody of Dante, it is better to think of it as a self-parody in short couplets brought on by the overwhelming experience of reading the *Commedia*. When Chaucer follows Dante ("Io non Enëa, io non Paolo sono," *Inferno* 2, 32) in protesting that he is not equipped for such a journey, he protests so much that we are compelled to believe him:

> I neyther am Ennok, ne Elye,
> Ne Romulus, ne Ganymede,
> That was ybore up, as men rede,
> To hevene with daun Jupiter,
> And mad the goddys botiller.
> (*The House of Fame*, 2, 588–92)

This pattern of imitating Dante before retreating into humorous or rueful self-parody is repeated throughout the poem. At the beginning of book 3, for example, he imitates Dante's invocation of Apollo in *Paradiso* 1, 13–27: but whereas Dante proposes to crown himself with laurel if his poetic task is completed, Chaucer promises to slap a kiss on a laurel tree (1091–1109). Not surprisingly, *The House of Fame* ends incomplete, just as Chaucer catches sight of a "man of gret auctorite" who, one supposes, will resolve all the doubts and questions engendered by this sorry poetic performance.

Mindful of such shortcomings, Chaucer entered into a period of poetic experimentation that saw him lengthening his line, varying his meters, and struggling to incorporate lessons and phrasings learned from the *Commedia*. In *A Compleynt to His Lady*, he tries his hand at *terza rima*, an experiment wisely abandoned, since (as he says elsewhere) English contains a great scarcity of decent rhyme words. The *proem* to a lengthy *compleynt* from *Anelida and Arcite*, another "workshop" or experimental poem in a variety of meters, sees him fusing a phrase remembered from the *Purgatorio* ("la puntura de la rimembranza," 12, 20) with a conceit involving piercing swords borrowed from Machaut. It is remarkable to think that the poet responsible for the brilliant opening period of *The Canterbury Tales* could write so badly; the bloated lines sit, python-like, full of semi-digested matter:

> So thirleth with the poynt of remembraunce
> The swerd of sorowe, ywhet with fals pleasaunce,
> Myn herte, bare of blis and blak of hewe . . .
> (*Anelida and Arcite*, 211–13)

By the time he came to write *Troilus and Criseyde*, however, Chaucer had mastered a stanzaic form and could sustain extended narrative in English (*rhyme royal*, ababbcc) and was ready to write a poem of Dantean scope and grandeur. Although his immediate source-text was the *Filostrato*, one of Boccaccio's earliest compositions, it is clear that Dante is his master in matters of prosody and intellectual organization. The beginning of his very last stanza is modelled on a tercet from the *Paradiso*:

> Thow oon, and two, and thre, eterne on lyve,
> That regnest ay in thre, and two, and oon,
> Uncircumscript, and al maist circumscrive.
> *Troilus and Criseyde*, 5, 1863–65;
> see *Paradiso* 14, 28–30)

By the time he had completed *Troilus and Criseyde*, Chaucer was as confident of his poetic credentials as Dante was in beginning the *Inferno*: he too awards himself sixth place (after Virgil, Ovid, Homer, Lucan, and Statius) in a line of poetic descent that connects pagan antiquity with the Christian present (*Troilus and Criseyde* 5, 1792; compare *Inferno* 4, 94–102). He opens his *Legend of Good Women*, written as a penance for the supposed anti-feminist leanings of the *Troilus*, with a joke (so it seems) at Dante's expense: there is nobody in *this* country, he says, "That eyther hath in helle or hevene ybe" (*Legend of Good Women* G, 6). The *Canterbury Tales* is an enterprise where the precedent of Boccaccio's *Decameron*, rather than of Dante's *Commedia*, seems more relevant: and yet there are many fascinating citations of, or brushes with, Dante to consider. The Wife of Bath, in her *Tale*, makes good use of Dante's discourse on true nobility in *Convivio* IV and finds a tercet from the *Purgatorio* (7, 121–23) to epitomize the theme (3, 1125–30). It is not surprising that the Wife, who has prospered through trade in textiles and skill in marriage, should wish to incorporate such sentiments into her text: many upwardly mobile Italian merchants were fond of citing *Convivio* IV by way of arguing that progress in the world (rather than noble birth) should be taken as proof of noble status.

Earlier in this fragment of *The Canterbury Tales*, Dante is cited in the role that remains his primary identification in the English-speaking world: as an authority on Hell (3, 1520). The drama in *The Friar's Tale* of the mysterious yeoman (a fiend in disguise) who attempts to maneuver the summoner into damning himself has a great deal in common with the drama of *Inferno* 27 (Guido da Montefeltro). Both narratives feature devils who observe punctilious accuracy in matters of linguistic logic in attempting to distinguish a man's words from his true intentions, his *entente*; both devils are successful and take their victims to Hell. There is no evidence that Chaucer's tale, which takes place in rural England, is directly indebted to *Inferno* 27. But the reference to Dante early on confirms that the English and Italian authors may be read within a common cultural matrix. It often proves profitable and enlightening to read Dante and Chaucer in tandem even when no explicit verbal parallels are forthcoming. No English writer comes closer than Chaucer to sharing Dante's literary and metaphysical parameters; no other English poet before Milton produces anything that rewards close comparison with the text of the *Commedia*.

The uniqueness and precocity of Chaucer's engagement with Dante becomes readily apparent once we turn to his immediate successors. Although John Gower tells one anecdote that has "Dante the poet" answering a flatterer (*Confessio Amantis* 7, 2329–37), he shows no knowledge of Dante's writings.[2] In *The Fall of Princes* (1431–38), John Lydgate speaks of Chaucer's having written "Dante in Inglissh" (1, 303), a reference (it is presumed) to *The House of Fame*.[3] Lydgate's *Fall*, which runs to more than 36,000 lines, contains two further references to Dante which derive (via a French prose translation) from Boccaccio's *De casibus virorum illustrium*. In 1418, Nicholas Bubwith, bishop of Bath and Wells, returned home from the Council of Constance with a Latin translation of the *Commedia* made for him by an Italian bishop (who had spent time in England); the book was still at Wells in the 1530s. In 1443, Duke Humphrey, Lydgate's patron, presented Oxford University with an Italian text of, and a Latin commentary on, the *Commedia*: both books have since disappeared, and nothing appears to have been learned from them. From this point on, for more than a century, Dante becomes little more than a name, and a source for a word or two in Italian dictionaries. His fortunes revive somewhat after the Reformation, when he is appealed to as an authority against Rome. The Protestant John Foxe, who fled from England at the accession of Queen Mary, saw Dante's *Monarchia* through the press at Basle and quotes from this work in his *Book of Martyrs* (1563). John Jewel, bishop of Salisbury, avers in his *Apologie of the Churche of Englande* (1567) that "Dantes, an Italian poet, by express words calleth Rome *the whore of Babylon*."[4] In 1570, Queen Elizabeth decreed that every church in England should have Foxe's *Book*, Jewel's *Apologie*, and a Great Bible. The name of Dante, then, could be found all over England in the late sixteenth century as part of the apparatus of Protestant reform. Intelligent Elizabethans, however, could recognize that there was much in Dante that their monarch would not approve of. Edmund Spenser, who was well acquainted with Italian literature, nowhere mentions Dante by name; John Florio, son of a Florentine Protestant, studiously avoids the text of Dante in compiling *A Worlde of Wordes* (1598), his Italian and English dictionary. Evidence for some surreptitious familiarity with the *Commedia* is provided

by *Tarlton Newes out of Purgatorie* (1590), an anonymous pamphlet supposedly written by the actor Richard Tarlton two years after his death in
1588. The notion that there is nothing in the afterlife but Heaven and Hell
is ironically opposed by the assertion that

> there is *Quoddam tertium* a third place that al our great grandmothers have
> talkt of, that *Dant* hath so learnedly writ of, and that is Purgatorie.
>
> (*DEL* I, p. 80)

It is not until we come to John Milton (1608–74) that we find an English
poet with the education, intelligence, and political opportunity to sustain
a close engagement with Dante. Milton was familiar with a wide range of
Dantean texts: he knew the *Monarchia*, owned a copy of the *Convivio* (1529,
third edition), and was familiar with the *Vita nuova* (from the 1576 *editio
princeps*, published in the same volume as Boccaccio's *Trattatello in laude
di Dante*); he quoted from Daniello's edition of, and commentary on, the
Commedia. His intimate knowledge of Dante allowed him to find passages
that offer a more refined critique of papal power (and a more accurate reading
of Dante) than those offered by John Foxe and Bishop Jewel. Milton's manner
of incorporating a Dantean tercet into *Of Reformation* (1641) is typically
ingenious in both respecting and amending Dante's text; Dante's "matre"
("mother"), which completes the Italian hendecasyllabic line, must lose a
syllable, become "cause," and so serve the cause of English pentameters:

> Ahi, Constantin, di quanto mal fu matre,
> non la tua conversion, ma quella dote
> che da te prese il primo ricco patre!
>
> (*Inferno* 19, 115–17)

> Dante, in his 19. *Canto of Inferno*, hath thus, as I will render it to you in
> English blank Verse:

> Ah Constantine, of how much ill was cause,
> Not thy conversion, but those rich demaines
> That the first wealthy Pope receiv'd of thee.[5]

Dante's insistence upon the separation of papal and imperial powers proved
useful to Milton in his attack upon English absolutism (the attempt to unite
religious and secular powers ever more closely in the figure of the monarch).
And the ringing condemnation by Dante's Beatrice of preachers who neglect
the faithful and pervert the gospel (*Paradiso* 29) is translated to the cause
of English Puritanism, as articulated by Milton's St. Peter, with remarkable
ease:

sì che le pecorelle, che non sanno,
tornan del pasco pasciute di vento.
(*Paradiso* 29, 107–08)

The hungry Sheep look up, and are not fed,
But swoln with wind, and the rank mist they draw.
(*Lycidas*, 125–26)

There is, of course, much in Dante's Catholicism that proves incompatible with Milton's Puritanism. But Milton showed a remarkable ability to separate poetics from politics in the poets he admired: he admired Spenser, for example, in spite of Spenser's championing of royal absolutism. He shows a sympathetic understanding of the Dantean scheme of Purgatory in assuring Henry Lawes, the celebrated musician, that

Dante shall give Fame leave to set thee higher
Than his *Casella*, whom he woo'd to sing,
Met in the milder shades of Purgatory.
(*Sonnet* 13, 12–14)

The earliest version of this sonnet reads "mildest," rather than "milder": Milton was concerned to mark the difference between the souls in Ante-Purgatory and in Purgatory proper. Not that Milton believed in Purgatory, of course. His rejection of the organizational structures and religious hardware of Catholicism is abundantly clear in *Paradise Lost* book 3, where "Cowls, Hoods and Habits . . . Reliques, Beads, Indulgences, Dispenses, Pardons, Bulls" are tossed by a whirlwind in "The Paradise of Fools" (3, 490–96). A little later in the same book, however, we find a description of Jacob's ladder which has much in common with the ladder that rises up in *Paradiso* 21.

Milton is rewarding to read in conjunction with Dante because he falls into neither of the two forms of response that have been most prevalent in England: abject praise, or fierce and uncomprehending rejection. Milton's uses of Dante in *Paradise Lost* often offer a witty and critical commentary on Dante's poetic project. Here, for example, the lines

Thou art my Father, thou my Author, thou
My being gav'st me.
(*Paradise Lost* 2, 864–65)

might be paired with the celebrated threefold acclamation of Virgil at the opening of the *Inferno*:

Tu se' lo mio maestro e 'l mio autore,
tu se' solo colui . . .
(*Inferno* 1, 85–86)

In Dante's text, Dante is acclaiming Virgil; in Milton's, Sin is acclaiming Death. Parallels like these, if we hear them, may be read as a positive or negative critique of Dante, or as a mapping of independent ground. The first such opportunity comes early on, with Milton's description of Hell as a place where "hope never comes/That comes to all" (*Paradise Lost* 1, 66–67). Having evoked Dante's famous Hell-gate description ("LASCIATE OGNE SPERANZA," *Inferno* 3, 9), Milton immediately counter-distinguishes his own Hell by defining it, simply, as a place "prepar'd" by "Eternal Justice" (*Paradise Lost* 1, 70). This at once parallels the second tercet of *Inferno* 3 ("GIUSTIZIA MOSSE") and parts company with it, since no mention is made of God in his Trinitarian aspects of divine power (Father), highest wisdom (Son), and primal love (Holy Spirit). The effect of the *absence* of these divine attributes makes Milton's Hell seem a more terrible construct than Dante's, as indeed it is: for there is to be no passing *through* it (for protagonist, or reader) to learn how "'L PRIMO AMORE" could sanction such a place. The power, wisdom, and love of Heaven is evoked not as instrumental in the making of Hell, but as an absence, a place fallen away from:

> Such place eternal justice had prepar'd
> For those rebellious, here thir Prison ordained
> In utter darkness, and thir portion set
> As far remov'd from God and light of Heav'n
> As from the center thrice to th' utmost Pole.
> O how unlike the place from whence they fell!
> (*Paradise Lost* 1, 70–75)

Dante's *Commedia* is a poem written in political exile that ends with a homecoming in, as part of, "the Love that moves the sun and the other stars" (*Paradiso* 33, 145); *Paradise Lost* is a poem completed in political exile that begins with the exile of rebellious angels and ends with the exile of humanity from Eden. In Milton, stirring talk of a journey upward from Hell – "long is the way/And hard, that out of Hell leads up to light" – comes only from Satan (2, 432–33; compare *Inferno* 34, 95–96). The terrain that Milton returns us to is the troubled "World" (12, 646) of the postlapsarian present. Differences between Dante and Milton prove, finally, more striking than affinities. Milton's debt to Dante (not as immediately obvious as his debt to Ariosto and Tasso) is profound: the transformations of Satan into serpents in *Paradise Lost*, books 9 and 10, for example, could scarcely have been written without the Ovidian-inspired precedents of *Inferno* 24 and 25. But Dante's debt to Milton is also considerable: that is, our debt to Milton as readers of Dante. A single phrase from *Paradise Lost* can often bring us a new sense of the singularity, the strangeness, of Dante's poem. In 1, 227, for example, Milton speaks of the air of Hell feeling "unusual weight" as Satan flies through it. This is "unusual" for Hell because nothing has ever flown through it before, not even a fallen angel. Far stranger, however is the "novo carco," "unusual weight," experienced by the rocks of Hell as Dante, a living human being, scrambles over them (*Inferno* 12, 30). The historical, third-person perspective that predominates in Milton's poem only serves to remind us that Dante's intimate, first-person journey is very strange indeed.

Milton's conviction that Italian was the greatest of European languages and cultures went against the grain of English fashion: the seventeenth century saw French replace Italian as the most favored vernacular in court and educational circles. Voltaire's dismissal of Dante, popularized through his *Dictionnaire Philosophique* (1764), was often repeated in England and sums up the fortunes of Dante in English for much of the eighteenth century: "Twenty pointed things in him [Dante] are known by rote, which spare people the trouble of being acquainted with the remainder."[6] Odd phrases from the *Commedia* were circulated by the leisured classes returning from the continental tour; the periodical *Doddsley's Museum* (1746) features an alphabetical accounting ("the Ballance") of twenty poets which ranks Dante above Boileau but below Corneille. He scores respectably in "Pathetic Ordonnance" (fifteen marks out of twenty, with eleven poets scoring higher), but somehow ranks dead last in "Dramatic Expression"; only Shakespeare gets lower marks for "Taste" (*DEL* 1, p. 242). In paraphrasing the *Commedia* in the course of his *History of English Poetry* (4 vols., 1774–81), Thomas Warton, Poet Laureate, condemns the "disgusting fooleries" of *Inferno* 16 before turning with relief to Voltaire's parody of *Inferno* 27. Guido da Montefeltro, dressed as a Franciscan, dies and meets Beelzebub:

> Monsieur de Lucifer!
> Je suis un Saint; voyes ma robe grise:
> Je fus absous par le Chef de l'Eglise.[7]

"Dante thus translated," says Warton, "would have had many more readers than at present" (*History of English Poetry*, III, p. 253).

The need for a decent "Englishing" of Dante becomes ever more painfully evident in this period: but before 1782, published translations from the *Commedia* were restricted to single episodes. In that year, however, William Hayley translated three cantos of the *Inferno* as a footnote to his *Essay on Epic Poetry*, and William Rogers published a blank verse translation of the entire *Inferno*. Rogers' work is neither accurate nor poetically accomplished; the quality and tenor of Hayley's work may be gauged from an earlier rendition of the famous Hell-gate inscription in his *The Triumphs of Temper*

(1781): "Thro' me ye pass to Spleen's terrific dome" (*DEL* i, p. 361). In 1802, the first complete English translation of the *Commedia* was published by an Irishman, Henry Boyd. It was not until 1814, however, that H. F. Cary, an Anglican clergyman, brought the English-speaking world face to face with a powerful, accurate, and poetically moving translation of Dante. The revolutionary importance of Cary's astringent, disciplined verse can best be grasped by contrasting it with Boyd's luxuriant, archaic, six-line stanzas:[8]

> When life had labor'd up her midmost stage,
> And, weary with her mortal pilgrimage,
> Stood in suspense upon the point of Prime;
> Far in a pathless grove I chanc'd to stray,
> Where scarce imagination dares display,
> The gloomy scen'ry of the savage clime.
>
> (Boyd, 1)

> In the midway of this our mortal life,
> I found me in a gloomy wood, astray
> Gone from the path direct: and e'en to tell,
> It were no easy task, how savage wild
> That forest, how robust and rough its growth,
> Which to remember only, my dismay
> Renews, in bitterness not far from death.
> Yet, to discourse of what there good befel,
> All else will I relate discover'd there.
>
> (Cary, 1–9)

Boyd's stanzas, which wander from the path early on and tell of things never encountered in Dante, is intended as a substitute for the original: Cary encourages us to keep abreast of the Italian text, line by line (nine lines for three *terzine*). Following enthusiastic endorsement by Samuel Taylor Coleridge in a lecture on Dante in 1818, Cary's work became a bestseller and was later acknowledged by Wordsworth as "a great national work" (*DEL* i, p. 466). Keats carried Cary's three volumes in his knapsack during his 1818 tour of the Lake District and the Highlands of Scotland; Blake, with Cary's text close at hand, produced ninety-eight colored drawings of the *Commedia*, and was busy engraving scenes from the *Inferno* within days of his death in 1827. Cary achieved minor celebrity status, becoming in turn Curate of the Savoy and Assistant Keeper of Printed Books at the British Museum; schoolboys were assigned the task of turning passages from his *Commedia* into Latin verse.

The next most important *dantisti* among the English Romantic poets (if Blake is counted as a brilliant illustrator of Dante rather than as a poetic imitator) are Coleridge, Byron, and Shelley; the greatest of these is Shelley. Coleridge was a discerning reader of the *Vita nuova*, the *Convivio*, and (as is evident from his *Biographia Literaria*) the *De vulgari*; his notebooks show him worrying away at the meaning of the canzone "Tre donne intorno al cor" for more than a decade (1806–19). The 1818 lecture makes its pioneering approach to Dante's poetry via a political and economic assessment of Dante's Italy: "Never was the commercial spirit so well reconciled to the nobler principles of social polity as in Florence" (I, p. 151).[9] Byron and Shelley shared such interest in political and historical matters, especially as they affected the contemporary struggle for Italian liberation. Byron's *terza rima Prophecy of Dante*, in which a first-person Dante reviews the whole course of Italian history down to the present, was written in Italy for Italians in the hope that it would be translated as an aid to the nationalist cause; "Italy," Byron wrote to his publisher, urging the publication of his Dantesque poems, "is on the eve of great things."[10]

Byron's experiments with *terza rima*, "of which your British Blackguard reader as yet understands nothing,"[11] include a translation of *Inferno* 5, dubbed "Fanny of Rimini." But it was Shelley, at the end of his abbreviated career, who was to produce what is easily the greatest English poetry in *terza rima*, his *Triumph of Life*.[12] Shelley (1792–1822) spent the last four years of his life in Italy. His *A Defence of Poetry* (1821) pairs Dante and Milton as preeminent epic poets preceding and following the Reformation. Dante is characterized as "the congregator of those great spirits who presided over the resurrection of learning"; his every word is "a burning atom of inextinguishable thought . . . pregnant with a lightning which has yet found no conductor."[13] Shelley clearly aspired to become, through his own painstaking craft, a conductor of the political and poetic energy that he found latent in Dante. His translation of the difficult canzone "Voi che intendendo il terzo ciel movete" (and his study of Cavalcanti) clearly prepared the way for *Prometheus Unbound*: Dante, "more than any other poet," he tells us in prefacing that poem, has succeeded in giving poetic expression to "the operations of the human mind" (p. 163). In introducing his *Epipsychidion*, Shelley recognizes parallels with the *Vita nuova* and endorses Dante's insistence that a poet is obliged, upon request, to distinguish "colore rettorico" from "verace intendimento" (p. 298). *The Triumph of Life* shows a remarkable understanding not only of the entire *Commedia*, but also of the poetic traditions that precede and follow from it, from Brunetto Latini to the Petrarchan *Trionfi*. Shelley was so eager for his verse to be understood in Italy that he translated key passages (such as the first thirteen stanzas of his "Ode to Liberty") into Italian. His *terza rima Triumph of Life* is perhaps the most Italianate poem ever written in English.

Shelley's poem begins with a triumphal procession that obviously owes much to the *Commedia*'s Earthly Paradise: a ghostly figure, bent beneath "a dusky hood & double cape" (89), moves forward on a chariot, preceded by dancing youths, followed by the aged, and accompanied by "the great, the unforgotten" who are "chained to the car" (208–09). The first-person narrator is joined by "what was once Rousseau" (204); his guide identifies the figures in the triumph and then describes his own life's journey, beginning with "the shape all light" (352) that first urged him to enter the world. This brilliant female apparition, we deduce, is to be identified with the shrouded figure that has passed before us on the chariot. When our attention is directed back to this figure, the triumph that now surrounds her is one of grotesquery and physical disintegration, death rather than life. It seems that we are following the sequence of the Petrarchan *Trionfi*, moving in a direction that rejects the metaphysics of the *Purgatorio*. And yet, at the very moment of signalling this transition, Shelley invokes Dante rather than Petrarch in an extended rhetorical figure that, like a bolt of poetic lightning, offers an itinerary that seems to move counter to his own poem-in- progress:

> Before the chariot had begun to climb
>   The opposing steep of that mysterious dell,
> Behold a wonder worthy of the rhyme
>
> Of him who from the lowest depths of Hell
>   Through every Paradise & through all glory
> Love led serene, & who returned to tell
>
> In words of hate & awe the wondrous story
>   How all things are transfigured, except Love;
> For deaf as is a sea which wrath makes hoary
>
> The world can hear not the sweet notes that move
>   The sphere whose light is melody to lovers –
> A wonder worthy of his rhyme – the grove
>
> Grew dense with shadows . . .
>
> (469–81)

These beautifully crafted, heavily enjambed tercets offer something approaching a paraphrase of the entire *Commedia*, while supporting Shelley's declared preference for the *Paradiso* above the other canticles. The poem breaks off, unfinished, some eighty lines later, amid scenes of fatigue and death that provoke the narrator to cry, "Then, what is life?" (544). The last page of the autograph manuscript is given over to sketches of sailboats; Shelley drowned at sea shortly afterwards, on July 8, 1822.

No English poet of the later nineteenth century rivals Shelley as a student of Dante. Tennyson's famous "Ulysses," which takes its point of departure from *Inferno* 26, 90–142, is the outstanding example of the widespread Victorian habit of translating or embellishing "scenes from Dante" – almost always the same two or three scenes (Paolo and Francesca, Ugolino) popularized by paintings hung at the Royal Academy.[14] Arthur Hallam, mourned by Tennyson's *In Memoriam*, translated the Ugolino episode into Greek iambics while a thirteen-year-old schoolboy at Eton, and showed considerable promise as a Dante scholar before his death at twenty-two: but Tennyson himself learned little from Dante. Thomas Carlyle found reading the *Inferno* "uphill work" (*DEL* II, p. 480); his writing and lecturing on Dante is full of sloppy mistakes and mistranslations. Robert and Elizabeth Barrett Browning lived for many years with a portrait of Dante hanging in their house at Florence, but Robert's "Sordello" expresses a yearning for a history of poetry that might have evolved in a different, non-Dantean, direction.[15] A broader shift in taste is exemplified in the translating, painting, and poetry of Dante Gabriel Rossetti: the turn from the *Commedia* (particularly the *Inferno*) to the *Vita nuova* and the cult of Beatrice. This coincides with, or facilitates, a shift from a public and political Dante to a private and subjective one. Rossetti's early poem "Dante at Verona" (*c.* 1848–52) portrays the exiled poet as a moody and isolated individual who thinks of nothing but the death of Beatrice. This prepares the way for Matthew Arnold's characterization of Dante as "essentially aloof from the world, and not complete in the life of the world," as "the grand, impracticable Solitary."[16] The Romantics' hope that the text of Dante might work changes in the contemporary political world is here quite lost. The most accomplished political Dantist in Victorian England was, in fact, a professional politician: four-time prime minister W. E. Gladstone published translations from all three canticles (including an Ugolino) and declared, late in life, that he had learned "a great part of that mental provision" requisite for public life "in the school of Dante" (*DEL* II, p. 601).

The revitalization of Dante in English poetry was to come, eventually, from outside England – chiefly from Ezra Pound and T. S. Eliot, American poets who (until very recently) defined the possibilities of artistic response to Dante on both sides of the Atlantic. The origins of American Dante studies are traditionally associated with the long and eventful life of Lorenzo Da Ponte (1749–1838), born in the Jewish Ghetto of Ceneda (now Vittorio Veneto), who began his professional life as Mozart's librettist and ended as (unsalaried) Professor of Italian at Columbia University.[17] The American edition of Cary's translation (1822) sold rapidly; Henry Wadsworth Longfellow worked steadily at his own translation (published 1867) for three decades, aided by the criticisms and support of Charles Eliot Norton and James Russell Lowell, fellow members of the "Dante Club" (later the Dante Society of

America) at Harvard. Nineteenth-century Americans experienced a difficult, triangulated relationship with English and Italian cultures as they struggled to define their own experience of the *Commedia*: "If [I were] an Italian," commented Fanny Appleton, "I should believe it like the gospel, its stern simplicity and majesty have such a stamp of divine authority, more than Milton, I think, with his poetic vagueness."[18] Such uncertainty in native terms of reference perhaps explains why American poets (notably Longfellow and Pound) took an especial interest in the *De vulgari eloquentia*, Dante's handbook for "making it new" in an emergent vernacular tradition.

Although Ezra Pound (1885–1972) was distantly related to Longfellow, he made a point of avoiding (sometimes belittling) the "Cambridge School" of American Dantists; his early translations of Cavalcanti (1912) claim Rossetti as "my father and my mother."[19] His plans for an epic that would rival or rewrite the *Commedia* were first hatched in the course of undergraduate studies at Hamilton College: the first part, in *terza rima*, would concern itself with emotion, the second (pentameters) with instruction, the third (hexameters) with contemplation. In "Scriptor Ignotus" (published in 1908), the "English Dante scholar and mystic" Bertold Lomax (Pound's middle name was Loomis) dreams of writing a forty-year epic, "though sight of hell and heaven were price thereof."[20] Pound's unfinished *Cantos* took, in fact, more than fifty years to write; they chronicle a dismal itinerary that leads through support of Italian Fascism, anti-Semitism, postwar imprisonment in a cage at Pisa, and confinement in a mental hospital to, finally, long silence. The so-called "Hell cantos" (14–15, 1930) open by quoting *Inferno* 5, 28 in Italian, and borrow motifs from the Dantean Malebolge; historical personages that Pound finds offensive are dipped in excrement. The latter part of the "Fifth Decad" (1937) sees Dante's Geryon deployed as a figure of fraud, "twin with usura" (51, p. 251; see also 46, p. 235, "Hic Geryon est").[21] Canto 92 (from "Rock Drill," 1955) opens on a "Mount," designed to recall the Dantean Earthly Paradise; canto 93 is concerned with issues of *cortesia* and *civilitas* that reflect a belated rereading of *Convivio* III and IV. The last line of "Thrones" (1959, "You in the dingy (piccioletta) astern there!," 109, p. 774) echoes Dante's words of warning and encouragement to those who, "in piccioletta barca," contemplate following him into the heavenly spheres (*Paradiso* 2, 1–18). Pound achieves no brilliant ascent after "Thrones," however: old and infirm, he turns back to consider what has already been written and "the take-off" he cannot make (116); this last canto meditates on attainments, and on "errors and wrecks"; the last "note" records memories of birds, rising and falling (p. 803).

The *Commedia* serves, finally, as both model and antitype for Pound's *Cantos*. Dante's poem lays down a pattern of exile and return: Pound follows

Dante into exile (the culture of Europe before and after the First World War), but then travels further into exile by placing himself on the wrong side of the century's great political arguments. Academics form his only real audience, and some academics (Harold Bloom, for example), have closed the lid on him; the political record has annulled the poetry.[22] Eliot, by contrast, appears to have judged his itinerary to perfection: he left Harvard to follow Pound into European modernism, but later changed course to embrace orthodox Christianity and mediate modernism to an enervated postwar world. While Pound was languishing in the Chestnut Ward of St. Elizabeth's Hospital, Eliot had embarked on a grand tour, collecting honorary doctorates and (in 1948) the Nobel Prize. His work has exerted a powerful, long-lived influence in English-speaking classrooms; his use of Dante (whom he claimed as his single greatest poetic influence) established terms of engagement for thousands of people in their first reading of the *Commedia*.

Eliot, like Pound, was at first heavily influenced by, and later dismissive of, Rossetti's reading of Dante. He remained convinced, however, of the preeminent importance of the *Vita nuova*, a poem which (he tells us in his famous 1929 "Dante" essay) teaches us "to look to *death* for what life cannot give."[23] The long and painful conversion experience of the *Vita nuova* is re-enacted at even greater length through the sequence of Eliot's writings. Eliot spends a lot of time in the modern equivalent of *Inferno* 3, the vestibule of Hell: Prufrock (despite the lines from *Inferno* 27 that hang over his head, an epigraph on deception that itself deceives, p. 13) belongs there; Gerontion's predicament is "neither . . ./ Nor . . . Nor" (p. 39). *The Waste Land* 1, 62–3 (and its attendant note) alludes to *Inferno* 3, 55–57 by way of describing people walking to work over London Bridge; a more rousing Dantean imitation (the voyage of Ulysses) was cut from the typescript *Wasteland* by slashes from Pound's pencil. When Eliot hits rock-bottom with *The Hollow Men* (1925) he still seems closer to the cries and grumbles of *Inferno* 3 than to the horrors of Cocytus; Malebolge he side-steps entirely (leaving the mud and crud to Pound). "Animula" (1929) finds its point of departure in *Purgatorio* 16, 85–93, in which Marco Lombardo tells how "l'anima semplicetta" ("the simple little soul") springs from the hand of God at birth to pursue "ciò che la trastulla" ("things that bring delight"). Dante (and Shelley after him) emphasizes the energy and joy of the new-born: Eliot's infant creature, however, is more fearful from the first and soon takes refuge behind the pages of the *Encyclopedia Britannica* (21–23, p. 113).

Eliot's upward ascent begins, in hesitant and painful fashion, with *Ash Wednesday* (1930). This poem is pitched somewhat uncertainly between cantos 25 (the purgation of lust) and 28 (the Earthly Paradise; Matelda) of the *Purgatorio*. The three stairs of section 3 recall the three steps at the gate of Dante's Purgatory (*Purgatorio* 9, 94–102); a deliberate but imperfect echo of *Paradiso* 3, 85 ("E 'n la sua voluntade è nostra pace") is heard towards the end of the sixth and final section. We look to the fourth part of *Four Quartets* (1935–42) for the conclusion of this difficult ascent. It seems appropriate that Eliot should save his most extensive tribute to Dante for the journey's end of "Little Gidding" (1942). Eliot might have chosen a Cacciaguida figure (*Paradiso* 15–17), a distinguished ancestor, to point him to the summit: instead, he chooses to meet a "familiar compound ghost," bearing the "brown baked features" ("cotto aspetto"; Eliot borrows phrasing here from his Temple Classics Dante) of Brunetto Latini.[24] The future that Eliot is promised here, in the bombed-out landscape of wartime London, is far from cheering; he has little to look forward to this side of death. The substitution of a Brunetto for a Cacciaguida relieves Eliot of the burden and responsibility of political prophecy: but it remains a brilliant poetic stroke, true to Eliot's personal itinerary.

The Brunetto episode is the *only* dramatic encounter in *Four Quartets*. The isolation of Eliot's narrative voice and the lonely idiosyncrasy of Pound's *Cantos* (Pound travels without companions) are antithetical to the *Commedia*. Lack of dialogue, for Dante, signals the absence of political life. In the course of a dialogue with Dante in *Paradiso* 8, 116 (which goes on to elaborate a theory of estates, what we would call the division of labor), Charles Martel asks whether things would be worse "for man on earth, were he not a citizen?" ("per l'omo in terra, se non fosse cive?"). Pound picks up just the last three words of this line (beginning with the negative) and translates them "Dant' had it,/ some sense of civility" (p. 624). The feebleness of this translation, which returns Pound to the pre-Raphaelite mannerisms of Rossetti, is matched by the failure of Eliot to capture any of the political intelligence developed through the *Paradiso*. Eliot's reading of Dante is Augustinian (sometimes Manichean), rather than Thomistic-Aristotelian: his "Dante," we have noted, teaches us "to look to *death* for what life cannot give" (p. 275). Paradise, for Dante, is a model of what human society can be made to be: paradise, for Eliot, is where dead people live.

The bridging of American, English, and continental Dante traditions effected by Eliot and Pound has facilitated some important poetic work, such as the *Divine Comedies* of James Merrill.[25] But the last century has seen a different Dante that is almost always at odds with that of Eliot and Pound: the Irish Dante of Yeats, Joyce, Beckett, and Heaney. Yeats' understanding of Dante owes something to Pound (who worked as his secretary at intervals between 1913 and 1916), but it was an *idea* (rather than the text) of Dante that Yeats found most inspiring. In the dialogical poem "Ego

Dominus Tuus" (1917), the voice, *Hic*, is fascinated by Dante's achievement in making "that hollow face of his" better known to the mind's eye than any other face, "But that of Christ"; the voice, *Ille*, thinks that such an image is a fabrication, "fashioned from his opposite."[26] *Hic* argues that a literary style can only be achieved by "sedentary toil" and "the imitation of past masters," but *Ille* counters that "I seek an image, not a book." Dante provided Yeats with the supreme example of a fabricated image of poetic identity: he also provided the greatest example of a poetic system through which it might be exercised. When Yeats came to invent his own system in *A Vision* (1938, revised 1956), he situated Dante in Phase Seventeen of the lunar cycle as "the *Daimonic* man" who achieves "Unity of Being" and who wears the true mask of "simplification through intensity."[27]

Yeats knew little Italian and probably never read any translation of the *Commedia* from cover to cover: Joyce, by contrast, knew Dante as well as, and Italian better than, any other writer in this survey. Joyce grew up knowing of Dante as part of the Catholic culture of Ireland: he had a dour governess called "Dante" Conway; he lived in a house at Blackrock with stained-glass panels in the hall door depicting Dante and Beatrice. His Jesuit educators (like their counterparts in Italy) employed the *Commedia* to enforce Catholic orthodoxy, "the spiritual-heroic refrigerating apparatus invented and patented in all countries by Dante Alighieri."[28] Joyce revelled in the anti-clerical Dante while separating the poetics of the *Commedia* from the accretions of post-Tridentine Catholic dogma. His decision to stick with Dante (rather than to turn to pre-Christian epic or peasant song) indicates different ambitions for Irish identity than those essayed by Yeats and Synge: the insular culture of Ireland must realize its European (and later its global) affiliations. As Dante is the poet of Florence (even as he writes a poem of universal scope), so Joyce will be the poet of Dublin.

Joyce's journey into exile is more authentic (more Dantean) than that of Pound: Joyce struggled long and hard to find a place for his work in Ireland until 1912, when a nervous Dublin printer destroyed the sheets of *Dubliners* (and Joyce left Ireland for good). His early novel, *Stephen Hero* (1904–06), has a chapter that is clearly modelled on *Inferno* 15 (Brunetto): but it is *A Portrait of the Artist as a Young Man* that plots the Dantean itinerary, or his variant of it. Joyce acquired a copy of the *Vita nuova* at Trieste as he was writing the *Portrait* (1914–15), a novel that brings us to *Paradiso* 33 at its midpoint (Stephen sees the world as "a theorem of divine power and love and universality", p. 150; *Paradiso* 33, 133–36), but concludes with many echoes of Dante's *libello* as Stephen registers the presence of his beloved. Joyce's play *Exiles* features a twenty-seven-year-old music teacher called Beatrice Justice;[29] the first Dantean echo of *Ulysses* ("Now I eat his salt bread," p. 17) recalls the prediction of exile in *Paradiso* 17, 58–59.[30] *Ulysses* contains many lines and phrases from the Italian text of the *Commedia*, including (under the rubric "RHYMES AND REASONS," cut from the Gabler edition) three successive rhymes from *Inferno* 5 (92, 94, 96; p. 114). It also incorporates the line "Ed egli avea del cul fatto trombetta" (p. 151; *Inferno* 21, 139): the scatological Dante that finds no place in Eliot becomes one of Joyce's choicest voices. In the "Eumaeus" section, Stephen makes a rambling reference to "the impetuosity of Dante and the isosceles triangle miss Portinari he fell in love with" (p. 521); in writing "Penelope," Joyce originally had Molly Bloom contemplating the wearing of a white rose, but (with an impetuous stroke of his own in page proof) changed the color to red: "or shall I wear a red yes and how he kissed me . . . and yes I said yes I will Yes."

The poetic prose of *Finnegans Wake* (1922–39) contains few Italian phrases (Joyce is writing a new vernacular), but adapts many "dantallising peaches" (Dantean tropes) from "the lingerous longerous book of the dark" (the *Inferno*; p. 251). The salt bread motif is sounded again (pp. 247, 483), and Guelfs and Ghibellines do battle in a gaudy assortment of linguistic dresses. Joyce's "trifolium librotto" (p. 425) contains a very short paraphrase of "Unterwealth" and "Uppercrust," the first two canticles (pp. 78–79), but, in "touring the no placelike no timelike absolent" (p. 609) of sleep, owes most to the *Paradiso*. The perfect circular, circulating structure of the *Wake* represents Joyce's grandest bid for equivalence with "the divine comic Denti Alligator" (p. 440).

The claiming of Dante as poetic mentor and ancestor has obvious advantages for Irish poets writing in English. Irish Catholicism brings them (for better or worse) closer to the urban, national, and universalizing culture of Dante than any American or English poet can imagine. From the Irish vantage point, T. S. Eliot (despite his striving for the imperial and impersonal authority of *Latinitas*) may look parochial and eccentric in mutating from (in Heaney's words) "the intellectual mysteryman from Missouri" to "the English vestryman."[31] Aspects of Catholic dogma and practice that have long proved a stumbling block to the Anglican English – as comically chronicled by Barbara Pym – offer rare expressive opportunities for Irish poets. Heaney's "The Strand at Lough Beg," for example, opens with a dedication to a relative slain in sectarian violence and a tercet describing the "tall rushes" at the foot of Purgatory (*Purgatorio* 1, 100–02).[32] The poem begins by associating the landscape in which the murder took place to the road "Where Sweeney [seventh-century Ulster king] fled"; it ends by rewriting *Purgatorio* 5, 91–129 (the bloody death of Buonconte, fleeing the battle of

Campaldino, by a stream). The poem's last lines effect a remarkable fusion of ancient Ireland, Dantean Purgatory, and modern Ulster:

> With rushes that shoot green again, I plait
> Green scapulars to wear over your shroud.
>
> (p. 18)

But in "Station Island," the title-poem of his next collection,[33] this act of familial piety comes back to haunt Heaney as he moves somewhat uncertainly among pious pilgrims at Lough Derg, "St Patrick's Purgatory." Colum McCartney, the murdered boy, appears to denounce him

> for the way you whitewashed ugliness and drew
> the lovely blinds of the *Purgatorio*
> and saccharined my death with morning dew.
>
> (p. 83)

The reading of Dante, then, offers both good and bad temptations for the Irish poet; Heaney is finally escorted away from the Island by James Joyce, greatest and least pious of all Irish Dantists. Samuel Beckett, Joyce's amanuensis for *Finnegans Wake*, read Dante with late-Joycean pathos and humour. The status of souls in Ante-Purgatory, an intense but passing concern for Heaney, was a lifelong obsession for Beckett. *More Pricks than Kicks* (1934), his early sequence of short stories, follows the adventures of Belacqua, a character named after the sublimely indolent Florentine lute-maker of *Purgatorio* 4, 103–35. "Dante and the Lobster," the first story in the sequence, finds Belacqua "stuck in the first of the canti in the moon":[34] not literally stuck (it transpires), but figuratively, in his reading of *Paradiso* 2 (where Beatrice explains the moon's mysterious spots). Belacqua struggles to make progress with the text, but snaps it shut on the stroke of noon and goes out to lunch; he thus becomes one of those readers who, at the beginning of *Paradiso* 2, are advised to turn back and not put forth "to the open sea" ("in pelago," 5). Dante's Belacqua is not allowed to make progress up the mountain because he repented late on earth: he will lounge in the shade of Ante-Purgatory until his time comes round. This motif of long, seemingly endless (but not quite hopeless) waiting in a strange, transitional space becomes, of course, the dominant motif of Beckett's drama. The strange predicaments in which his protagonists wait (Winnie, in *Happy Days*, buried to her neck in sand, etc.) recall the full, strange range of Dantean postures.

More Pricks than Kicks cannot sustain the brilliant start made by its opening story; its relative failure is typical of most novelistic adaptations of Dantean texts. One temptation for novelists is to let a Dantean work supply their narrative structure; the novelist then concentrates on working out local details. William Golding's *Free Fall* (1959), in which the painter Sammy Mountjoy sights Beatrice in an art class, tries to rework the pattern of the *Vita nuova*; the pulp-novel *Inferno* (1976) by Larry Niven and Jerry Pournelle, which features Benito Mussolini as guide through the underworld, is the worst of many attempts to repeople or relocate the first canticle. The best remains Joseph Conrad's *Heart of Darkness* (1899).

The most interesting appropriations of Dante in the late twentieth century are by African-American and Caribbean writers; interest centers on the act of appropriation itself, which remains intensely problematic. In *The System of Dante's Hell* (1965), Amiri Baraka seems at once to envy Dante the security of his metaphysical system ("But Dante's hell is heaven," p. 9) and to scorn it.[35] In his "Makers of Discord" section, in which a Newark gang runs amok with a meat cleaver at a basement party, the following sentence is framed, before and after, by strong obscenities: "Lovely Dante at night under his flame taking heaven. A place, a system, where all is dealt with . . . as is proper" (p. 99). The novel struggles, by turns, to imitate, outdo, and throw over Dantean metaphysics and its great white continuators (Eliot, Pound, and Joyce). Gloria Naylor's *Linden Hills* (1985) follows two young black male poets on their downward journey through a prosperous community built for blacks who aspire to live out a white-patented dream of social advancement. Naylor's appropriation of Dante's *Inferno* as master narrative for this landscape of private torments (a white model for black society) replicates the choice made by Linden Hills itself. The ironies of this are rich and difficult to control: but the attention paid to the sufferings of women in this arrangement adds something quite new to the English-language Dante tradition. Derek Walcott's *Omeros* (1990), full of otherwordly meetings, continues the lifetime's agon with Dante initiated by his *Epitaph for the Young* (1949).

Dante's unfinished engagement with English language film, video, and television reflexively examines the very nature, the *modus agendi*, of codex, screen, and audio technologies. It is a striking and consistent feature of such engagement, now a century old, that visualizing Dante comes easier than voicing him. William B. Ramous' 1907 short *Francesca da Rimini* was followed by *Dante's Inferno* by Henry Otto (1924), an ambitious attempt to realize the *cantica* in the style of Gustave Doré. The sound era shifted from direct imitation of Dantean locales to allusive atmospherics; dark or subterranean scenes in Manhattan or Gotham City seem perennially evocative of the *Inferno*. The *TV Dante* (1988) of Peter Greenaway and Tom Phillips baffled or unnerved most critics on its first British broadcast in 1990; it deserves revisiting as a precocious meditation on high and low art, on the history of moving images, and on the digitized future of television.[36] New English translations of the *Commedia* continue to appear with extraordinary frequency. Tom Phillips has made a notable contribution to this effort; so too has Seamus Heaney, who ends *Field Work* with a translation of *Inferno* 32–33, "Ugolino." Translating this episode, we have noted, has become commonplace since Chaucer's first effort some six centuries ago. But history continually finds new paths to the *Commedia* as contemporary writing. The savage sectarian violence running through *Field Work* (now itself a retreating memory) finds perfect summation in Heaney's "Ugolino." The silence that hangs once the "song" is over is eerie, not quite perfect poetic closure:

> Your atrocity was Theban. They were young
> And innocent: Hugh and Brigata
> And the other two whose names are in my song.
>
> (p. 64)

NOTES

1 References follow Larry D. Benson, ed., *The Riverside Chaucer* (Boston: Houghton Mifflin, 1987). For more detailed discussion of the Dante–Chaucer relationship, see Howard H. Schless, *Chaucer and Dante* (Norman, OK: Pilgrim Books, 1984); David Wallace, "Chaucer's Italian inheritance," in Piero Boitani and Jill Mann, eds., *The Cambridge Companion to Chaucer* (Cambridge: Cambridge University Press, 2nd edn., 2003), pp. 36–57; David Wallace, "Italy," in Peter Brown, ed., *A Companion to Chaucer* (Oxford: Blackwell, 2000), pp. 218–34; Warren Ginsberg, *Chaucer's Italian Tradition* (Ann Arbor: University of Michigan Press, 2002); Karla Taylor, *Chaucer Reads the Divine Comedy* (Stanford: Stanford University Press, 1989).

2 G. C. Macaulay, ed., *The English Works of John Gower*, 2 vols., Early English Text Society, Extra Series 81–82 (London: Oxford University Press, 1900), II, p. 296. This passage does not appear in all manuscripts.

3 Henry Bergen, ed., *Lydgate's Fall of Princes*, 4 vols., Early English Text Society, ES 121–24 (London: Oxford University Press, 1924–27), I, p. 9.

4 Quoted from the text in Paget Toynbee, ed., *Dante in English Literature: From Chaucer to Cary (c. 1380–1844)*, 2 vols. (London: Methuen, 1909), I, p. 52. This work is henceforth referred to as *DEL*. Toynbee's findings for the earlier period have been more than doubled by Jackson Campbell Boswell, *Dante's Fame in England: References in Printed British Books 1477–1640* (Newark, NJ: University of Delaware Press, 1999); see further Nicholas R. Havely, "'An Italian Writer Against the Pope?' Dante in Reformation England," in Eric G. Haywood, ed., *Dante's Metamorphoses: Episodes in a Literary Afterlife* (Dublin: Four Courts Press, 2003), pp. 127–49. On the Latin *Commedia* at Wells, see David Wallace, *Premodern Places* (Oxford: Blackwell, 2004), pp. 139–80.

5 Douglas Bush et al., eds., *Complete Prose Works of John Milton*, 8 vols. (New Haven: Yale University Press, 1953–82), I, p. 558. All other references to

Milton follow Merrit Y. Hughes, ed., *John Milton. Complete Poems and Major Prose* (New York: Macmillan, 1957). For detailed accounts of the Dante–Milton relationship, see A. R. Cirillo, "Dante," in William B. Hunter, Jr., *A Milton Encyclopedia*, 9 vols. (Lewisburg: Bucknell University Press, 1978–83), II, pp. 102–08; Irene Samuel, *Dante and Milton: The Commedia and Paradise Lost* (Ithaca: Cornell University Press, 1966).

6 *DEL*, I, p. 423, quoting from the English translation of 1786. This view of Dante, first published in 1756, was incorporated into the first edition of the *Dictionnaire* (1764; London edn., in French, 1765).

7 Thomas Warton, *History of English Poetry*, 4 vols., facsimile of the 1774 edn., introduced by René Wellek (New York: Johnson Reprint Corporation, 1968), III, p. 253.

8 Quotations follow Henry Boyd, trans., *The Divina Commedia of Dante Alighieri*, 3 vols. (London: Cadell and Davies, 1802); H. F. Cary, trans., *The Divine Comedy of Dante Alighieri* (New York: Colonial Press, 1901). On post-Caryan Dantes in English, see Ralph Pite, *The Circle of Our Vision: Dante's Presence in English Romantic Poetry* (Oxford: Clarendon Press, 1994) and Nick Havely, ed., *Dante's Modern Afterlife: Reception and Response from Blake to Heaney* (Basingstoke: Macmillan, 1998).

9 References to Byron follow E. H. Coleridge, ed., *The Works of Lord Byron*, revised edn., 13 vols. (London: John Murray, 1918–24).

10 Letter dated August 17, 1820 (vol. XII, p. 65).

11 Letter dated March 20, 1820 (vol. XI, p. 419).

12 See Donald H. Reiman, *Shelley's The Triumph of Life: A Critical Study* (Urbana: University of Illinois Press, 1956). I quote from this variorum edition; references to other poems follow Newell F. Ford, ed., *The Poetical Works of Shelley* (Boston: Houghton Mifflin, 1975). See also Stuart M. Sperry, *Shelley's Major Verse: The Narrative and Dramatic Poetry* (Cambridge, MA: Harvard University Press, 1988), pp. 183–201; Timothy Webb, *The Violet in the Crucible: Shelley and Translation* (Oxford: Clarendon Press, 1976), pp. 276–336.

13 David Lee Clark, ed., *Shelley's Prose* (Albuquerque: University of New Mexico Press, 1954), p. 291.

14 See (in addition to Toynbee, ed., *Dante in English*) Paget Toynbee, *Britain's Tribute to Dante in Literature and Art: A Chronological Record of 540 Years (c. 1380–1920)* (London: Oxford University Press for the British Academy, 1921); Deidre O'Grady, "Francesca da Rimini from Romanticism to Decadence," in Haywood, ed., *Dante's Metamorphoses*, pp. 221–39.

15 See Steve Ellis, *Dante and English Poetry: Shelley to T. S. Eliot* (Cambridge: Cambridge University Press, 1983), pp. 66–101; Alison Millbank, *Dante and the Victorians* (Manchester: Manchester University Press, 1998).

16 See the essay "Dante and Beatrice" (1863), conveniently available in Michael Caesar, ed., *Dante: The Critical Heritage 1314(?)–1870* (London: Routledge, 1989), pp. 608, 612.

17 See Joseph Louis Russo, *Lorenzo Da Ponte: Poet and Adventurer* (New York: Columbia University Press, 1922); see also A. Bartlett Giamatti, *Dante in America: The First Two Centuries* (Binghamton, NY: MRTS, 1983).

18 Journal entry for January 25, 1841 as quoted in Edward Wagenkneeht, ed., *Mrs Longfellow: Selected Letters and Journals of Fanny Appleton Longfellow (1817–1861)* (New York: Longmans, Green, 1956), p. 74.

19 Hugh Kenner, ed. and intr., *The Translations of Ezra Pound* (London: Faber and Faber, 1970), p. 20.

20 Ezra Pound, *A Lume Spento* (New York: New Directions, 1971). Pound paid $8 to have this (his first) volume of poems printed in an edition of 100 copies at Venice in 1908; the title is from *Purgatorio* 3, 132.

21 References follow *The Cantos of Ezra Pound*, 4th collected edn. (London: Faber and Faber, 1987).

22 See Harold Bloom, ed., *Modern Critical Views: Ezra Pound* (New York: Chelsea House, 1987), p. viii.

23 *Selected Essays* (London: Faber and Faber, 1951), p. 275. References to Eliot's poetry follow T. S. Eliot, *Selected Poems 1909–1962* (London: Faber and Faber, 1974); Valerie Eliot, ed., The Waste Land: *A Facsimile and Transcript of the Original Drafts Including the Annotations of Ezra Pound* (New York: Harcourt Brace Jovanovich, 1971).

24 For excellent analysis of this episode see A. C. Charity, "T. S. Eliot: The Dantean Recognitions," in A. D. Moody, ed., *The Waste Land in Different Voices* (London: Edward Arnold, 1974), pp. 117–62; Ellis, *English Poetry*, pp. 236–43. See also D. Manganiello, *T. S. Eliot and Dante* (Basingstoke: Macmillan, 1989).

25 See Rachel Jacoff, "Merrill and Dante," in David Lehman and Charles Berger, eds., *James Merrill: Essays in Criticism* (Ithaca: Cornell University Press, 1983), pp. 145–58. Prospects for an Australasian Dante may be gauged from Gaetano Rando, ed., *Language and Cultural Identity* (Wollongong, NSW: Dante Alighieri Society, 1990); Margaret Baker and Diana Glenn, eds., *Dante Colloquia in Australia, 1982–1999* (Adelaide: Australian Humanities Press, 2000).

26 Daniel Albright, ed., *W. B. Yeats: The Poems* (London: J. M. Dent, 1990), pp. 210–12.

27 W. B. Yeats, *A Vision*, revised edn. (New York: Macmillan, 1956), pp. 140–45.

28 James Joyce, *A Portrait of the Artist as a Young Man*, ed. Richard Ellmann (New York: Viking, 1966), p. 252. References to other works by Joyce employ the following editions: James Joyce, *Ulysses*, corrected text, ed. H. W. Gabler (New York: Random House, 1986); James Joyce, *Finnegans Wake* (London: Faber and Faber, 1975). Some aspects of Gabler's editorial practice remain controversial; compare his text with James Joyce, *Ulysses* (Harmondsworth: Penguin, 1971).

29 In sketching out this play in a notebook, Joyce wrote: "Beatrice's mind is an abandoned cold temple in which hymns have risen heavenward in a distant past but where now a doddering priest offers alone and hopelessly prayers to the Most High" (James Joyce, *Exiles*, ed. Padraic Colum [London: Jonathan Cape, 1952], p. 168).

30 Gabler, ed., *Ulysses*, pp. 643–44; for a facsimile of the relevant page proofs, see the excellent work by Mary T. Reynolds, *Joyce and Dante: The Shaping Imagination* (Princeton: Princeton University Press, 1981), pp. 80–81.

31 Seamus Heaney, "Envies and Identifications: Dante and the Modern Poet," *Irish University Review* 15 (1985): 7.

32 See *Field Work* (London: Faber and Faber, 1979), pp. 17–18. Heaney's engagement with Dante develops further in *Seeing Things* (London: Faber and Faber, 1991) and in ongoing translations. For the importance of Osip Mandelstam's "Conversation with Dante" (to Heaney and *tout court*), see Bernard O'Donoghue, "Dante's Versatility and Seamus Heaney's Modernism," in Havely, ed., *Dante's Modern Afterlife*, pp. 242–57; Wai Chi Dimock, "Literature for the Planet," *PMLA*, 116 (2001), pp. 173–88. On Barbara Pym's *Excellent Women*, see David Wallace, "Dante in England," in Teodolinda Barolini and H. Wayne Storey, eds., *Dante for the New Millennium* (New York: Fordham University Press, 2003), pp. 422–34.

33 See *Station Island* (London: Faber and Faber, 1984), pp. 61–94.

34 *More Pricks than Kicks* (London: Calder and Boyars, 1970), p. 9.

35 Quotations follow Imamu Amiri Baraka (LeRoi Jones), *The System of Dante's Hell* (New York: Grove Press, 1966).

36 See Amilcare A. Iannucci, "Dante and Hollywood," in Iannucci, ed., *Dante, Cinema and Television* (Toronto: University of Toronto Press, 2004), pp. 3–20; Tom Phillips, *Works and Texts* (London: Thames and Hudson, 1992), pp. 219–51; Nancy J. Vickers, "Dante in the Video Decade," in Theodore J. Cachey, Jr., ed., *Dante Now: Current Trends in Dante Studies* (Notre Dame: University of Notre Dame Press, 1995), pp. 263–76.

SUGGESTED READING

Griffiths, Eric and Matthew Reynolds, eds. *Dante in English* (London: Penguin, 2005).

Hawkins, Peter S. and Rachel Jacoff, eds., *The Poets' Dante* (New York: Farrar, Straus, and Giroux, 2001).

FURTHER READING

The most useful reference book at present is *The Dante Encyclopedia*, ed. Richard Lansing (New York: Garland. 2000). For those who know Italian the *Enciclopedia dantesca*, ed. Umberto Bosco (Rome: Istituto dell'Enciclopedia Italiana, 1970–78) is a valuable resource. The journal *Dante Studies* publishes a yearly "American Dante Bibliography."

DANTE TRANSLATIONS

I have listed below some of the most reliable and well annotated translations, all of which are now available in paperback.

Durling, Robert M. and Ronald L. Martinez. *Inferno and Purgatorio*. Oxford: Oxford University Press, 1996 and 2003.
Hollander, Robert and Jean. *Inferno and Purgatorio*. New York: Doubleday, 2000 and 2003.
Mandelbaum, Allen. *Inferno, Purgatorio, Paradiso*. New York: Bantam Classic, reissued 2004.
Singleton, Charles S. *Inferno, Purgatorio, Paradiso*. Princeton: Princeton University Press, 1970–75.

WEB RESOURCES

The following sites are among the many now available; most of them contain links to other sites as well.

The American Dante Bibliography: www.brandeis.edu/library/dante/
Dante Online: www.danteonline.it
Dante Society of America: www.dantesociety.org
Danteworlds: danteworlds.laits.utexas.edu
The Dartmouth Dante Project: www.dante.dartmouth.edu
Digital Dante: www.ilt.columbia.edu/library/index.html
The Princeton Dante Project: www.princeton.edu/dante
The William and Katherine Devers Program in Dante Studies: www.dante.nd.edu
The World of Dante: www3.iath.virginia.edu/dante/

COLLECTIONS OF CRITICAL ESSAYS

Barolini, Teodolinda and H. Wayne Storey, eds. *Dante for the New Millennium.* New York: Fordham University Press, 2003.

Bergin, Thomas Goddard, ed. *From Time to Eternity.* New Haven, Yale University Press, 1967.

Bloom, Harold, ed. *Dante.* New York: Chelsea House, 1986.

Cervigni, Dino, ed. *Dante and Modern American Criticism,* special issue of *Annali d'Italianistica* 8 (1990).

Freccero, John, ed. *Dante: A Collection of Critical Essays.* Englewood Cliffs, NJ: Prentice Hall, 1963.

Ianucci, Amilcare A., ed. *Dante Today,* special issue of *Quaderni d'Italianistica* 10, nos. 1–2 (1989).

Lansing, Richard, ed. *The Critical Complex* (8 volumes). New York: Routledge, 2003.

Mazzotta, Giuseppe, ed. *Critical Essays on Dante.* Boston: G. K. Hall, 1991.

CRITICAL WORKS

The number of books and articles on Dante is staggering. The selective list here of critical works supplements the bibliographies at the conclusion of the essays and includes several books that have appeared since the first edition.

Anderson, William. *Dante the Maker.* New York: Crossroad, 1982.

Auerbach, Erich. *Dante, Poet of the Secular World.* Chicago: University of Chicago Press, 1961.

Barolini, Teodolinda. *The Undivine Comedy: Detheologizing Dante.* Princeton: Princeton University Press, 1992.

Boitani, Piero. *The Tragic and Sublime in Medieval Literature.* Cambridge: Cambridge University Press, 1991.

Botterill, Steven. *Dante and the Mystical Tradition: Bernard of Clairvaux in the Commedia.* Cambridge: Cambridge University Press, 1994.

Boyde, Patrick. *Dante Philomythes and Philosopher: Man in the Cosmos.* Cambridge: Cambridge University Press, 1981.

Perception and Passion in the Divine Comedy. Cambridge: Cambridge University Press, 1993.

Cassell, Anthony K. *Dante's Fearful Art of Justice.* Toronto: University of Toronto Press, 1984.

Cestaro, Gary. *Dante and the Grammar of the Nursing Body.* Notre Dame: University of Notre Dame Press, 2002.

Chiarenza, Marguerite Mills. *Tracing God's Art.* Boston: Twayne, 1989.

Cogan, Mark. *The Design in the Wax: The Structure of the Divine Comedy and Its Meaning.* Notre Dame: University of Notre Dame Press, 1999.

Cornish, Alison. *Reading Dante's Stars.* New Haven: Yale University Press, 2000.

Ferrante, Joan. *The Political Vision of the Divine Comedy.* Princeton: Princeton University Press, 1984.

Foster, Kenhelm. *The Two Dantes and Other Studies.* London: Darton, Longman and Todd, 1977.

Gragnolati. Manuele. *Experiencing the Afterlife: Soul and Body in Dante and Medieval Culture*. Notre Dame: University of Notre Dame, 2005.

Harrison, Robert Pogue. *The Body of Beatrice*. Baltimore: Johns Hopkins University Press, 1988.

Havely, Nick, ed. *Dante's Modern Afterlife: Reception and Response from Blake to Heaney*. New York: St. Martin's Press, 1998.

Hawkins, Peter. *Dante's Testaments: Essays in Scriptural Imagination*. Stanford: Stanford University Press, 1999.

Hawkins, Peter and Rachel Jacoff, eds. *The Poets' Dante: Twentieth-Century Reflections*. New York: Farrar, Straus, and Giroux, 2001.

Hollander, Robert. *Dante: A Life in Works*. New Haven: Yale University Press, 2001.

Iannucci, Amilcare, ed. *Dante: Contemporary Perspectives*. Toronto, University of Toronto Press, 1997.

Dante, Cinema and Television. Toronto: University of Toronto Press, 2003.

Kleiner, John. *Mismapping the Underworld: Daring and Error in Dante's Comedy*. Stanford: Stanford University Press, 1994.

Lewis, R. W. B. *Dante*. New York: Viking Penguin, 2001.

Mazzeo, Joseph A. *Structure and Thought in the Paradiso*. Ithaca, NY: Cornell University Press, 1958.

Mazzotta, Giuseppe. *Dante, Poet of the Desert*. Princeton: Princeton University Press, 1979.

Dante's Vision and the Circle of Knowledge. Princeton: Princeton University Press, 1993.

Moevs, Christian. *The Metaphysics of Dante's Comedy*. Oxford: Oxford University Press. 2005.

Morgan, Alison. *Dante and the Medieval Other World*. Cambridge: Cambridge University Press, 1990.

Raffa, Guy P. *Divine Dialectic: Dante's Incarnational Poetry*. Toronto: University of Toronto Press, 2000.

Schildgen, Brenda Deen. *Dante and the Orient*. Urbana: University of Illinois Press, 2002.

Scott, John A. *Understanding Dante*. Notre Dame: University of Notre Dame Press, 2004.

Shapiro, Marianne. *Dante and the Knot of Body and Soul*. New York: St. Martin's Press, 1998.

Williams, Charles. *The Figure of Beatrice*. New York: Noonday, 1961.

INDEX

CAMBRIDGE COMPANIONS TO LITERATURE

The Cambridge Companion to
Philip Roth
edited by Timothy Parrish

The Cambridge Companion to
Margaret Atwood
edited by Coral Ann Howells

CAMBRIDGE COMPANIONS TO CULTURE

The Cambridge Companion to Modern
German Culture
edited by Eva Kolinsky and Wilfried
van der Will

The Cambridge Companion to Modern
Russian Culture
edited by Nicholas Rzhevsky

The Cambridge Companion to Modern
Spanish Culture
edited by David T. Gies

The Cambridge Companion to Modern
Italian Culture
edited by Zygmunt G. Barański and
Rebecca J. West

The Cambridge Companion to Modern
French Culture
edited by Nicholas Hewitt

The Cambridge Companion to
*Modern Latin American
Culture*
edited by John King

The Cambridge Companion to Modern
Irish Culture
edited by Joe Cleary and
Claire Connolly

The Cambridge Companion to Modern
American Culture
edited by Christopher Bigsby